Hello...

There are almost as many definitions of 'design' as there are colours in the spectrum. At its most basic, though, we can say that it's the creation of any inanimate object that motivates a fellow human being. That motivation could be anything from going out to buy a new car – the point of vehicle design and of those adverts that trumpet their benefits – to simply stopping for a moment and appreciating the art before them.

Design is a deeply ingrained part of the human psyche. Since the earliest days when we were painting on cave walls, we have been interested in creating objects that tell a story or simply brighten up our surroundings, proving that the need to design is an inherent urge in all of us. Over the years, of course, things have changed, tastes have evolved and technology arrived, but still that desire remains. The advent of the computer elevated design into a whole new level. No longer were we restricted to sculpting, painting or drawing with physical objects; now we could create in a virtual space on a screen, change our creations as often as we wanted and finally output a definitive copy to share with family, friends and the world at large.

And that's where *The Ultimate Guide to Graphic Design 2nd Edition* can help. Over the course of almost 200 pages, we'll show you how you can harness the power of your computer to create more professional, appealing and engaging work that you'll be proud to show, and which will impress those who see it.

With full coverage of Photoshop, Illustrator, InDesign, QuarkXPress and more, our team of expert writers will guide you step by step through each task at hand. And, if you need to brush up on your skills before launching yourself into some of the more ambitious projects, check out the comprehensive A to Z of Design in the second half of the book, where we explain key concepts that every professional or aspiring designer should have in their armoury.

Happy designing.

Nik Rawlinson

A note about the text: The examples shown in screenshots throughout this book use the Mac interface, and we have used Mac-based shortcuts in the text. However, the majority of the applications covered – in particular, Photoshop, InDesign and QuarkXPress – work on both the Mac and Windows-based PCs and the on-screen interfaces are close to identical on each platform. In most cases, keyboard shortcuts can be easily translated from one platform to the other. 'Command' on the Mac is usually replaced with Ctrl on the PC; 'Option', where used, is replaced with 'Alt', and when we make reference to control-clicking on a Mac, PC users need only right-click in the usual manner.

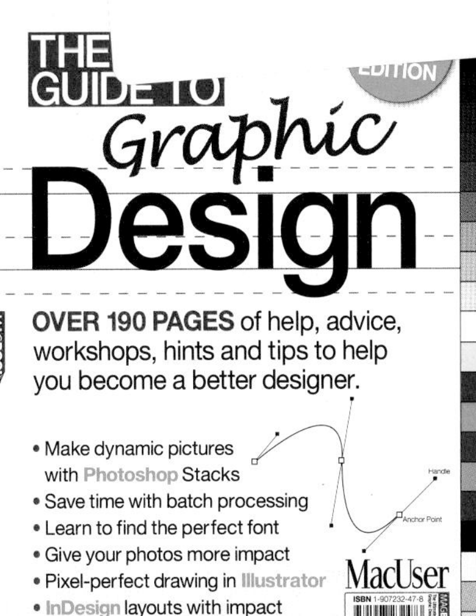

The Ultimate Guide to Graphic Design

EDITORIAL
EDITOR Nik Rawlinson
ART EDITOR Camille Neilson
PRODUCTION EDITOR Jon Lysons
SUB-EDITOR Kirsty Fortune
DEPUTY EDITOR Kenny Hemphill
CONTRIBUTORS Adam Banks, Steve Caplin
IMAGES Danny Bird, Steve Caplin, Chris Robson, Hugh Threlfall

ADVERTISING
020 7907 6000, Fax 020 7907 6600
ads.macuser@dennis.co.uk
ACCOUNT MANAGER Alexandra Skinner 020 7907 6623
AD PRODUCTION EXEC Michael Hills 020 7907 6129
DIGITAL PRODUCTION MANAGER Nicky Baker 020 7907 6056
US ADVERTISING MANAGER Matthew Sullivan-Pond ++1 646 717 9555 *matthew_sullivan@dennis.co.uk*

PUBLISHING & MARKETING
020 7907 6000, fax 020 7636 6122
MANAGING DIRECTOR Ian Westwood 020 7907 6355
PUBLISHER Paul Rayner 020 7907 6663
BOOKAZINE MANAGER Dharmesh Mistry 020 7907 6100
LIST RENTAL INSERTS EXECUTIVE John Perry 020 7907 6151 *john_perry@dennis.co.uk*
MARKETING MANAGER Claire Scrase 020 7907 6113

MAGBOOK

DENNIS PUBLISHING LTD
MANAGING DIRECTOR TECHNOLOGY AND MOTORING Ian Westwood
MANAGING DIRECTOR OF ADVERTISING Julian Lloyd-Evans
NEWSTRADE DIRECTOR Martin Belson
CHIEF OPERATING OFFICER Brett Reynolds
GROUP FINANCE DIRECTOR Ian Leggett
CHIEF EXECUTIVE James Tye
CHAIRMAN Felix Dennis
Typography Neue Helvetica © Heidelberger Druckmaschinen AG, licensed by Linotype *linotype.com*
Collis © 1993 The Enschedé Font Foundry *teff.nl/fonts/collis*
Printed in England by BGP Print Ltd, Chaucer International Estate, Launton Road, Bicester OX6 7QZ

HOW TO CONTACT US
MAIL MACUSER, 30 Cleveland Street, London, W1T 4JD
EMAIL *mailbox@macuser.co.uk* **WEB** *www.macuser.co.uk*
PHONE 020 7907 6000 Fax 020 7907 6369

The paper used within this magazine is produced from sustainable fibre, manufactured by mills with a valid chain of custody.

Contents

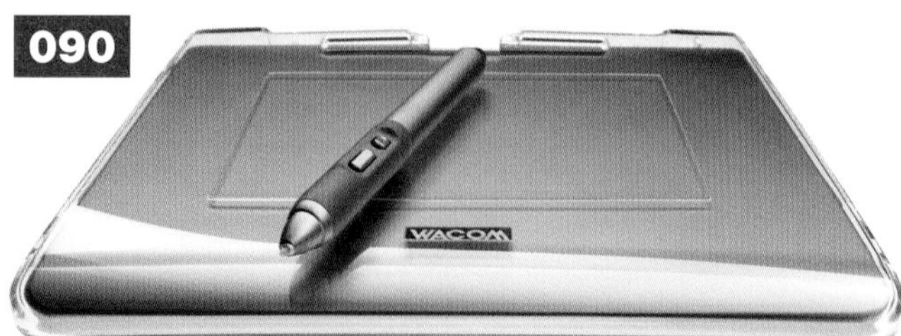

Design Techniques ... 007

Hints, tips and techniques that will inspire your designs, allowing you to produce impressive results and, if you're working professionally, an income, too.

A to Z of Design 049

A comprehensive guide to the most commonly used terms in the world of design to enhance your knowledge of the techniques employed by experienced designers.

168
Single
Double
>14.0 0.0/14.0
>14.0
1.0× 0.0/7.0
1.0× 0.0/6.0
>14.0 0.0/9.0
0.7× >12.0
18.0 -12.0
>7.0
1.0× 0.0/8.0
Other...
& Cheese
NICULTURAL FROMAGERIE SOCIETY
A history of innovation
More info

174
LOVE
192 PAGES OF Design KNOW-HOW

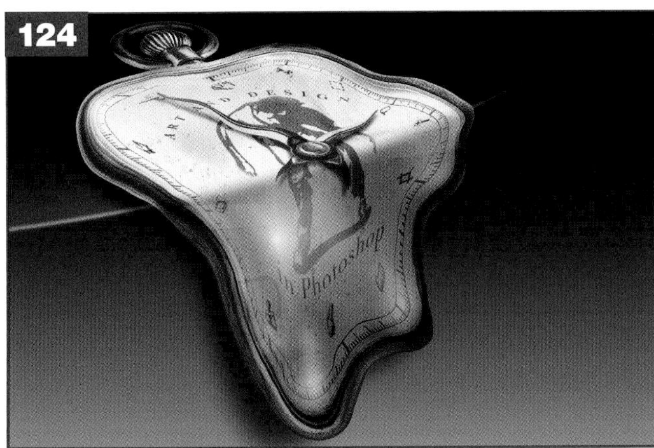
124

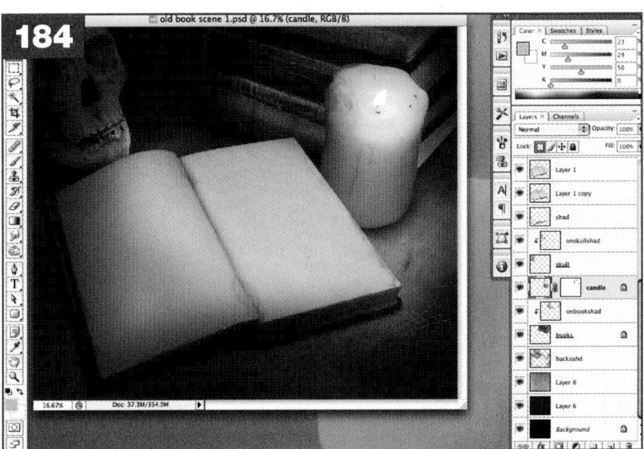
184

Design Techniques

If you came to *The Ultimate Guide to Graphic Design* for inspiration and advice, then this is where you'll find just that. Over the next 39 pages, we'll walk you through the techniques required to produce the kind of impressive effects that deliver the results you're after and, if you're working professionally in the field of graphic design, deliver an income, too.

None of these creative workshops assume any level of prior expertise. However, if you're having trouble understanding some of the basic concepts covered in each one, then be sure to check out the A to Z of Design section, which starts on p49.

In each of these Masterclasses, we have used either the latest version of each application, or one of its predecessors published within the past couple of years. In most cases, you should be able to complete each project in an earlier edition, too, although we have made every effort to highlight any features that are unique to only the latest versions.

If you don't have the most up-to-date editions of each application covered, you can download trials of most applications from their vendors. For Adobe Creative Suite application trials, check out *adobe.com/downloads*. For QuarkXPress, click to *http://8.quark.com/downloads/login.aspx*.

To get your creative juices flowing, we kick off this section of Design Techniques with an interview with David Carson, perhaps the most influential designer of his generation.

DAVID CARSON

We talk exclusively to US typographic design legend David Carson, the founder of *Ray Gun* magazine, who notoriously rewrote the rule book on graphic design.

Words Adam Banks **Photography** Gary Sims

It's not everyday that you get to meet the world's most famous graphic designer. Not even when it's in his diary. I was scheduled to interview David Carson in 1998, and the convention-smashing, deconstructive, who-says-you-have-to-learn-the-rules-before-you-break-them-style he'd pioneered on the US magazines *Beach Culture* and *Ray Gun* was beginning its crossover into the mainstream. Nobody was hotter than Carson, and as I waited for him in the foyer of a London boutique hotel that day, there was a mounting sense of expectation. It kept mounting for two hours. He never showed.

Fast forward more than 10 years, and there's still nobody hotter than Carson. Quark has brought him back to London as part of its campaign to make friends with designers, and I have been promised half an hour of his time before a public event at Hammersmith's Riverside Studios. This time he's only slightly late, completely charming, talkative and very funny. Then he gets up on stage and gives the audience more than their money's worth.

No PowerPoint here. Carson simply fires up his MacBook, revealing the same chaotic Desktop that you can see at *ilovedesign.com*, and starts pulling bits of work out of folders. It's shambolic, but nobody cares, even when he overruns his allotted time and just carries on. And on.

Then he moves onto the slide projector. Slide carousels, like deckchairs, have built-in comedy potential, as Carson knows perfectly well. The first technician goes off shift, defeated, as the event spirals on into the night. At one point slides are popping out like toast. Carson has deconstructed presenting. It's not supposed to be like this, but it's a lot more fun.

Amid the chaos we see plenty of good stuff, from the first *Ray Gun* covers to the latest commissions for po-faced blue-chips. When Carson finally gives way to Q&A, my neighbour in the audience asks how he persuaded BMW to let him cut up the letters of their logo. He pauses. 'Well… Those pieces didn't actually get accepted.' Still not quite mainstream, then.

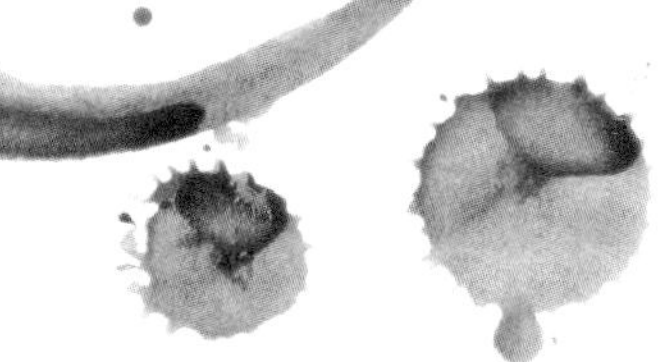

'The first rule of graphic design is don't announce you've got a book coming out when you haven't done it.'

On *The Rules of Graphic Design*, the book for which this was supposed to be the promotional tour.

'I did a BIG poster for the movie Helvetica. I set it in Franklin Gothic.'

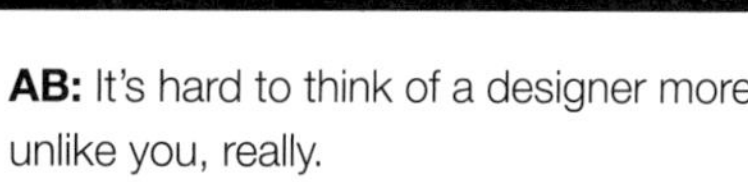

Adam Banks: You've just arrived in the UK?
David Carson: Yes, I just got in from Zurich and I'm not quite all here. But that's maybe not unusual.
AB: I like your Desktop. It kind of looks like our office.
DC: And the funny thing is, that's not even particularly bad.
AB: It gets worse?
DC: Someone sent me an email and I couldn't get it to open. Then I realised it *was* open, it had just blended in.
AB: It's a creative way of working. You have music on as well?
DC: I literally can't work without music.
AB: I think that goes together, because there's chaos and there's stimulation. You once said: 'Don't mistake legibility for communication.' Sometimes people misinterpret that and think you're not trying to communicate, that maybe it's just some designer's game, but that's not it at all – it's about engaging and stimulating, isn't it?
DC: It's trying to communicate an idea, and in doing that, sometimes something became a little harder to read, but I think the whole 'hard to read' thing got way overblown.
AB: Well you did set a whole article in Dingbats…
DC: [Laughs] That's what I always hear about. Thirty issues, and one article. Well, I admit that was one you could not actually read. But it has a lot to do with what you're interested in reading, too. People who weren't into the music or that particular band tended to write the whole thing off as being unreadable.
AB: The reader has to make an effort, too.
DC: Yes. When I first redesigned *Surfer* magazine, they took a copy to the famous American designer Milton Glaser, and surprise, surprise, he hated it.
AB: It's hard to think of a designer more unlike you, really.
DC: [Laughs] Yeah. But my thing is to take it to an 18-year-old kid coming out of the water. If he loves it, it's probably working. That's kind of what happened with *Ray Gun*. The publishers were worried about the first issue. Maybe we've gone too far. But then from the start it got a good reaction, advertisers came in.
AB: It was hugely influential obviously, *Ray Gun* and *Beach Culture*…
DC: Yeah, well I tend to think *Beach Culture* was actually a better magazine, but fewer people saw it. If you can somehow, which you can't, construct a tree of influence, it would be more than people realise. When I show some of that early work tonight, to students, for example, they might think what's the big deal, but in the early 1990s there wasn't anything like that.

'I LIKE to show a client a LOT of stuff. But don't show them anything you HATE, because you know if you do they'll PICK it.'

AB: You edited a book about lucky accidents…

DC: It should have been called *Happy Accidents*, I think, but it's actually called *Lucky Disasters*.

AB: And there's a lot of that in the process.

DC: Yes, you have a general direction where you think you're going, but you have to be able to do things along the way that maybe you weren't expecting. It maybe happens a little less now. Earlier, things would fall on the ground, and you would go ooh, that could work. Maybe I can pick that up and scan it in… It had to have some relevancy, it wasn't just 'that's weird, let's throw that in'. It's easier, in a sense, to do simple, classic design – you can get people off the sidewalk and teach them to do a newsletter. It's harder to do the freeform, expressive stuff well. You read an article, what do I get from that? That's the starting point. I look at a photo and I say, wooh, that needs to bleed. Maybe I'd find a section of the photo and blow it up…

AB: And again, you often see that done now, and before the mid-1990s, you just wouldn't see it done, but now everybody's kind of got permission to do it.

DC: Yeah, I was talking to an educator from Cranbrook [Academy of Art, Michigan] just a year or so ago, and he was very matter of fact and saying, well, it's over, we won. I hadn't really thought of it like that, but watch the news, watch CNN, everything's flying up, you've got the type doing all these things…

AB: Do you think that as the tools get more sophisticated, and places like Cranbrook are now teaching people how to do the kind of stuff that you do, is there a danger that we lose those happy accidents?

DC: Well, there is… It's not about all the tools, it's really gotta come from the individual. The only way you can do anything really unique or different is utilise yourself.

AB: I suppose we have to mention Quark… It seems to me that Quark and you are quite a good fit, because I always think of QuarkXPress when we were all just starting to use it and it was exciting, and it was quite a primitive tool at that point. When I think about the new versions, I guess… I guess you don't sit around a lot putting soft drop shadows on things…

DC: [Laughs] You know, just recently getting introduced to some of the newer functions, I had a couple of clients that I had done that on. I had done what I accused other people of doing – I had found the button. And to their credit, both those clients said, umm, do you think maybe we should lose that drop shadow?

AB: Your first book was *The End of Print*. Obviously, you can take that in two ways:

'Never having learned all the things you're NOT supposed to do helped a lot.'

'You can't put your own FACE on the front cover unless you're AUSTRIAN.'

Referring to the self-promotional tendencies of Stefan Sagmeister, the world's second most famous graphic designer.

that it's the end of print in that it finishes, or we've got to make it into something else.

DC: I think there was a lot of confusion that we were trying to say it's the end of writing or it's the end of reading. But I've come to think it probably was the early stages of the end of print as a primary source of information. I think most of the major newspapers and magazines, circulation is down…

AB: But that's not the only form of print – you still get masses of mailings through your door…

DC: Exactly, it just changes into something else. Neville Brody actually came up with the quote, he looked at *Ray Gun* and he said, well, this is the end of print. That's it, we've taken it as far as we can. I think he was a little early on that, but it's more and more true. It becomes more of a novelty item, like vinyl records…

AB: Like McLuhan said, when it outlives its relevance it becomes a work of art. Do you think we might all be in the heritage industry in a few years' time?

DC: [Laughs] It was also David Byrne who talked about that in the intro to *The End of Print*. He said: 'Print is no longer obligated to simply carry the news.' It had been given freedom to serve other purposes. This may not relate, but I was on a panel for this movie *Helvetica*, and this guy [type design guru] Erik Spiekermann went on and on about the amazing alphabet, that can tell you everything you need to know with just these few symbols. Well, something didn't hit me right about that, but it took a student to say afterwards, 'What's he talking about? The alphabet has failed miserably. We have to invent smiley faces, LOL, this whole other language. Laughter, sarcasm…

AB: Which is kind of doing the same thing you're doing: rather than just conveying the text, you're conveying the state of mind.

DC: Well exactly, see that's an interesting analogy. I think that's maybe a different interview… Sometimes I think that Neville Brody was right, that *Ray Gun* was this last gasp of print being important. And I don't think you can point to something since then that has had as much effect.

AB: And yet, look at everything that's happened, I mean the Internet barely existed.

DC: Yeah, I think it's specifically because they were all of a sudden doing websites, it dispersed a lot of very creative people that would have done the next thing.

AB: Well, those ripples are still going out. David Carson, I think we need to end there, so thank you very much, that was great.

DC: That seemed a little scattered… But *I'm* scattered.

Art is a selective re-creation of reality according to an artist's metaphysical value judgments. An artist recreates those aspects of reality which represent his fundamental view of man's nature.
Every child is an artist. The problem is how to remain an artist once he grows up.

Line art

Creating a line art illustration is a great way of making the most of a photograph and, thanks to handy tools in Photoshop and Illustrator, it's not as hard as you might think. We walk you through a couple of very different approaches.

Words and illustrations Steve Caplin

The idea of converting photographs or paintings into line art has been around since at least the 15th century. The technique coincided with the invention of printing, because printing machines could either print black or not at all – with no shades of grey available – the only option for reproducing images was to convert them to pure black and white.

From the earliest engravings to the latest computerised etchings, we've seen the form elevated to an unprecedented degree of sophistication. But the underlying method remains the same: using different densities of crosshatching to simulate lighter and darker shades of grey. Because all the shading is made with fine lines, the technique is referred to as 'line art'.

William Blake began his career as an engraver, while Gustav Doré perfected the technique in the 19th Century. Even as late as the 1980s, photographs were painstakingly rendered as etchings for use in newspaper advertisements. Because papers were notoriously inaccurate in their blotchy reproduction of photographs, advertisers who wanted their products to look their best would routinely have the images hand drawn in a photo-realistic etching style instead of relying on the hit-and-miss dot screen process.

There are a number of different methods of converting images into line art. Some require painstaking effort on the part of the artist, while others can be more or less automated. We'll look at a couple of very different approaches.

THE ILLUSTRATOR METHOD

Adobe Illustrator is the perfect tool for creating line art illustrations, since it's designed from the ground up for drawing smooth, clean lines with simple flat fills. The fact that every element is a separate editable object makes it easy to apply different fills and strokes to them, and to change these values at a later point. It's also possible to repurpose artwork created in Illustrator. This means that if, for example, you've produced a complex illustration, like the one shown in workthrough one, you can reuse the illustration elsewhere with comparative ease.

Illustrations have far more clarity than photographs, and can be reproduced far smaller without loss of information. This is why technical manuals always use line art illustrations rather than photographs, even though, like here, they will almost certainly have started with photographic images, which were then traced. When producing these illustrations, you don't have to worry about clean backgrounds, professional photographic lighting or even dirty fingernails. You just need to get the raw image into Illustrator, so that you can produce the perfect illustration from it.

When drawing over a photograph, the problem, initially, is that the drawings will cover the image to such an extent that you may no longer be able to see what you're trying to reproduce. It's possible to get around this problem by lowering the opacity of the objects as you draw them, using the Transparency palette – you can always return them to their full strength later on.

The question when producing technical drawings of this kind is how much detail do you include? The answer is to add in enough detail to make the illustration clear to the viewer, but not so much that the space is cluttered up. You don't need to add in every bump and screw head, every character of button text and every bevel.

THE PHOTOSHOP METHOD

There are many ways of creating line art effects from images in Photoshop, and many of the built-in 'artistic' and 'sketch' filters will attempt to produce one-shot results for you. But these methods always look forced and artificial; it's possible to do better with a little human intervention. We've tried a couple of different approaches here, which produced two different results.

The first method involves tracing over the image by hand with the Pen tool; then you can 'stroke' the resulting Pen path by switching to the Brush tool (with the Pen path still visible) and pressing Enter. This applies the current Brush as a stroke to the path, and is a useful Photoshop technique. You then use a copy of the original photograph, highly stylised using the Stamp filter, to add in the hair and eyes, before adding colour on a separate layer. The result of this method is to produce a highly stylised, yet recognisable portrait. It does, however, require a certain degree of skill, as you will need to know where to draw in the Pen lines, and some judgement is needed in this process.

The second approach is more automated, and requires no drawing skills. It relies on using the Threshold adjustment to produce three copies of the original photograph, each at a different threshold level. A diagonal pattern can then be applied to the lightest of these three copies, filling the final (and most minimal) copy with black to add definition. Although it's remarkably easy to achieve, the results can be impressive, with the diagonal lines giving the image a cross-hatched look that's fully in keeping with the traditions of etching. For a more naturalistic approach, try using concentric circles or wavy lines instead of straight diagonals – although this takes some time to arrange the curves convincingly.

WORKTHROUGH ONE: ILLUSTRATOR

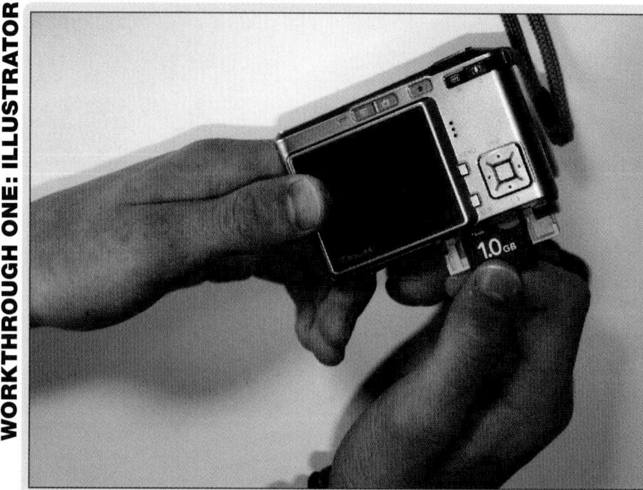

▲ **STEP 01** This photo shows how to insert a memory card into a camera. But it's far from clear, even at high resolution. When printed very small in a user manual, it would be hard to tell what's going on. Open the image in Illustrator to begin tracing, and scale it so that it's an appropriate size for the illustration.

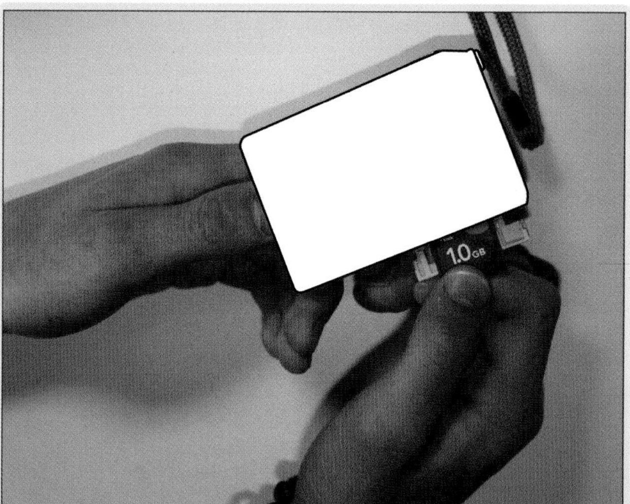

▲ **STEP 02** With the image in Illustrator, first lock the layer it's on. That way it can't be moved. Then create a new layer on which to create the illustrations. By doing this, you can hide the original photo to see how it is progressing. Start to trace the first shape with the Pen tool, starting with the main shapes.

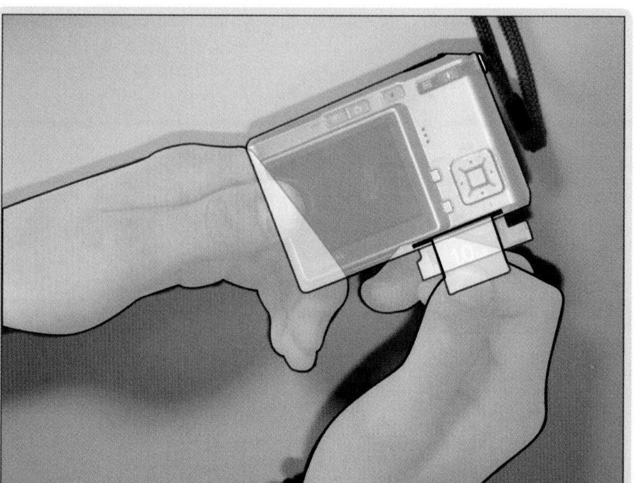

▲ **STEP 03** You'll soon find that it's hard to see what's going on when the photo is covered with objects. You could apply no fill, but this would make it harder to see the shape of your drawings. A better solution is to fill the objects with white, and lower their opacity to about 50% so you can see through them.

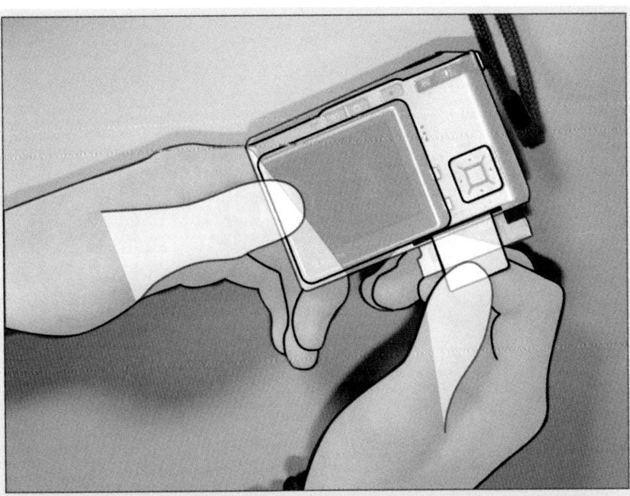

▲ **STEP 04** Continue adding objects. Those that appear in front of other items, like the thumbs here, will need to be filled with white; some are just unfilled lines, such as the lines marking the fingers. When drawing rotated rectangles, such as the screen, draw the first one using Effect > Stylize > Round Corners.

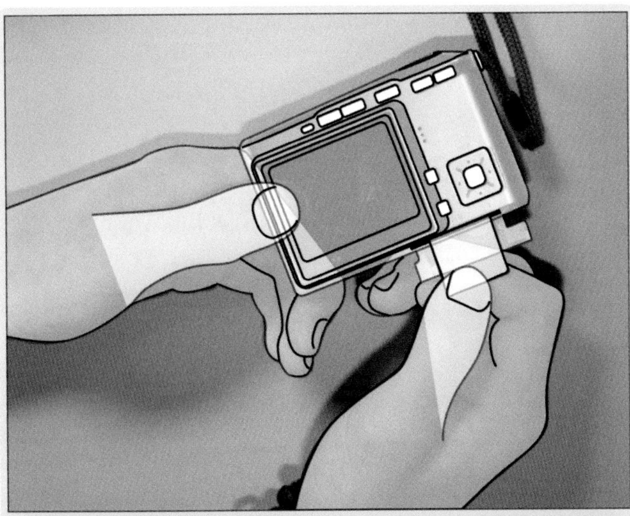

▲ **STEP 05** All the screen insets and buttons on the back of the camera are made by duplicating the first rectangle and moving it to each new location. When you select a rotated rectangle, the side and corner handles appear in their rotated position, allowing you to easily reshape and scale them.

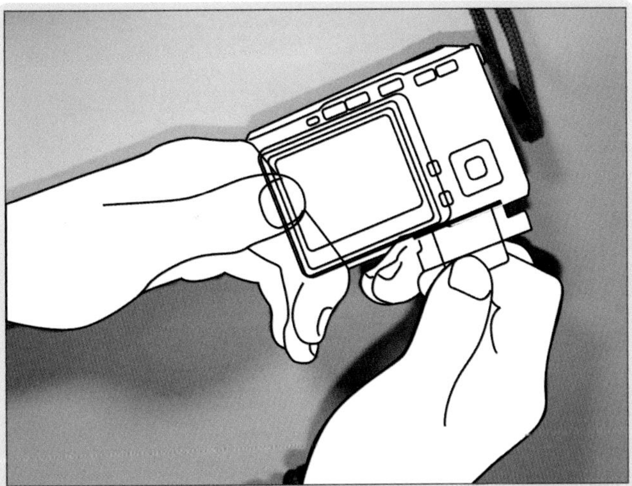

▲ **STEP 06** Once the lines are filled in, you can bring the transparency of all the objects back to 100%. Clearly, some reordering needs to be done here. The order in which the elements were created doesn't match the stacking order required for the illustration. Fortunately, it's easy to move them up and down.

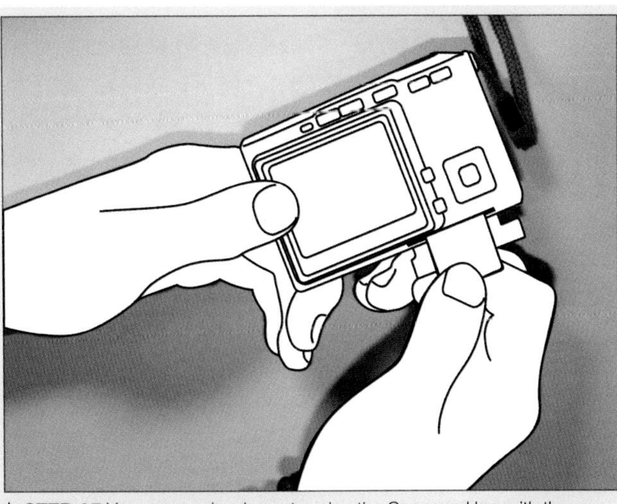

▲ **STEP 07** You can reorder elements using the Command key with the square bracket keys to move items up and down in the stack. If you cut an item with Command-x, use Shift-Command-f to paste it in front of any other selected item – a useful way to set the stacking order of Illustrator objects.

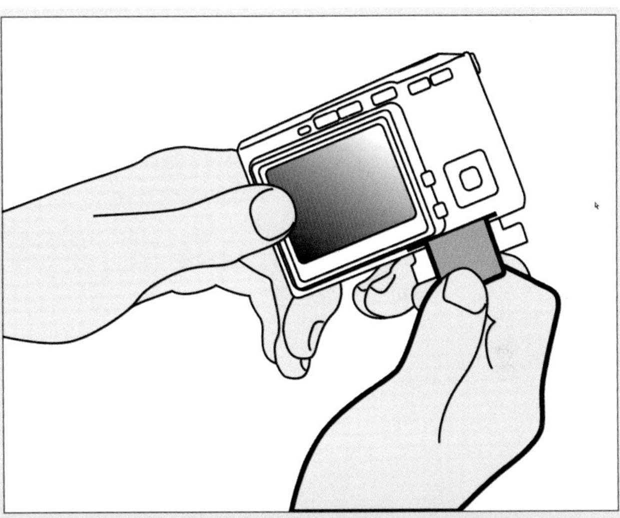

▲ **STEP 08** With the line artwork complete, you can hide the original photo far more easily as it's on a separate layer. A little colour can be added to the image and the key region of the hand inserting the card can be outlined in a bolder stroke. The simple gradient on the screen also gives the image a lift.

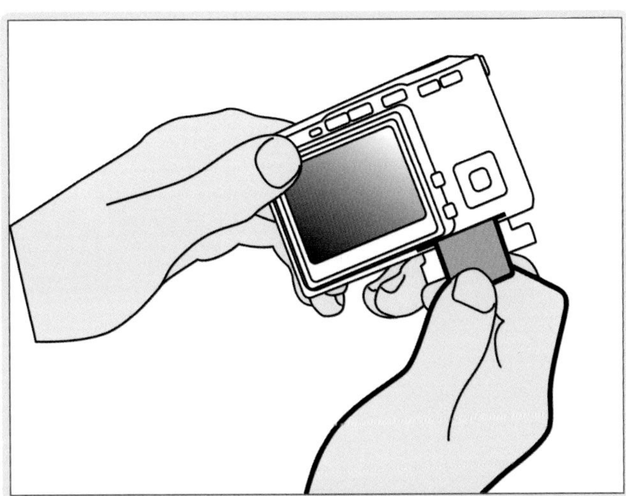

▲ **STEP 09** Because each object is a separate element, you can correct mistakes easily. You shouldn't, for example, show the thumb smudging the screen, and it's easy enough to move the whole hand in Illustrator. This operation would be more difficult if you were using the original photo instead.

WORKTHROUGH TWO: PHOTOSHOP 1

▲ **STEP 01** We'll use this photo as the basis for an illustration in Photoshop. There are tricky elements here – the lack of side lighting (which would have helped), and the wispy hair (which would be difficult to redraw). We'll show how almost the entire process can be automated, with no drawing required.

▲ **STEP 02** Begin by duplicating the photograph as a new layer – you'll need a couple of copies of the original later. Use Smart Blur, with the pop-up Mode set to Edge Only. This will produce the inverted outline seen here. It's not perfect, but it's a good place to start generating your line art image.

▲ **STEP 03** Invert the line art using Command-I, the results will be ragged and bitmapped. Apply the Poster Edges filter to the result to create a smoother finish. It doesn't matter how you set the Poster edges settings, as it makes little difference in this instance. Hide this layer for later use.

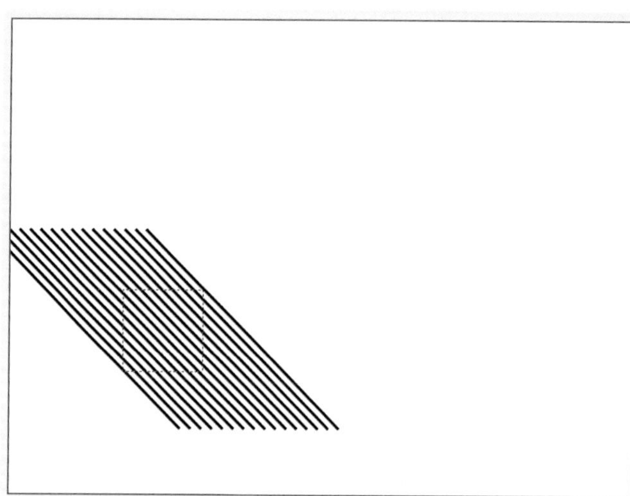

▲ **STEP 04** You now need to create a crosshatch pattern to shade the image. Draw a line at 45° on a new layer, and select it; use Alt-Shift-Command and the right cursor to nudge a copy of it 10 pixels to the right. Continue until you have a set of stripes, then select a square area and define it as a pattern.

▲ **STEP 05** Take another copy of the original image, and use the Threshold dialog (Image > Adjustments) to create a deliberately dark version of the face: we want to include most of the skin in this example. Then use the Magic Eraser tool to delete all the white from this layer, leaving just that black shadow visible.

▲ **STEP 06** Open the Layer Styles dialog box, and use Pattern Overlay to apply diagonal stripes to the layer. They'll only show up over the black area, producing this result. Because you applied the texture using Layer Styles, you can reduce the size of the texture.

▲ **STEP 07** Take another copy of the original photo and use Threshold to produce a paler version of the black-and-white image. Make a new version of the diagonal stripe texture, with the stripes going the other way, and use Pattern Fill on this version; set the mode of this layer to Multiply.

▲ **STEP 08** Reveal the original inverted Smart Blur outline layer and bring it to the top of the layer stack. Set the mode of this layer to Multiply, so you can see the shading layers through it. So far, so good: but more definition is needed in the deep shadows, and especially within the pupils of the eyes.

▲ **STEP 09** Take yet another copy of the original photo and use the Threshold adjustment. This time, you only want to see the very darkest parts of the image, so drag the slider until everything but the deepest shadows disappears. Set the layer mode to Multiply, so you can see through to the layer beneath.

▲ **STEP 01** This image uses the same photographic original as used in workthrough 2. The outline and main elements are drawn using the Pen tool; then, on a new empty layer, switch to a hard edged Brush (around four pixels) and press Enter to stroke the Pen path with that brush.

▲ **STEP 02** A copy of the original photograph is treated using Filter > Stylize > Stamp to produce a smooth-edged black and white effect. It's similar to the Threshold adjustment, except that a far smoother result can be created this way. Erase any unwanted stray clumps of pixels.

▲ **STEP 03** Finally, make a new layer and paint colour into it. The blush on the cheeks is made by using the Burn tool, set to Midtones, on the pale skin colour: in this mode, it darkens and enriches the colour.

PHOTOSHOP FOR FREE

With the growth of web-based applications, Adobe has made the bold move in developing a free online version of its heavyweight image editor, Photoshop. We take a look to see how it compares to its big brother.

Words Kenny Hemphill + Alan Stonebridge

ONLINE IMAGE EDITOR
Photoshop Express

Price Free
Contact Adobe + *photoshop.com/express*
Needs PowerPC G4 or better + Mac OS X 10.4 + 1GB Ram
Pros Fantastic interface + Slick + Lots of editing features
Cons None

It's been obvious for some time that more and more of the work we do on our Macs and PCs will be done online in web-based applications, rather than locally on our own machines. Email, word processing, spreadsheeting and project management can already be performed, albeit at a reasonably basic level, without ever opening an application on your hard drive. Photoshop Express, however, is something very different. This isn't some tiny start-up launching an Ajax-based application that looks and performs well within strict limitations. Nor is it an online giant like Google or Yahoo! making a play for markets dominated by multinational software houses. This is Adobe taking its flagship application, Photoshop, and putting it online. At least, that's what it is on the surface. It doesn't, however, take long once you've started using Photoshop Express to realise that while it may carry the Photoshop name, this has more to do with leveraging a powerful brand than any relationship it has with Photoshop CS4 or Elements. While Express allows you to edit photographs and display them in galleries, share them with friends and download them again for printing, it does it differently from CS4 and Elements. Nor does it have much in common with Lightroom's room-based approach. But enough of what Photoshop Express isn't. What is it?

▲ The Photoshop Express interface is clean and easy to navigate. Once you've uploaded your photos, you can edit them and share them in a gallery or email them.

▲ In addition to adjustments such as exposure and saturation, Express allows you to apply effects. This one is called Sketch and can be applied in varying degrees.

Put simply, Photoshop Express is a beautifully designed, easy to use and surprisingly powerful tool for uploading, manipulating and sharing your digital pictures. And for a program still in beta testing it's remarkably polished and stable.

It's worth noting a couple of things at this stage. Firstly, the beta is technically only open to US residents. This restriction can, however, easily be overcome by selecting 'US' when prompted for your country of residence during the sign-up process. The only personal information required to create an account is a valid email address. The second restriction is that Express only supports Jpeg images, and they must be no more than 10MB in size and have a height and width of 4000 pixels or less. Images larger than 2880 x 2880 pixels are reduced in size after editing. And you can only store 2GB of images per account. None of those limitations should present too much of a problem for most people.

To upload pictures to your account, you just click on the Upload Photos button on the top-left of the interface. At this point, you'll spot two of Express' neatest features: the tooltips that pop up whenever you hover over a button, and the way that user interface elements fade in and out rather than flash on and off. Clicking on Upload presents you with a Finder window and highlights compatible images. Click on an image or Shift-click multiple images to upload. You can then elect to upload the pictures to your Library, create an album to upload them to, or upload to an existing album.

Adobe recommends that you don't upload any more than 100 photos at a time, but, while upload times are reasonable given that the servers that host the application are in the US, we'd stick to smaller batches of 20 or so images. In our tests, a folder containing nine images totalling 25MB took around 10 minutes to upload. You can work directly with photos from your Facebook, Picasa, or Photobucket accounts by clicking on the relevant log-in link under Other Sites in the left interface pane. There's no support yet for Flickr or MySpace. We'd also hope to see the introduction of support for photo printing services such as Snapfish and Photobox. Whether that happens may depend on whether Adobe plans to offer its own printing service from Express.

At this stage, you may feel that working inside a browser window is less than ideal. If so, click the icon in the top-right corner of Express' interface. This switches to full-screen mode and means that Express becomes indistinguishable from an application on your hard drive. The full-screen mode really is beautifully implemented.

There are a number of options for editing your images. The simplest is to click on the image you want to adjust and then click on the Edit Photo button. However, hovering over an image displays a menu that drops down from the bottom of the photo and allows you to choose Edit, as well as perform basic functions, such as rotating, emailing an image, or downloading it. From this menu you can also revert to the original image after performing an edit. This is another neat feature of

▲ The editing features are limited but very well-implemented. When you click on a command, such as Exposure, you can quickly preview each of the available options.

Express; all changes are completely non-destructive and you can revert back to an original or to a previous edit at any stage.

Once in the editing window, you'll find all the features you'd expect: crop; rotate; remove red-eye; alter exposure, white balance, or saturation and sharpen. There are plenty of effects too, like PopColor, which isolates a single colour in an image and turns everything else black and white, and Sketch, which does as its name suggests. The editing features are very neatly implemented. Click on the one you want and you're presented with seven thumbnails, representing different degrees of application of the adjustment or effect. Hover over a thumbnail and its effect is previewed in the main window. Click on it to apply it. You can then apply other adjustments or effects. Reverting to the original is a matter of pressing one button on the bottom toolbar, but, cleverly, you can remove each effect in isolation by deselecting it in the left-hand pane. The editing features are far from comprehensive, but they provide most of the features that you're most likely to need for making basic adjustments to photos before sharing them or printing them.

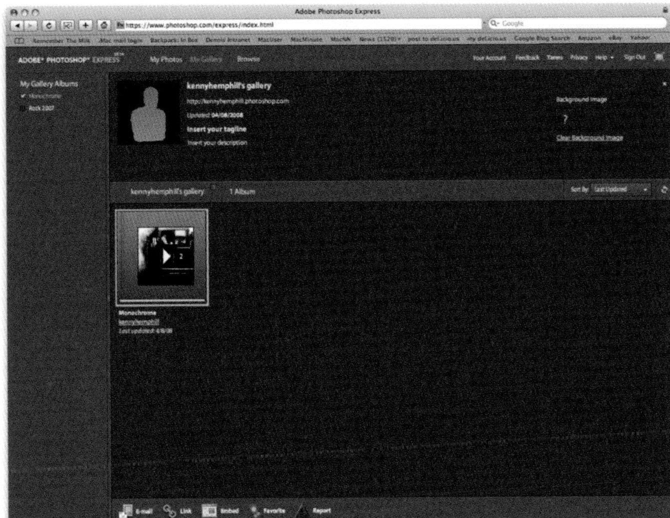

▲ Images remain private until you elect to share them on an album-by-album basis and you can refer friends to them with a link or embed them in a web page.

Albums are private by default, you elect to make them public by clicking on My Gallery and selecting the albums you want to share. At this stage you can also copy a link to an album or copy code to embed it in a web page.

Photoshop Express isn't perfect. It can be a little slow to access from the UK because it's currently only hosted in the US. And, as you would expect, it has a limited feature set. But Adobe has created a stunning online photo editor that looks sensational and works brilliantly. It won't replace any desktop application, let alone its namesake, but as a way of uploading and editing pictures so you can display them or email them to friends, it's unbeatable. ⊕

UPLOAD AND DOWNLOAD PHOTOS WITHOUT THE PAIN

Photoshop Express has a real wow factor – it's amazing to have so much power at your disposal when editing images in a web-based application, but you'll have to contend with a couple of issues to get photos in and out of Express. Manually converting images begins to grate under heavy use, especially with the inevitable delays that come with the existing servers being based in the US.

The first limitation will only affect those whose cameras shoot in Raw mode – only Jpegs can be uploaded to Photoshop Express. This isn't, however, likely to be a problem for most people, especially for snaps taken with a compact or camera phone. If you're shooting as Raw, try setting your camera to shoot a Jpeg version too.

Don't give up on Express if you don't want to make the change – it doesn't matter if the Mac or PC you've dragged halfway across the world doesn't have an up-to-date version of Photoshop's Raw converter that works with your camera. So long as you're running a recent enough version of Mac OS X that supports your camera's Raw format or have another converter on your PC, then you will already have the tools at your disposal to convert the images to Jpeg.

A bigger stumbling block lies in the supported resolutions. You'll probably be shooting in the highest resolution that your camera supports. Unfortunately, images bigger than 2880 pixels in height or width are shrunk down after editing, although photos up to 4000 x 4000 pixels in size can be uploaded – fine if you're lucky enough to take perfect photos every time, but you're bound to take at least a few photos that need a little cropping or colour correction, and you can save time and bandwidth by uploading smaller images in the first place – vital if you're on borrowed time, especially in an Internet café.

To help Mac users cope with these irritations, we've put together two Automator workflows, which need either Tiger or Leopard. The first creates a standalone Automator application onto which you can drop photos to convert them. Since it's an application in its own right, you can leave it on the desktop or in the Dock, plug in your camera and drag its contents onto the icon. Leave it to do its magic while you catch up on email and check a few news websites and, after a few minutes, you'll have a folder full of photos ready to upload to Express.

After spending time turning good shots into ones that you're keen to share, you probably don't want to lose the end results. Express lets you download your images at the original or a lower resolution, but it's a real hassle to do so – you have to select the photo, choose the resolution and decide where to save it. Unfortunately, there's currently no way to mark multiple photos and download them all as an archive.

This makes downloading a whole reel of edited photos a real chore, but our second workflow cuts out a lot of the hassle. It'll download all of the photos to one location – and all at the original resolution in which they were uploaded, and ready to send to a photo-printing service.

If you're using Express, it's unlikely you'll have the power of Photoshop and it's excellent droplets to hand. It's worth keeping these workflows on your portable Mac or, if you're going to use someone else's Mac while on your travels, put them on your memory card. They're small enough not to eat up valuable space that would be better used to store photographs, and they will save you plenty of time converting images.

Converting photos for upload

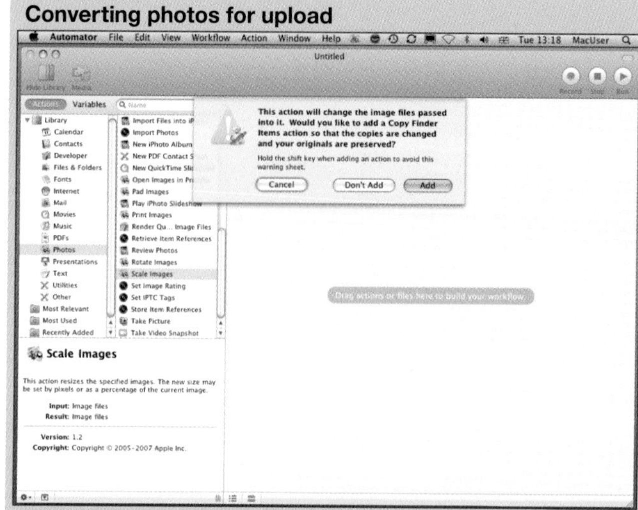

▲ **STEP 01** Create a custom workflow in Automator and add the Scale Images action to it. When asked, add the Copy Finder Items action so that Automator doesn't alter the original photos on your camera. Set it to copy to a new folder and turn off the option to replace existing files.

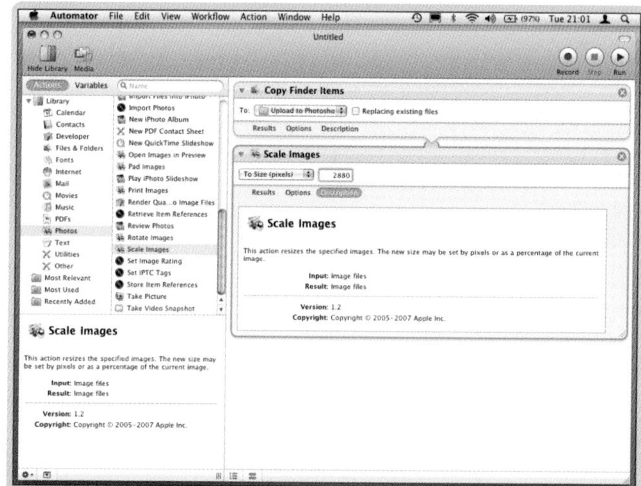

▲ **STEP 02** Set the scaling method to reduce images to a specific size in pixels. If you intend to edit the images, set it to 2880 pixels or less. Images are scaled in proportion and the larger dimension – width or height – is scaled to your chosen value. This ensures images are small enough for Express to handle.

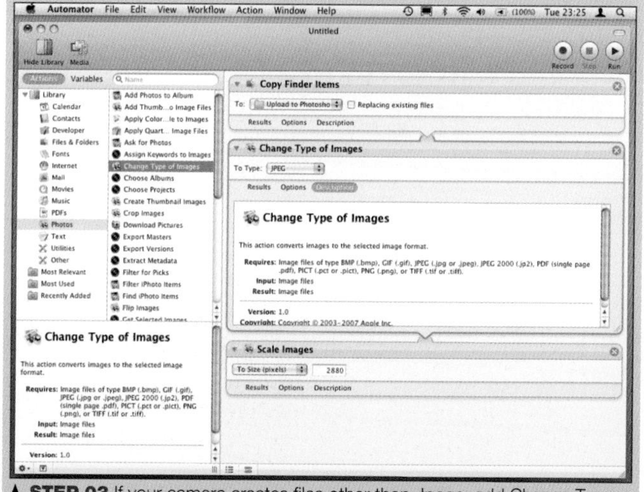

▲ **STEP 03** If your camera creates files other than Jpegs, add Change Type of Images between the two existing actions and set the type to Jpeg. Save the workflow, then choose File > Save As and save it as an application onto which you can drop images to convert them.

Quickly download multiple photos

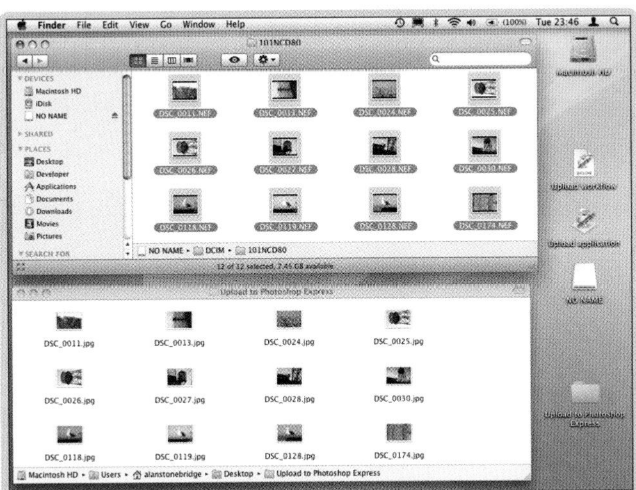

▲ **STEP 04** Plug in your camera and locate the photos for upload in the Finder. Drag them – not the folder that contains them – onto the application from Step 3. Progress is shown in the menu bar; when it disappears, look in the folder from Step 2 to find Express-compatible files ready for upload.

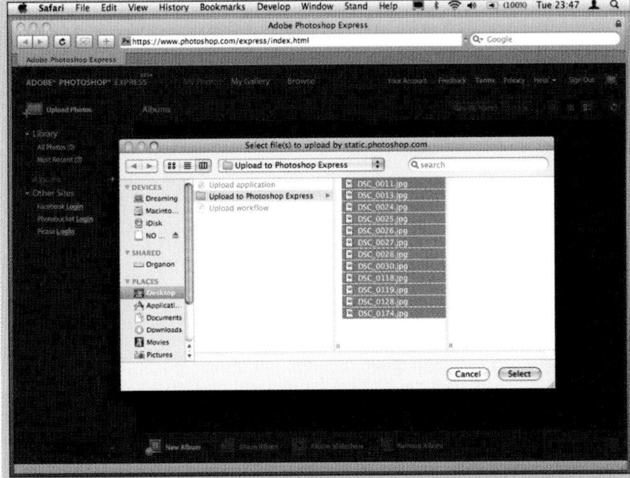

▲ **STEP 05** Log into Express and click on the Upload Photos button on the welcome screen. Browse to the folder that contains the converted photos. This dialog box recognises standard Mac shortcuts, so press Command-a then press the Select button to upload multiple photos at once.

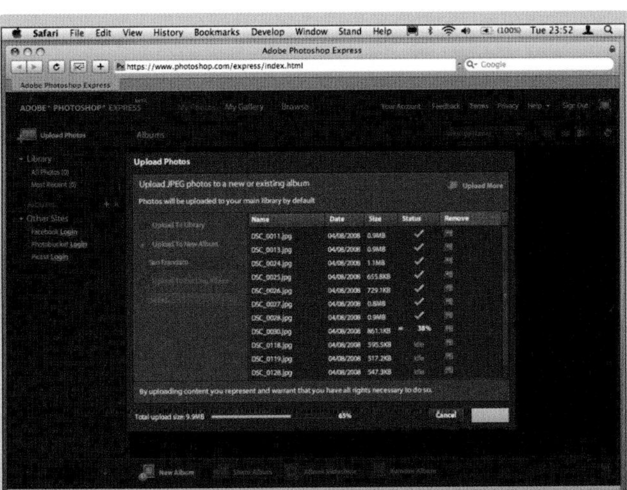

▲ **STEP 06** In the next dialog, choose whether to upload directly to the library, create a new album, or add them to an existing one. When you're ready, hit Upload and wait for the progress bar to hit 100%, then press the Done button. All of your images will appear, ready to be edited and shared with the world.

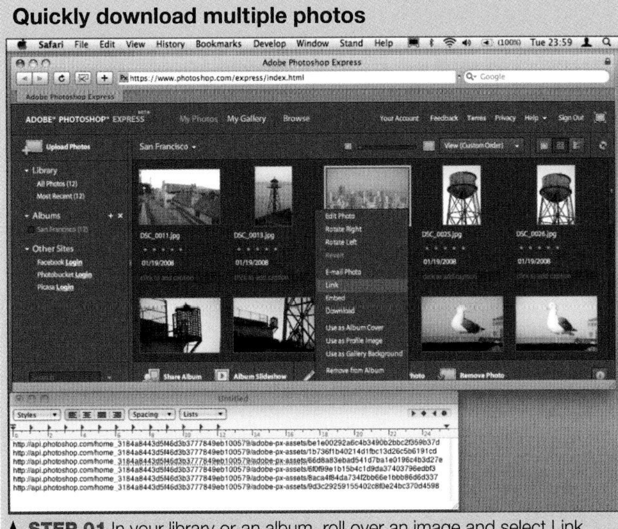

▲ **STEP 01** In your library or an album, roll over an image and select Link from the Photo Options menu. Create a new document in TextEdit and press Command-V to paste the address of the full-resolution photo. Press Return. Keep doing this until you've gathered links to the photos you want to download.

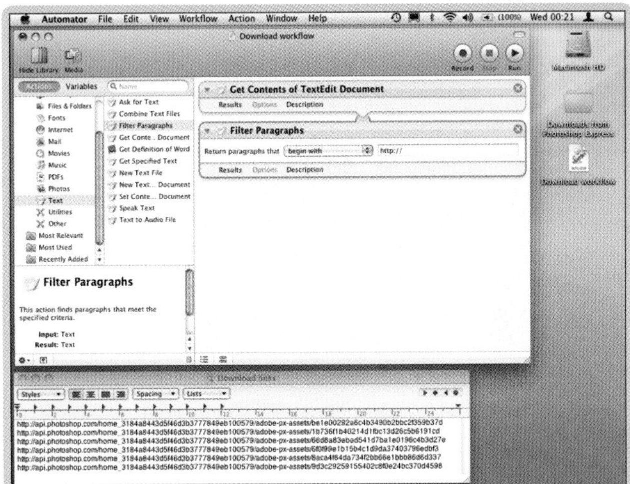

▲ **STEP 02** Create a new custom workflow in Automator. Under the list of text actions, drag Get Contents of TextEdit Document into the workflow, then add the Filter Paragraphs action beneath it. Set it to return paragraphs that begin with http:// so that it separates the links for the final action.

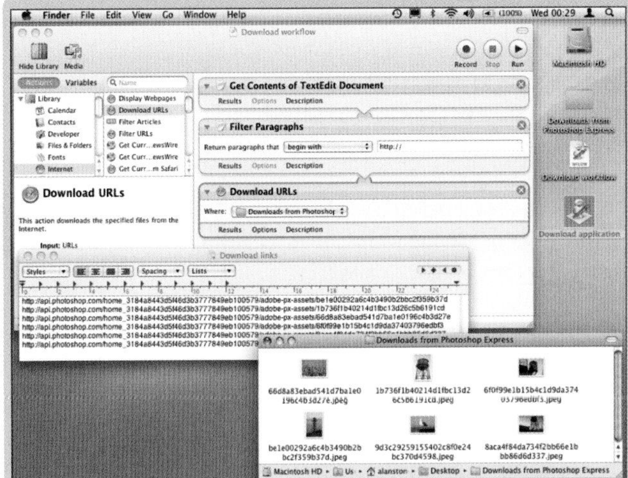

▲ **STEP 03** Finally, add Download URLs from the Internet actions. Set it to download to a new folder. Save the workflow as an application so that it runs without opening the Automator application. Bring the TextEdit document of links to the front and run the application. All the images in it will be downloaded.

Managing your photos

Words Lukas Aleksandr

The digital age has all but wiped out the need for storing hard copies of your images, and with Mac OS X's Time Machine it's now easier than ever to keep up-to-date backups of your files. But there are other ways to protect your precious photos and keep them safe.

Photos are captured moments in time and – by all logical accounts – time is linear and can't run backwards. As such, your photos are unique, so deserve particular care and attention to keep them safe.

Once you have imported your photos onto your Mac, you have at least one backup of your originals. Except that's not true for long. The whole idea of digital photography is that by doing away with negatives and prints, we can also do away with film. Instead, we use memory cards, which as soon as we've imported their contents, we wipe clean to use again. And in the process, those backups on our Mac suddenly become the masters.

With Time Machine under Leopard, it is now far easier for us all to keep up-to-date backups of our files, as we no longer have to make a conscious decision to connect an external drive, instigate a backup

▲ Leopard's Time Machine creates links to any unchanged files, so when you travel back in its history, you see the entire contents of your Mac on a given day.

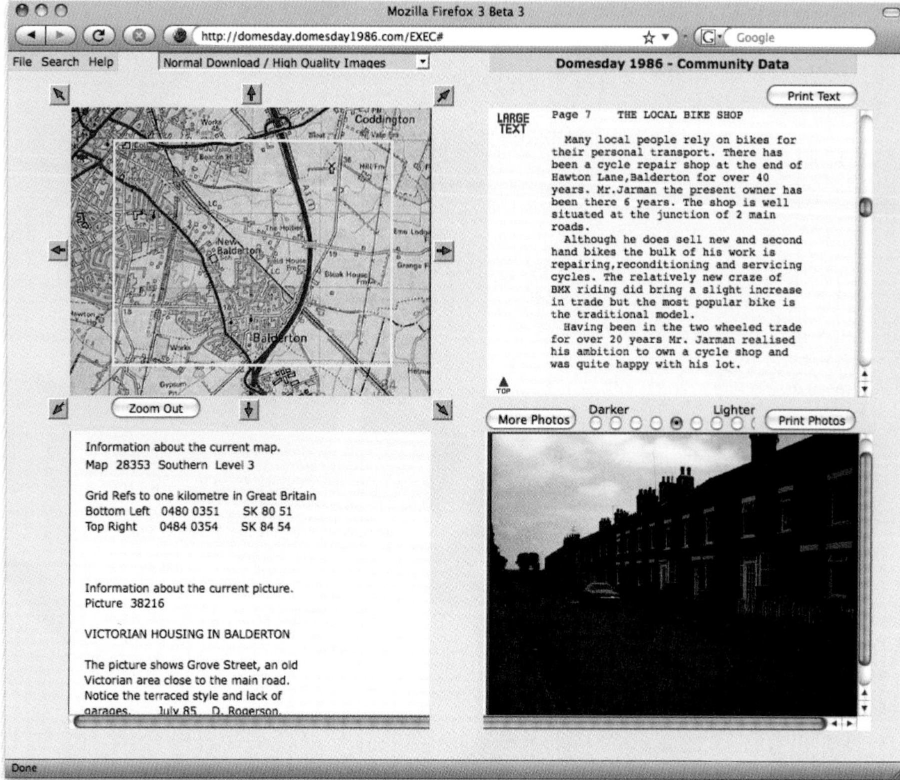

▲ The BBC's Domesday project, which created a modern-day, digital edition of the *Domesday Book* to celebrate its 900th anniversary, used Laserdiscs for storage. It is often cited as an example of digital obsolescence.

script and then disconnect the same drive, and move it offsite every time we want to import new pictures.

But whether you're running Leopard or not, you should have a supplementary system in place that will keep your photos safe. In an era where we can email them to friends, delete the blurred, unflattering or poorly framed shots and put the rest online, we are becoming increasingly blasé about our digital assets and often only realise quite how careless we've been when it's too late. In this feature, we'll take you through the steps to ensuring you keep your photos safe, and useful, for years to come.

FORMAT FIRST

Times move on and standards change. Try opening an old MacWrite file on a modern Mac, for example. While you may be able to extract the physical text, the chances are you'll lose most or all of your formatting. Do the same with MacPaint, and you'll have an even tougher job on your hands. Why? Because as software houses evolve their products they slowly change their file formats and, eventually, one-time standards become obsolete. See Microsoft's ground-up rewriting of the Office file formats if you don't believe us.

The same is true of physical media, such as the close-to-obsolete floppy disk, and the LP-sized laserdisc that was usurped by the smaller, more convenient, more capacious DVD. Laserdiscs were once held up as the future of data storage, and they were used for everything from feature films (*Terminator 2: Judgement Day*, *Cliffhanger*, *Back to the Future* and others appeared on the format) to concerts (Madonna, Janet Jackson) to software. Laserdisc provides us with the most famous example of digital obsolescence, after it was used by the BBC to produce a digital update of the entire *Domesday Book* in the mid-1980s. It was a massive project that involved the construction of a special Domesday Player designed to play back the discs when connected to a BBC computer.

However, Laserdisc fell out of favour as other formats came along, and then Jpeg arrived as the predominant image format (it wasn't around when the Domesday discs were produced) and suddenly the BBC's hard work was made obsolete. An extensive preservation project saved some of one of the discs, there were two in total, which has now been published online at *domesday.domesday1986.com*.

So if someone as big and well resourced as the BBC can fall into the format obsolescence trap, there is no reason why the same can't happen to the rest of us. When you import your pictures, then, you should

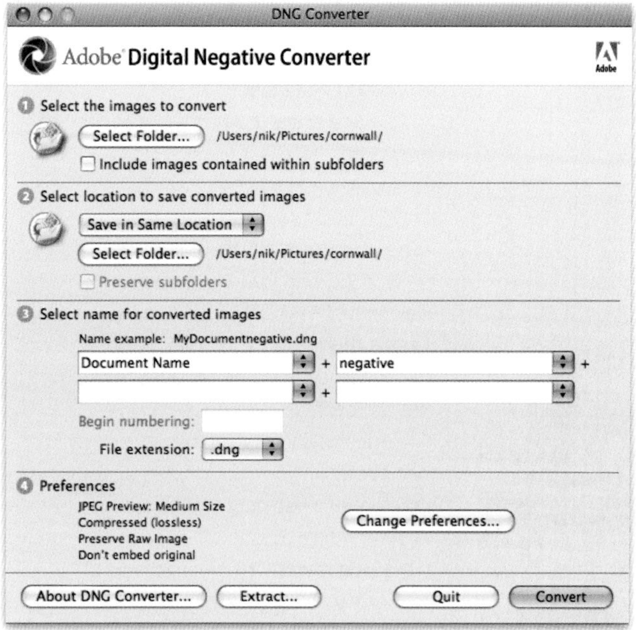

◄ Adobe's Digital Negative (DNG) Converter is a free download for Mac and Windows users. It allows you to translate your proprietary Raw format files to a more open standard. A companion plug-in also allows you to handle DNG files in various editions of Photoshop and Photoshop Elements.

consider their format and how long you can expect to be able to continue reading it. Jpeg is unlikely to go out of fashion any time soon, but proprietary Raw formats may. You should therefore consider converting your camera's native Raw-format images to an open standard like Digital Negative (DNG).

Adobe developed and announced the Digital Negative format in 2004. It is royalty-free, and the specification is open for examination, allowing third-party developers to incorporate it into their own applications. Why not just use the widespread Jpeg format, which can be read by pretty much any application or web browser going? Because conversion to Jpeg makes fundamental changes to the file, reduces the amount of data it contains, introduces compression artefacts, and reduces the range of editing options open to you in the future.

Some cameras, including models from Hasselblad, Leica and Pentax, can shoot DNG files natively, and for those that do not, Adobe offers a free converter, which works as a standalone application on both Mac OS X and Windows (see the downloads link on the right of the Adobe Digital Negative page at *adobe.com/products/dng*).

Once converted, you can open your images without further conversion in Photoshop and Photoshop Elements, Aperture 2, Corel Paint

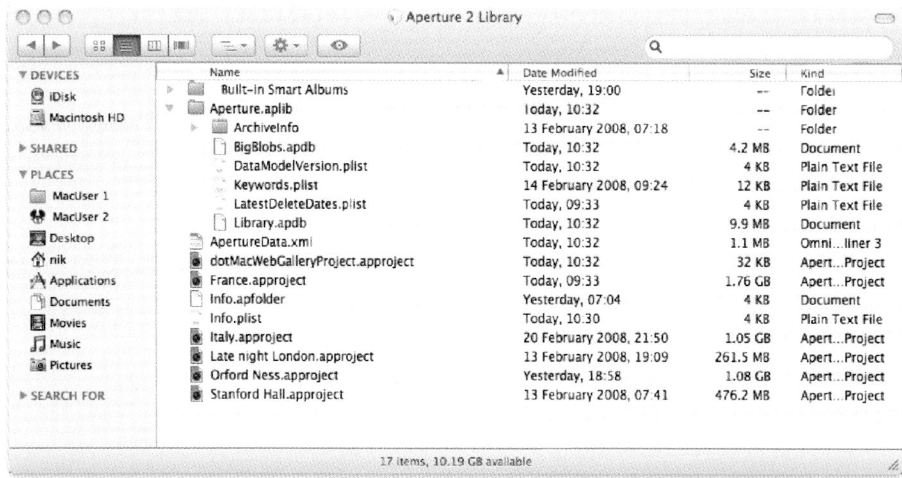

▲ **iPhoto and Aperture store their Libraries in packages rather than regular folders. You can examine these by right-clicking the Libraries in your Pictures folder and picking Show Package Contents. Looking is fine, but don't mess with the contents or you could corrupt your Libraries.**

Shop Pro X and a wide range of applications from leading developers, such as Canto, Lemkesoft and Extensis.

iPHOTO AND APERTURE LIBRARIES

Once you have secured the format of your images, it's time to start looking at the best strategy for backing them up.

If you use iPhoto or Aperture to manage your libraries, your images are safely stored in packages, which both keeps them safe from fiddling on your hard drive and makes them easy to back up. You'll find them in your user folder's Pictures folder, which will probably appear in the Finder's sidebar.

You can browse the contents of a Library by right-clicking its icon in the Finder and choosing Show Package Contents. Inside each one you'll find a series of sub-folders. Inside the iPhoto package there's a folder called Originals, with every import session organised by year and event inside it. If your library ever becomes corrupt, you may be able to retrieve your originals from this folder by manually dragging them out.

In Aperture things are a little more complicated. Again, you can view the contents of your Library in-situ on the hard drive by right-clicking and picking Show Package Contents, but inside you'll find more embedded packages, rather than folders. These are opened from a context menu in the same way as the master library, with each one containing an import folder, inside of which are folders for your original images and their associated metadata.

Aperture doesn't ever touch your original images as they are considered to be Digital Masters from which all adjusted versions are derived, and so you can always be sure of being able to retrieve them from here. If you are working with Raw image files, which offer the greatest flexibility inside Aperture, it also creates thumbnails and Jpeg previews of each one, which can also be retrieved from within these folders.

While it is fine to view these folders and their contents, you should never alter their structure or delete any of their contents. Doing so could seriously corrupt your Library and make it unusable. The simplest way to back up your complete libraries offsite is to create ⊕

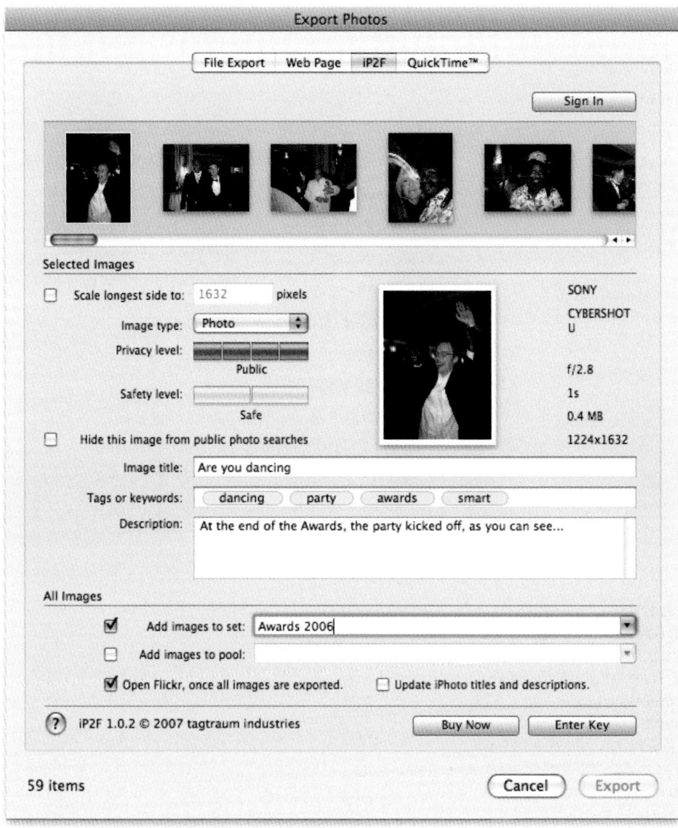

◄ **Plug-ins, like iP2F, make it easy to upload your photos to Flickr by adding new features to the Export menu in iPhoto. From here you can also assign your photos to groups, tag them and set their privacy levels.**

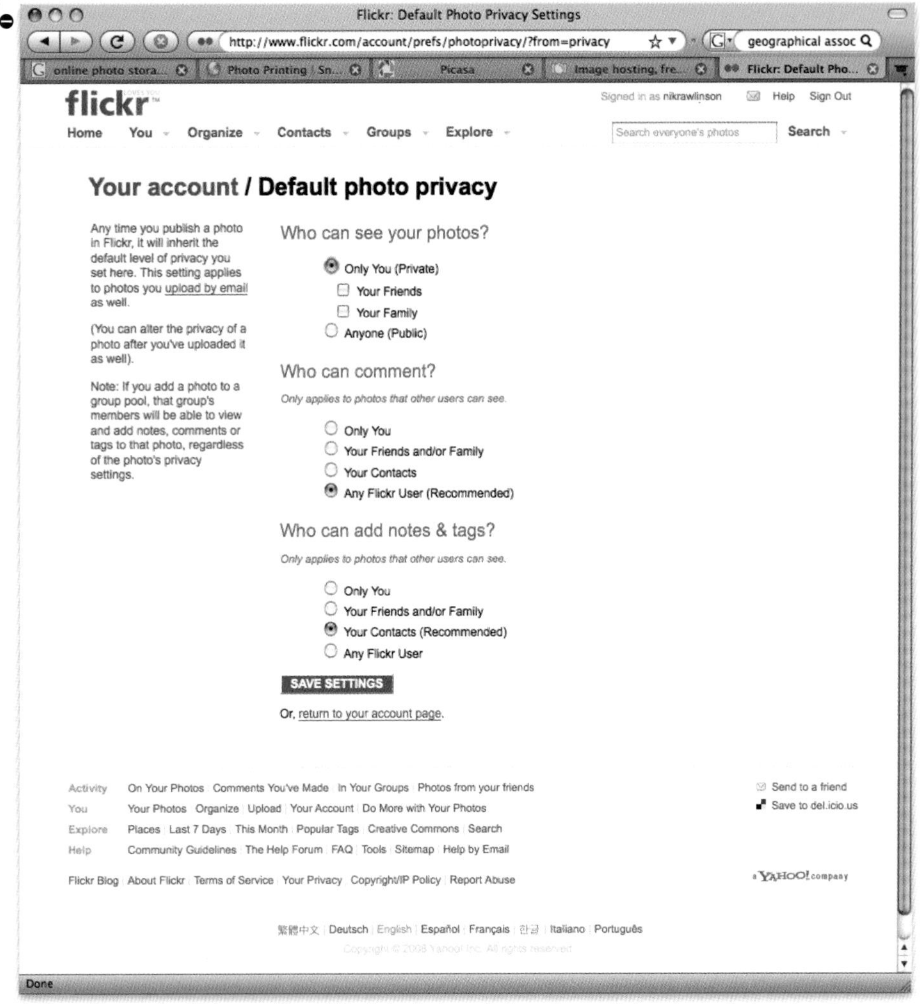

▲ If you plan on using Flickr or another public photo-sharing website, make sure that you have set adequate and appropriate rights on your images, preventing visitors from using them. You might also want to make your libraries private so that only you and your invited guests can see them.

▲ Online photo printing sites, such as PhotoBox and Snapfish, also offer storage facilities. These are password protected, and are a good way to keep a selected number of photos backed up offsite in a secure manner.

an archive of each one and copy it to a MobileMe iDisk, assuming you have sufficient space. Why create an archive? Because of the way that the Mac handles transfers to mounted remote volumes, in which it will copy, check and close off every file in a folder individually, rather than handling the folder as one entity and then checking it off just once.

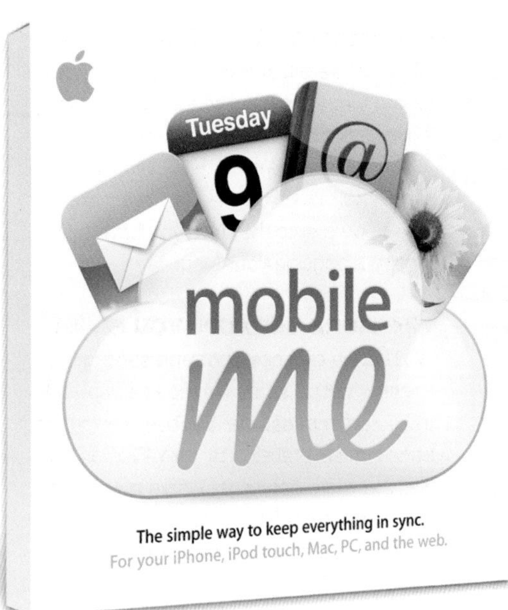

Tuesday
9
@
mobile
me
The simple way to keep everything in sync.
For your iPhone, iPod touch, Mac, PC, and the web.

◄ The MobileMe service is one of the best integrated backup and storage services for Macs. However, the amount of space on offer, when you consider how much it costs, may be too limiting for anyone with an extensive photo library.

This is logical, since the FTP equivalent of copying a folder would be to create a new directory on the remote server and then copy all of the contents to it.

BACKUP, BACKUP, BACKUP

The range of backup tools at the Mac user's disposal is as impressive as it is diverse, but two are of greatest interest, as they ship for free with the hardware: Backup and, for Leopard users, Time Machine. However, it's worth thinking beyond these conventional tools to ensure the safety of your images – as each has its own set of limitations.

Backup may offer to save a copy of your files online and offsite, but only for so long as you continue paying the MobileMe membership fee of £69 a year, and even then your storage space is far from generous at just 10GB. Time Machine, meanwhile, only backs up onsite, either to a connected drive or wirelessly to a Time Capsule device. This is insecure as it means that a fire could wipe out both the originals on your Mac's hard drive, and the backups on your Time Capsule.

Fortunately there are a growing number of online photo storage services, which are both free and, in some cases, integrate with Mac OS X. The best known is, of course, Flickr, which integrates directly with iPhoto and Aperture using FlickrExport (*connectedflow.com/flickrexport*). There are three editions: one for iPhoto (£12) and two for Aperture. Of these, one is a free 'lite' edition, which drops esoteric functions such as geotagging and the ability to store your Flickr ID in the application, and one is a £14 power users' edition that includes everything. iP2F, from *tagtraum.com/ip2f.html* and priced at $14.95 (about £7.50) with a 14-day free trial, performs a similar function, uploading your pictures through iPhoto's Export tool.

If you are uploading your images to Flickr for backup purposes, you should ensure that you don't inadvertently make them available for free use by third parties. Check that you have selected an appropriate rights level, and that you haven't applied a Creative Commons licence, which actually gives other users permission to republish them or incorporate them into their own work. You should also

10 steps to keeping your photos safe

1 Consider the format of your photos and how long they are likely to remain readable. Even popular formats of old have become obsolete over time.

2 Formats such as Adobe's DNG raw file are fairly software- and platform-agnostic, so it could offer better future proofing.

3 Avoid using Jpeg as a means of saving space when this was not your images' original format. This throws away data and can introduce compression artefacts.

4 Consider using online storage tools, such as Flickr and Snapfish. Paying for an upgrade to Flickr Pro is a sensible, low-cost way to enhance its feature set.

5 Protect any images you store online by applying relevant privacy controls if you are using public storage tools.

6 The MobileMe service is one of the simplest conduits to making online backups of your data, but space is limited and it remains relatively expensive.

7 Consider making compressed archives of large image folders before uploading them to a server to save time.

8 Optical discs degrade over time and should only ever be considered as a temporary storage and transport medium – not for long-term backups.

9 The simplest backup routine involves two hard drives, used to create complete copies of your Mac's internal storage.

10 The more backups you make, and the better distributed they are, the safer your images will be.

check that your Flickr privacy settings are appropriate to archive use rather than public display. Log in to your account, click your member name at the top of the screen, just above the search box, and pick the Privacy and Permissions tab. Working through the entries in the Global Settings section, you should then pick the options that make them visible only to yourself.

Flickr is by no means the only option for storing your photos online either, and you may find that you are better served by a printing service, such as Snapfish (*snapfish.co.uk*) or PhotoBox (*photobox.co.uk*), which give you server storage space from which you can then share your photos with friends and family, or use their services to make prints.

▲ Optical media, such as high-capacity Blu-ray discs, offers a good medium-term storage solution, but should not be your only backup source. Over time, optical media can degrade through exposure to the sun, so should be kept in a dark environment if possible.

BACKING UP TO CD AND DVD

The traditional means of backing up your images was to burn them onto CD or DVD, and this remains a fair short-term solution. CDs can store about 640MB of data, regular DVDs are happy with 4.7GB, and high capacity Blu-ray discs can handle 25GB on a single layer, and 50GB on a dual-layer disc. The all-but defunct HD-DVD format, which was so spectacularly dumped by almost all of its supporters, was capable of holding 15GB and 30GB on single and dual-layer discs respectively.

Apple played it safe in the format war by supporting encoding for both disc formats in its professional video formats, but never made it possible to burn directly to either disc from its own computers, and never shipped a Mac with either Blu-ray or HD-DVD built in.

Now that Blu-ray has won this modern-day VHS/Betamax battle, Apple remains reluctant to add Blu-ray drives to any of its machines because of what CEO Steve Jobs describes as licensing complications, and so third-party drives remain the only option for the time being.

However, as has been known for some time now, optical discs are not an everlasting storage medium. Home-burnt discs work in a fundamentally different way to commercially produced software, audio and video discs. Pre-recorded discs are pitted, with long and short indentations along the recorded spiral providing a physical means of adjusting the reflection of the drive's laser. Home-burnt discs, on the other hand, remain unpitted at all times – instead, the writing drive's laser changes the colour of a layer of dye sandwiched between two clear faces, emulating the same light-changing features.

However, this means that home-recorded optical discs are susceptible to corruption if left in bright light. As such, any discs you use to back up your photos should be stored in a light-tight box. Even with these precautions in place, you should seriously consider re-recording each disc every 12 months or so, which makes optical media a less suitable means of backup.

And as optical media becomes less well suited, hard drives become more attractive, particularly as prices continue to fall. A simple backup routine would involve buying two large hard drives that you use to make a complete copy of your image folders. Store one of these offsite, and swap them every time you make a new copy of your folders onto the drive you have been storing alongside your Mac.

THE MORE BACKUPS YOU HAVE...

While each of these photo-preserving routines will go some way to keeping your treasured images safe, the best advice would be to run several side by side. Remember that the more copies you have of your files, the safer they will be, and the greater will be your confidence when it comes to editing and working with them on a daily basis.

MASTERCLASS

Using Photoshop CS3 to create convincing rain effects

In this Masterclass, we show you how to create convincing rain using noise, motion blur, layer masks and custom brushes downloaded from the web.

Kit required Photoshop CS3 or later
Time About 1 hour
Goal To create convincing rain effects
Skill level Advanced

In this Masterclass, we're going to play with rain by inverting a common scenario of an umbrella protecting you from a heavy shower. The effect is surprisingly easy to achieve with the use of custom brushes downloaded from the web and a little digital noise. The result, though, is quite spectacular, and it goes against the idea of subtle editing and the theory that the best edits are impossible to spot.

It's all done with noise and interference. Noise is rarely desirable – particularly when it's created in your digital camera as the sensor gets overloaded, and we usually try to remove as much of it as we can from our photos. However, if you know how to manipulate it, you can use noise to your advantage, as it creates truly random results, an effect that would be time consuming and repetitive when done by hand. In this tutorial, we'll be adding noise inside Photoshop and then applying a motion blur that turns it into streaks. Once carefully blended and masked, that noise will be transformed into a rain shower coming out of an umbrella. The result, as you'll see, is impressive and, although impossible, surprisingly realistic. The same principles can be used to apply rain to less-imaginary scenarios, such as a regular street scene. Just don't forget to change your colour temperature and lighting as appropriate to get the best results.

We've used Photoshop CS3 in this Masterclass, but it will also work with earlier versions and, obviously, CS4.

▲ **STEP 01 PREPARATION** A great end result starts with a good opening photo. This source image was shot in a confined space with poor light. Because of the small room in which it was taken, we avoided using the flash so that we didn't cast any harsh shadows and instead increased the ISO to 400. We also included as many props as we needed to avoid having to add them as a montage at a later point.

▲ **STEP 02 RAW ADJUSTMENTS** Shoot your image in both Raw and Jpeg, as this enables you to review the file as a Jpeg and then process it in Raw. This gives you access to all of the information as captured by the camera's sensor, and means you have the maximum possible flexibility when it comes to editing. Here, we used Adobe Raw Converter to lower the colour temperature slightly and increased the exposure to counter the poor lighting.

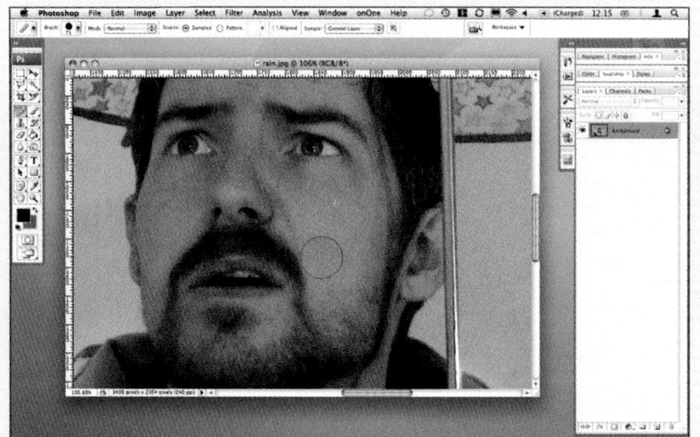

▲ **STEP 03 CLEANING THE SUBJECT** We're all prone to unwanted blemishes, and at a high ISO there will also be artefact interference. Your first job is to remove these using a soft, small healing brush. Try not to go too far, though, as imperfections make the picture look real. If you overdo it, the subject will end up looking plastic.

▲ **STEP 04 CLEAN UP THE BACKGROUND** Shooting in a confined space often results in unwanted shadows. Remove these using a large, soft brush and blend the colours of the background by sampling them using the eyedropper tool. Here, we've used several layers and varied the opacity, leaving us with a smooth, uniform background.

◄ **STEP 05 CLOTHING SPLASHES** To give your image a sense of reality, the rain needs to react with the subject. As such, we want to add splashes to the coat. Photoshop doesn't include any brushes for doing this, but you can download new ones from the web. (Try *bit.ly/3hg6*). Each splash is placed on a new layer, allowing us to change its opacity, blend mode and position individually, and blurred to match the original image.

◄ **STEP 06 THE FIRST RAIN DROPS** With the splashes in place, you now need to add the rain that creates them. Here, we used another custom brush to save us creating our own droplets (rain brushes can be downloaded from *bit.ly/O0R6* and *bit.ly/GJVA*). You aren't adding the full shower at this stage of the process – just the highlight details that will give it life – so don't look to fill the whole area, but rather add a curtain to each edge of the umbrella. Mask out areas where the rain might be obscured, such as below the spoke ends, to vary the effect.

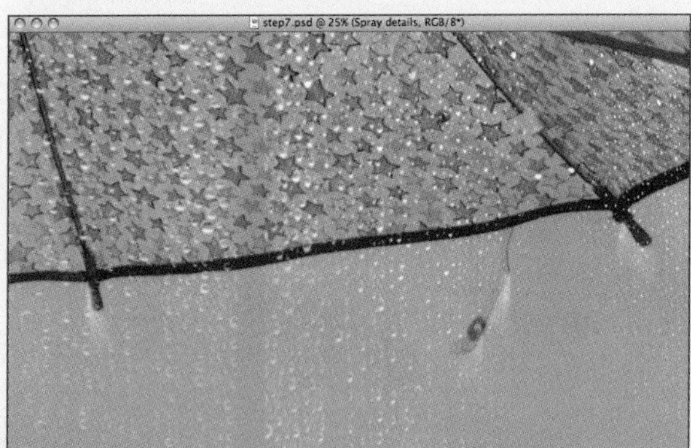

▲ **STEP 07 UMBRELLA SPRAY** Real rain would never simply run off an umbrella – it would always bounce on its taught surface. As such you need to add some small details that increase the sense of realism. Reduce the size of your rain brush and use it to add a fine spray coming off the points of the umbrella to show the rain running off. Make your strokes short and fade them off fairly quickly by adjusting the opacity of your brush.

▲ **STEP 08 FOCUS THE VIEWER'S EYE** Add a simple vignette by creating an oval marquee in the centre of the picture to cover the main area, inverting it, feathering it as much as possible and then filling it with black. Adjust the layer transparency to 70% to reduce the impact. Create a new layer with its opacity set to about 30% and paint over the umbrella with black to darken it a little.

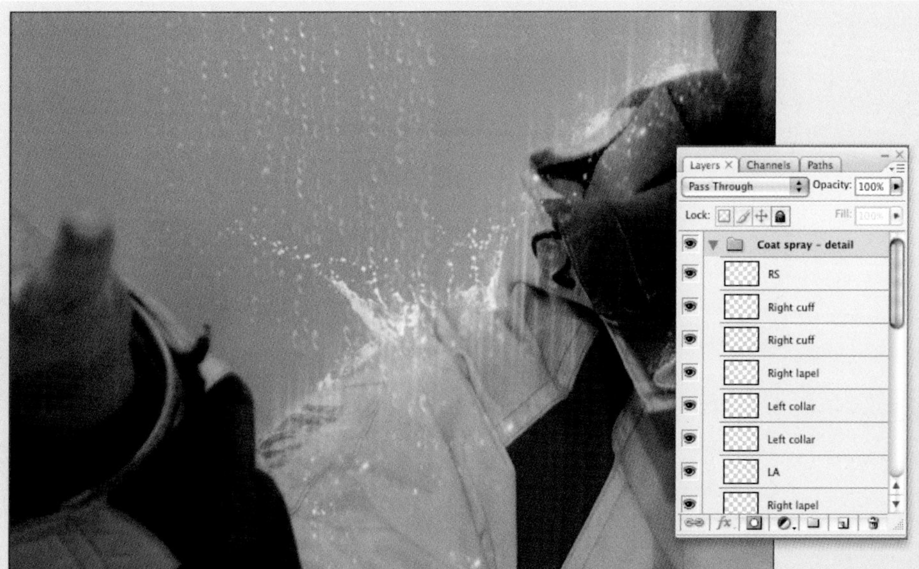

◄ **STEP 09 BUILDING THE SPRAY** The basics of your picture are now in place and you can start to build up the effects. Zoom in close and use small particle brushes around areas of the coat that the rain would hit. Switch to the base picture layer and dodge the area behind these painted parts to create a slight glow behind the upper layers, and then blur the spray to match the picture.

► STEP 10 THE MAIN SHOWER Add a new layer and fill it with black. Don't add a new fill layer or the next step won't work. Now add noise (Filter > Noise > Add Noise) with the settings at 60%, Gaussian, monochromatic. Set the layer blend mode to Screen using the opacity drop-down at the top of the Layers palette.

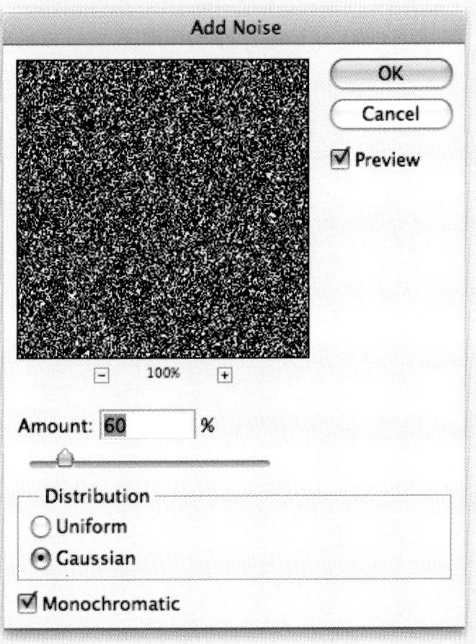

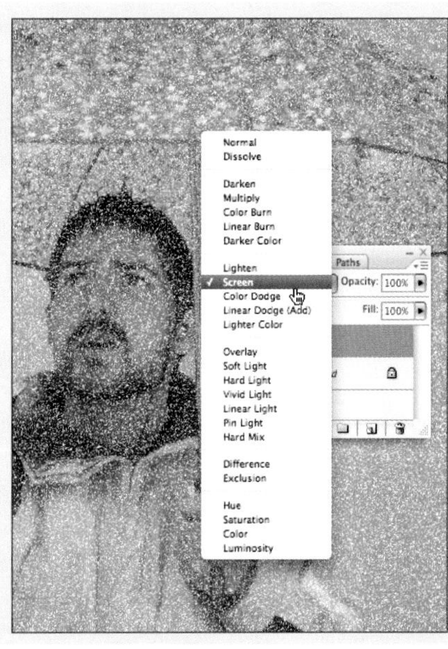

▲ STEP 11 MAKE THE RAIN MOVE At the moment, the rain looks like random snow, so you need to make it fall by adding a blur. Pick Filter > Blur > Motion Blur and set the angle to 90°. Adjust the Distance measurement by using the slider at the bottom of the dialog box until your raindrops are a believable size. We found about 25 pixels to be ideal, but it will vary according to the size of your image.

▲ STEP12 REFINE THE RAIN You only want it to fall from inside the umbrella, so add a new layer mask and use a large, soft brush to remove any rain falling outside the umbrella. Use a smaller, semi-transparent brush on the same mask layer to remove drops from inside the umbrella for a more random effect.

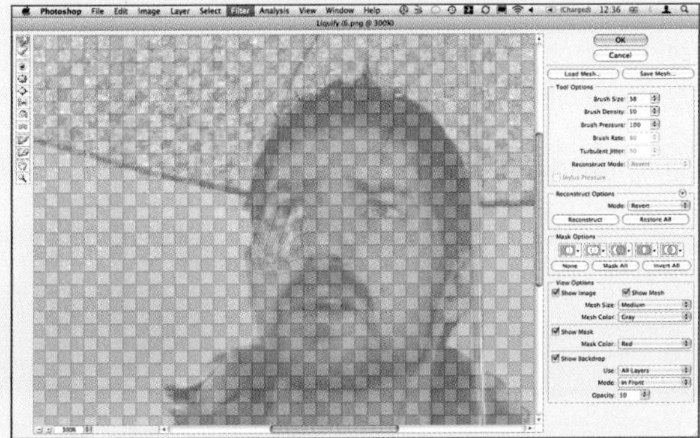

▲ STEP 13 FINAL TOUCHES The umbrella is still doing too much of a good job, so let's add some more splashes – this time to the face. Use a droplet brush to add rain to the face and then liquify (Filter > Liquify or Shift-Command-X) to mould them to the contours of the face. Make sure you add the raindrops on a new layer to avoid liquifying the face, and check the Show Backdrop box in the Liquify dialog box to show the underlying image.

▲ STEP 14 COLOUR ADJUSTMENTS This is a matter of personal preference, but for this picture we used a selective colour adjustment layer to adjust the black and neutral colour ranges to a cyan/blue hue, which enhances the skin tones. Cyan and blue are also cold colours, which give the finished image a feeling of true discomfort.

MASTERCLASS
Create realistic, torn notebook paper in Photoshop

Discover how to create a realistic scrap of notebook paper using simple selections, clipping masks, gradients, blurs and custom brushes.

Kit required Photoshop CS3 or later
Time About 30 minutes
Goal To create realistic, torn notepaper for use on websites
Skill level Intermediate

In this tutorial, you'll learn how to create a torn page from a notebook. When flattened and used as a background image, you can superimpose a list of recent posts on your blog, or use a handwriting typeface in Photoshop to add clever little notes to a design-led website, such as a digital scrap-booking project.

Creating a page and adding ruled lines is the easy part. We'll begin by using basic selections to create the paper and remove the initial holes along the top. However, it's the extra effects added to the page that give it a real sense of depth. Tearing out a page in the real world would leave a rough, uneven edge where it was bound. You can achieve this by using a layer mask to add a distressed look around the paper's edges, and to create a natural-looking tear along the holes. So that our fake piece of paper emulates the real world even more closely, we'll add creases with one click of a custom brush to instantly add realistic folds and wrinkles to the paper and, of course, any text or images you place upon it. Rather than leave the paper lying flat, we'll further enhance the effect by lifting the paper from the page using the Warp function. Then we'll use the same tool in the opposite direction to create a realistic shadow technique that will make bog-standard drop shadows a thing of the past.

You might also try these final steps on your favourite photographs to reduce their uniformity and add a little punch to an otherwise flat presentation.

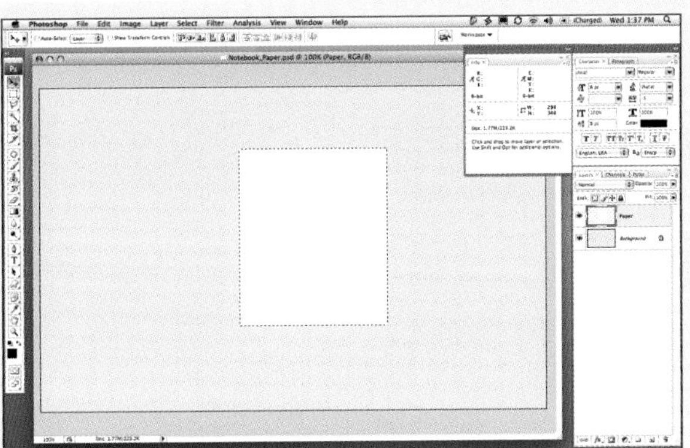

▲ **STEP 01 PREPARATION** Begin by opening a new document in Photoshop. Since the paper will be white, set a background color that makes it easy to see the paper as it's created. On a new layer, use the Rectangular Marquee tool to create an appropriately sized box and fill it with white. Rename this layer 'Paper'.

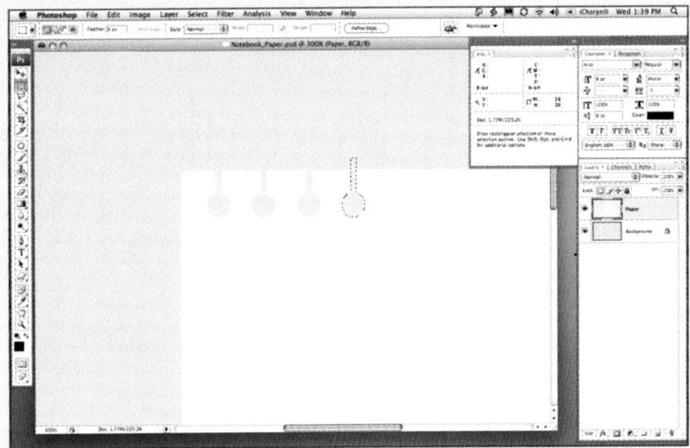

▲ **STEP 02 ADDING RING HOLES** Use a combination selection made with the Elliptical and Rectangular Marquee tools to create the initial hole and tear mark at the top of the paper. Once the selection is created, position the first hole and delete its contents, then using the Arrow keys, move the selection across the top of the paper making holes at even increments. (Holding down the Shift key while pressing an arrow key moves the selection 10 pixels at a time.)

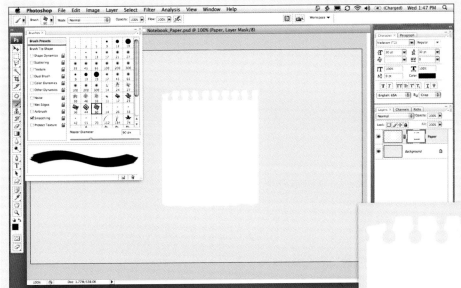

▲ **STEP 03 GIVE THE PAGE A TORN-OFF LOOK**
Add a Layer Mask to the Paper layer and using a rough-edged brush such as the Chalk 60 Pixels brush found in Photoshop's default brushes collection, paint away tear marks between the holes and along the bottom edge of the paper. Remember that sometimes the little tabs at the top of notebook paper get torn off completely.

▲ **STEP 04 PUTTING LINES ON THE PAGE** On a new layer, use the Single Row Marquee tool to create the blue lines across the paper. Use Shift along with the arrow keys to move the selection 10 pixels at a time. Space the lines 30 pixels apart. Next, on another new layer, use the Single Column Marquee tool to create two vertical red lines three pixels apart. Set this layer's opacity to 30% and clip both layers to the Paper layer.

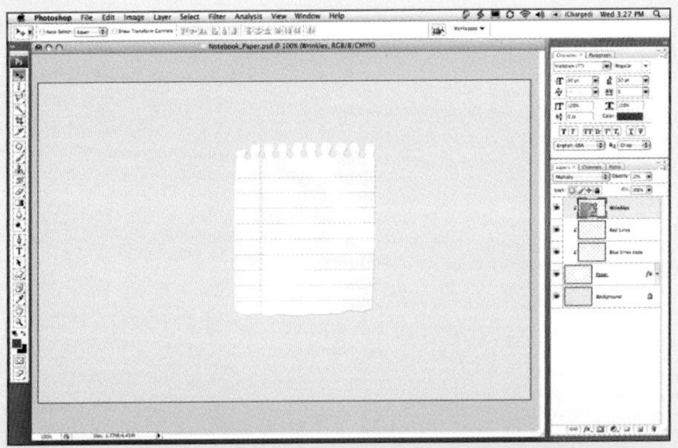

▲ **STEP 05 ADD A WRINKLED TEXTURE TO THE PAPER**
Create a brush from wrinkled paper, or download one (from *bit.ly/3ieTfy*), and load it into the Brushes palette. Set the foreground colour to black, size the brush to fit and click once to add a wrinkled texture to the paper. Clip this layer to the Paper layer and lower its opacity to 10%. The effect should be noticeable but subtle. Call this layer 'Wrinkles'.

▲ **STEP 06 WARP THE PAGE TO ADD DEPTH** Select the Paper layer in the Layers palette, Ctrl-click on the layer mask and choose Apply Layer Mask. Holding down the Alt key, click and drag a copy of the Paper layer below itself. Rename this new layer Shadow and hide it by clicking on the eye icon next to the layer thumbnail. Using the Free Transform tool in Warp mode, click and drag the corners of the paper inward to create the illusion that they're lifting off the background surface.

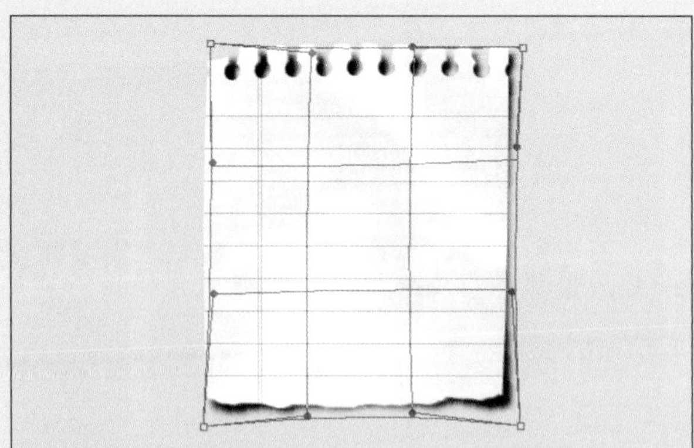

▲ **STEP 07 CAST A REALISTIC SHADOW** Select the Shadow layer and make it visible. Invert the colours on the layer by pressing Command+I to turn it black. Apply a three-pixel Gaussian Blur and then Warp this layer as well, this time pulling the corners and bending the sides until a realistic shadow has been achieved. Notice that the corners of the transformation pull away, but the sides arch back towards the paper.

▲ **STEP 08 ADD CONVINCING LIGHTING** Create a new layer at the top of the layer stack also clipped to the Paper layer and draw a black-to-transparent linear gradient from the upper left corner at an angle into the document to create a shadow on this corner. Set this layer's opacity to about 10%. Repeat this process on a new layer using a white-to-transparent gradient, dragging from the lower-right corner to create a highlight. Change its blend mode to Screen and its opacity to 80%.

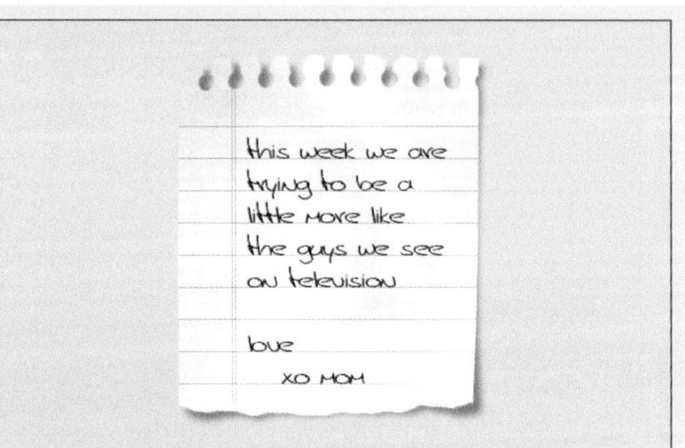

▲ **STEP 09 ADD SOME TEXT TO THE PAGE** A blank page isn't very exciting, so choose the Text tool, set the character's leading in the Character palette to 30px to match the spacing of the lines on the paper, then enter your text using a handwriting font such as Jerry's Handwriting (available for free at *bit.ly/11hHU*), adjusting the font size accordingly. For an even more convincing effect, lower the text layer's Opacity to about 80% and place it below the Wrinkles layer.

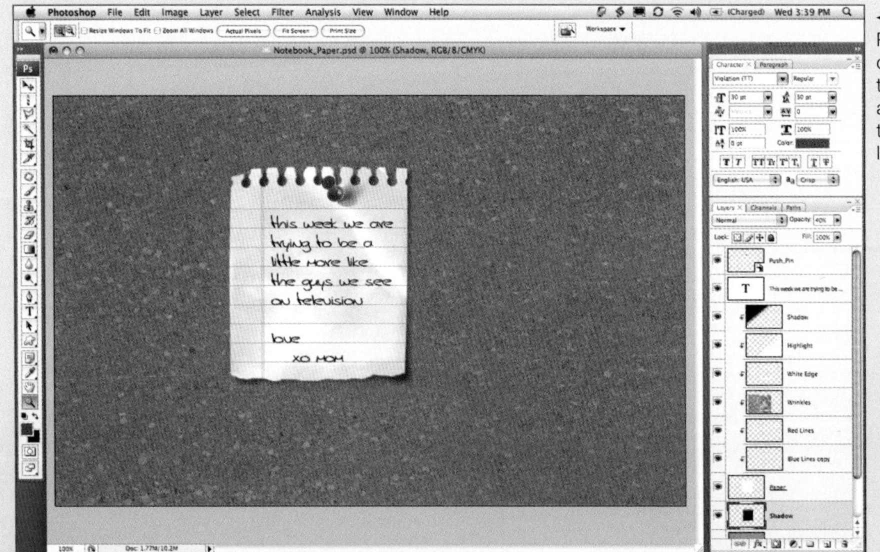

◄ **STEP 10 FINAL TOUCHES** Polish off the project with a push-pin and some corkboard, upload it to the sidebar of your blog to make an announcement or you could make a note about your vacation to Hawaii next to that photo of you and the surfboard in your latest scrapbook entry.

MASTERCLASS
Creating panographic collaged images

Producing images by assembling many different shots can create eye-catching results, and can be done in many different applications.

Kit required Adobe InDesign CS3 (or any DTP, graphic layout or bitmap editing application) + Multiple photographs of a scene
Time 30 minutes
Goal To produce a large composite image from multiple photos
Skill level Beginner

Panorama photography, ultra-wide views stitched together from multiple photos, is growing in popularity, but it requires specific equipment and software to do it with real precision. Panographs, on the other hand, are made with a more cavalier attitude to photorealistic perfection.

These are composite images, too, but made with the seams and differences between the individual shots used as part of the final effect. Individual photographs are collaged together to produce a final larger artwork, with the different photos being distinguishable, to a greater or lesser degree, in the end result. David Hockney used this technique a few decades ago, but it also echoes the work of cubist painters almost a century back. Panographies – the results of this kind of image collaging – can be used to show a wider view than with normal lenses, but the possibilities go much further

You make them simply by shooting overlapping images and putting them together. Depending on the effect you want, you can tilt your camera as you move across the scene to create a sense of movement, enlarge a specific area, take shots at different times, move around to capture more viewpoints than can be seen from one spot and so on. The photos can be put together in Photoshop, a DTP or graphics tool, such as InDesign, QuarkXPress or Illustrator, or Apple's Pages in layout mode.

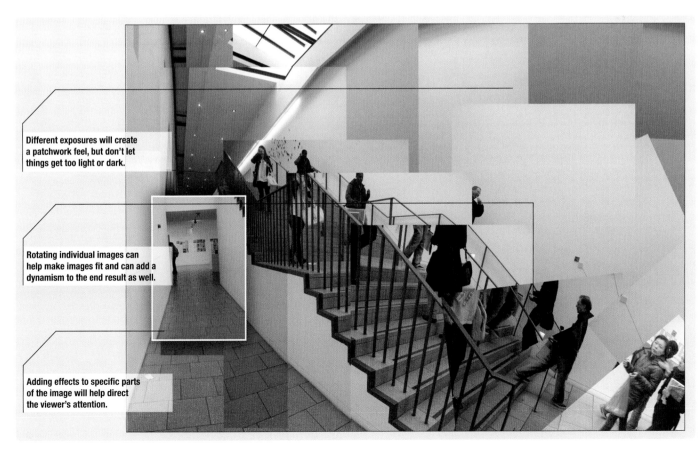

Different exposures will create a patchwork feel, but don't let things get too light or dark.

Rotating individual images can help make images fit and can add a dynamism to the end result as well.

Adding effects to specific parts of the image will help direct the viewer's attention.

▲ **STEP 01 SHOOTING IMAGES** Pick your scene and think about it as a broad view, a wider vista than you can capture in a single shot. You may prefer to fix your exposure, if your camera allows this, so that you don't end up with lighter and darker overlapping shots, Here, however, we've left the controls on auto – the opposite of what's normally done for panorama photography.

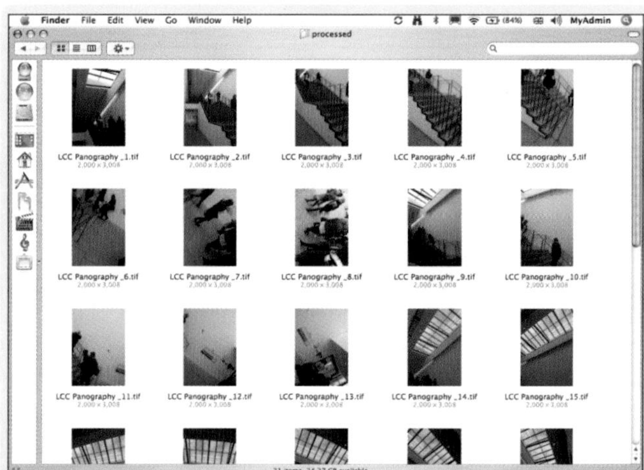

▲ **STEP 02 PREPARING PHOTOS** Shoot your images, making sure to capture a generous number of images. You're unlikely to use every image you shoot, but you'll find it useful to have a wide selection from which to make your selection. Save them in whatever format your process can use – we've used Tiff, but Jpegs will normally do as well.

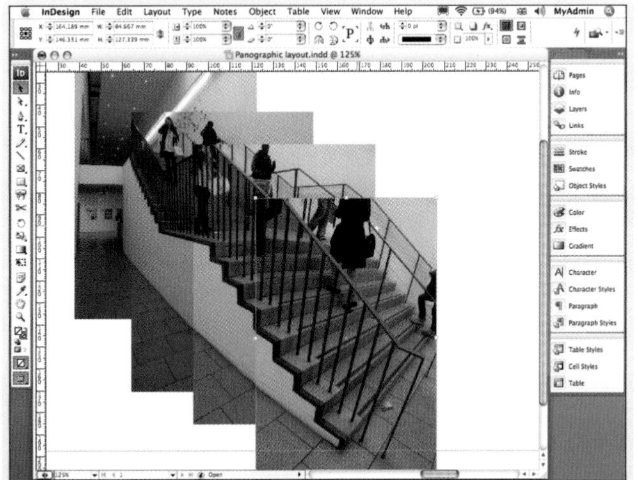

▲ **STEP 03 LAYING OUT** We'll use InDesign, as this is more object orientated than Photoshop. Place a few images on the page and try aligning them to make a larger image. Find significant parts of the image and work with those, don't worry about fitting every element.

▲ **STEP 04 TILTING IMAGES** You may need to tilt some of the photos as you go towards one end of a large sweep, especially if the camera was turned as you went when you took the shots. With the right subject, this can be very effective – but you'll probably have to practise visualising this when you take your shots in the first place.

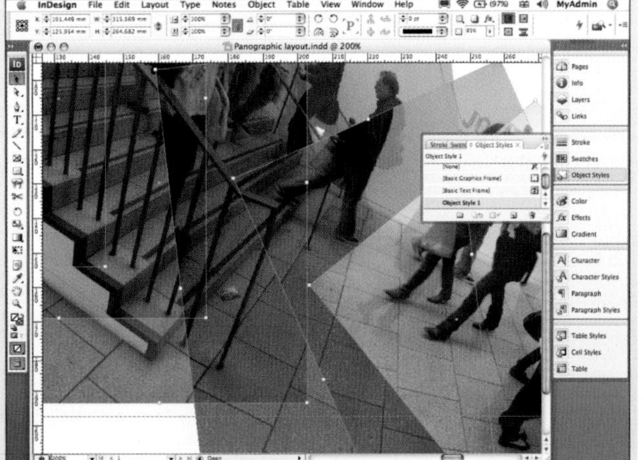

▲ **STEP 05 SETTING OPACITY** Try dropping the opacity of one or more of the images to blend the images together. With InDesign, select one or more graphics and choose Object > Effects > Transparency. This can be surprisingly effective with the right set of images. Here, we have set an object style with opacity set to 85% and then applied that to every image in the arrangement.

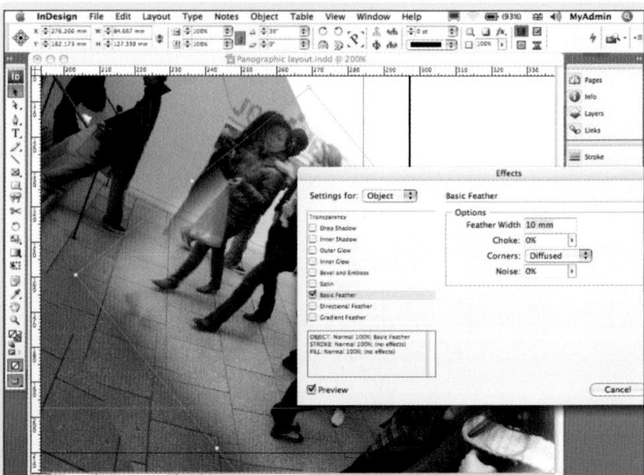

▲ **STEP 06 FEATHERING EDGES** Although you shouldn't concern yourself too much with blending images together as seamlessly as possible, sometimes using feathered edges can be a useful technique. It is particularly effective with scenes with cloudy skies, but it can help patch in sections with all sorts of subjects.

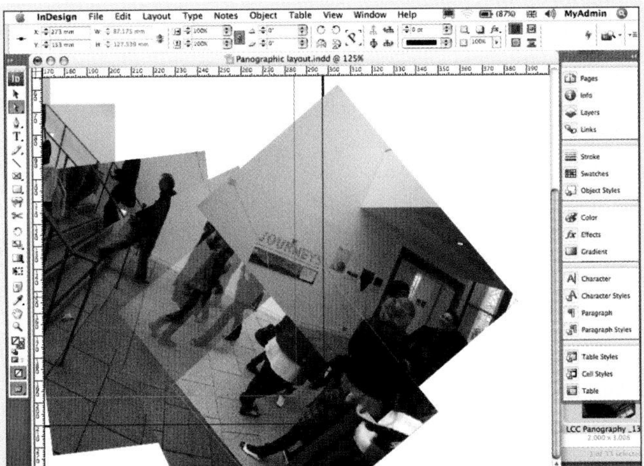

▲ **STEP 07 RESHAPING IMAGES** Sometimes it may be necessary to alter the shape of the graphic frame itself (or in Photoshop, just mask or delete parts of an image layer) so that the image is cropped to remove distracting image elements. This goes beyond the simple concept of using equal-size rectangular photos, and could lead to a more cubist effect if done carefully.

▲ **STEP 08 ADDING ROWS** If you've taken multiple rows of images you should start importing and collaging those into your existing set. If you've left the exposure to auto you may find some extreme variations of lighting. Here, the bright windows made the meter stop down the image. If this is too strong then adjust in Photoshop, otherwise just go with it.

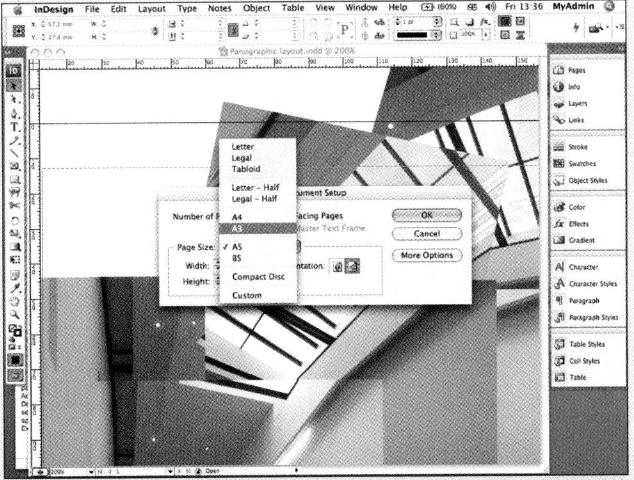

▲ **STEP 09 RESIZING THE PAGE** You'll probably find that you misjudged the page size you'll need for this project. In InDesign and other similar programs, set the document size to something larger. We've now moved up to an A3 page. In Photoshop, increase the canvas size to give yourself lots of room – you can always crop it down afterwards.

▲ **STEP 10 ADJUSTING PLACEMENT** With multiple rows of images you'll find that it can get hard to align things well. Don't be too put off by this, but do make use of the rotate tool and transparency effect to help get things into position. If necessary, resize within the frame, or even (if you can) go back and reshoot the scene.

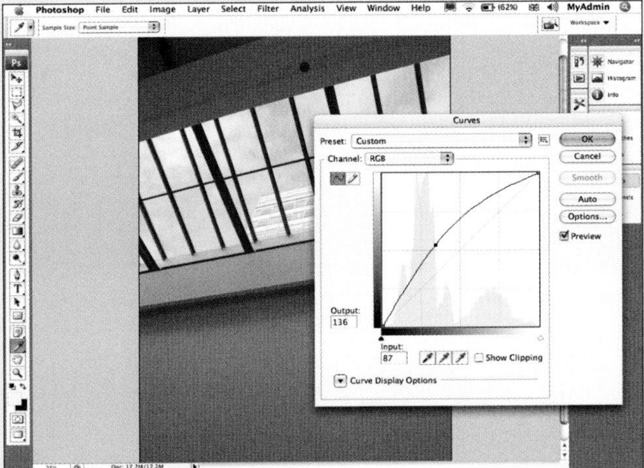

▲ **STEP 11 IMAGE ADJUSTMENT** At this stage, with this set of images, it is clear that the darker ones are just too dark. In this situation, you should perform whatever kind of Photoshop adjustment you prefer to these images. If you've been assembling in InDesign just update the linked files, or re-import if you're using a less-capable layout tool.

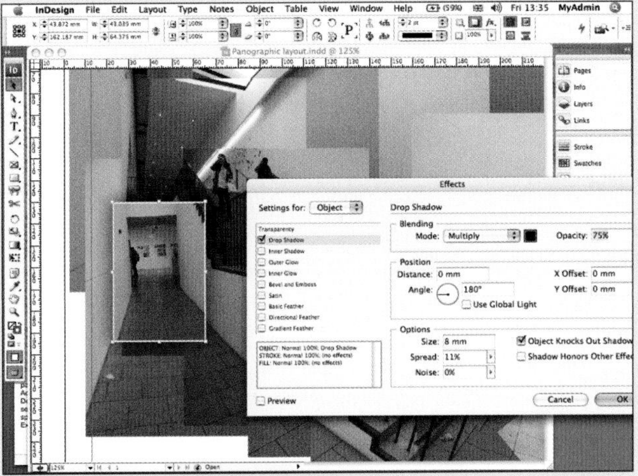

▲ **STEP 12 ADDING FINAL TOUCHES** Don't forget that you have far more options at your disposal than just rotating and sending things forward and back. This cropped view shows a glimpse of the exhibition space at the end of the passage, and is picked out with a shadow and white stroke. Export as a PDF or use your Photoshop file directly when you're finished.

MASTERCLASS

Create isometric projections

Using scale, shear, rotate (SSR) to key complex objects onto an isometric grid – in this case, to create the back view of an iMac.

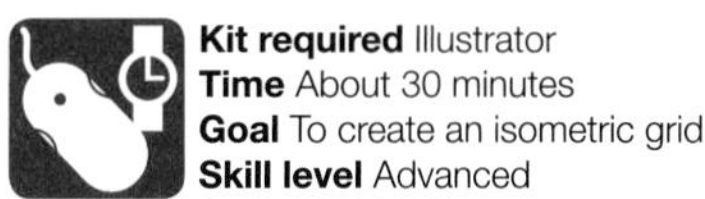

Kit required Illustrator
Time About 30 minutes
Goal To create an isometric grid
Skill level Advanced

Isometric projections are from the family of axonometric projection systems. Isometric comes from Greek for equal measure. This is because isometrics don't use a vanishing-point system; instead, lines fall onto a 30° grid. There are many other systems that don't require vanishing points or horizon lines, but give you similar benefits. However, isometrics is the only one of these systems to make the jump from the technical illustrator's toolbox to a useful skill for all graphic artists.

Building basic blocky shapes on an isometric grid is very fast and easy, but when you're dealing with curvy or complex objects, using a grid alone can quickly become a daunting task. Here, you'll learn how to use the scale, shear, rotate method (SSR) to key complex objects onto an isometric grid, and discover how to handle surfaces that don't fall neatly onto the x, y or z planes.

To begin, we've created a set of orthographics by tracing several reference photos. For this project, we've used a front view, a side view and a back view of the current iMac, but you don't need these to follow along as the orthographics can be downloaded from *http://bit.ly/Xjb4*. The iMac poses additional challenges in the varied angles of the stand and the curved back. You won't be using any exotic tools, but a basic understanding of setting up actions will speed up the whole process. As such, we'll start by explaining the SSR method.

About the SSR method

Let's build a cube to show how SSR applies perspective. Aligning a cuboid's sides isn't difficult, but creating 30° and 150° scrap lines to represent the isometric grid will assist with tricker objects. Just draw a horizontal line and apply the x- or y-axis transformations.

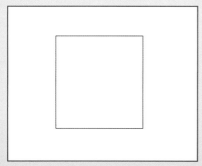

Use the Rectangle tool with the Shift key held down to draw a square. Make two copies. They will become the three visible sides of your cube along the x-, y- and z-axes.

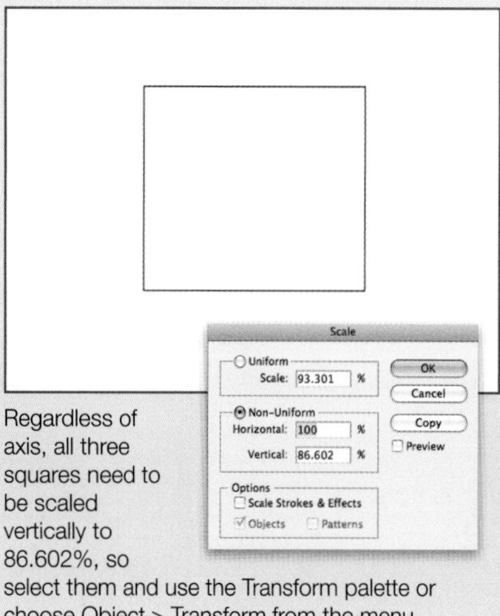

Regardless of axis, all three squares need to be scaled vertically to 86.602%, so select them and use the Transform palette or choose Object > Transform from the menu.

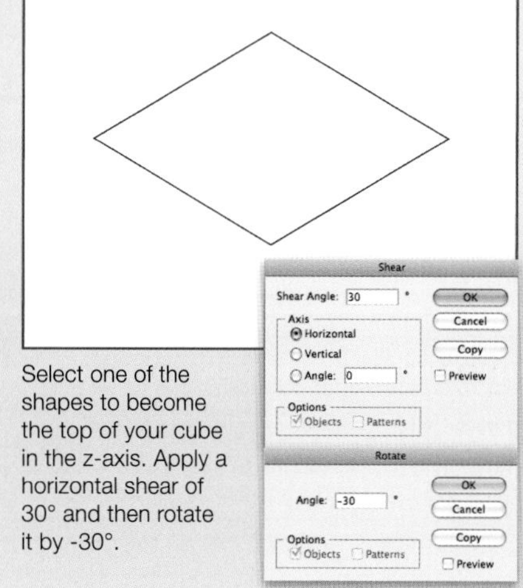

Select one of the shapes to become the top of your cube in the z-axis. Apply a horizontal shear of 30° and then rotate it by -30°.

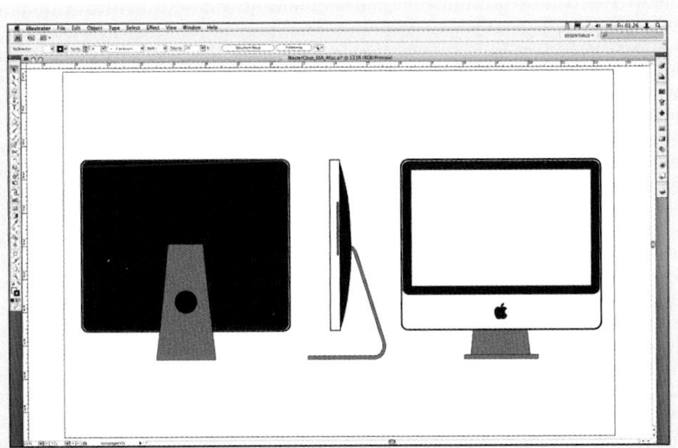

▲ **STEP 01 STARTING WITH PLAN DRAWINGS** To begin an isometric drawing using this method, start by making a set of orthographics, or plan drawings. Our front, side and back view were drawn from reference photographs, and a three-quarter view is often a useful reference. Depending on the complexity of your object, you may need more views. Trace the photos to get your orthographics. You don't need to be too detailed, just trace the shapes you want to be in your final illustration.

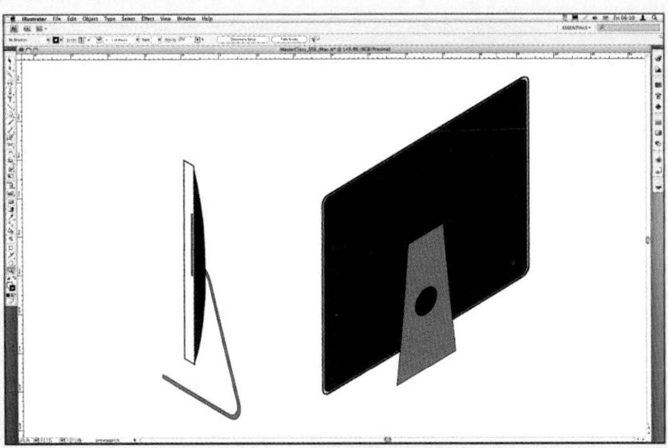

▲ **STEP 02 ESTABLISH YOUR OBJECT'S ORIENTATION** We'll place the back of our iMac along the x-axis, so select the back view orthographic and apply the correct values for scale, shear and rotation to transform it onto this plane (see About the SSR method, below). This sets up the back as your right side. Next, select the side view of the iMac, which will be placed on the y-axis. Apply the correct values for that plane so the side view is ready to be used as the left side of your isometric object.

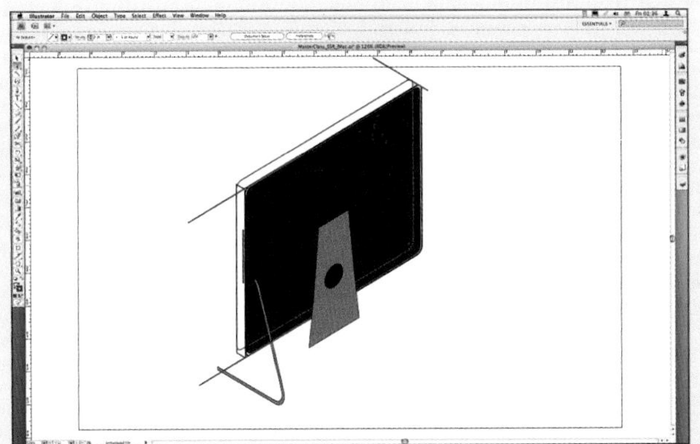

▲ **STEP 03 ALIGN THE SIDES** Place 30° lines on the back view as shown in blue, and align the side and back at the closest edge of the object. The side view now conveys the computer's thickness. Next, you'll create the outline of the iMac's front by Alt-dragging the outside line of the back view. The iMac's curved corners pose an extra challenge, so place a 150° scrap line at the top-right corner to help position the shape.

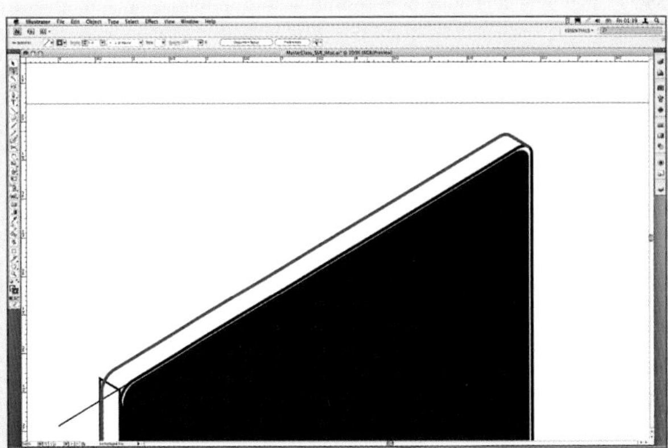

▲ **STEP 04 CLEAN UP ROUGH EDGES** With the wireframe established, you can clean up the shape with the Scissors and Direct Selection tools. Cut the part of the far outline that will be hidden when the shape is complete. Move 150° scrap lines into place to connect the corners at the top right and bottom left of the front and back sides. The rounded corners mean there's nothing to be done at the top-left corner. Finally, cut the scrap lines to size and join the points (Command-J).

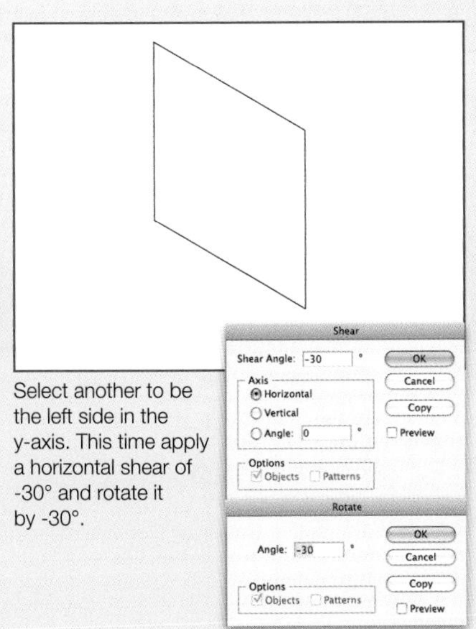

Select another to be the left side in the y-axis. This time apply a horizontal shear of -30° and rotate it by -30°.

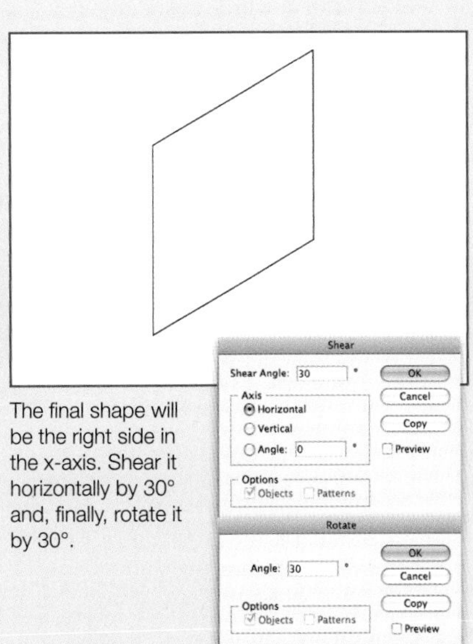

The final shape will be the right side in the x-axis. Shear it horizontally by 30° and, finally, rotate it by 30°.

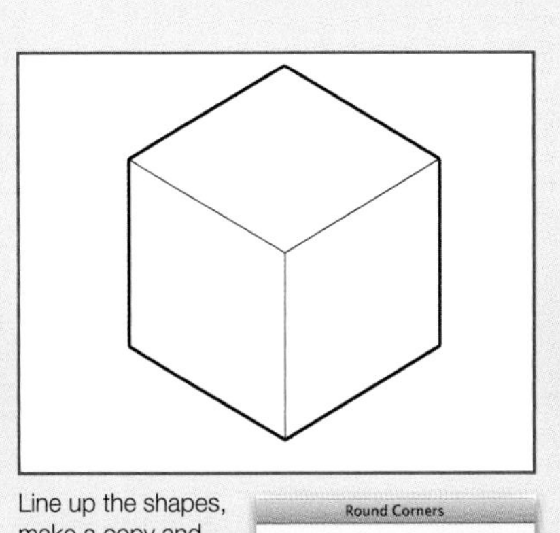

Line up the shapes, make a copy and send it to the back. Increase its stroke to 6pt for a thick outline. Apply Effects > Stylize > Round Corners with a value of 1pt to tidy the joints.

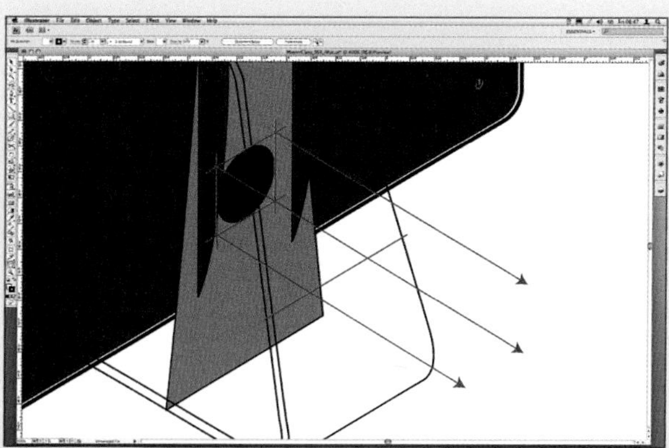

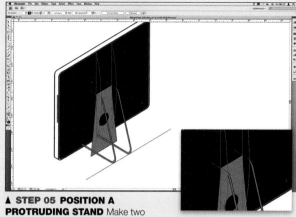

▲ STEP 05 POSITION A PROTRUDING STAND Make two copies of the curved back and stand from the side view orthographic and apply the y-axis transformation to them. Position them so their vertical lines run through the top corners of the back view's stand. Place 150° scrap lines that project from these top corners through the curved back to form two connection points. Move the stand outlines into position at the connection points where the curve and scrap lines intersect.

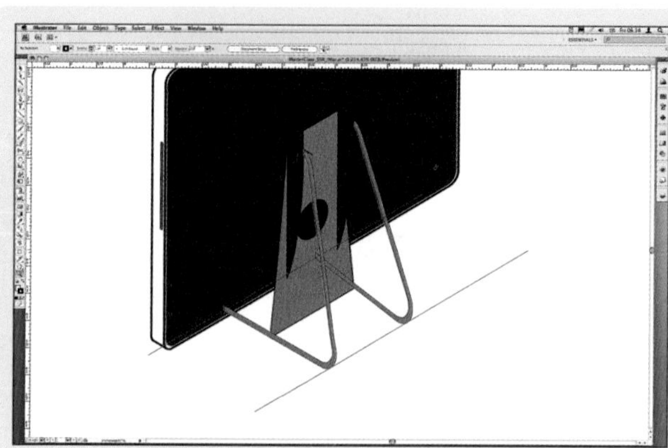

▲ STEP 06 WIDEN THE BASE You've established the thinnest part of the stand, but the back view shows it should be wider where it passes under the Mac. Place long, 30° scrap lines that connect the two sides of the stand at the front and rear edges, select the scraps and turn them into guides (Command-5). To widen the stand's bottom, select groups of anchor points and move them along the guides until the base of your protruding stand matches that of the flat back view.

▲ STEP 07 ADD PROJECTION LINES Build a square around the flat circle on the back view by making a square (in the x-axis) out of 30° scraps and vertical lines. Position them so each side touches the circle. Next, create four 150° scraps and position them through the square's corners so they project outwards through the angled stand. By eye, mark off where the bottom two lines cross the middle of the stand and connect with a 30° scrap line.

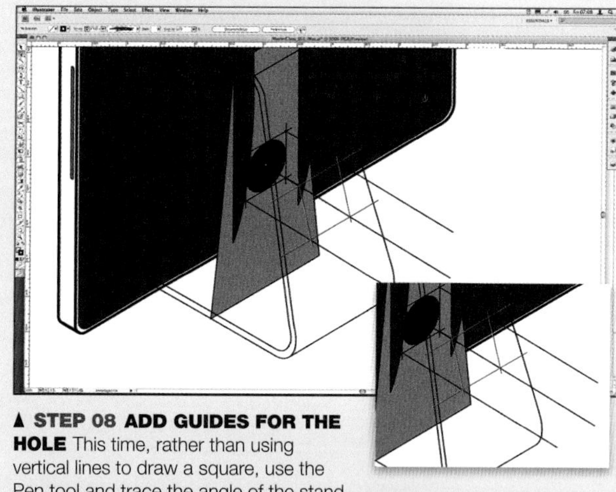

▲ STEP 08 ADD GUIDES FOR THE HOLE This time, rather than using vertical lines to draw a square, use the Pen tool and trace the angle of the stand. The two sides of the stand will be different angles because the stand is wider at the base than the top. Find the approximate median of the two lines and use it to build the sides of the new square. Connect the top of the square where these lines cross the projected lines.

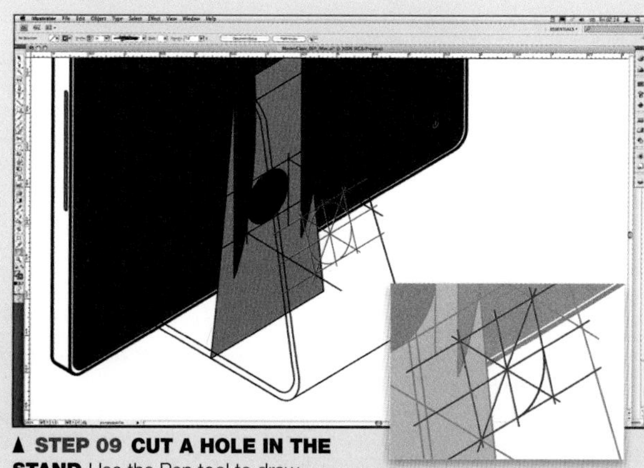

▲ STEP 09 CUT A HOLE IN THE STAND Use the Pen tool to draw diagonals and a cross through the square. Click in the centre of one side and drag half way towards the closest corner before releasing. Click the centre of the next side and drag half way towards the next corner, and continue in this manner until you've finished the ellipse. Smart Guides (CS2 or later) will help keep the control points in line with the square's sides. Finally, hide the back view's stand as it's no longer needed.

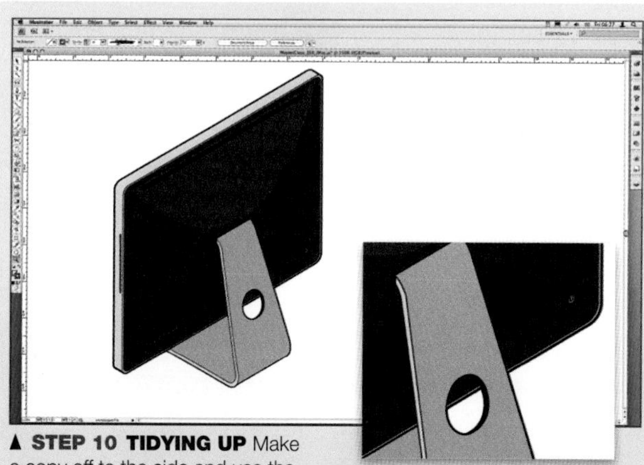

▲ STEP 10 TIDYING UP Make a copy off to the side and use the Pathfinder tools to reduce it to an outline. Increase the line weight and fill with white. Move the outline back into place and send it to the back. Tidy up the object by hiding any remaining guides and lines that should logically be obscured from this perspective. Keep colour and shading to a minimum, but add some simple shading to show the back's curved form, and fine details such as port depth.

MASTERCLASS
Create your own customised maps

In this Masterclass, we show you how to create your own maps for use in brochures, magazines and leaflets with Adobe Illustrator.

Kit required Illustrator
Time About 30 minutes
Goal To create customised maps for use in print and online
Skill level Intermediate

Although the Internet is awash with mapping websites, you can't just take screen grabs and use these maps in published material: everything is copyrighted.

You could publish a link to, for example, Google Maps, but if you want to include the same information in leaflets, magazines and brochures, you'll either have to pay to license Ordnance Survey maps or draw them yourself. The advantage of creating your own maps is that they can be customised to fit the available space. You can highlight landmarks of interest or adjust the colour scheme to match the rest of your publication, and Adobe Illustrator is the perfect application for the job.

Maps appear complex, but they can be surprisingly simple to draw. The technique we use here employs minimum effort for maximum effect. We can't remove the work involved in tracing an existing map, but we can ease the pain through some basic fill and stroke techniques.

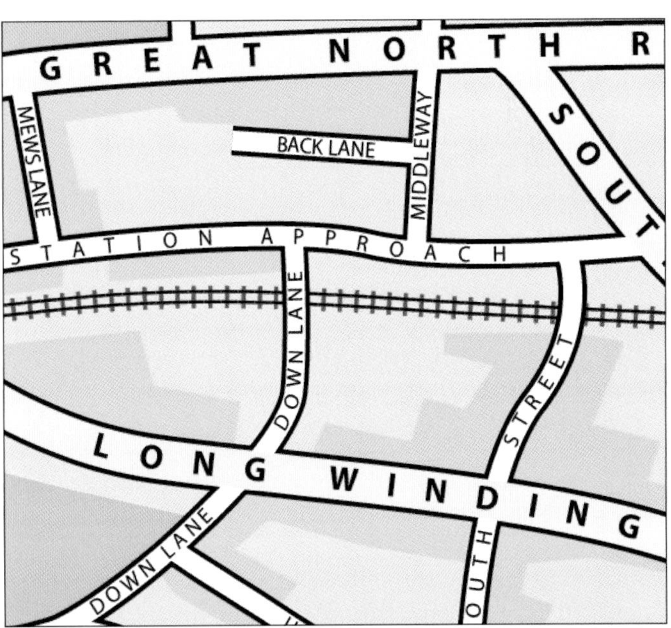

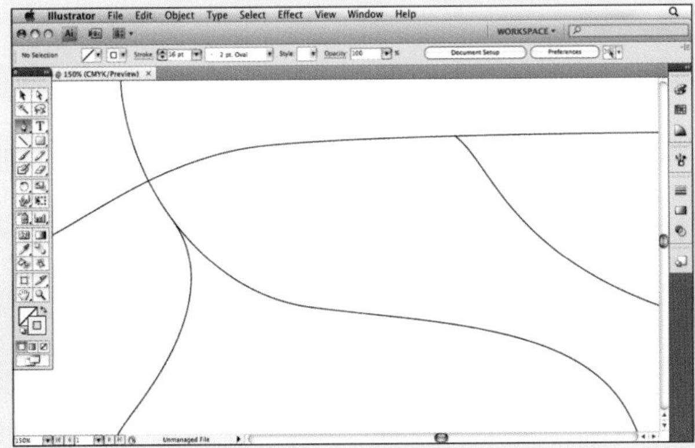

▲ **STEP 01 CREATE THE LAYOUT OF THE MAJOR ROADS** Begin by drawing the major roads only. Make sure your paths are set to have a stroke but no fill. A white fill is the default drawing method, and if you leave it visible, you'll find sections of previously drawn paths become mysteriously covered up. Use the Pen tool, drawing the lines as smoothly as you can. Any sudden changes in direction will make adding text difficult later on. If you have trouble with the Pen tool, the Pencil tool will draw Bézier curves for you.

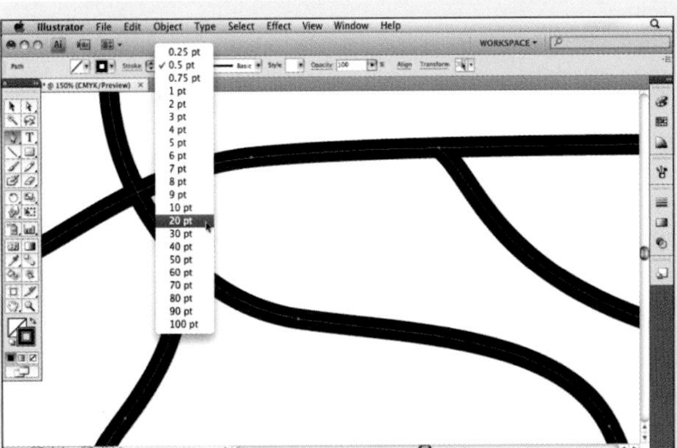

▲ **STEP 02 ADD A FAT STROKE** Select all the major roads and set a fat stroke. The precise size depends on the size of your map and the complexity of the road system – for example, we've used a stroke setting of 20pt for the main roads, but we'll need a smaller value when it comes to drawing the minor roads. If you notice any awkward joins or errors, fix them now; otherwise, you'll end up with two further copies of this network, and changes will become more difficult later.

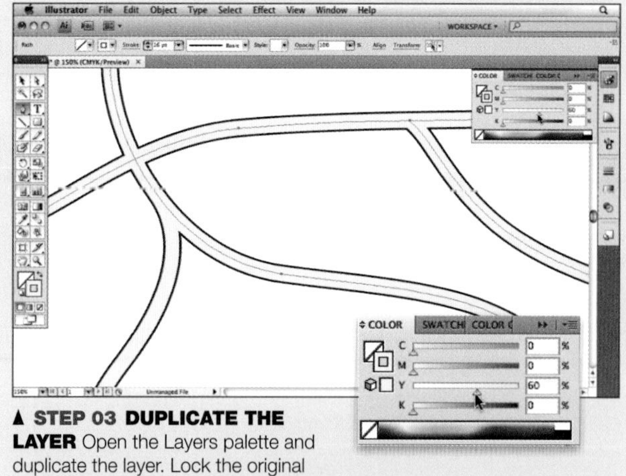

▲ STEP 03 DUPLICATE THE LAYER Open the Layers palette and duplicate the layer. Lock the original layer and on the new one, select the roads and lower the stroke value and change to yellow. The difference produces the thickness of the road edges. Here, a 16pt yellow stroke is 4pt smaller than the original 20pt stroke, creating a thickness of 2pt on either side.

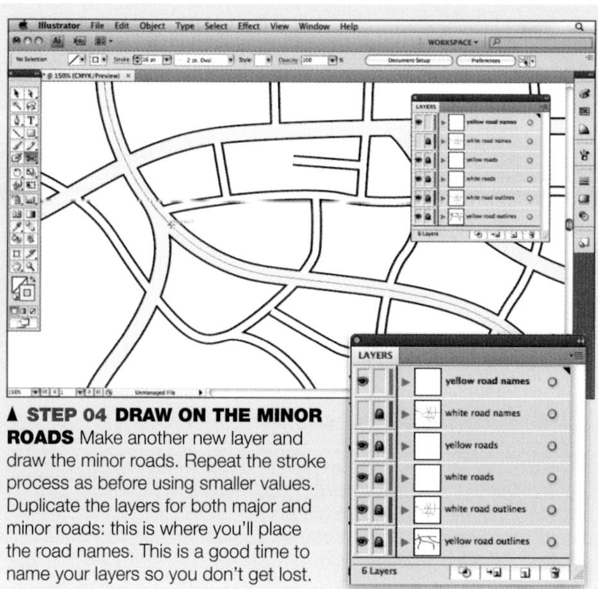

▲ STEP 04 DRAW ON THE MINOR ROADS Make another new layer and draw the minor roads. Repeat the stroke process as before using smaller values. Duplicate the layers for both major and minor roads: this is where you'll place the road names. This is a good time to name your layers so you don't get lost.

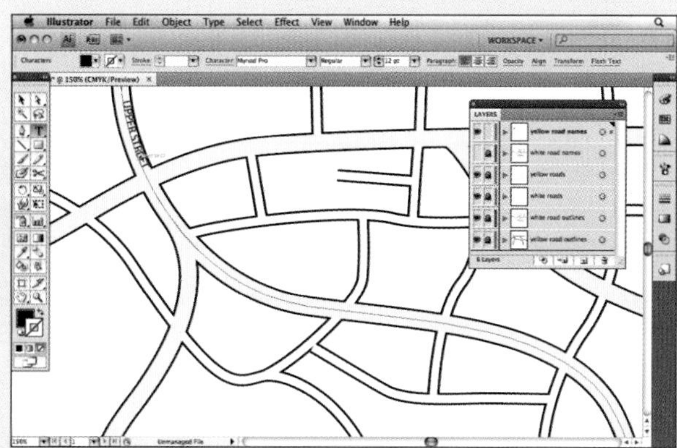

▲ STEP 05 TYPE IN THE ROAD NAMES Lock all the layers except one of the road name layers so that they aren't edited accidentally, and click on one of the roads with the Text tool. This will create line text that follows the drawn path. Type the first road name here in the font of your choice and you'll see how it flows along the road. This process will also remove the stroke from the path, which is why we duplicated it first.

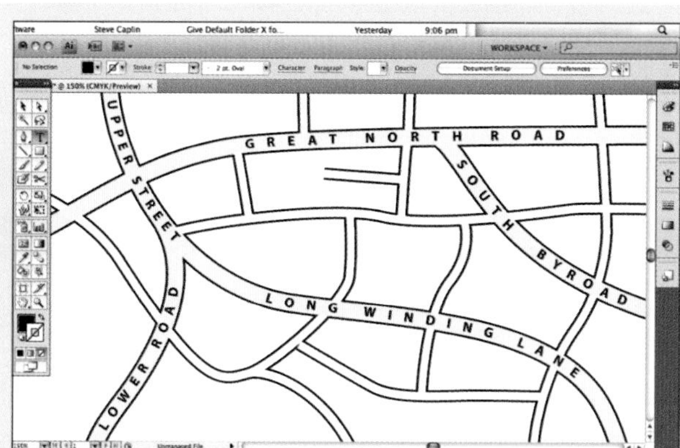

▲ STEP 06 POSITION THE ROAD NAMES You need to baseline shift the lettering downwards so that the path runs through the middle of the words: use Alt-Shift and the down cursor to do this. Words can be spaced out to fill the length of the road by selecting all the text and using Alt-Shift and the right cursor; hold down the Command key and a marker handle appears that enables you to drag the text left and right along the path.

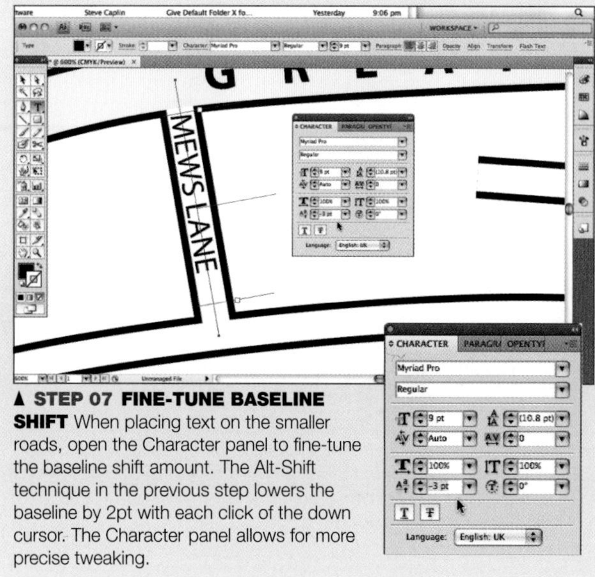

▲ STEP 07 FINE-TUNE BASELINE SHIFT When placing text on the smaller roads, open the Character panel to fine-tune the baseline shift amount. The Alt-Shift technique in the previous step lowers the baseline by 2pt with each click of the down cursor. The Character panel allows for more precise tweaking.

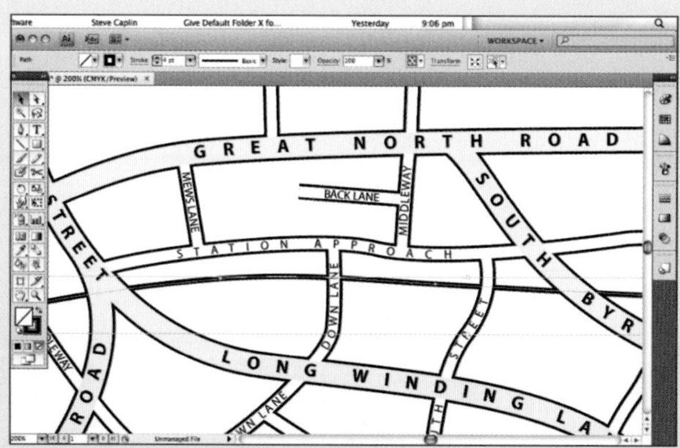

▲ STEP 08 ADD IN RAILWAY LINES Continue until all the road names are in place. You can always switch to a condensed version of the font (if available) if you need to fit a long name onto a short road. With all the names present, you can draw in the railway. Initially, this is a simple path drawn on its own layer, beneath all the road layers.

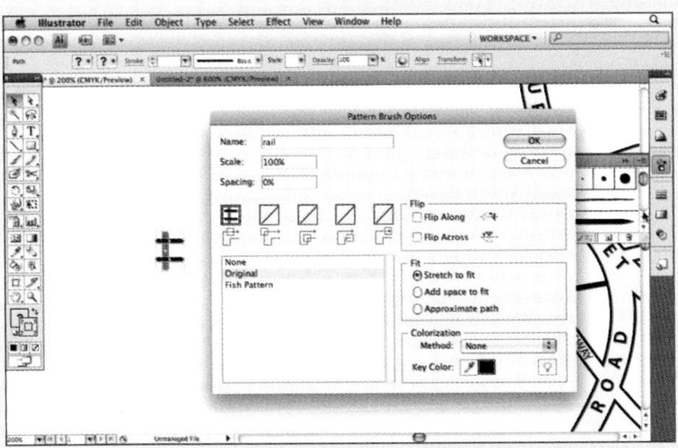

▲ **STEP 09 CREATE A BRUSH FOR THE RAILWAY** You can create the pattern for the railway in just a few seconds: it's just two horizontal black bars (for the rails) with one vertical brown bar behind (for the sleeper). Select the assembly and choose New Brush from the pop-up menu in the Brushes panel. Define the selection as a Pattern brush, which will repeat itself smoothly along any selected path. The various options allow you to define corners, starts and finishes that don't concern us here.

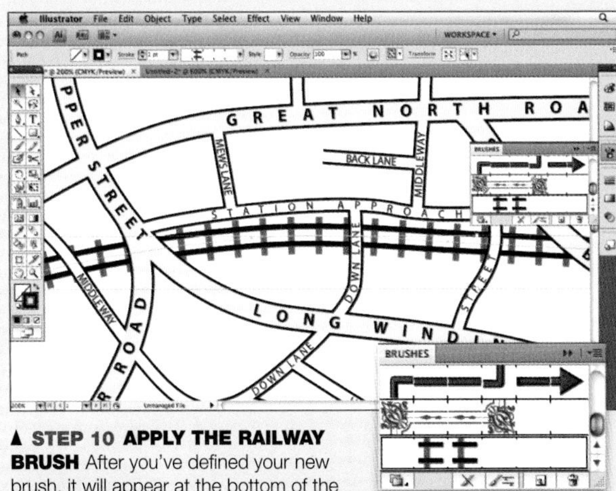

▲ **STEP 10 APPLY THE RAILWAY BRUSH** After you've defined your new brush, it will appear at the bottom of the Brushes panel. To apply it to your railway, select the railway path with the Selection tool and then click on the new brush. The rails will now run along the shape of the path.

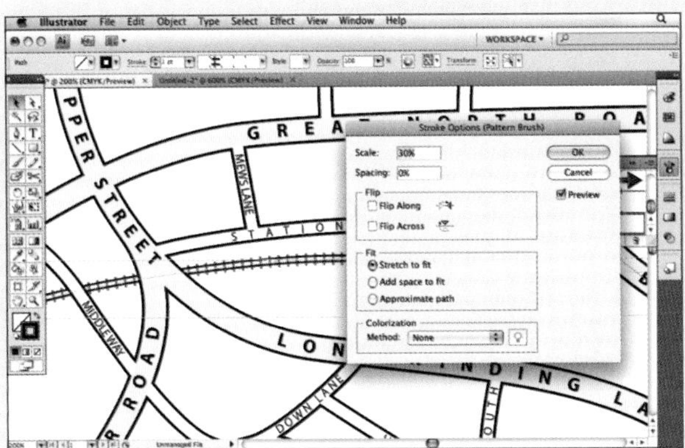

▲ **STEP 11 ADJUST SIZE OF RAILWAY BRUSH** Because the rail segment was drawn at a size that was large enough for us to work on, the rails are far too big for the map. To put it right, make sure the rail path is selected and choose Options of Selected Object from the pop-up menu in the Brushes panel. You can now reduce the size of the brush (make sure the Preview button is checked in order to see what's going on).

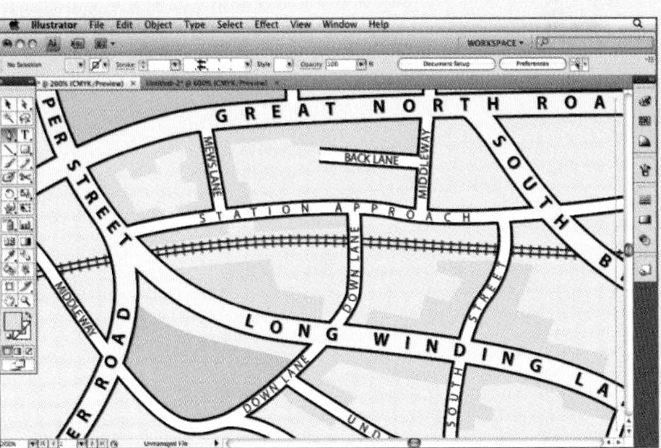

▲ **STEP 12 ADD ANY EXTRA FEATURES TO THE MAP** Any large areas marked out for parks, buildings, water and other large landmarks should be created on a new layer behind all the roads and railways. You'll end up creating far more layers than you'd expect in an Illustrator document, but the ability to lock all except the one you're working on makes editing and adjustment far less prone to accident.

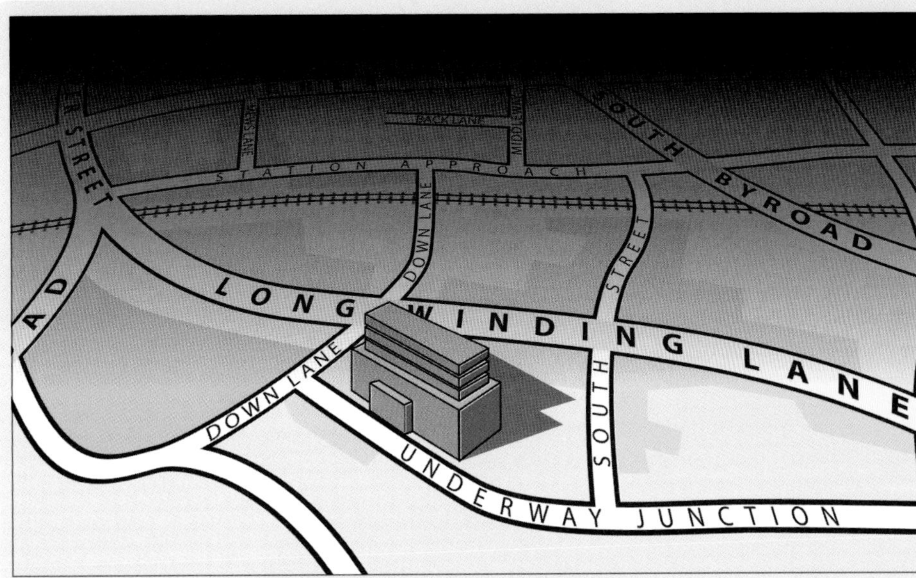

◄ **STEP 13 GIVE IT SOME DEPTH** To create a 3D version of a map, select it all and use Command-G to group all the elements together. Then use Effect > 3D > Rotate. Begin with a front view, and rotate backwards – adding some perspective – until the correct view is achieved. The map remains editable, which is useful when you need to move road names in order to fit in the new perspective view.

A to Z of Design

Are you foxed by common design terms? Do you find yourself stumped when trying to understand Photoshop displacement maps, InDesign paragraph rules, or simply the jargon used by printers when you need them to output your work?

The world of design is as broad as it is deep, and few of even the best and most experienced professionals have an intimate knowledge of all of the techniques they will need to employ in their day-to-day activities. The chances are that right beside their computer they'll have a comprehensive library of how-to books to keep them up to speed.

Building up such a library is expensive, and much of what you'll find in each volume will be irrelevant to the vast majority of users on a daily basis. Fortunately, with our A to Z guide to the concepts of design, you don't need to build up that library, as we've picked out the most important parts and brought them all together here.

Written by professional montage artist Steve Caplin, whose work appears every week in national newspapers and magazines, this carefully ordered section not only defines the most common terms in modern graphical design, but also shows you how to achieve common tasks in Photoshop, InDesign and other core software. It's the ideal place to start learning about the cornerstone applications used in graphic design today without spending a fortune on your own home library.

A: Actions

These essential Photoshop time-savers let you automate repetitive jobs, saving you the time and tedium involved in performing less creative tasks.

Some Photoshop work requires inspiration, artistic judgement and a flair for composition. This is the fun stuff – the creative, cutting-edge work that allows us to explore our creativity. But there's another side to Photoshop that we know all too well – the mundane processing of images for the web or for publication, the repetitive colour correction, and the resizing and repurposing of shot after shot. Yet it's precisely in this area that Photoshop can offer the most assistance.

Photoshop Actions provide a straightforward, but deceptively powerful, way to automate just about any repetitive task. Easy to create and quick to apply, they're the single biggest productivity enhancer the application has to offer. And yet, surprisingly, a great number of experienced Photoshop artists make no use of them whatsoever.

To begin making a new Action, open the Actions palette and select the New Document icon at the bottom. A dialog will appear, prompting you to enter the name of the Action and a location for it. This step is important. If you create Actions for specific jobs, it's worth creating a new set to hold them, so that they can be retrieved easily.

You'll also be asked to designate a keyboard shortcut for the Action. These can be any of the Function keys on the top row of the keyboard – there are 16 on modern Macs, 15 on older ones and 12 on laptops. The keys can be combined with the Command and Shift keys, giving 64 combinations, but bear in mind that several of the Function keys are by default used for system operations, such as Exposé and Spaces.

Assigning a keyboard shortcut means you can play back any Action instantly, as long as you can remember the combination. If you prefer, you can choose to view the Actions palette in 'button' mode, where each Action appears as a clickable button for easy selection. Once you've finished the setup process, you can begin recording your Action. This can be almost any combination of Photoshop steps, and can include any menu item, processing operation, filter or layer effect. You can also set Actions to open files from your hard disk, resize them and copy them into your current document.

Actions can even remember specified locations on your Mac. So, for example, this is an Action I created to resize images for a photo library. It first deletes any working paths I may have created, then changes the resolution of the image to 300dpi without resizing it, and saves the file in Tiff format in my High Res

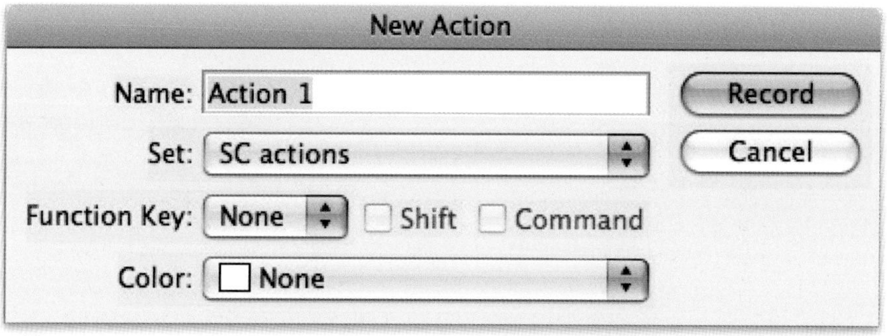

New Action

Name: Action 1 | Record
Set: SC actions | Cancel
Function Key: None | Shift | Command
Color: None

▲ **When you make a new Action, you're prompted for a name, a set to save the Action into and a keystroke. You can also add a colour if you wish – handy when you're viewing the Actions in Button mode.**

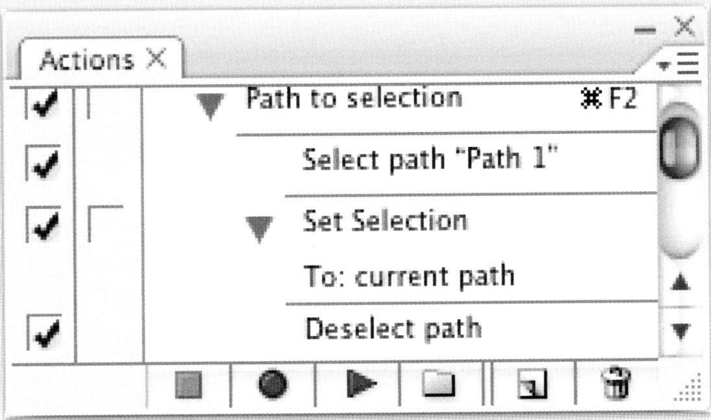

▲ **This simple Action loads a path named Path 1 and turns it into a selection. It then deselects the path.**

folder. It then resizes the image to a maximum of 1000dpi in either dimension (using the Automate > Fit Image command, found in the File menu) and changes the resolution to 72dpi, and saves the image in the Low Res folder. It then produces a thumbnail version of the image by resizing, and saves it using Save for Web in my Thumbnails folder. Finally, it closes the image and returns to Bridge, ready for me to select the next image. The entire Action takes just a couple of seconds to perform and is started with a keystroke.

Not all Actions need to be so complex, though. I use another, far simpler one, for removing the white fringe often seen on cutout objects. This first selects all the pixels present in a layer (by Command-clicking on the layer's thumbnail in the Layers palette), then contracts the selection by one pixel. It then inverses this selection and deletes, to remove a 1-pixel border from around the image.

Once you've finished recording your Action, press the Stop button on the palette. You'll see every step listed in the Actions palette – expand each step to see the precise details of every resize, every filter and Adjustment. If one item is incorrect, it's easy to edit it – double-click the item in the palette, change the settings with reference to the current image and the new settings will be recorded instead of the old ones.

The Batch command (File menu) can apply an Action to a whole folder full of images, and the dialog box here allows you to override open and save locations defined within the Action. So it's possible to take a folder of incoming images, process them (resizing, converting to CMYK, sharpening and so on) and specify a location for the new images to be saved into. Run the Action, go and make a cup of coffee, and when you come back

► **This more complex Action is used for adding new eyes to faces. After having drawn a pen path to outline the eyes, the Action makes a new layer named 'eyeball', fills it with white and then feathers the selection. The Action stops at this point, so we can change the feather size depending on the context. The Action then continues to shade the edge of the eyeball, and opens an iris from a Photoshop file saved to disk, pasting it into the eye area and changing its mode to Multiply before making a clipping mask with the eyeball layer.**

hundreds of images can be processed in your absence. Or just sit back and watch the show.

As well as running batch actions on whole folders of images, they can be called up directly through Bridge. This makes it easy to select a group of images visually, and run the Action on the selection – for example, brightening a whole range of images that have been shot on the wrong exposure. You only need to perform the task once as you record it, and the Action will repeat it indefinitely.

We sometimes want to make decisions in the middle of an Action. For example, we might want to specify the amount of Unsharp Mask applied to an image, choose a Blur value on a colour channel, or set a new name for a file. It's easy to do this by setting a Stop point after the Action is recorded – simply click in the row of boxes to the left of each Action step and it will be flagged with a marker. When the Action is played back, it will pause at that point.

After closing the current dialog box, the Action will continue playing. Actions can improve your productivity – and your sanity – to a huge degree. But be sure to save any sets of Actions you create, using the Save option in the pop-up menu at the top of the palette – otherwise, if Photoshop should crash or you experience a system freeze, any newly-created Actions will be lost. ⊗

A: Adjustment layers

Edit your pictures the non-destructive way by applying adjustment layers to your stack, rather than adjusting the images themselves.

Adjustment layers are powerful tools for Photoshop users, but they're often overlooked in the flurry of special effect filters and layer styles. The 15 adjustments available include Curves, Levels, Hue/Saturation, Selective Color, as well as all the standard adjustments you'd expect to find. However, there are also special-purpose adjustment layers, such as the Gradient Map, which appear nowhere else in Photoshop.

Adjustment layers allow you to apply standard adjustments in a non-permanent, editable way. For instance, rather than simply modifying a layer's appearance with Curves, you could use an adjustment layer version of Curves instead. The most obvious advantage is that this adjustment can be reopened at any point, and tweaked or removed entirely. You choose adjustment layers from the pop-up list at the bottom of the Layers palette, or by selecting New Adjustment Layer from Photoshop's Layer menu.

There's far more to the technology than this, though. First, an adjustment layer will apply its effect to all the layers beneath it. Think of it as a layer of translucent glass over your layer stack: anything seen through it will show the adjustment set within it. If you only want the adjustment to apply to a single layer, then the easiest solution is to use the layer beneath as a clipping mask. This can be done after the adjustment layer is created, by pressing Alt-Command-G. Alternatively, if you hold down Alt while selecting the relevant adjustment layer from the pop-up list, you can specify the clipping mode.

▲ **Here, the adjustment layer applied to the top, Solid Color layer has been set to Multiply so you can see through it to the image beneath – in this case, to give the picture a sepia effect.**

Adjustment layers [**01**] can be applied at all the standard layer modes, which greatly increases their range of use. So a Solid Color layer placed above this image would, by default, simply fill the workspace with that colour. When we change the mode of the adjustment layer from Normal to Multiply, though, we see through it to the image beneath: it's a simple way of creating a sepia-like effect without changing the pixels on the layer itself. And because the effect can apply to all the layers, we can use it to turn a whole set of layers to sepia.

Adjustment layers can, of course, be duplicated and moved around just like regular layers. As such, when you apply an effect to one layer, it's easy to duplicate it and apply it to other layers within the same document, or even in different ones. Furthermore, because they're editable, you can change the effect at any time. Again, as they behave like regular layers, it's a simple matter to reduce the opacity of an adjustment layer to reduce the strength of its effect, which gives increased flexibility without permanently changing the state of any of the layers in your document.

Adjustment layers can also have masks applied to them so that they affect only a portion of the layers beneath. In this example [**02A**], we want to take some of the blue out of this man's face. We can begin by making a new Curves adjustment layer, with which it's a trivial matter to achieve our goal. The trouble is that the Curves process has affected the suit as well [**02B**]. The adjustment layer already has a built-in mask when we create it, so by simply painting out the suit area on the mask, we can restore that region to its original state [**02C**].

The Gradient Map is a special adjustment layer that uses the foreground and background colours to add colour to the image. It works particularly well when using

▲ This man has an unhealthy blue cast, so we want to make a new Curves adjustment layer.

▲ However, the Curves adjustment layer affects the man's suit as well as his skin tone.

▲ By painting out the suit on the layer's built-in mask, we can restore that area to its original state.

▲ An image with strong colours can benefit greatly from being converted to black and white. The Gradient Map adjustment layer is a great way to do this.

black and white, as it produces a strong, crisp greyscale image that's far sharper than you could be achieved simply by converting an RGB picture to greyscale. In this example [**03A**], the original image is strong in colour. When it's simply converted to greyscale [**03B**] it loses all its power. The Gradient Map [**03C**], on the other hand, brings far more definition and contrast to it: when now converted to greyscale, this image will retain all that enhancement. One clear advantage of this method is that if you're creating an image which may or may not need to be in greyscale, you can work in RGB with a Gradient Map layer present, and see exactly how it will work in mono without permanently affecting any of the constituent layers.

Another, more controllable way to create a greyscale effect is to use the Channel Mixer adjustment layer. This lets you set the strength of each of the red, green and blue channels in an RGB document: by checking the Monochrome box at the bottom of the dialog, you can produce precisely the greyscale mode you need.

Some effects depend on applying an adjustment after a filter, such as turning objects into metal. Here's a mannequin's head [**04A**], which we're going to make appear to be made of bronze. The first step is to add a Curves adjustment layer with a stepped effect [**04B**]. But this affects the object's colour as well, resulting in an unwanted rainbow texture [**04C**]. We can fix this by changing the mode of the adjustment layer, using the pop-up menu in Layers palette. When we change it from Normal to Luminosity, only the brightness of the object is affected: the colours remain unchanged [**04D**].

The trouble now is that there's too much surface detail for a convincing metallic look. To remedy this, we lock the transparency of the layer and apply Gaussian Blur to it until we achieve the effect we want [**04E**]. If we were just using straight Curves, we'd have to apply the blur first – guessing the right amount. With the adjustment layer, we can apply blur to the head while looking through the Curves effect: this way, we can see precisely what we're going to get.

▲ Simply converting the image to greyscale results in the image losing its impact.

▲ The Gradient Map layer brings much more contrast and definition to the picture.

▲ We want to make this head appear as though it has been made of bronze.

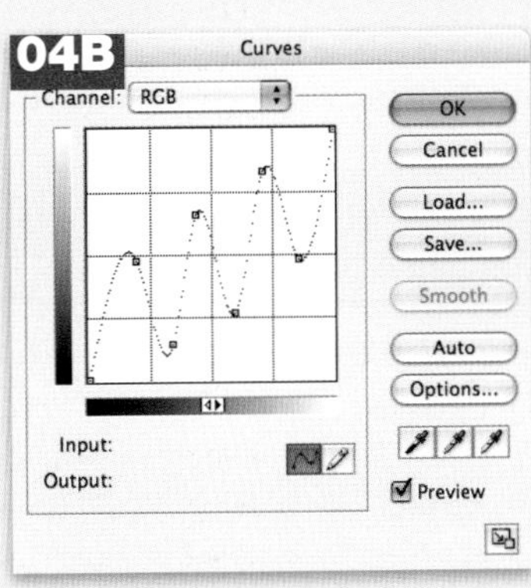

▲ First, add a Curves adjustment layer with a stepped effect.

▲ However, this affects the colour of the head and has added unwanted texture.

▲ We can fix this by changing the mode of the adjustment layer to Luminosity, whereby only the brightness is affected.

▲ Now there's too much surface detail, so we lock the transparency and apply Gaussian Blur until we get the desired effect.

A: Adobe Bridge

It may have started life as a simple image browser for Photoshop, but Bridge has evolved into a powerful asset management tool.

Adobe Bridge started life as the File Browser, a simple utility that allowed Photoshop users to see all the contents of a folder as thumbnails, rather than the text list seen in the standard Open dialog. The benefits were immediately obvious: users could browse files visually, rather than having to remember their name.

Now a standalone application, Adobe Bridge has evolved into a powerful asset management tool that spans the entire Creative Suite. Its toolset and functionality have increased with each release, and it's now a powerful, comprehensive utility that's capable of far more than basic image browsing.

Unlike static image databases such as Extensis Portfolio, Bridge works only with online collections – you can't use it to catalogue images on removable hard disks or DVDs. But with hard disk storage getting both larger and cheaper every year, more designers are keeping their entire image libraries instantly to hand rather than in drawers and on shelves.

The advantage of the online-only approach is that Bridge can scale thumbnails and previews to any size on-demand. Static databases, on the other hand, generate fixed-size thumbnails when files are imported, which often means users have to peer at a tiny image and need to open it in Photoshop in order to see the contents. Bridge's iPhoto-like system has a slider, which can be used to scale thumbnails, as you judge your preferred trade-off between clarity of preview and number of images displayed at a time.

Bridge includes a Preview pane in which any selected image will appear magnified to the maximum size of the pane itself. It's fully customisable, so users can choose its size – bearing in mind that the larger the Preview pane, the smaller the area devoted to the image thumbnails. Clicking on the Preview pane will bring up a 100% loupe.

With the most recent versions, however, the Preview pane has become almost an irrelevance. Pressing the Spacebar when any single image thumbnail is selected will enlarge that image to fill the entire monitor. Clicking anywhere within this preview will zoom in to a 100% view of the image, showing it at actual pixel size. You can pan around the image by dragging, and it will remain at actual size until you click the mouse button. When a single image is selected and zoomed to fit, pressing the left and right cursor keys will step through all the images in the folder. But here are a couple of useful extras: if you're zoomed in to 100%, stepping through the images will retain the same view size and position on successive images, which is a great way to compare details across multiple shots of the same

▲ In Review mode, you can cycle through a virtual carousel of images, rejecting those you don't want by pressing the down cursor key.

scene. And if two or more images are selected before zooming, then the cursor keys will cycle through only those selected images.

Bridge now includes a Review Mode in which all the images in a folder are displayed in a virtual carousel. Pressing the left or right keys will move to the next or previous image; pressing the down key will reject an image. It's an easy way to make comparison choices of a folder full of photographs. When exiting Review Mode, all the images are selected except those that have been rejected, allowing the kept images to be batch processed, labelled or moved to another folder. Alternatively, you can hide rejected photographs from the thumbnail display.

▲ As an image browser, Bridge is speedy, comprehensive and fully featured. Selected images are displayed on the right in the Preview pane.

Sometimes, you may have many similar images in a single folder. If shooting a wedding, for instance, you might have a dozen pictures of the bride's family, half a dozen of signing the register, and so on. To make the sorting process easier, Bridge lets you manually group similar images together into 'stacks'. These are represented by a single thumbnail, which can be expanded to show all of its contents by clicking on it.

The working environment in Bridge is highly customisable. You can choose to concentrate on thumbnails, text keywords, favourite folders, and so on; each appears in its own separate pane, which can be moved around and sized as you like. Recognising that you need different layouts for different purposes, Bridge lets you create as many layout variations as you like, all of which are instantly retrievable from a menu. When it comes to the metadata panel, you can customise the data included to a precise degree.

Bridge will open Raw files in its own Camera Raw dialog, without the need to open Photoshop first. An added bonus is the ability to open any file – Jpeg, Tiff and so on – into this dialog. This allows you to adjust contrast, colour fringing, white balance

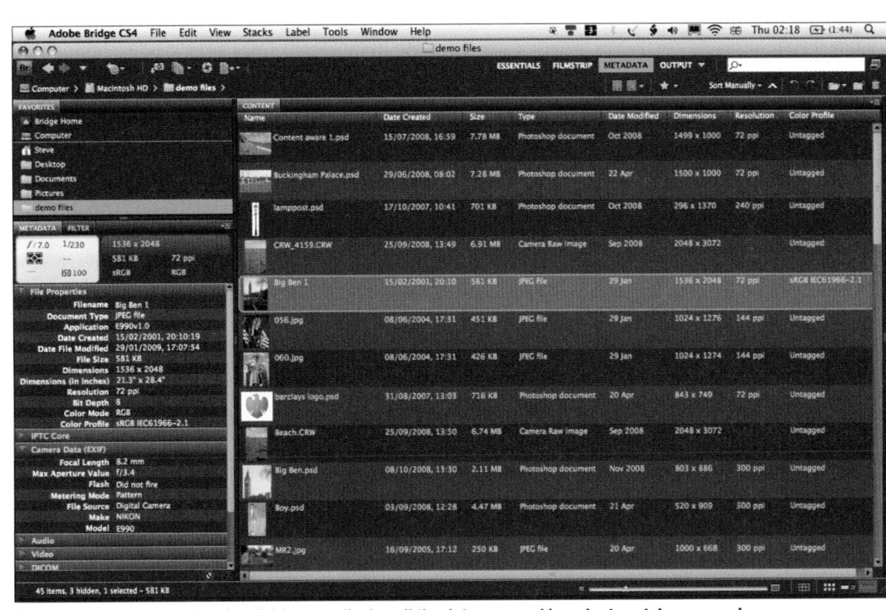

▲ If it's information you're after, Bridge can display all the data you need in order to catalogue your images.

and more, in a non-destructive manner. Of course, Bridge still retains its core role as an image browser for Photoshop, allowing you to apply batch Actions to selected images, place artwork into Photoshop documents, and open multiple images as separate layers within a single document.

Bridge can also be used as a slideshow application, in which images can be displayed full screen and cycled through with the cursor keys. Alternatively, you could opt for automatic display, in which you can set the period for which each image is viewed, choose from one of a dozen transition methods, and even zoom in and out of successive images.

Folders or selected images in Bridge can be published to a web gallery, using a variety of built-in templates. These can either be saved to disk, or uploaded directly via ftp to users' websites. Surprisingly, the major shortcoming in Bridge is its inability to print images directly; this capability has simply never been built in. You can, however, automatically combine images into PDF documents, which can then easily be printed from Preview. ⊗

B: Backgrounds

The secret of a successful montage is picking the right background and fully integrating it with the foreground subjects in your image.

It can come as a surprise to those unfamiliar with photomontage that the background in a composite image is frequently one of the last items to be added to the mix. While it might appear as though it's the background that unites and holds all the other elements together, it's often – but not always – the case that the focus of the illustration is created first, and a suitable background chosen once all the other objects are in place.

Think of any great work of art – the famous Mona Lisa, for example. It's unlikely that Leonardo da Vinci would have begun by painting in the hills and sky behind his enigmatic subject: far more plausible, surely, for him to have painted the scene into the gaps left behind La Gioconda's head and shoulders. However, there are certain issues you face when it comes to choosing the right background.

Clearly, it has to match the feel of the piece and be relevant to the foreground subject: if your main image shows an exploding computer, there's no advantage to placing it in the middle of a field or on a seashore when a home or office environment would be a much more appropriate setting. Similarly, a montage of ex-US president George W Bush featuring whatever added elements you feel will make him appear the most ridiculous will look much better set against a background of the White House or Iraq. The background provides the setting for your scene, reinforcing the message of the illustration.

The hardest part about selecting a background lies in choosing a view that matches the perspective of the foreground elements. When the focus of the image is a person, it is important that the horizon appears in the right location: a misplaced background can throw the whole image off-balance.

The way to make a background appear in the right place is to position the horizon on the same level as the eyes of the people in the image. If there isn't a clear horizon, it's easy to work out where it is by drawing vanishing lines from horizontal cues: where these lines meet you'll find the vanishing point, and hence the horizon.

Many good montages are often let down by having the focus of the image placed against backgrounds of wildly different colour. It's not that the background needs to be exactly the same colour as the foreground, but that the lighting of one needs to match that of the other.

Let's say, for example, that you have a studio shot of a woman in skiwear. Once you've removed the original backdrop, it

▲ **The background for this skateboarder was photographed on an overcast day – and it doesn't match the studio lighting of the subject (left). By warming it up (right) we can make the two elements look as though they belong together.**

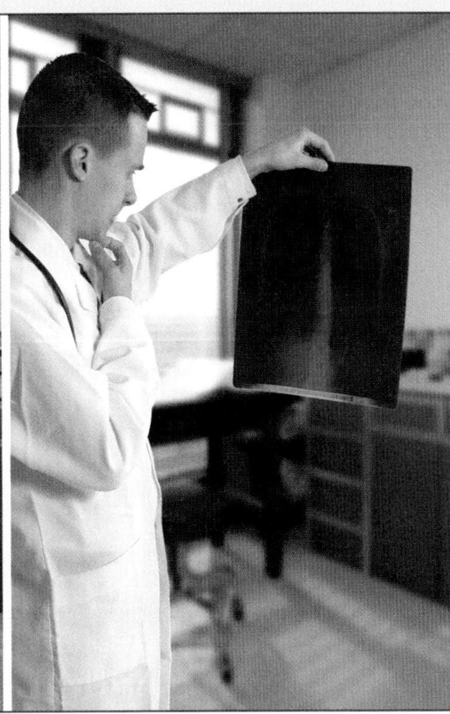

◄ This doctor's surgery makes a suitable background for our medic with his x-ray. But the fussiness of the background detracts from the subject (left). When we blur it to give the impression of limited depth of field (right), we bring the subject into stronger focus.

makes sense to place a snow scene behind her in order to enhance the overall image. But while the woman might have been shot in a studio using tungsten lights, the outdoor view will most likely have a strong blue cast, together with harsher, stronger shadows. When combined, the two will appear mismatched; you'll need to adjust the foreground image so that it matches the background, using Curves or Levels, to ensure that both elements of the montage appear to occupy the same colour space.

The snow example here is a special case: we can't easily 'warm up' the snow without it appearing artificial. But for most other scenes, adjusting the background colour to match the foreground is going to be an easier and more effective solution. There's no hard and fast rule to gauging this adjustment: if it looks right, then it is right. To be on the safe side, use an Adjustment Layer, placed directly above the background, to change the colour. That way you'll always be able to tweak it later if the need arises.

Sometimes you might have found the perfect background picture only to discover that it appears too fussy and complicated when placed in the montage. Too much detail in the background can easily detract from the focus of an illustration, making it harder for the reader to take the scene in at a glance. A useful technique here is to blur the background to give the impression of limited depth of field. Because this is an appearance we're used to in traditional photography, it doesn't appear unnatural, but serves to highlight the essential areas of the image without swamping them.

So far, we've been looking at backgrounds placed after the rest of the image has been completed. But sometimes we want to start with a background shot, and add elements to it: we might want to place people or objects in a well-known view. The problem here is slightly different. How do we add new objects so that they appear to be part of the landscape, rather than simply superimposed upon it? For example, how can we place a giant pig in Trafalgar Square and make it seem to be really there?

Adding appropriate shadows and matching the colouring is, of course, essential. But there's another way to integrate items into a view, and that's to place them so that they're partly obscured by elements in the original scene.

Try tucking your placed item behind a car, or a railing, or a bush, and you'll be surprised at how much difference it makes to the overall sense of realism. This can be easily achieved using a layer mask, which will allow you to paint out your object where the background is placed in front of it, without irrevocably erasing any part of it. ⊗

▲ This plastic rabbit in Parliament Square looks as though it has been plonked on top of the image (left). By moving it higher in the frame and tucking it behind the railings (right), even this absurd combination takes on a form of realism.

B: Baseline grid

Misaligned text is both sloppy and amateurish. Here, we show you how to set up and use a baseline grid to give your layout a more professional look.

Neatly aligned text is one of the features that distinguishes a professional layout from an amateur one. Whether you're working in InDesign or QuarkXPress, if the bottom lines of two adjacent columns of text are misaligned, it can cause your pages to look badly planned.

By default, most applications will apply 'auto' leading to type, which is generally 20% greater than the point size of the font. So if, for example, you're working with 10pt type, auto leading will be set to 12pt. Leading is designed to add extra space between lines of text to increase legibility; the word comes from the thin strips of lead that traditional typesetters used physically to insert between lines of movable type.

Professional designers will set an absolute figure on leading, allowing them to customise the type's appearance depending on the job – and they'll often use the 20% setting as a starting point. The difference is that if type is specified as 10/12pt (that is, 10pt in size on 12pt leading), then if an inline subhead or dingbat is increased to, say, 18p for dramatic effect, the leading will remain at 12pt. If the paragraph is set to auto leading, the line with the oversized character can receive extra spacing, resulting in an ugly mismatch.

Basic text alignment is easy to control using the Baseline Grids feature found in all good page layout applications. In InDesign and XPress, the grid is set in a Preferences dialog box: choose a value that matches the leading you're using for your main body text. As such, if the bulk of your publication is set in 10pt type with 12pt leading, for instance, you'll probably want to set the baseline grid to 12pt increments. Be sure to check the 'align to grid' option for the text you're using to make the text automatically snap to the next baseline.

As well as setting the incremental value, you can also set the distance down the page the baseline grid starts. This is important when ensuring that type aligns with your bottom margin. If you're placing graphics – boxes, pictures and so on – that snap to the bottom margin of the page, the text will look awkward if it falls short. The best approach is to type a column of text and adjust the First Line setting in Preferences, so the bottom line of the type falls exactly on the bottom margin of the page.

If the leading for a piece of text is less than the specified grid increment, its leading will be expanded to fit the grid. So if you're working on a 12pt grid and you have a piece of text set in 6/8pt, the leading will be expanded to 12pt so that it fits the grid. If, on the other hand, you're placing a block of text that already has leading greater than the baseline value – 12/14pt, for instance – the leading will be expanded to the next multiple of 12pt, so the text will end up being 12pt on 24pt leading.

This text is set in 12pt Times Roman with auto leading. Look what the 18pt dingbat symbol here✎ does to the leading of this paragraph: there's now an ugly gap in the middle which makes the text unaligned.

This text is set in 12pt Times Roman with 14.4pt leading. Now, when we use an 18pt dingbat ✎, the leading of the paragraph remains unaltered, because the leading was specified absolutely.

▲ **When leading is set to 'auto', over-sized characters such as the dingbat (left) can increase the leading of the entire line. If a leading value is specified, this can't happen (right).**

This text is set in 10/12 Myriad and is set to snap to a 12pt baseline grid.

Subhead in 18pt runs on two lines

When the subhead is on the same leading as the body text, it's clearly very much too tight.

This text is set in 10/12 Myriad and is set to snap to a 12pt baseline grid.

Subhead in 18pt runs on two lines

When the subhead is set on double the body text leading, it's now far too loose.

▲ **Oversized text, such as these subheads, look ugly when they snap to the standard text baseline – it's either too tight (left), or too loose (right).**

This text is set in 10/12 Myriad and is set to snap to a 12pt baseline grid.

Subhead in 18pt

The subhead above is in 18pt and is not aligned to the grid, so there's a thin space after it that works fairly well with this leading. But we can't always assume that our subheads will fit on a single line.

Sometimes, the subhead needs to be longer than a single line.

Subhead in 18pt runs on two lines

There's now too much space after the sub-head, because the following text snaps to the baseline grid.

▲ **Setting the subheads not to snap to the baseline grid is one solution, but this can result in uneven spacing between the subhead and the text that follows.**

This text is set in 10/12 Myriad and is set to snap to a 6pt baseline grid.

Subhead in 18pt

When the baseline grid is set to half the desired leading, the space after the subhead can be kept consistent. The only problem now is that the text on this side is half a line shorter than the text in the next column, which can look clumsy.

This text is set in 10/12 Myriad and is set to snap to a 6pt baseline grid.

Subhead in 18pt runs on two lines

Even when the subhead is on two lines, there's still the same space following it. But the text in this column and the one to the left now don't align correctly, as the baseline grid is half the leading height.

▲ **If you set your text to snap to a grid that's half the leading size, you can achieve good subhead spacing and equal spacing before the subsequent text. However, the columns are now uneven.**

This text is set in 10/12 Myriad and is set to snap to a 6pt baseline grid.

Subhead in 18pt

When the baseline grid is set to half the desired leading, the space after the subhead can be kept consistent. The only problem now is that the text on this side is half a line shorter than the text in the next column, which can look clumsy.

This text is set in 10/12 Myriad and is set to snap to a 6pt baseline grid.

Subhead in 18pt runs on two lines

Even when the subhead is on two lines, there's still the same space following it. A simple workaround is to set the entire text box to be vertically justified, which spaces out the text to fit top and bottom.

◄▼ **Changing the vertical alignment method to Justified using the Text Frame dialog allows you to balance two ragged columns of text – but it's a cheat.**

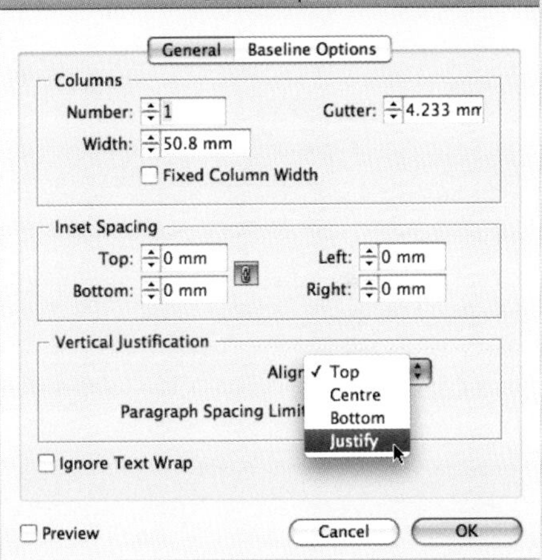

This oversized leading issue tends to occur when you're setting inline subheads that are larger than the type size. You can't set the subhead on the same leading as the rest of the text, or it will be too tight – especially if the subheads run onto more than one line. However, if the subhead leading is double the baseline, it will appear too spaced and too far away from the text that follows. One option is to set the subhead not to align with the baseline grid, but this means there would then be uneven gaps between the subhead and the text that follows it, as the body type snaps to a grid that's now a variable distance from the subhead.

A simple workaround is to set the baseline grid to be half the leading value, so our 10pt text will now be set on a baseline grid with increments of 6pt. This gives you the flexibility to use larger type and give it more appropriate leading; you're no longer constrained to multiples of 12, but multiples of 6. The leading within multi-line subheads, and between the subheads and the text that follows, can now be standardised.

Setting a baseline that's half the leading value also enables you to insert half line spaces between paragraphs – a useful technique for features such as interviews, where the question and answer format benefits from clear spaces dividing the journalist and the subject. A whole line space is too much; a half line space is usually just right. There's no need to specify this space precisely, as a 'space after' value of just 1mm will normally be sufficient to bump the text down to the next baseline.

The only difficulty arises when there are uneven numbers of subheads or half line spaces on corresponding sides of a multi-column text box. You can all too easily end up with text that, even though it snaps to a baseline grid, now appears ragged at the bottom of the page, because one side is half a line longer than the other. There are, however, ways of dealing with this problem. The simplest is to change one of the half line spaces to a full line space somewhere in the short column. If chosen with care, it's unlikely the casual reader would notice the deception, and the end result would be more pleasing.

InDesign offers a clever cheat, hidden in the Text Frame Options dialog accessed from the Object menu (or hit Command-B). Towards the bottom of this dialog is a Vertical Justification pop-up menu, in which one option is 'justified'. Just as standard justified text will be spaced out to fit the column width, vertically justified type is spaced out so that the top and bottom of the type matches the top and bottom of the enclosing text box. The type in between, of course, will no longer be aligned to the grid, as spacing is added evenly between all the lines. It's not a perfect solution, but it's a straightforward quick fix that can get you out of a problem.

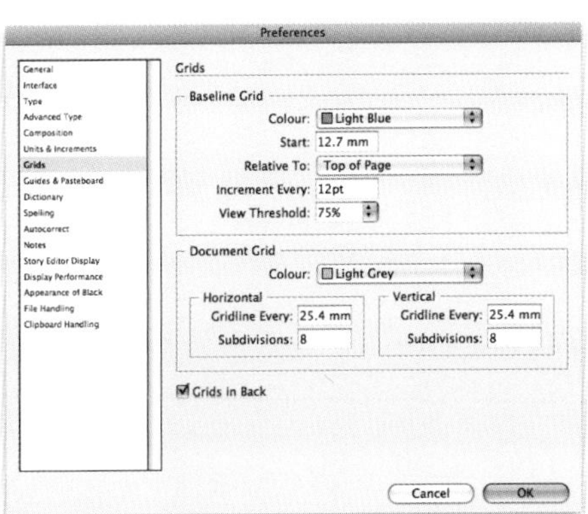

▲ **In InDesign, baseline grids are set in the Grids section of the Preferences dialog.**

B: Batch processing 1

We explain how to take a folder full of photographs from different sources and reduce them all to the same size and colour space.

One of the most often-overlooked features in Photoshop is its ability to deal with multiple files, processing each one according to a set of rules. There are many reasons why you might wish to batch process images. Here, we'll look at reducing all the images in a folder full of photos from different sources to the same size and colour space for use on a web page and in a slideshow.

In order to apply a process to a batch of images, you first need to define that process. You do this by building all the steps in a new Action. So to start, make sure the Actions panel is open and choose New Action from the pop-up menu at the top of the panel.

Give the Action a name and choose a set in which to save it [**01**]. If for any reason Photoshop crashes or freezes, you'll need to reload this Action from the set. While you can use the default set, which includes the sample Actions that ship with Photoshop, it's better to create your own so you can keep it separate – and share it among multiple workstations. With the Action defined and named, you have the option of choosing a keyboard shortcut and colour for it. Both of

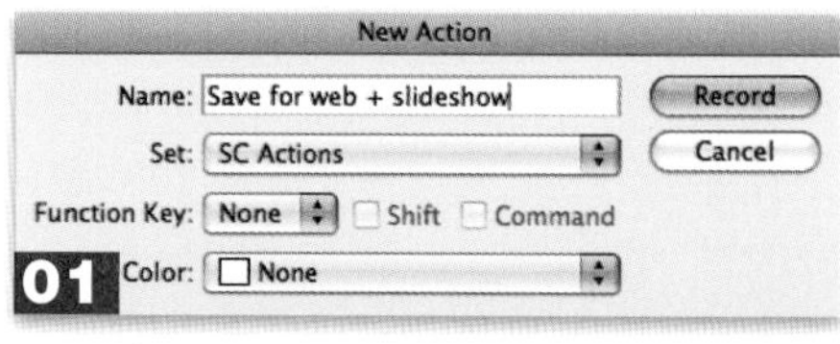

01

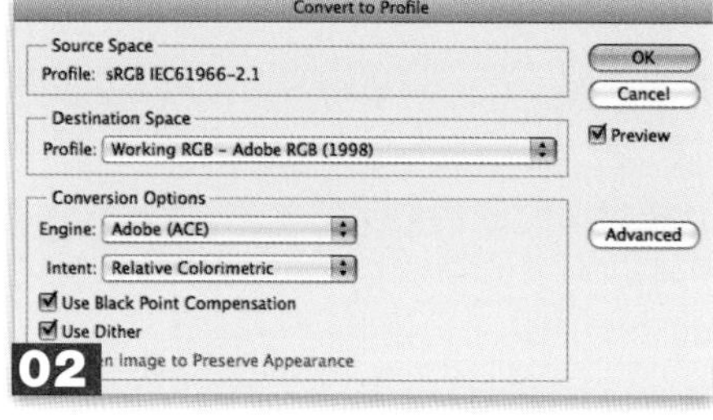

02

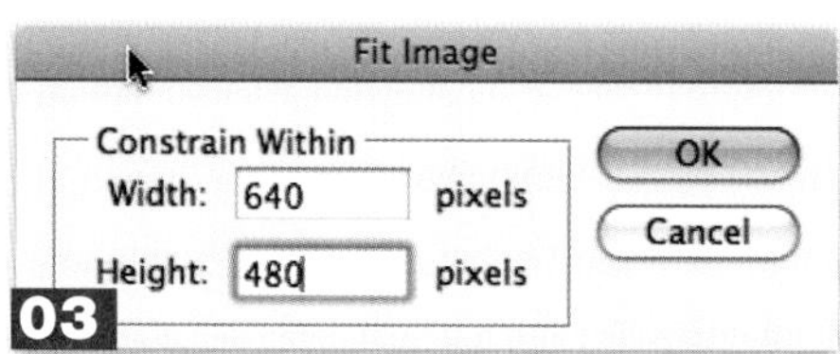

03

these steps are unnecessary for batch processing. Press the Record button to begin recording the Action. First, you need to open an image that's typical of the kind you're going to want to process. The first step is to make sure all the images are in the same colour space. This is straightforward enough: choose Edit > Convert to Profile, then choose the RGB mode you want (Adobe RGB 1998 is generally the most suitable). Note that you can choose this option if the image is in another colour space, such as sRGB, in which case it will make the conversion, or if it's already in Adobe RGB 1998, in which case, it will have no effect [**02**].

Next, you need to shrink the image to the size you want it – let's say 640 x 480 pixels. Here, you hit a snag. You can use the Image Size dialog to set the current image to be 640 pixels wide x 480 pixels high, with no difficulty. However, if the image isn't in a standard 4:3 ratio – if it's portrait rather than landscape, for instance – then choosing these values will produce an ugly distortion. The solution is to use File > Automate > Fit Image. This opens a dialog in which you can enter the maximum dimensions in which you want the image to appear – 640 x 480 in this case. Now, when you press enter, the image will be shrunk so it fits within this defined size [**03**].

If this is the image as you'd like to use it on your website, you can choose File > Save for Web & Devices. This dialog shrinks images down to a manageable size, partly by using

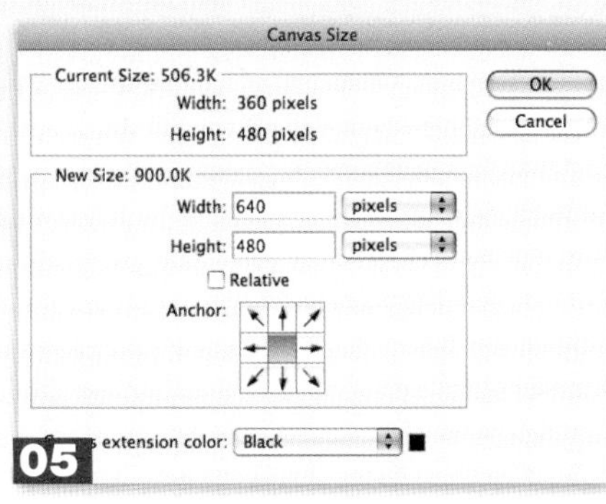

Jpeg compression and partly by stripping out any extra paths, channels or metadata that simply take up file space. Here, we've chosen a Jpeg setting of 40 to produce a small file that's still of good enough quality for on-screen display [**04**]. Hit Enter, choose a location – it's worth setting up separate folders for the results of the batch processing – and the Save for Web component will be added to the list of Actions.

You need to make a further tweak to prepare the images. The size is fine, but you want all the images to be exactly the same size – 640 x 480 – with a black background where the image is smaller than the preset size. You can do this in a single step, using the Image > Canvas Size dialog. Here, you can set the dimensions to be 640 x 480 pixels, leaving the 'anchor' setting where it is to guarantee that the image will be placed right in the centre. Rather than just clicking OK, you can use the Canvas Extension Colour pop-up menu to set the background colour to black [**05**]. With the image complete, you can use Edit > Save As (so you don't overwrite the original file) to save this completed image in the folder of our choice.

The last step is to close the window, after which the Action is now complete. If you look at it in the Actions panel, you can see each step listed in order, and you can pop open each one, as we've done here with the Canvas Size step, to see exactly what each action will accomplish [**06**]. If you were to pop open the Save for Web step, you'd see a huge range of entries detailing precisely what this step entails down to the smallest detail.

In fact, the Action is a little too complete. It includes the Open step you used right at the beginning to open our sample image. If you were to run this Action now, it would open the same file over and over, repeating the process just on this one. As such, you need to select it in the list and click the Trash icon at the bottom of the panel to delete it.

The Action is now finished, so you can begin your batch process. Choose File > Automate > Batch to open the dialog. The most recently created Action will already be loaded up for you, so all you need to do is to specify that the Source folder will be the folder that contains all the images for processing. You don't need to specify a Destination folder, as the two locations for finished images are already specified within the Action [**07**]. Photoshop will now run the Action on all images in the source folder, producing both web and slide show versions of your files automatically.

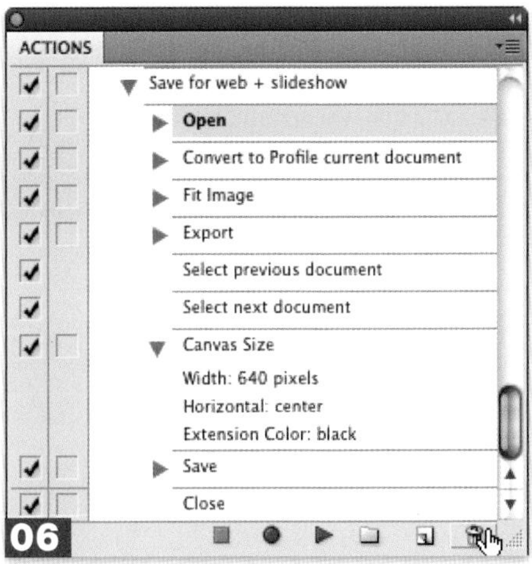

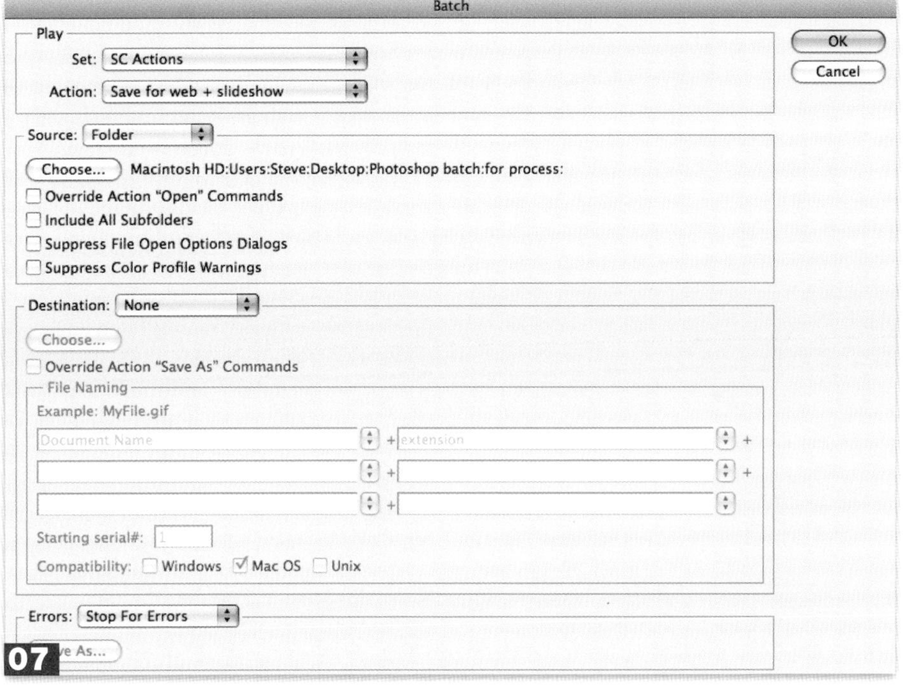

B: Batch processing 2

As we saw in the previous tutorial, batch processing can save hours of tedious work, so here's how to take it even further using Adobe Bridge.

In the previous A to Z, we introduced the idea of batch processing in Photoshop. We looked at how to create an Action to perform a set of tasks, and how to use the File > Automate > Batch menu to apply that Action to a folder full of files. In this issue, we'll see how we can take batch processing further, using Adobe Bridge to extend its use.

When you use Photoshop to select a group of files to which you want to apply a single Action, you have to specify an entire folder full of images. You can, however, use the visual interface in Bridge to select exactly the images you wish to process, using the standard Mac shortcuts for selecting several files. Click to select one, Shift-click to select the whole range of files between the first and second clicks, and Command-click to select or deselect individual files. Once you've selected all the files, use Tools > Photoshop > Batch to choose any Photoshop Actions that have already been created. The dialog from here is identical to the one you see in Photoshop, and that's because Bridge is calling Photoshop to run the process. The only difference is that, as you'd expect, 'Bridge' is selected as the source of the files.

You can also use Bridge to rename a batch of files, without having to set up a Photoshop Action first. If you choose Tools > Batch Rename, you're presented with a comprehensive dialog that enables you to build sets of names to your precise specification. You can choose a generic name for all the files, followed (if you wish) by the date and time of renaming in a variety of

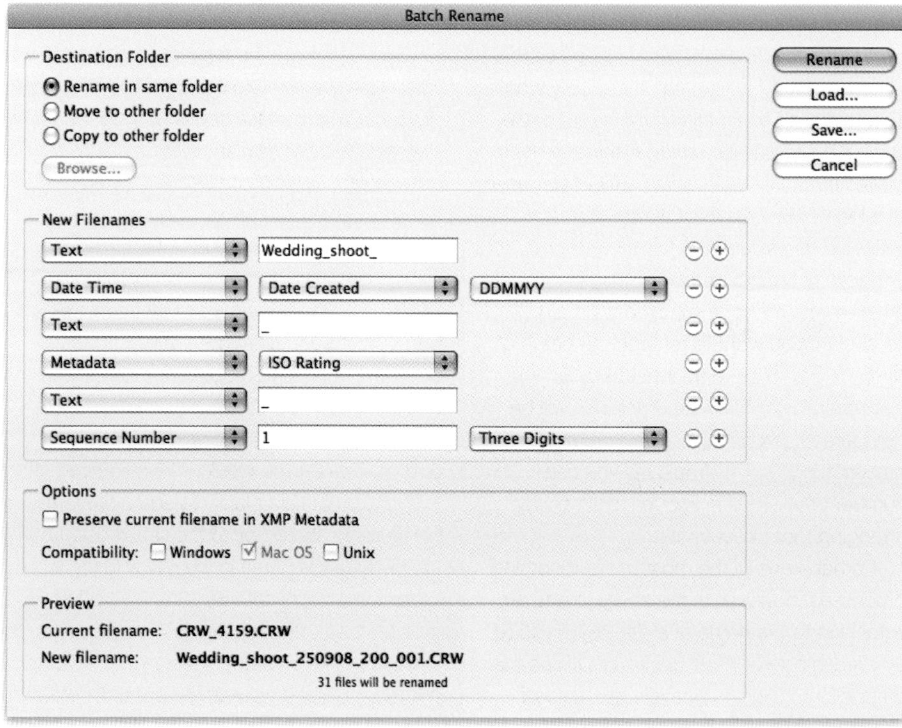

► **The renaming process in Adobe Bridge is comprehensive. Here, we're giving all our files the text 'Wedding_shoot_', followed by the creation date. This is followed by an underscore, then the ISO rating, another underscore, and finally a three digit number starting with 1. The result is that the original file (in this case, CRW_4159.CRW) now becomes 'Wedding_shoot_250908_200_001.CRW', which gives us all the information we need at a glance.**

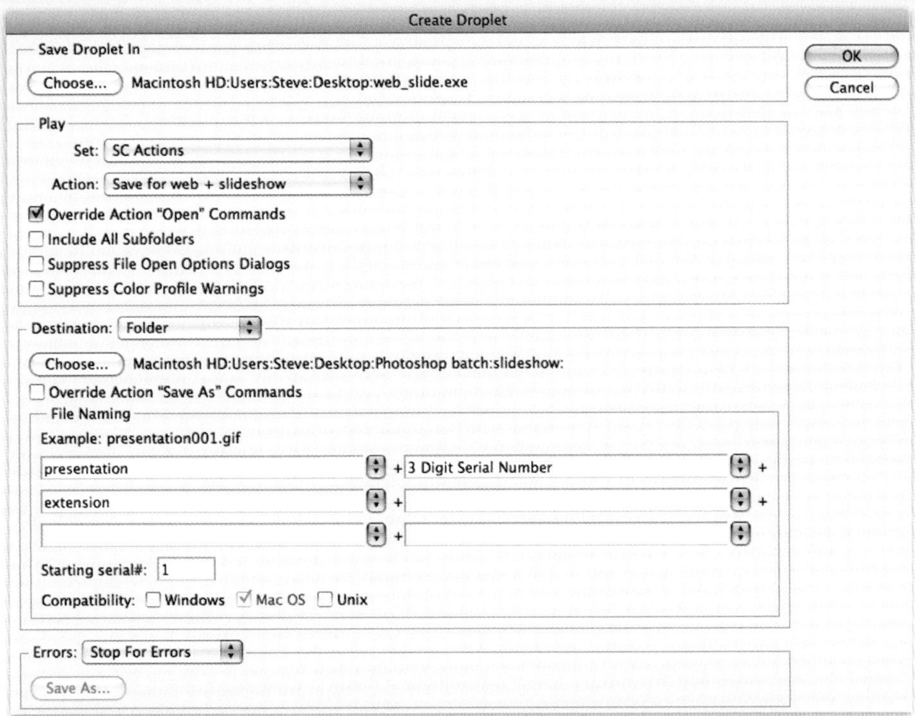

▲ **The Create Droplet dialog allows you to specify what it should be called, which Action the droplet should trigger and how the resulting files should be named.**

formats. You can add supplementary text or a sequence number – which you can specify as being between one and six digits – or a sequence letter. You can append the name of the current folder or add any metadata you like, such as the aperture value, exposure time, focal length, and so on. To the right of each option, you'll see small '+' and '-' buttons: click these to add a new name process or to remove an existing one.

Under the Options section of the renaming dialog is a checkbox marked 'Preserve current filename in XMP Metadata'. It's usually worth checking this, so a permanent record of the original name can be stored within the file. It makes it much easier to find should you need to relocate the original at a later date.

When you select files for renaming in Bridge, the order that they appear is the order in which Bridge will process them. As such, if you want to renumber a batch of files, you can drag them into the order you want them and that's the order they will be numbered. This is handy when creating presentations, for example, as you can number your slides in sequence simply by arranging them visually first.

Perhaps one of the most useful renaming processes, however, is the ability to add an extension to the name of a file. When you're emailed images – particularly from those using email clients such as Lotus Notes – you'll frequently find that the extensions have been stripped off them. This leaves Photoshop not knowing how to handle the image. In most cases, appending '.jpg' to the file name will fix the problem, after which the icon will immediately change to a full-sized image icon, and double-clicking the file will open it straight into Photoshop.

There's an alternative to selecting batch processes from either Photoshop or Bridge, and that's to instruct Photoshop to create a 'droplet' to initiate the task for you: choose File > Automate > Create Droplet to begin the process. You're presented with a similar dialog to the one you see when you run a batch process: you can choose the Action you want to play, and you can set the file names if you wish. The naming process is slightly differently presented to that used in Bridge: you're allowed up to six name fields and you choose what goes in each one by selecting from the up/down pop-up button at the right of each field.

If you don't want to use all six fields – and it's unlikely you would – then you can just leave that field blank. To add a custom name to be shared by all the saved files, you simply type the name in the first field (or wherever you want it). Be sure to add the extension field though, to make sure the resulting files can easily be opened. If the files are to be passed to users on either Windows or Unix platforms, check the boxes for compatibility. This won't change the files themselves, but will ensure the names are appropriately formatted.

Right at the top of the dialog is the 'Save Droplet In' field, which includes a single button named Choose. This is a critical step, as it enables you to set the name and location of the resulting droplet. Although this isn't an automatic option within the dialog, it's essential to add the extension '.exe' to the name of the droplet. This allows it to be used by Windows users.

Once the droplet has been created, it behaves – as its name implies – by drag and drop. You can select either a single file or a group of files in the Finder (or in Bridge), drag them onto the droplet and the specified Action will be performed. For Actions that are used regularly, this can be a much easier solution than going through the batch menu process in Photoshop.

There's just one minor downside to droplet creation. The '.exe' extension allows Photoshop, both on Mac OS X and Windows, to see the droplet as an application – and that's what lets it work via drag and drop. The problem, however, is that if you ever Control-click or right-click a file in the Finder or in Mail, and choose Open With, you'll find all your droplets listed along with Photoshop, Preview and any other image handling applications you have. It's a minor irritation, but if you've created a lot of droplets, it can sometimes entail a lengthy scroll before you locate the application you want.

web_slide.exe

▲ **The resulting droplet has an icon that clearly shows you're supposed to drop an image onto it to trigger a Photoshop Action. Make sure that you include '.exe' at the end of the filename.**

B: Bézier curves 1

Originally designed to help in the design of new cars, Bézier curves are versatile and, once you've mastered them, very useful tools.

Bézier curves are the building blocks of graphic design. They're used in vector applications such as Adobe Illustrator for drawing shapes, in page layout applications such as InDesign and QuarkXPress for reshaping picture boxes and fine-tuning text runarounds, in 3D modelling applications for defining revolve profiles, and even in pixel editing applications such as Photoshop for creating clipping paths. Indeed, without Bézier curves, it would be impossible to create the rich and varied designs with which we're familiar.

And yet few technologies cause as much consternation among designers. Unlike most design tools, which are becoming ever more intuitive, Bézier curves are difficult to control unless you take the trouble to learn how to use them. Here, we'll look at where they come from and how they work, and show you how to manipulate them to get the best out of them.

Bézier curves describe a curve by first specifying the end points of each section, known as 'end points', 'anchor points' or sometimes 'nodes'. These are the fixed locations that mark where a curve begins or where it changes direction. The shape of the curve between any pair of points is defined by 'control handles', which mark both the direction and the strength of the curve as it leaves the anchor point. The greater the distance from the anchor point to the handle, the more pronounced the curve that follows it will be.

When drawing Bézier curves, it's important to remember that the line between the handle and the anchor point always forms a tangent to the curve at that point – that is, it's as if the handle forms the end of a stick resting on the curve, which touches it at the anchor point but doesn't cross it. (There are special cases where the curve can change direction at an anchor point so that the handle does indeed cross it, but it forms a tangent on either side.)

In general, the handles of a curve should extend roughly one third to one half of the way to the next anchor point. This is clear when we look at a segment of a circle, which may be drawn in any graphics application. Here, the hollow blue squares are the anchor points and the red dots mark the handles [**01**]. When a circle is drawn in, say, Illustrator or XPress, it's formed of Bézier curves automatically. Selecting any of the component arcs will display the controls with which the curve has been created.

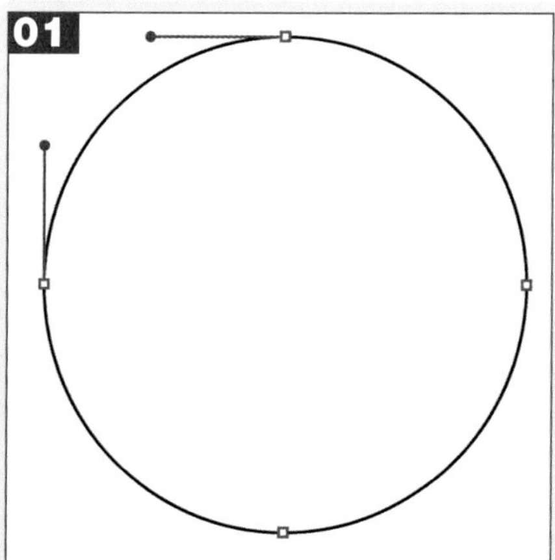

▲ **When a circle is drawn in InDesign or QuarkXPress, it's automatically made up of Bézier curves. Selecting any of the component arcs will display the various controls.**

PIERRE BÉZIER

Pierre Bézier was a designer at the Renault car company from 1933 to 1975. In 1962, he was looking for a way to describe a curve with mathematical precision that would enable it to be scaled and copied without loss of accuracy. Although he used a 3D form of the curve to specify a solid car body model, it's the 2D version that has become the mainstay of computer graphics applications.

MANIPULATING BÉZIER CURVES

There are several ways to manipulate Bézier curves. We'll examine the methods with reference to this simple diagram [**02**], which shows a curve drawn between two anchor points (hollow blue squares), which has been specified using the control handles (red dots). Note how the red lines that connect the dots to the anchor points form tangents to the curve.

One way to adjust the curve is to drag a control handle. Here, we've shortened the length of the handle, dragging it from point A to point B [**03**]. The original curve is shown in pale blue: note how the new curve is much shallower near the anchor point that has been adjusted.

As well as changing the length of a handle, you can also change its direction. Here [**04**], dragging the handle from A to B makes the curve rise rather than fall as it leaves the anchor point. The handle still forms a tangent to the curve, which is reshaped accordingly.

Bézier curves can also be adjusted by dragging the curve itself [**05**]: you can grab it anywhere and pull it to a different location. Here, moving or dragging an arbitrary point A on the curve to point B has the effect of changing the length of the control handles. Note, however, how dragging a curve in this way doesn't alter the direction of the handles, just their strength.

The final way to adjust a curve is to drag one of the anchor points. The direction and strength of the handles remains the same – the curve here has been shortened, and skewed up slightly [**06**], but it's essentially the same curve.

A FIELD GUIDE TO BÉZIER CURVES

This simple illustration [**07**] uses a variety of different anchor points. Point A shows a tangent to the curve, with equal-length handles either side. B is a tangent on either side, but the curve crosses over at the anchor point. C is a corner point, with two handles defining the curves on either side. At the corner point D, the curve to the right of it is defined by a control handle; the one above it is defined solely by the handle leaving the anchor point above it. The corner point E has no handles; the curves touching it are both defined by the control handles on the anchor points on either side.

USING BÉZIER CURVES AS CLIPPING PATHS

It's standard practice in Photoshop to define a clipping path using Bézier curves, and then to delete the area outside the path to create a cutout object on a white background. The path is maintained even when the image is saved as a flat Jpeg file, so it's easy to load the path and retrieve the cutout later.

The trouble is that when the object is cut out and placed onto a dark background, the anti-aliasing process means that a certain amount of the white background will creep in, creating a white fringe.

The solution is to draw the path just inside the object's boundary. To achieve this, turn the path into a selection, and then expand that selection by one pixel before inversing the selection and deleting the background: this makes a one-pixel fringe outside the pen path area.

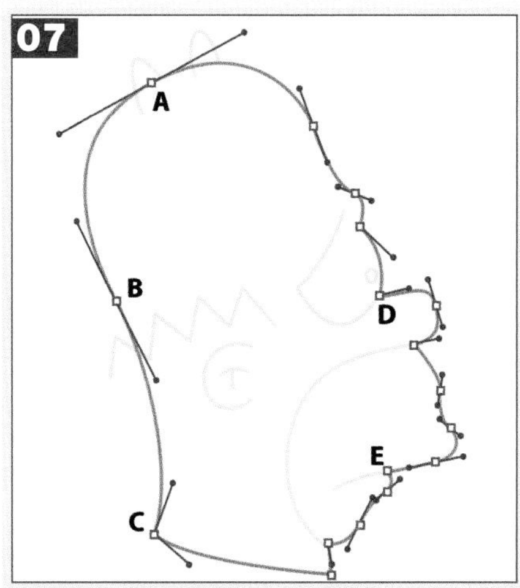

▲ This simple illustration uses a range of different anchor points..

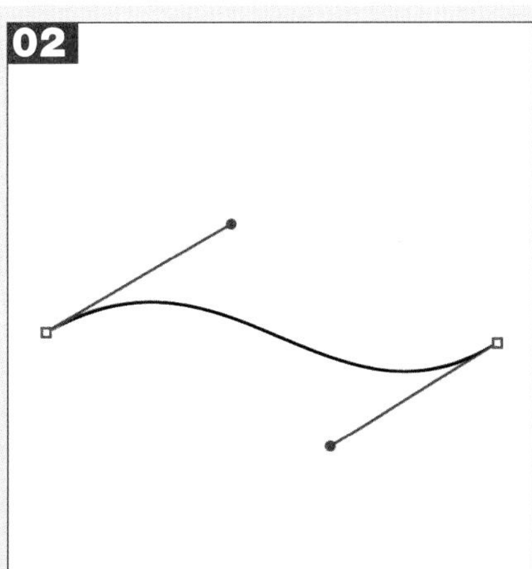

▲ The curve between the two anchor points is specified using the control handles (red dots).

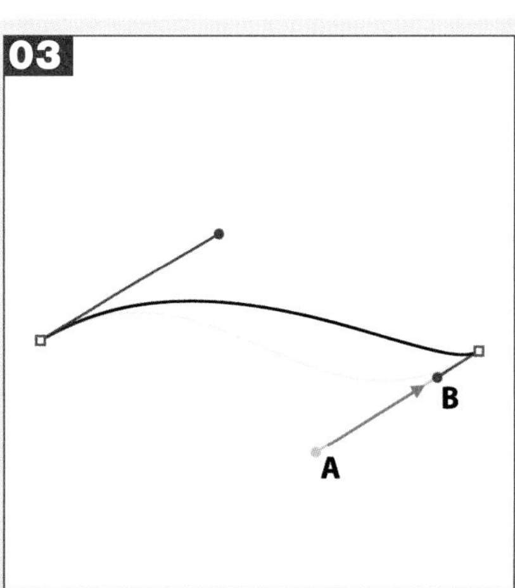

▲ You can adjust the curve by dragging the control handle (the original curve is shown in pale blue).

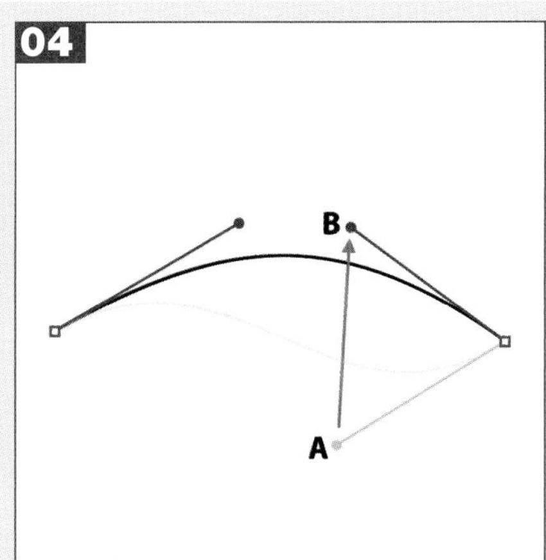

▲ Dragging the handle from A to B makes this curve rise rather than fall as it leaves the anchor point.

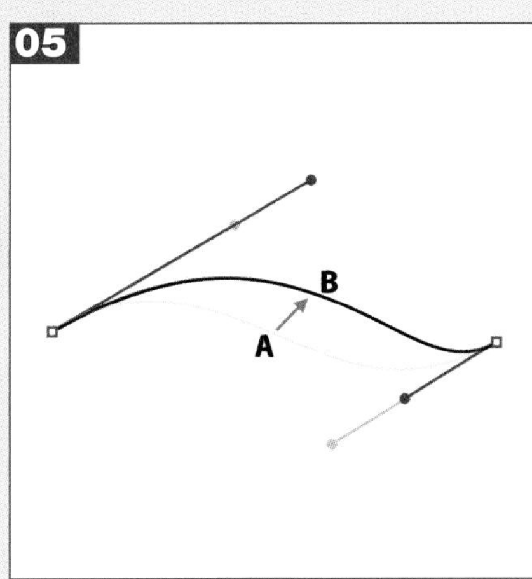

▲ You can adjust Bézier curves by dragging the curve itself, which alters the strength of the handles.

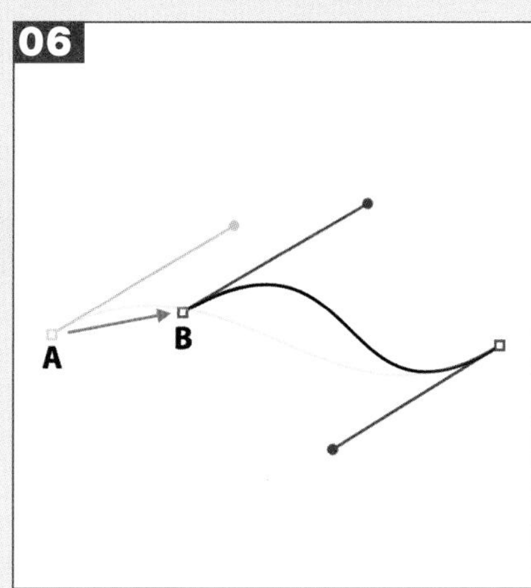

▲ You can also change the shape of the curve by dragging the anchor points.

B: Bézier curves 2

Illustrator's Pencil tool can be used instead of the Pen tool to create smooth, editable paths and curves. Here, we explain how.

The Pen tool is the main drawing tool in Illustrator, producing smooth, editable Bézier curves. However, the Pen tool is notoriously difficult to master, combining a steep learning curve with an often counter-intuitive operation. For those who really have trouble getting to grips with this one, the Pencil tool is a handy alternative.

The Pencil tool is used much like the pencil after which it's named: pick it up and sketch with it. As you draw, a dotted blue line will trace the movement of the tool, as if you were drawing with a very scratchy, dried-up ballpoint. The real magic happens when you release the mouse button: the dotted line is instantly replaced by a smooth, editable path, just as if it had been drawn with the Pen tool.

Once the path has been created, it's possible to use any of the standard path editing techniques to move the anchor points, redirect the Bézier handles and adjust the curves. You can reshape any curve simply by drawing over it again with the Pencil tool. As long as the path is active, drawing a new line that both begins and ends near the curve will reshape the curve between those two points.

An active path is one that displays its anchor points along its length – a selected path, in other words. If the path has become inactive, clicking on it with the Move tool will reselect it – or use the shortcut of holding down the Command key to access the Move tool temporarily.

If you draw a new path with the Pencil tool starting at the endpoint of an existing, active path, you can continue to draw the path from where you left off. This is a huge help when drawing long or complex paths that would be unwieldy to create in a single drawing action.

If you retrace the path by starting on an active path and finishing at a point away from the path, then the redrawn version will terminate where you stop drawing, ignoring the whole section of path that you created initially that led from your redraw point to the terminus. This can happen accidentally if you don't start and finish close enough to the original path. And while it can be disconcerting to see half your creation suddenly vanish, it's easy enough to Undo and then redraw the path correctly.

The process that turns the initial blue dotted line into a path will always smooth the path, producing an evened-out version of your initial sketch. The tool will smooth out minor wiggles in your sketch, but will retain

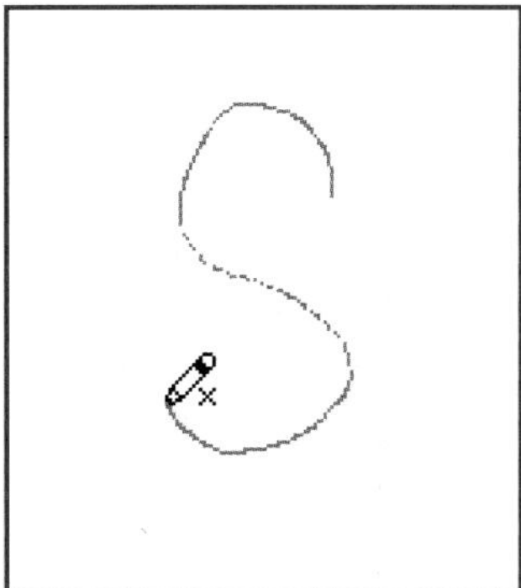

▲ When you draw with the Pencil tool, you see a blue dotted line that traces your movements.

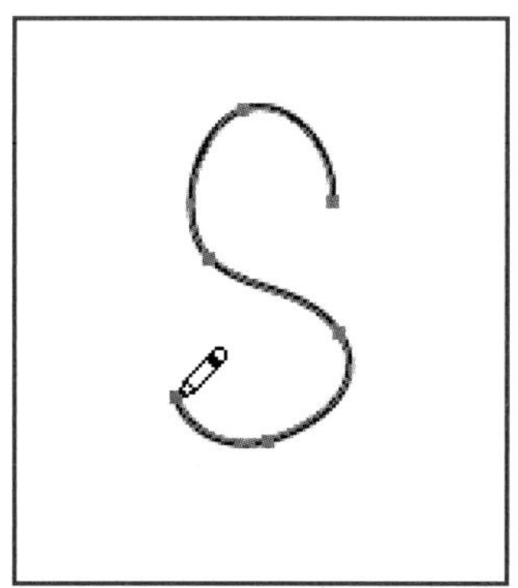

▲ Releasing the mouse button produces a smooth curve as a new path, replacing the dotted blue line.

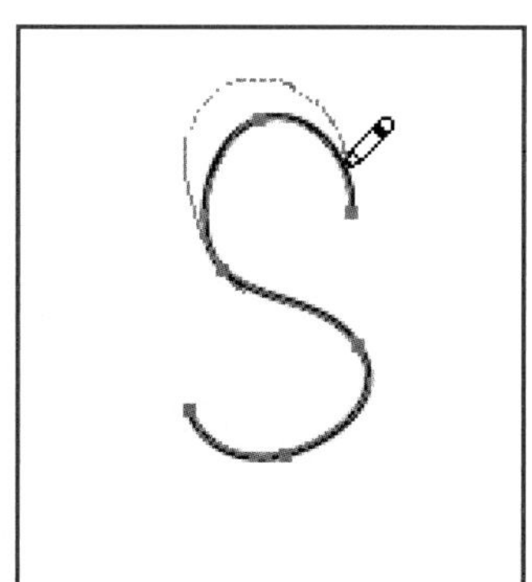

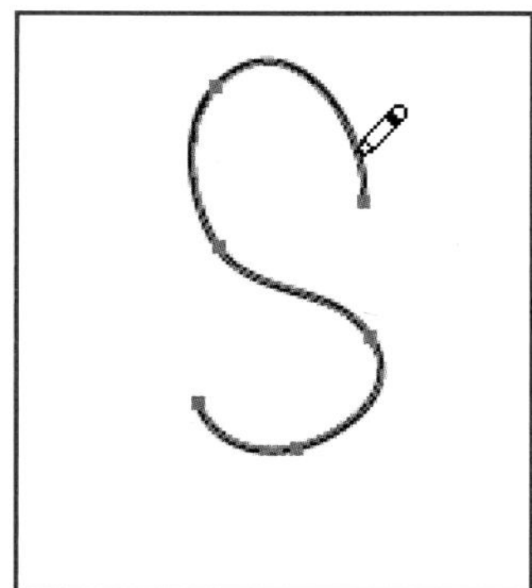

▲ If you draw over an existing path, the path is reshaped between the start and end points when you release the mouse button.

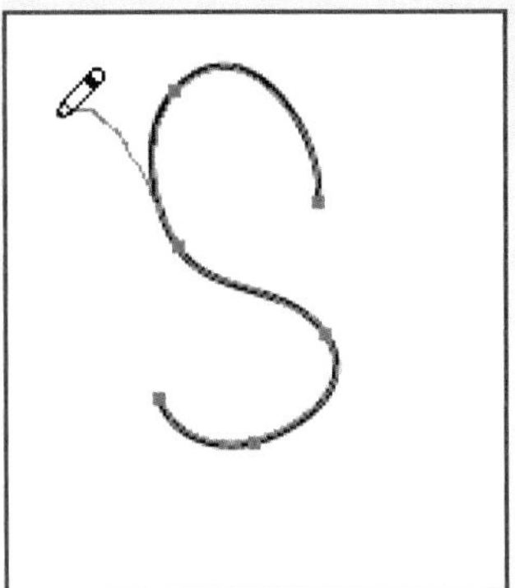
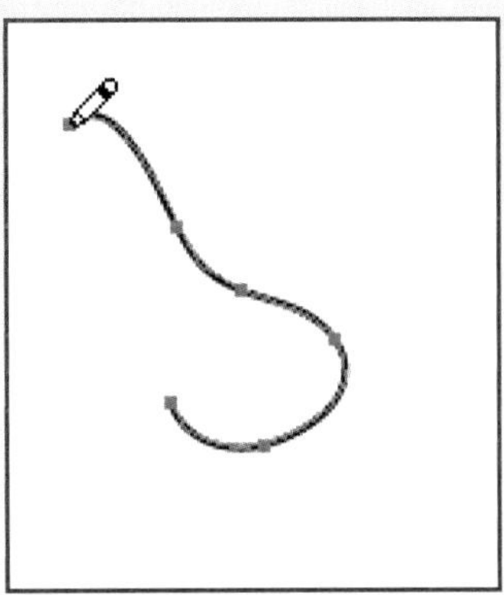

▲ If you retrace a path that starts on your initial path and ends away from it, the path will be redrawn between the start and end points, removing the original path from the start point onwards.

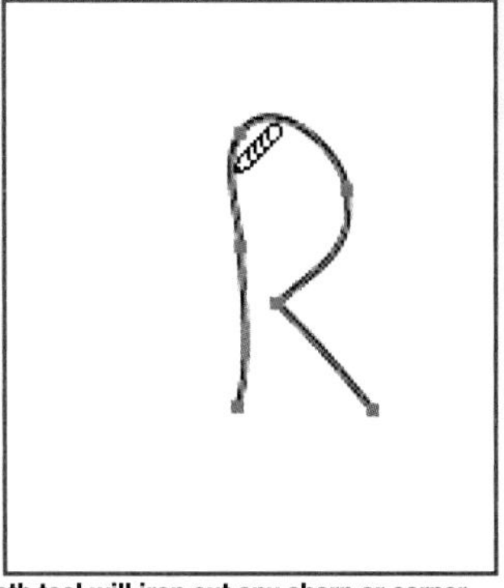

▲ Tracing over a Pencil tool path with the Smooth tool will iron out any sharp or corner points, producing a smooth curve.

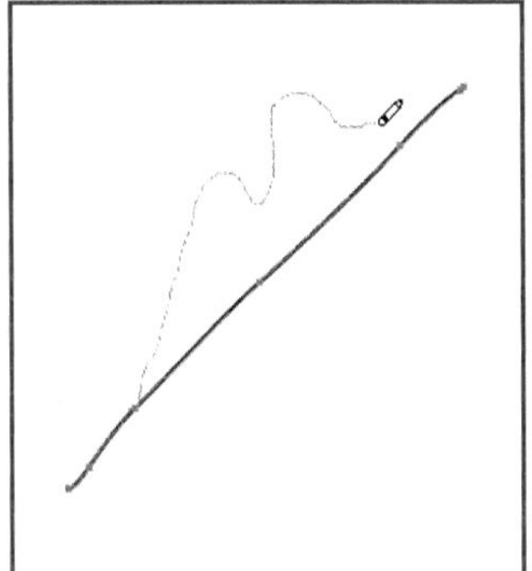
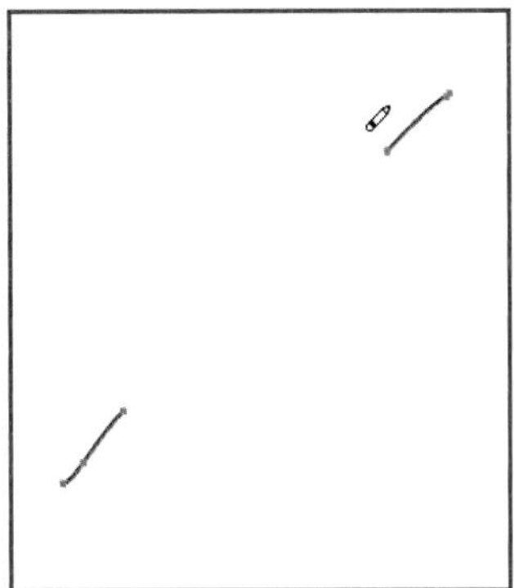

▲ The Path Eraser deletes the path from where you begin to trace to the point on the path nearest where you stop, irrespective of the line you trace in between.

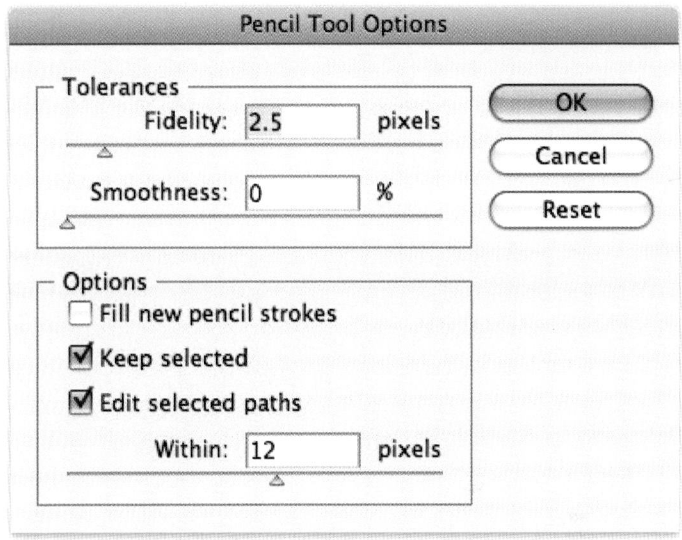

▲ Double-clicking on the Pencil tool in the Toolbar pops up its Options dialog, where you can set the behaviour of the tool.

any hard corners it thinks are deliberate. If you use a second sketch to add to an existing path, the join between the two will almost always result in a hard corner point, rather than a smooth curve point.

Fortunately, it's easy to correct hard corners. You can simply draw over them with the Pencil, in which case the new path will smooth out any unwanted bumps in the original. Alternatively, you can use the tool's variant, the Smooth tool. This is nested beneath the Pencil tool in the Toolbar. As its name implies, the Smooth tool is used to smooth away unwanted bumps in a Pencil-drawn path. It works in a similar way to the Pencil itself, as you simply drag it over a section of the curve to smooth it. Unlike the Pencil tool, though, the Smooth tool won't redraw the shape exactly where you drag, but will only iron out bumps and wrinkles.

The other variant of the Pencil tool is the Path Eraser tool, which is nested beneath it in the Toolbar. When you trace with this tool, you'll see the familiar dotted blue line, but when you release the mouse button the path you trace over will be erased between your start and end points. It's curious behaviour, as it doesn't matter where you draw with the Path Eraser tool, as the path is always erased between the first point on the path where you clicked and the point on the path closest to the point at which you stop drawing. What happens in between is immaterial.

Your accuracy when drawing with the Pencil tool depends on many factors. If you're using a Wacom tablet, you might expect a high degree of fidelity when drawing a curve; less so when drawing with a mouse, and much less when drawing with your finger on the trackpad of a laptop. So you need a way to adjust the Pencil's behaviour depending on your skill and hardware limitations. Double-clicking the Pencil tool's icon in the Toolbar brings up the tool's Options dialog, which lets you alter the settings that control the tool's behaviour. At the top are the settings for Fidelity and Smoothness. The Fidelity determines the minimum distance you can drag before another anchor point can be added. The higher the value, the less the path will resemble your initial drawing, but the smoother it will be. The default figure is 2.5 pixels. The Smoothness setting controls how much the path is smoothed out after it's drawn. Raise this figure for a looser, more stylised result.

There are three options. Fill New Pencil Strokes determines whether a new path is filled with the current Fill colour. Normally, you'd want this box unchecked, as it can be disconcerting to see your Pencil sketch suddenly filled with colour. The Keep Selected option tells Illustrator whether drawn paths remain selected, so they can be easily edited, or are deselected, enabling the easy drawing of a new path. The final checkbox, Edit Selected Paths, determines whether the Pencil tool can be used to reshape an existing path. If the box is checked, there's then a slider to set how close you have to draw to the initial path in order for it to be activated and reshaped.

The Pencil tool can be used to reshape any path, even one drawn with the Pen or Autotrace tools. Even proficient users of Bézier curves will often use it to reshape paths quickly and easily, and it's the ideal drawing tool for the novice Illustrator user. ⊗

C: Colour balance

Get the colour balance wrong and you can drain all of the life and realism out of your work. Get it right and you'll produce stunning results.

There are many ways to change the colour of a layer or a selection in Photoshop – so many, in fact, that the choice often seems bewildering. But then there are many reasons why you might want to change an item's colour. Adjusting a head to match a new body will require different colour-correction techniques compared to turning a green car into a red one or making a black-and-white drawing look like a blueprint. Each circumstance needs a different method, as we'll see here.

The simplest of all colour corrections is the Color Balance dialog box (Command-B), which offers three sliders for adjusting the red, green and blue components. It's a somewhat crude approach but is most useful for adding a touch of colour to grey artwork. If you're painting a gold ball, for example, it's a lot easier to begin with a grey-filled circle and use the Dodge and Burn tools to add highlights and shadows to it. Working in grey scale, we don't need to worry about how these tools will affect the colour. Then, when the ball is shaded, it's easy to turn the colour of the ball to gold by adding plenty of red and yellow, using Color Balance.

We get more control over colour changes with the Hue/Saturation dialog box Command-U). Here, dragging the Hue slider will cycle all the colours in the selection or layer through the entire spectrum. It's very different to the Color Balance approach of adjusting each channel individually; this is a global modification that produces far more pronounced results. This method is useful when we've selected an item of clothing, for instance, and want to change its colour so it stands out better in a composition. Dragging the Hue slider will enable us to see the element in every colour there is, making the choice much easier.

But this method of changing colour can easily produce hues that are garish, over-bright and unnatural. When using this dialog box it's frequently necessary to use the Saturation slider as well: dragging it to the left will lower the intensity of the colour, generally producing more realistic tones.

For more precise control over each colour channel, the Levels dialog box (Command-L) provides sliders that set the brightest, darkest and midtone points for each colour. This is most useful for changing the overall colour tint of an image when subtlety is required: Levels is the preferred method of colour correction for photographers. When you first open the dialog box you'll see the RGB composite histogram, which displays the spread of tonal range for the whole image. This is where we can apply a quick fix to rectify poorly balanced images: dragging the end sliders to match the ends of the histogram will generally produce a better-contrasted, higher-quality image.

▼ Beginning with a grey disk we can shade it to resemble a ball – then turn the ball to gold using the Color Balance dialog box.

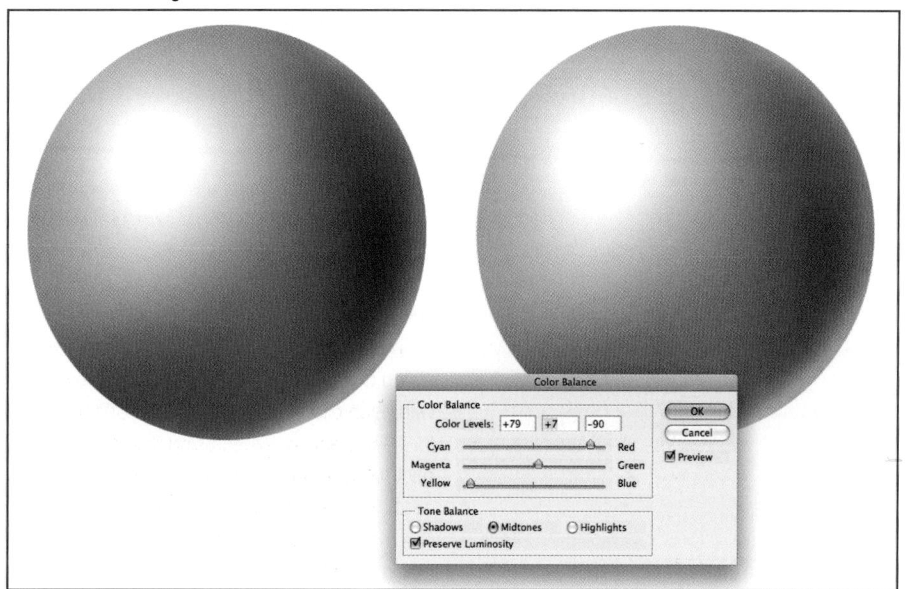

◄ Using the Hue/Saturation dialog box we can make radical changes to an item's colour – such as this girl's red shirt. Note how we frequently need to lower the saturation to retain a natural appearance.

For adjusting each colour, though, we need to look at the small pop-up menu that, by default, reads RGB – the Red, Green and Blue composite view. We can change this so we can concentrate on each of the Red, Green and Blue channels individually, and by dragging the sliders for each channel we can control the overall hue of the image with great accuracy.

Best of all we can apply changes to each channel without committing ourselves: it's always possible to go back to a channel that we've already worked on and tweak the settings there. Uncheck the Preview box in this dialog to see how the image looked before the adjustments – a useful way to see the progress that you've made.

The Curves dialog (Command-M) offers a similar functionality to Levels but without the histogram function. Instead we get the ability to add additional control points between the brightest and darkest points rather than just a single midpoint as Levels offered. As with Levels, Curves offers per-channel adjustment; but the ability to drag the curve up and down, producing smooth colour changes, makes it very useful for such delicate tasks as matching skin tones.

It's often necessary to 'think backwards' when using Curves: if a face needs more red in it, for instance, then lowering the amount of green and blue instead can often produce more realistic results than simply adding red, which may tend to oversaturate the image. Adding extra points to each colour Curve gives us more precise control but be aware that any significant movement in a single curve will produce outlandish, garish colour changes. It's great for special effects but needs to be used with caution.

One of the most intriguing colour adjustment methods in Photoshop is Replace Color (found under Image > Adjustments). With this tool we first select a colour range by clicking on it in the image: the selected area will show up in the preview window in the dialog. We can add to our selection by holding Shift and clicking on unselected areas within the image, and remove unwanted areas by holding down Alt and clicking on them. Interestingly, we can change a colour range to any hue, without having to make any complex selections first: dragging the Hue and Saturation sliders will affect just the range of colours we've selected. This tool is fantastic for changing a unique colour within a complex environment – for example we could change the yellow of a tiger behind bars to red or green, without having to select the yellow manually.

The Fuzziness slider in the Replace Color dialog box sets the range of the colours chosen with each click. Start with a value of about 40 for best practice. When using this dialog it's best to work on a copy of the target layer: it's all too easy to accidentally change the colour of a background element and not notice until it's too late.

▲ The Replace Color dialog box allows us to change a range of colours without making complex selections. Here, the red in the horseguards' tunics has uniformly been changed to green in an instant.

C: Colour spaces

The right colour space is essential to optimising your images for their intended output medium, pick the wrong one and the results are unpredictable.

Few concepts confuse designers as much as colour spaces. It's not just a question of choosing between RGB and CMYK: there are different flavours of RGB, for one thing, and then there's that rather baffling Lab colour that crops up in Photoshop occasionally. What on earth are they all for?

The problem arises from the fact that computer screens and printed items display colour in opposite ways. Computers work by starting with a black screen onto which they add combinations of red, green and blue pixels – just as if you were shining coloured torches onto a sheet of paper in a dark room.

The more light that is added, the brighter the image gets. Adding maximum amounts of all three colours produces pure white. Where the primary screen colours – red, green and blue – overlap, you get cyan, magenta and yellow [**01**].

Ink on paper, however, works the other way round. Starting with white paper, the more ink that's added, the darker the result. Print overlapping circles of cyan, magenta and yellow, and where they overlap you'll find red, green and blue. Mix them all together, and you get black [**02**]. Well, not quite – in actual fact, you end up with a rather muddy brown, which is why commercial printing always includes black as a fourth colour to fill in deep shadows and give depth to images.

Given that additive colours (RGB) and subtractive colours (CMYK) work in the opposite way, it's surprising that monitors can display CMYK with any accuracy at all. When working in Illustrator or FreeHand, always work in CMYK (unless you're designing exclusively for web work), or you'll encounter problems when your illustrations are imported into XPress or InDesign. When using Photoshop, you should generally work in RGB: the files are three-quarters the size, because there are only three channels, and many of the filters don't work in CMYK. But be sure to turn on CMYK Preview frequently (use command-Y) to check that the colours are compatible: images that look bright and well contrasted in RGB will often turn out dull and flat in CMYK.

This is because RGB is a much wider colour space (known as the 'gamut') than CMYK. This simply means RGB can display far more colours than CMYK [**03**]. One problem is that Photoshop uses a special colour space known as sRGB, which is a space designed to make business graphics look better under the Windows operating system. As the gamut chart shows, it's a very limiting space: for preference, designers will always change their working colour space to Adobe RGB, which gives a far more faithful representation of the way an image will look when it's printed.

The widest colour space of all is used in Raw, which is the format captured by high-end digital cameras. It's good for tweaking photographs, but is wasteful of resources, as

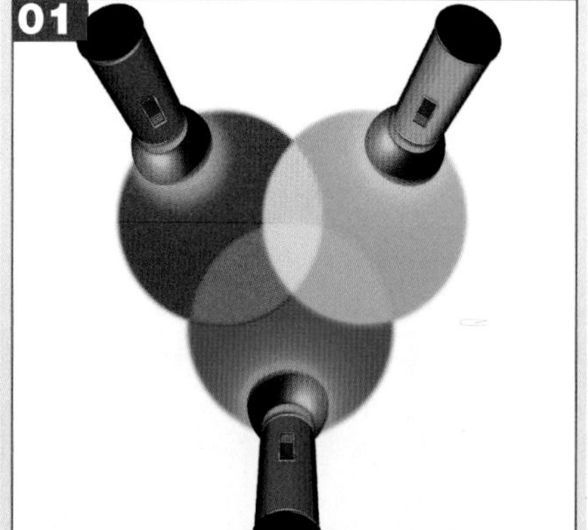

▲ **Monitors use additive colours, throwing light onto a dark screen. The more lights added, the brighter the result. Note that red and blue make magenta, red and green make yellow, and blue and green make cyan.**

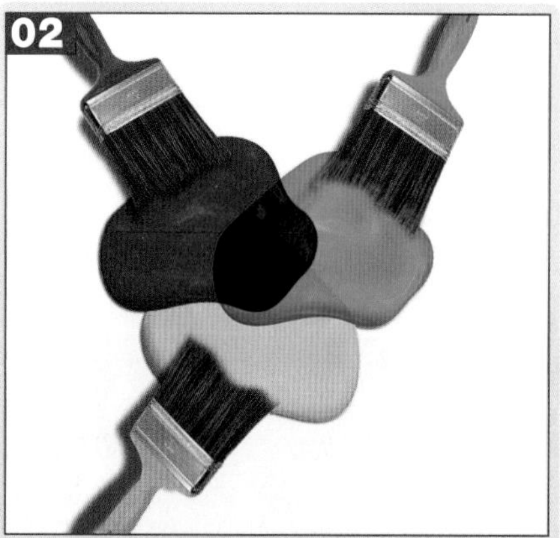

▲ **Printing inks start with white paper: the more ink is added, the darker it gets. Cyan and magenta make blue, yellow and magenta make red, and blue and yellow make green.**

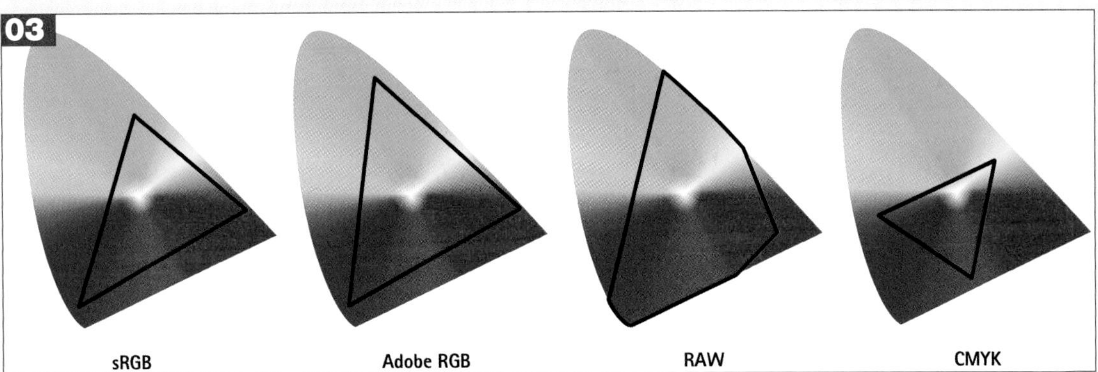

◄ **The overall shape shows the range of colours visible to the human eye. The range of colours in each of the different colour spaces lies within the black lines. sRGB (far left) is the narrow colour space used by default in Photoshop. Most designers change sRGB to Adobe RGB (second from left), which has a much wider colour gamut. The Raw space (second from right) is wider still. Note how the CMYK (far right) colour space is very narrow in comparison.**

the files tend to be very large. The Raw space is used mainly by professional photographers, rather than by designers.

To guarantee that the colour shown on your monitor matches printed output as closely as possible, ensure that it's well calibrated. We recommend the Gretag Macbeth Huey as an ideal first step: available for about £50, this is a tiny device the size of a pen, which you place on your monitor at regular intervals in order to calibrate it for the most realistic colour. In addition, the Huey sits on your desk in front of your monitor, constantly monitoring the ambient light in the room and adjusting your monitor to ensure consistent image display.

One colour space found only in Photoshop is Lab (sometimes written L*a*b), which is the space in which Photoshop performs all its calculations before converting them to either RGB or CMYK. The closest to the range of colours visible with the human eye, Lab is by far the widest colour space, but its also one of the most confusing. The word describes the three components that define the space. The brightness of an image comes from the luminosity (L) component, which is effectively a greyscale version of the image. The colour is made up of two separate channels labelled 'a' and 'b'. The 'a' channel contains colours varying between blue and yellow, while the 'b' channel contains colours between green and red. It's a tricky space to imagine, as there's no real-world model on which to base a solid understanding of the space.

There are only a few instances in which you'd convert an image to Lab colour. The most common is when trying to eradicate colour noise of the kind frequently produced by digital cameras shooting in low light. The limits of the CCD chip in the camera means that odd pixels of the wrong colour are created, which can be tricky to get rid of by conventional means. When converting an image to Lab space, however, it's possible to blur each of the 'a' and 'b' channels independently in order to smudge the stray pixels out of existence. Because all the sharpness and definition comes from the 'L' channel, you can blur the other two by a large amount without losing any detail in the original image.

Some applications, such as Painter, use a colour space known as HSV in their colour pickers. The three components here are Hue (the type of colour – that is, red, blue, green and so on); Saturation (the strength of the colour); and Value (the brightness of the colour). This space is also sometimes known as HSB, which stands for Hue, Saturation, Brightness.

If all this seems rather baffling, don't despair. For routine work, the colours remain the same in RGB, HSV and Lab spaces; it's just a different way of measuring and manipulating them. It's rather like a tin of beans, which could cost 44p, or 86 cents: the beans are just the same, it's only the measuring system that changes.

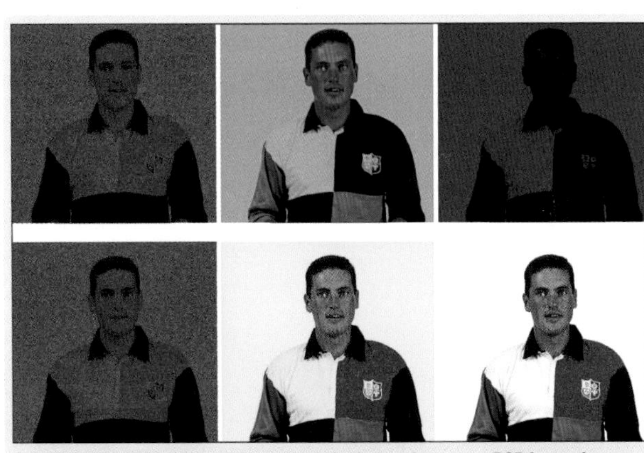

▲ **Each of the red, green and blue channels that makes up an RGB image is shown at the top, with the result of combining them below. Notice how the green and black on the shirt are identical on the red channel; the red and white are virtually indistinguishable here as well, because there's no red at all on either of the blue or yellow channels.**

▲ **Each of the cyan, magenta, yellow and black plates that make up printed colours are shown at the top, with the result of combining them below. It would be possible, in theory, to stop after adding just cyan, magenta and yellow, but the image is rather washed out. It takes the black plate to add definition and shadow.**

D: Distortion

There are many occasions when distortion can be desirable – particularly when you're trying to fit an image into an irregular space.

Whatever illustration program you're working in, the ability to distort elements to fit within a space is essential. Sometimes it's simply a matter of scaling and rotating an object or layer; frequently, more radical distortions are required in order to make the picture element look as though it belongs in the space.

Photoshop provides various ways to distort images. Free Transform is most commonly used to scale and rotate, but if you hold down the command key as you drag a corner handle, you'll distort just that handle; hold down Command and Shift to distort a single handle along a vertical or horizontal axis. More useful is perspective distortion: Command-Alt-Shift-drag a corner handle to mirror the distortion with the opposite handle on the same side as the one you're dragging. This technique is very useful for making a flat texture appear to be receding in three dimensions, giving the ability to create instant walls and floors.

If you distort a flat texture using this perspective process, there's a danger that the foreground will look artificial, as the pixels are enlarged to fill the space. A simple workaround is to move the texture layer half off the canvas to one side, and then to duplicate it, drag it to the other side of the canvas and merge the two layers together. This produces a texture that's twice as wide as the canvas, so when it's distorted you'll retain the integrity of the pixels.

The Image Warp feature introduced in Photoshop CS2 is a powerful tool that combines envelope distortion (which uses Bézier curves to control the shape of the outside of the bounding 'envelope') with mesh distortion (which allows the interior grid points to be moved independently). Image Warp enables complex distortions, such as wrapping a label around a curved surface. It can be tricky to manipulate so many anchor points, especially as dragging a corner will also affect the interior grid points, so it's frequently best to begin with one of the built-in preset distortions to get the basic shape, then modify that by changing the method to Custom using the pop-up menu, which will allow the individual points to be edited freely.

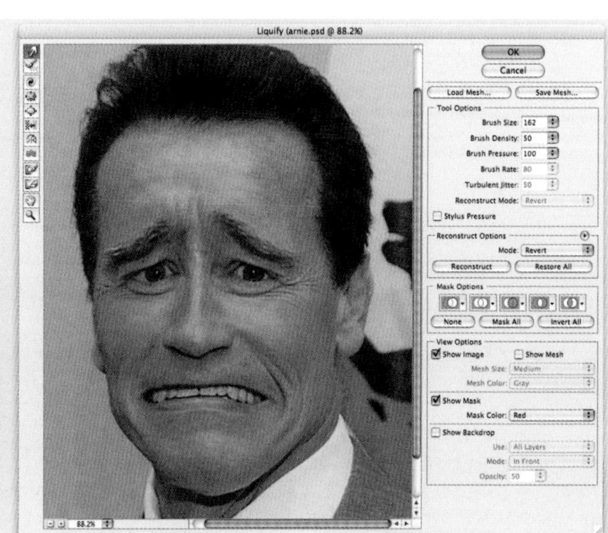

► Photoshop's Liquify filter can be used for caricatures, or to change expressions: making this publicity photo of Arnold Schwarzenegger look worried was a simple job for this tool.

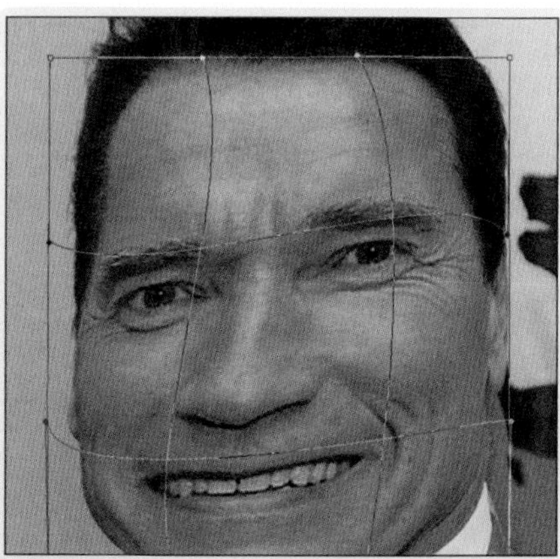

▲ By manipulating only the inner points on a Mesh Warp, we can be sure that the outside of the selection will still line up with the unselected area. Good to know there won't be a join in Arnie's hair line.

◄ Illustrator's Warp distortion allows shapes to be distorted using a variety of preset shapes, with a small number of controls to affect their strength.

◄ The Mesh distortion gives us as many anchor points as we want both around the periphery and within an object, providing many control vertices – but at the expense of ease of use.

◄ ▲ The flag (top left) is selected at the same time as the outline (bottom), ensuring that the outline is the topmost object in the selection. Choosing envelope distortion with the top object produces the perfect fit that slots the flat flag neatly into its distorted shape (above).

Like any pixel-based editing system, Image Warp is destructive: once the layer has been distorted, there's no easy way to return it to its original state, and further editing is tricky. A good solution is to convert the layer into a Smart Object first, which can still be distorted using Image Warp. The difference is that when you select it later, the previous Image Warp controls will appear, just as if you'd never committed to the operation: you can manipulate the control points further, or even remove the distortion. Best of all, Smart Objects can be created from multiple layers, which means you can distort a group of objects as one, while retaining full editing control over its content.

For more freeform distortion, Photoshop's Liquify filter provides a brush-based approach. Like a far more powerful version of the Smudge tool, Liquify allows you to push and pull great clumps of pixels exactly where you want them. It's perfect for minor adjustments, such as changing the expression on a face, slimming thighs and stomachs, and creating caricatures. It's also a powerful tool for creating whirling designs from basic photographs. This tool is best used with a graphics tablet, rather than a mouse, for more precise control.

There are three ways of distorting objects in Illustrator. The first is to use a Warp, which is a shape chosen from a menu of preset shapes. The direction and strength of each warp can be set, as can the amount of horizontal or vertical distortion, but you can't then edit the anchor points to produce a custom envelope as you can in Photoshop.

The second method is a Mesh distortion, in which you begin by choosing the number of horizontal and vertical grid points within the mesh (again, unlike in Photoshop, where these values are set). It's a powerful tool, as it allows you to customise the mesh precisely to the requirements of the object on which you're working. Each point within the mesh can be moved independently, and each is linked to those around it by Bézier-controlled curves that determine the shape of the object being distorted. The more mesh points, the more control you have, but the harder it is to manage all the vertices.

The third method is ingenious and requires no editing of anchor points or slider controls. This, the 'top object' method, automatically warps a selection to fit the shape of the uppermost selected object. It's useful in that it's easily replicable, so can be used to make a series of objects conform to a single shape. You might, for instance, draw a rippled flag outline; any flat EPS flag that's combined with this will take on the shape of that outline. If you add shading as separate objects, it's easy to apply both the distortion and the shading to a folder full of flat flags with no effort.

Both Photoshop and Illustrator also include a range of distortions that operate within the object or layer: these include a set of filters in Photoshop, such as Ripple, Spherize, Twirl and ZigZag, which move a layer's pixels around according to parameters set by one or more sliders. (The ZigZag filter, curiously, is the one to choose if you want to make ripples.)

Illustrator includes a smaller set of filters for randomising the line drawn between pairs of anchor points: these include Bloat, Roughen, Tweak and so on. These can be applied from the Filter menu, in which case the line segments will be moved, with anchor points added, in line with the filter's appearance. It's far better, though, to apply the same filters through the Effects menu: in this way, they remain live and editable – in a similar way to Photoshop's Smart Objects – and can be tweaked or even completely removed at a later point.

▲ This scene has been built entirely from a single photograph of a flat brick wall. The perspective mode of Photoshop's Free Transform creates convincing 3D effects with ease.

D: Dodge and Burn

Old-style analogue photo printing techniques have made the transition to Photoshop with these two essential tools for maintaining a well-balanced image.

The Dodge and Burn tools are among the most useful in the Photoshop toolset. And if you think the names are odd, wait till you look at the tool icons: the Dodge tool is represented by what appears to be a black lollipop on a stick, and the Burn tool by the sort of gesture that football supporters in the car behind shake at you when you're only doing 80mph in the fast lane.

The truth is that these tools are based on techniques used by traditional photographers in darkrooms. To lighten an area of an image, a photographer would wave a solid obstruction between the enlarger and the developing paper – the lollipop on the stick. This would prevent so much light from the projected negative reaching that area, and so would result in a brighter image. Similarly, if the photographer wanted a bright portion in the centre with darkened edges, he or she would make their hand into an O shape, allowing light through the middle but withholding it around the perimeter of the image.

In Photoshop the tools perform the same function: Dodge brightens the images, Burn darkens them. They both use standard brush sizes, using the square bracket keys to make the brush larger and smaller. As with all brushes, the strength of the effect – referred to in this instance as the exposure – is set using the number keys. So we'd type 2 for 20%, 5 for 50% and so on, up to 0 for 100%. But when using these tools, perhaps more than any other, Photoshop users will benefit from a pressure-sensitive graphics tablet. If you don't have access to one, then keep the tools to a low value and build up shadows and highlights with successive brush strokes.

The tools are commonly used to add highlight and shadows to images, and the result is far more effective than painting in white or black over the top. Because we tend to switch between the tools frequently when adjusting shading, there's a handy modifier key: with either tool selected, hold the Alt key to temporarily access the other one.

Dodge and Burn each have three modes of operation: they can lighten or darken shadows, mid-tones or highlights. The choice of mode makes a big difference to the result, as the face examples here show. Depending on the image,

▲ **We'll use this simple grey disk as the basis for drawing a ball using the Dodge and Burn tools. Grey, with no colour component, makes the perfect base.**

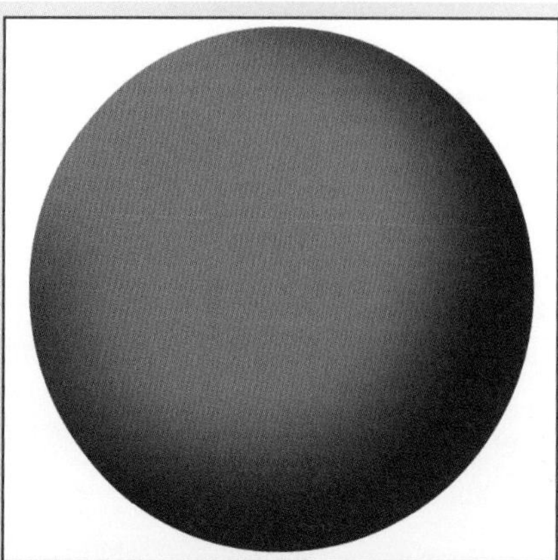

▲ **The Burn tool, set to Highlights, is ideal for adding basic shading around the right and bottom. Use a large brush size for a smoother effect.**

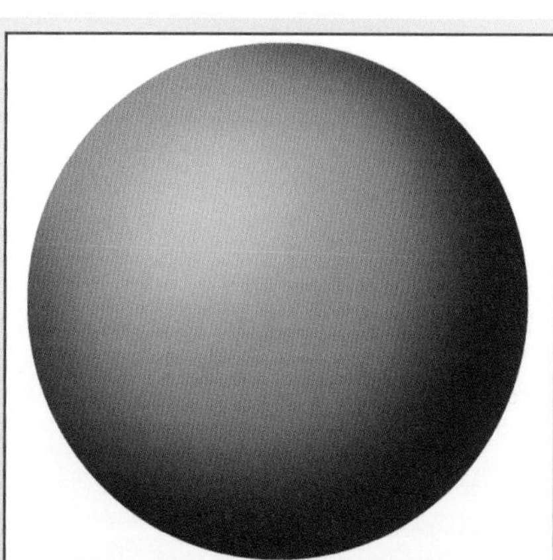

▲ **Holding the Alt key to switch to the Dodge tool, add the beginnings of a highlight on the left to begin to create a 3D effect.**

► This bland portrait has been lit mainly from the front. We'll use the Dodge and Burn tools to add more dramatic shading.

◄ When set to Highlights, the Dodge tool produces good results in brightening the face, adding saturation to the highlights. But notice how the Burn tool creates a greying effect as it darkens the skin.

► Set to Midtones, the Burn tool now produces rich, strong shadows. The Dodge tool, however, makes the brightened side look washed out and unnaturally bright, removing detail.

◄ Set to Shadows, the Burn tool creates an over-saturated look, while the Dodge tool brightens as if painting with white. In practice, we rarely use either tool in this mode.

▲ Best results are obtained from using a mixture of the modes. Here, we've used Midtones with the Burn tool to darken the left side of the face, and Highlights with the Dodge tool to brighten the right side.

the different modes can produce oversaturated results or, by contrast, turn a colourful image into one that's greyish and lacking in contrast.

Often, we find ourselves switching between Highlights and Midtones in order to work on different areas of an images. You can choose each mode from the Options bar at the top, but it's easier to use the shortcut. Hold Ctrl and Shift as you click, and a pop-up menu will appear beneath the cursor from which you can choose the mode you want.

The Dodge and Burn tools are useful for drawing realistic-looking 3D objects from scratch, simply by adding light and dark. We have used a ball as a simple example here, showing how successive strokes of the tools can turn a flat disk into a more convincing 3D form. When creating artwork in this way, it's generally best to start off with a mid-tone grey base, painting in the highlights and shadows using these tools. When the basic shading is complete, colour can be added using the Hue/Saturation, Color Balance, Curves or Levels dialog boxes. In theory, if we know we're going to be creating a red ball, we could begin with a red base; but the Dodge and Burn tools affect the saturation of the colour as well as the lightness, and it's all too easy to produce unexpected and unwanted colour shifts by accident. It's far better to work on a base that's already fully desaturated, then put the colour in at the end.

We'll frequently use the Burn tool to add shading to the edges of a scene, particularly if there's an artificial light source within it. This helps to focus the reader's attention on the salient elements, drawing them in from the edges. But if the scene is a montage, it would be an uneconomical use of our time to shade each layer in turn. A good solution is to make a new layer, and add shading to that. But if we simply make a new empty layer we'll be unable to use the Dodge and Burn tools: it's impossible to darken non-existent pixels. The answer is to create a new layer set to Hard Light mode, and filled with 50% grey – there's an option to do this automatically when making the layer. In Hard Light mode, grey is invisible; but when we darken or lighten it, we can see the effect clearly.

Adding shading to a separate Hard Light layer allows us to paint in complex shading, such as adding folds, creases and wrinkles to fabric. And unlike painting directly on to the target layer, when we work on a Hard Light layer we can always undo our mistakes by painting over the affected area with 50% grey.

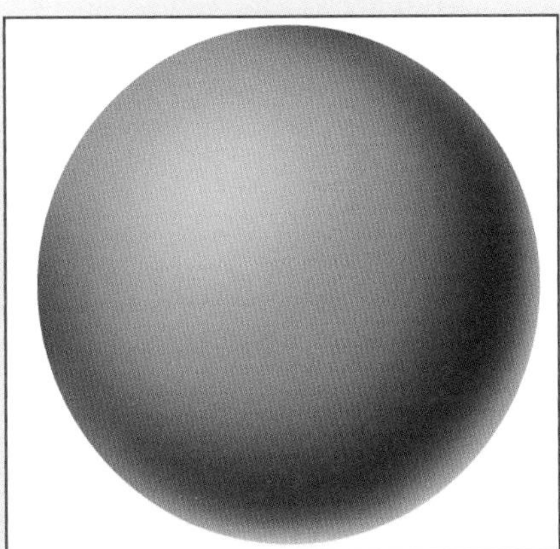

▲ Still using the Dodge tool, reduce the size of the brush and paint a bright rim beneath the darkened side, giving the impression of backlighting.

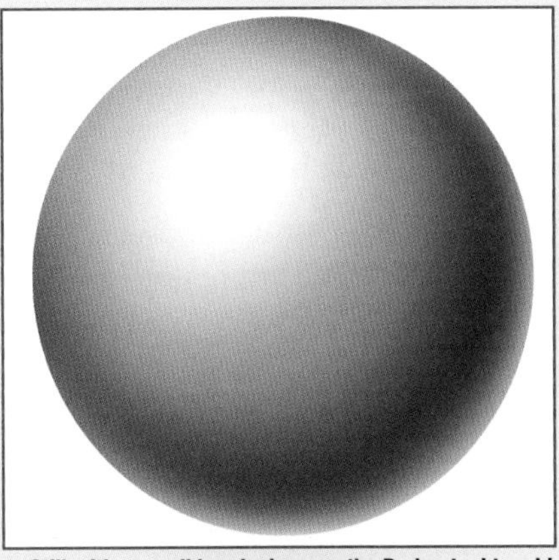

▲ Still with a small brush size, use the Dodge tool to add a bright hotspot in the middle of the lightened area.

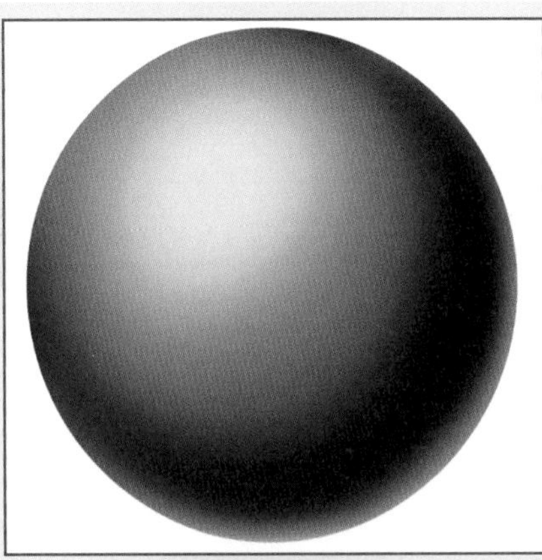

▲ Finally, use the Hue/Saturation dialog box to add some colour to the ball and finish the effect.

E: Embossing

Learn to master the embossing tools and you can easily give your images the 3D touch, pressing elements into or out of the page.

Photoshop's Layer Styles have the ability to add a range of effects to both regular layers and live type. They can be used to quickly add glows, neon and other effects to text, with the minimum amount of effort. Because these are live effects, rather than pixel-based filters, they're fully editable and can be tweaked, adjusted – or even turned off altogether – at any time.

One of the most useful effects is embossing, found in the Bevel and Emboss section of the Layer Styles dialog. Far from being a one-trick pony, this is a highly customisable, endlessly adjustable effect that can be used to simulate a range of real-world styles. Embossing adds a 3D quality to a layer, which can then be tweaked to look like stone, metal, plastic and so on. Yet it's this extended capability that can make the dialog box seem impenetrable at first: with so many options, it can be hard to know where to begin.

The default mode is Inner Bevel, which places the bevel – the raised edge of an embossed object – within the object's outline. Variations include Outer Bevel, which makes the bevel operation affect the underling layers, and the innovative Pillow Emboss, in which both the object itself and the layers beneath have the bevel effect applied to them.

A choice of three technique options is available. The default is Smooth, which is the one you'll want to use most often: it produces a clean, extruded effect. The other two are Chisel Hard and Chisel Soft, which are useful when making text look as if it's been carved into a stone tablet, but otherwise are of little interest.

The Up/Down direction buttons determine where the lighting on an embossed object appears to come from. When lit from above, an object will look raised; when lit from below, it will appear to be engraved into a surface. This is simply a result of our expectation that light will come from above.

Three sliders affect the magnitude of an emboss effect: Size (the width of the bevel within the object), Depth (the apparent height of the bevel) and Soften (the degree to which

▲ With a basic default bevel, an object or lettering has some apparent depth.

▲ By increasing the size and depth, we can make the embossing effect stronger.

▲ Raising the Soften value produces a smoother bevel.

▲ Adding a Gloss Contour gives us a metallic sheen to the emboss.

▲ As you can see here, adding a basic Contour produces a more complex inner bevel form.

▲ The Texture pane allows us to fill the object with an embossed pattern.

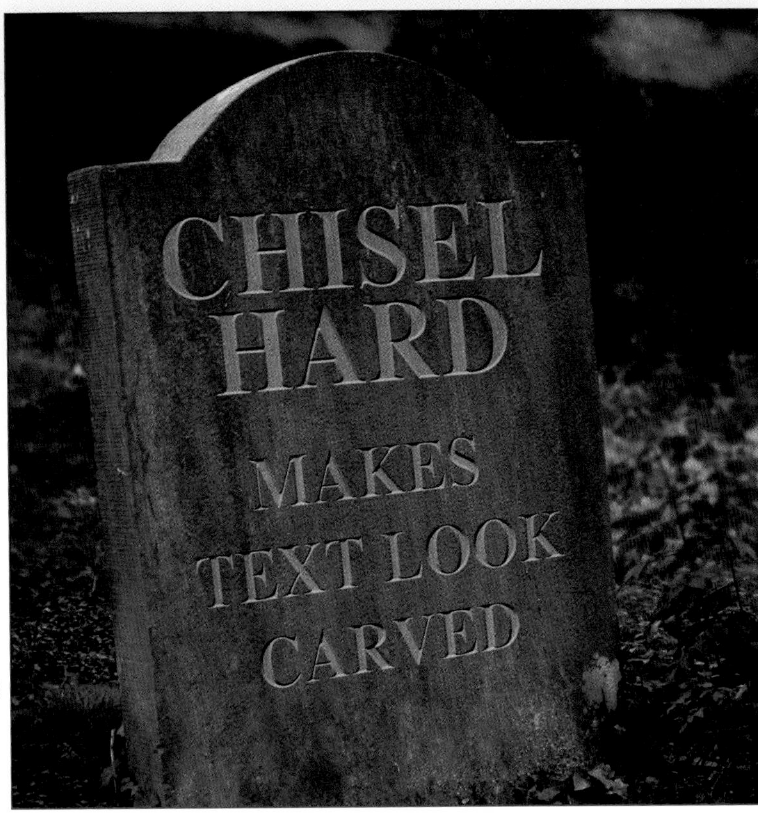

► A combination of Chisel Hard and a Down lighting direction makes this text look carved into the stone.

◄ We have the same effects applied to the letters E and B in this group.

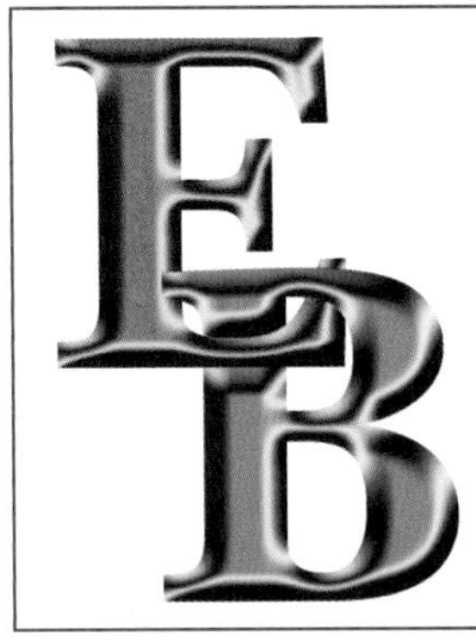

◄ To make them interact, we can mask the letter B so it goes behind the E, but the bevel effect treats the mask as a cut in the object.

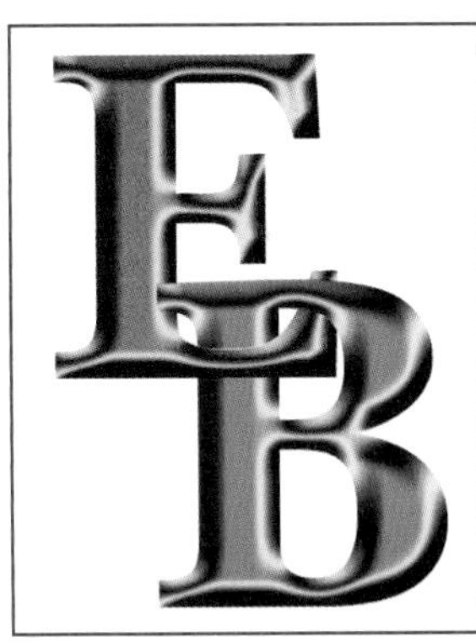

◄ Checking Layer Mask Hides Effects in the Advanced Blending pane produces the hiding effect we want.

bevelled edges are smoothed). The adjustment of each of these depends largely on the size of the type or object you're working with, and the crispness of the result you want to achieve.

The Shading section, at the bottom of the main Bevel and Emboss pane, is where we can set the lighting direction and altitude, the highlight and shadow colours, and the way in which these colours are applied. Here, too, we can set the Gloss Contour, which allows us to add the impression of shininess to a surface. Choose from one of the pop-up preset curves, or draw your own profile by editing one of the existing curves. The results are shown in real time, so we can see how our changes affect the artwork. Using Gloss Contour, we can impart a metallic flavour to artwork with ease.

Two further panes appear to be nested beneath the main Bevel and Emboss section: Contour and Texture. The contour isn't the same as Gloss Contour, but it does set the shape of the bevelled edge within the object itself. By default, this will use a straight, diagonal line – or in other words, no contour at all. By changing this to a pre-set curve, or drawing our own, we can then create the appearance of raised ridges within the object, as if the curve has been extruded following the outline of the layer.

It's a useful technique for creating, for example, picture frames: complex forms can be drawn on the curve associated with the contour, and the frame will then appear lit and rendered in effective 3D. Note the Anti-Alias button within this section: this smooths the edges, producing finer, more pleasing results – and the Range slider, which determines what proportion of an object's surface is affected by the contour effect.

The final Emboss pane is Texture, which overlays a textured pattern onto the artwork. Rather than simply imprinting it on top, the texture is itself embossed and lit using the lighting direction and strength set for the rest of the object. Any saved pattern can be used as an embossing texture, and any artwork can easily be turned into a pattern for this purpose.

Although applying an embossed texture can easily swamp artwork and hide the bevel applied beneath it, dragging the Depth slider will reduce the intensity of the effect: often, a small amount of texture can add a subtle distortion to an object's surface, making it look chipped and dented. We can also use the Scale and Invert controls to adjust the texture's appearance further.

Once the desired effect has been achieved, it can be saved as a preset so that it can be retrieved with a single click. Embossing operations can also be copied from one layer to another by holding the Alt key and dragging them within the Layers palette.

▲ The Pillow Emboss style produces an embossing both inside and outside the lettering, which is perfect for this embossed leather-effect look.

Because Layer Effects apply to entire layers as live effects, we can paint on a layer to which embossing has been applied and, as we paint, our brush strokes will appear embossed. If the original layer consists of text, we can change the font and wording and the effects will still be applied to that, too.

E: Extracting images

Have an image that is too complex to cut out the traditional way – such as hair or fur? Turn to the Extract filter and let Photoshop do the hard work for you.

Most Photoshop montage work involves extracting images from their backgrounds. If an object has been specially photographed against a white background, this is an easy task, the most basic selection tool, the Magic Wand, will be capable of selecting most of the white in the image with a single click. If there are non-contiguous areas of white – with a closed loop inside the object, for instance – then it's necessary to hold down the shift key as you click in those regions to add them to the overall selection.

Once you've selected all the white areas, inverse the selection using Command-Shift-I so that just the object itself is selected. You can then copy it to a new layer using Command-J.

The luxury of having a white background to work with isn't always available, however. If an object has been photographed outside a studio setting, the chances are that the background will be more complex and so more difficult to select. Multiple Magic Wand selections may still be able to isolate the image, but if any of the background colours are similar to those within the object, it will be a tricky task.

One solution is to select the object manually using the Lasso tool. You need a steady hand in order to follow the outline accurately. It can help to hold down the alt key as you drag, which will both enable you to trace straight lines between clicked points and to release the mouse button without the selection automatically closing off. If you make a small mistake, there's no need to start again: once you've made the selection, make an additional selection while holding down the shift key to add to the previous selection; hold down alt to subtract from it. Note that these keys must be pressed before beginning to trace with the tool.

Better still is the Pen tool, which is capable of drawing smooth curves as well as straight lines. Because the curves can be edited after they've been drawn, you can adjust the pen path until it fits your object perfectly. A further bonus is that any paths you draw can be saved within the file, so that next time you open it, you only need to turn the path into a selection with a single click in order to retrieve the cutout. The downside, however, is that the Pen tool is notoriously difficult to master.

Photoshop artists frequently have a hard time extracting people from backgrounds – not

▲ **MAKE NEW LAYER** Even though it's been photographed against a plain white background, this is a tricky cutout – so much fiddly hair and flowers. We begin by creating a new layer, filled with a contrasting colour, behind this one, so we can see what we're doing.

▲ **ISOLATE THE HAIR** With the Background Eraser tool, sample the hair colour and click on the background, dragging around the head until all the white is removed. Notice how the fine strands of hair are retained.

▲ **SAMPLE THE SHIRT** Because the shirt is a similar colour to the background, we need to sample it to make sure it isn't accidentally erased. We can now continue to remove the remainder of the background by painting it out with the tool.

▲ **TRICKY BACKGROUND** In the Extract filter, we begin with a brushstroke that covers the edge of Donald Rumsfeld.

▲ **FILL THE PORTION TO BE KEPT** We click once with the Fill tool within the outlined area to mark that as the part of the image we wish to keep.

▲ **PREVIEW** We can see the result by pressing the Preview button. There's a lot of unwanted transparency and scratchiness around the figure.

because of their bodies, but because of their hair. Even when photographed in a studio, just how do you remove the background from a full, flowing head of hair? The reality is that this is actually a simple task using Photoshop's Background Eraser tool. This uses a tolerance setting similar to that found in the Magic Wand; the higher the tolerance, the more similar colours will be removed. For hair, choose a tolerance of between 30 and 60, depending on the complexity of the background.

You can set the tool to protect the foreground colour, so check this box and hold down the alt key to sample a typical colour for the hair. Set the tool to Sample Once (otherwise you'll run the risk of sampling the hair colour by accident), and then click and begin to drag outside the image. As you move the tool over the hair, all the background colour within the hair will be removed, leaving just the hair visible. Because it's difficult to see the result clearly over the standard checkerboard background that indicates transparency, it's easier if you make a new layer behind the hair layer, filled with a contrasting colour – that way, you can see exactly what's been erased. This technique also works with fiddly objects such as trees, fences and so on.

▲ **DEFRINGE** We needed a low tolerance setting because the shirt is so close to the background, but this has left a fringe around the edge of the plants (left). To remove this, choose Layer > Matting > Defringe, with a value of just one pixel (right).

The Magic Eraser tool is similar to the Background Eraser, except that you click once in the image with this tool and all pixels of a similar colour are instantly deleted. Use this one with caution, as you may well find that highlights such as the whites of eyes and teeth are inadvertently deleted in this way. One useful remedy for this situation is to set a point in the History palette before beginning any erasing. That way, you'll always be able to use the History Brush to revert missing pieces of the image later.

The two Eraser variants work well when the background is of a reasonably uniform colour, such as extracting trees from a blue or cloudy sky. When there's more complexity in both the foreground and background, use the Extract filter instead. It's a little fiddly to use, but does a good job of removing difficult backgrounds.

Choose the Extract filter from the Filter menu, or press Command-Alt-E to enter its interface window. Begin by using the Edge Highlighter tool to trace around the outline of the object you want to extract, making sure the brush covers the edge of the object. Then use the Fill tool to select the interior of the object. Press the Preview button to see the result.

Unless you're lucky, the result you get won't be perfect the first time. Dragging the Edge Touchup tool over the edges will smooth them, repairing a lot of the image. Finally, use the Cleanup tool to paint any extraneous elements in or out.

▲ **EDGE TOUCHUP** The Edge Touchup tool, dragged around the perimeter of the head and shoulders, does a good job of smoothing the outline, but there are still places where some background has crept in, and there's a bite taken out of Rumsfeld's ear.

▲ **CLEANUP TOOL** The Cleanup tool, set to maximum pressure, provides a simple way to paint out the unwanted areas. By holding down the alt key as we paint, we can also restore that missing chunk of ear.

F: Fill and Stroke

Fill and Stroke define the interior and exterior of graphical elements in your work, and as such define its very essence: what you can and can't see.

The terms Fill and Stroke, as complementary properties of graphic objects, first appeared with the release of MacDraw, the first object-oriented graphics application on the Mac. Fill refers to the colour, pattern or texture contained within an object's boundaries; Stroke is the colour, pattern and thickness of the boundary itself.

With only two colours available – black and white – MacDraw could offer only non-scalable patterns, rather than shades of grey, for its fills. The strokes offered were a variety of thickness of black or white line, with the later option of a dotted or dashed line.

Adobe Illustrator, the natural successor to MacDraw, uses the same basic system – except that the Fill options now include colours, gradients, photographic images and scalable textures. The technology underpinning strokes has evolved further, with a wider range of options available. Illustrator users can now apply multiple strokes to a single object, permitting the creation of complex, multi-layered outlines that can be adjusted and edited at any time. This makes it easier to draw objects such as roads on maps, which can have two strokes applied – a thick stroke marking the path of the road itself and thinner strokes outside this to create the road's borders. In reality, the apparently 'thin' black border strokes would be a thicker black stroke created behind that making the path of the road.

Illustrator users have for some time had the ability to define patterns as stroke components, and additional variations on these patterns can also be defined to create corners and end points, so finishing off patterned strokes neatly. These patterns will, by default, bend to follow the direction of the path to which they're applied; so a linear pattern, such as a Roman key design, will look equally valid tracing the perimeter of a rectangle (in which case corner variants will be brought into play as required) as it will defining the edge of an ellipse.

Special stroke styles, known as brushes, can help to bring a hand-drawn quality to Illustrator

▲ **The figure on the left has a black stroke but no fill, which is why we can see right through it. The second has a basic fill and stroke: note how the fill hides stroke elements behind each object. The third uses Ink Brushes with coloured fills to create a hand-drawn effect; the fourth uses watercolour brushes with a gradient fill for a more painted look.**

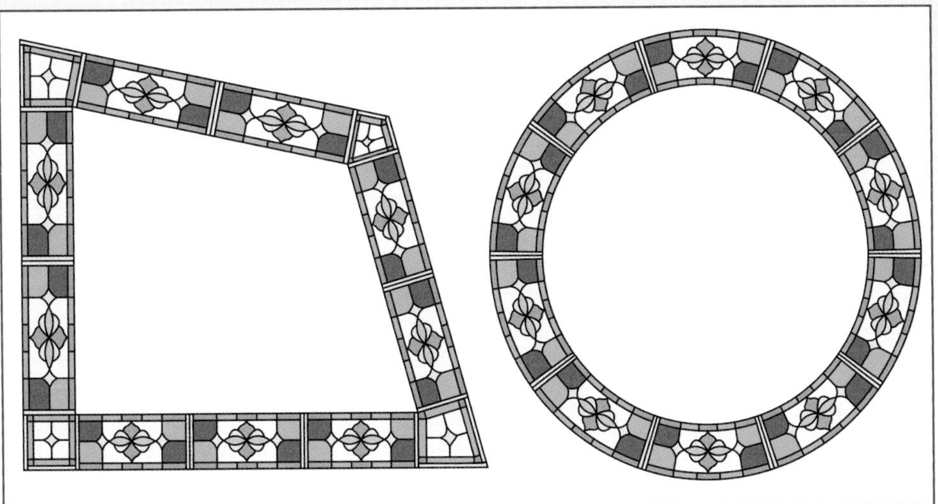

◄ **The pattern stroke technology in Illustrator is powerful enough to place and distort corners on an irregular polygon automatically, while still being able to make the stroke look perfectly acceptable when bent around a curved perimeter.**

artwork, simulating watercolour or pen-and-ink styles, among others. These strokes are no more than elongated designs in the form of a stroke that might be made by a leaky ink pen, or multiple random shapes in varying shades of grey; but when set to follow a drawn path, even the simplest Illustrator images can be made to look like naturalistic artwork with the addition of colour and a textured background. Each of these brush paths can then be modified individually, thickening and reversing their direction where appropriate to better imitate the hand-drawn effect.

Because a brush stroke in Illustrator will automatically be extended to wrap along the entire length of a path, the result can look overly drawn-out and artificial. The solution is to split the path into multiple segments with the Scissors tool, which will make the stroke reapply to each segment, producing a more appealing and convincing effect.

Photoshop also makes use of fill and stroke, in two different ways. Any selection can be filled with colour – use Alt-Delete to fill with the foreground colour, and Command-Delete to fill with the background colour. Pressing Shift-Delete will bring up the Fill dialog box, from which we can choose to fill at a lower than 100% opacity, or to fill with a predefined pattern or texture.

We can also apply a stroke to any object or selection using the Stroke section of the Edit menu, a technique that will draw a stroke of user-defined size around the perimeter of the object. It's less well known that Photoshop also permits us to apply a stroke to any Pen path: with the path active (and visible), choose a foreground colour and a brush size, and press Enter; the path will be stroked with that brush. It's a simple and foolproof way to draw smooth, curved lines. If the resulting stroke is too thick, undo the operation, reduce the brush size and try again. By combining a hard-edged brush stroke with a smaller, soft-edged brush in a lighter colour, we can create the instant impression of pipes and wires.

The second way of applying fill and stroke in Photoshop is by using the Layer Styles palette. These differ from the previous methods in that they're applied to layers as a whole, and remain 'live' – so if the layer is later edited, the styles will apply to the new layer elements automatically. Using Layer Styles we can apply colour, gradient and even texture fills, made from repeating tiled patterns; we can set the angle and type of the gradient, and the size and opacity of the textures.

The Stroke section of Photoshop's Layer Styles section can add strokes as flat colours, as patterns or as gradients. But we can also create multiple strokes, by adjusting the parameters for such Style components as Outer Glow and Drop Shadow. These both create soft-edged haloes around the artwork, the difference being that Drop Shadows can be offset while Outer Glows can't; but they're both effectively additional strokes that can be applied and controlled independently. Layer Styles can be edited at any point, as the effects are live rather than comprising editable pixels. In this regard they behave far more like Illustrator fill and stroke, with the exception that there's no easy way to make dashed stroke in Photoshop. We can simulate a dotted stroke, though, using the Pen path technique described above, stroking it with a hard-edged brush set to a wide spacing.

Both InDesign and QuarkXPress allow simple and complex strokes and fills, including gradients and patterns, to be applied to any objects within a page layout.

► **Photoshop allows us to apply patterns, gradients and bevels to filled objects – as well as creating multiple strokes using shadows and glows.**

F: Filters

The power of a graphics application is in its ability to apply filters to your image. Combine them to produce some stunning effects, as we show here.

Filters are a quick and easy way to apply special effects to images. Most are customisable, so you can adjust the strength and type of the effect to suit the image you're working on; one or two simply apply a preset effect with no user control.

Photoshop's filters fall into two broad categories: the Gallery set, which includes Artistic, Brush Strokes, Distort, Sketch, Stylize and Texture groupings; and all the rest. The Gallery filters were originally bundled as Gallery Effects, and were sold separately, but were later incorporated directly into Photoshop. Whether you choose one of these filters by navigating through the submenus, or by choosing Filter Gallery at the top of the Filters menu, you'll be presented with the same dialog.

The Filter Gallery also lets you combine multiple filters and apply them to the image in one go. The large preview pane shows the combined effect of as many filters as you choose to stack up. You can even change the order in which the filters are applied by dragging them up and down in the list. Hide the effects of individual filters by clicking on the eye icon next to the filter's name. To add a new filter, click the New Document icon.

What makes this approach so useful is that in order to achieve special effects such as watercolour, pen and ink drawing or whatever, you need to apply a range of filters one after the other. Rather than choosing a setting and hoping for the best before moving on to the next filter, the Gallery allows you how to modify each filter while seeing precisely how it will effect subsequent effects. Our example shows a sketch effect that uses three filters – Poster Edges, Diffuse Glow and Texturizer – all working in combination.

There are several things you can do after applying a filter or a set of filters using the Gallery. If you choose another layer, pressing Command-F will apply the same filter to that layer, in exactly the same way. This is useful when you want to treat a number of layers identically: the keystroke will apply the filter with no dialog box.

If you've applied a filter and want to change the settings, undo the filter's action and press Command-Alt-F. This will bring up the filter's dialog, with the settings you previously used – the difference is that you can adjust those settings before committing to them. If the previous filter comprised a multiple Filter Gallery

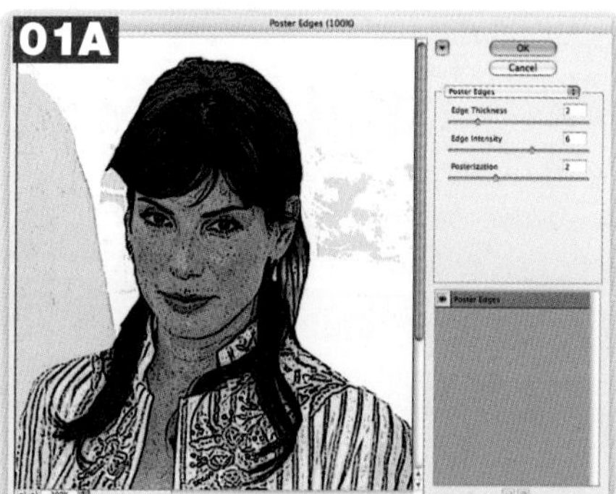

▲ **The Poster Edges filter, applied to this photograph of actress Sandra Bullock, produces a strong graphic effect. Our first step towards creating the impression of a hand-drawn image.**

▲ **Adding Diffuse Glow to the previous effect brightens the image, adding glowing highlights while hiding the background elements.**

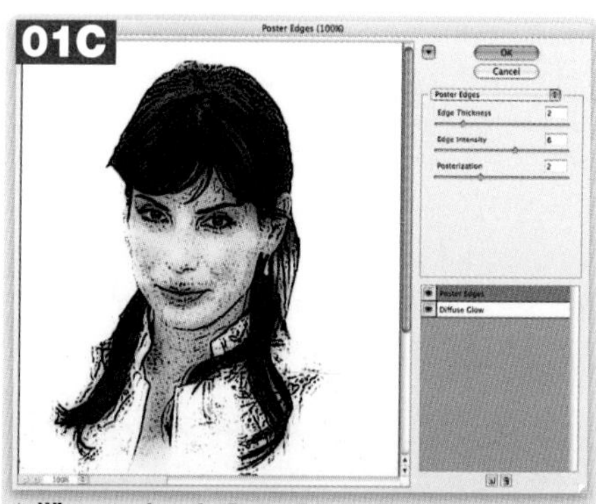

▲ **When you drag the Poster Edges effect so it applies after Diffuse Glow, we create a more ethereal feel, as the white shirt fades away into the background.**

► **When we apply a lot of Gaussian Blur to this photograph of the *Harry Potter* train, we appear to have damaged the image to the extent that it's now unrecognisable.**

stack, pressing this combination will load up the Gallery window with all the filters lined up as they were the last time you used them.

There's a third, very useful option: immediately after applying any filter, choose Undo and press Command-Shift-F to bring up the Fade dialog. This reapplies the filter exactly as before, but with a slider that enables you to fade the effect of the filter: dragging to the left will reduce the strength, allowing more of the original layer to show through. In addition, and most usefully, you can change the mode in which the filter was applied using Photoshop's standard light modes: Screen, Multiply, Hard Light and so on. Because you can see the effect of changing to each of these modes before you commit to any of them, it's easy to step through the different modes until you find one that does the job you want. The Fade command means you can greatly enhance each filter's range of operation using this range of extra settings. It's worth noting that you can invoke the Fade command after any brush stroke or adjustment, too.

While most of Photoshop's filters use the colour of the original image, most of those grouped under the Sketch menu (with the exception of Chrome and Water paper) instead produce a two-colour effect using the foreground and background colours. You can't change these colours while working in the dialog, so you have to guess them before you begin. This is another instance where the ability to repeat a filter comes in useful. If the effect isn't what you want, undo the filter step, adjust the colours and apply the same filter again. The foreground colour also effects one or two other filters, such as the leading in the Stained Glass filter.

► **Using the Fade command immediately after the filter, however, allows us to change its mode: here, Linear Dodge gives us a more magical image.**

▲ **Adding Photoshop's Texturizer filter with the Canvas setting completes the impression of a hand-drawn sketch on canvas.**

The Texturizer filter applies one of four preset textures to an image, distorting the image so it appears to have been printed on a textured surface. You can adjust the lighting direction, and the scale and the strength of the effect, but you can also load other textures to vary the effect. The Patterns folder, inside the Presets folder in your main Photoshop folder, contains a variety of useful textures, and you can also create your own: any Photoshop document can be used as a bump map within the Texturizer filter. So if you find, say, the pattern in the default Canvas texture too small and repetitive, you can substitute it with a much larger canvas texture of your own for a more convincing result.

Some of the filters make more controllable substitutes for other effects. The Threshold adjustment, for example, turns an image to pure black and white, with a slider that sets the cutoff point between the two. However, it frequently produces a very harsh effect, so it's far better to use the Stamp filter (in the Sketch menu), which offers the same light/dark balance slider, but also includes a Smoothness slider that can produce clean results with ease. You can get similar effects using the Note Paper filter, which adds both controllable texture and an embossing effect, and the Torn Edges filter, which produces a threshold image with roughened outlines.

Photoshop CS3 and CS4 include Smart Filters, which enable you to adjust the effect of any filter at a future point. In earlier versions, applying a filter to a Photoshop file is an irrevocable step: make sure you duplicate the layer first, so you can easily revert to it and adjust the filter settings as required. ⊗

F: Free-to-use pictures

When adding images to a website, be careful which ones you use – some of them need a licence. Here, we show you how to get pictures for free.

The Internet is awash with images. A simple Google search will turn up thousands of pictures that are more or less appropriate for your requirements, in just a fraction of a second. A tremendous bonus for the image-hungry designer, right?

Wrong. If you think that you can just grab images from the internet and use them in your work, you're falling into a dangerous and potentially very expensive trap. Last year a web designer told me how he'd set up his company's website using small, generic images found on Google – a container ship, a man holding a box, a man pushing a trolley, and so on. He used 10 images in all, none of them more than an inch square, and thought no more about it. Until his company received a letter from Getty Images, demanding payment of £800. Per image. Plus VAT.

Getty uses a company called PicScout, which trawls websites looking for unlicensed content. PicScout gets a percentage of the proceeds; Getty gets to levy a punitive fine. Everyone wins, except the poor sucker who has unwittingly used one of its images. In this case, the company had 21 days to pay the £8000 and remove all the offending images from their site.

The simplest solution is to buy your images from either a reputable online image library, or from a cut-price source such as iStockphoto (***istockphoto.com***) – which, ironically, is now owned by Getty. But does this mean there are no alternatives left for the truly cash-strapped designer?

Fortunately, there are several sources of genuinely free-to-use images available for both personal and commercial use. Your first port should be Wikimedia Commons (***commons.wikimedia.org***), the media wing of Wikipedia. It has more than 4.5 million images on all subjects, including celebrities and politicians, who are the hardest people to track down online (in a free-to-use capacity). Images are typically available in high resolutions, good enough for commercial publication.

Licence types vary from image to image, but any restrictions are clearly displayed alongside the image itself. In the main, all images on Wikimedia use the Creative Commons licence, which permits anyone to use the images for just about any reasonable purpose. The key word here is 'reasonable': you couldn't take an image of David Bowie, for instance, stick a copy of your latest Indie CD in his hand in Photoshop and use it to promote your music.

In the US, any images captured by a photographer in the employ of the government are by default owned by the taxpayers who ultimately pay his salary. Such images are said to be in the public domain, which means they

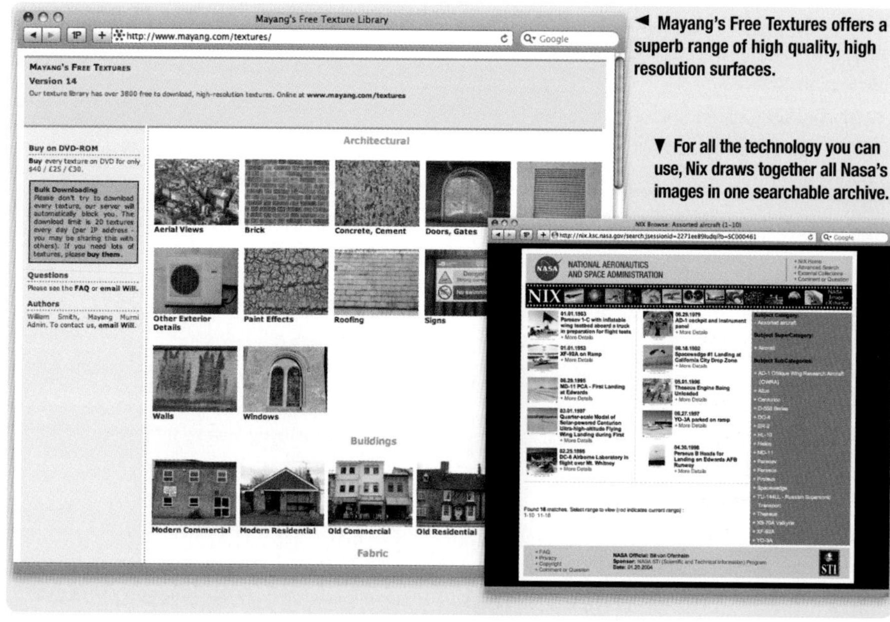

◄ **Mayang's Free Textures offers a superb range of high quality, high resolution surfaces.**

▼ **For all the technology you can use, Nix draws together all Nasa's images in one searchable archive.**

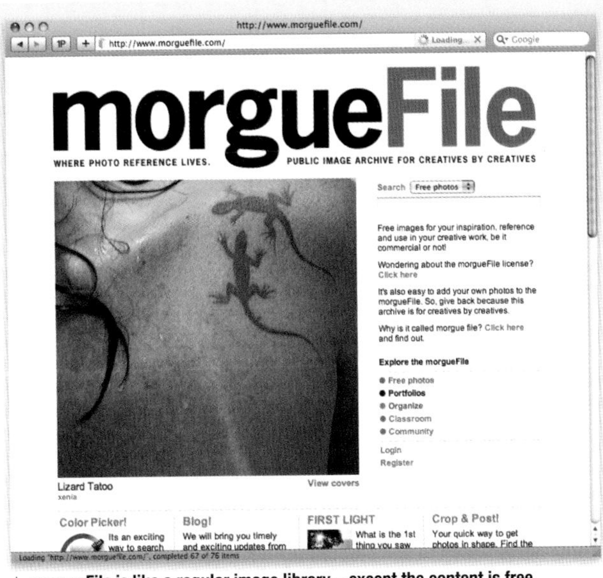

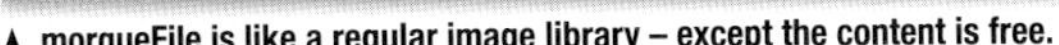

▲ **morgueFile is like a regular image library – except the content is free.**

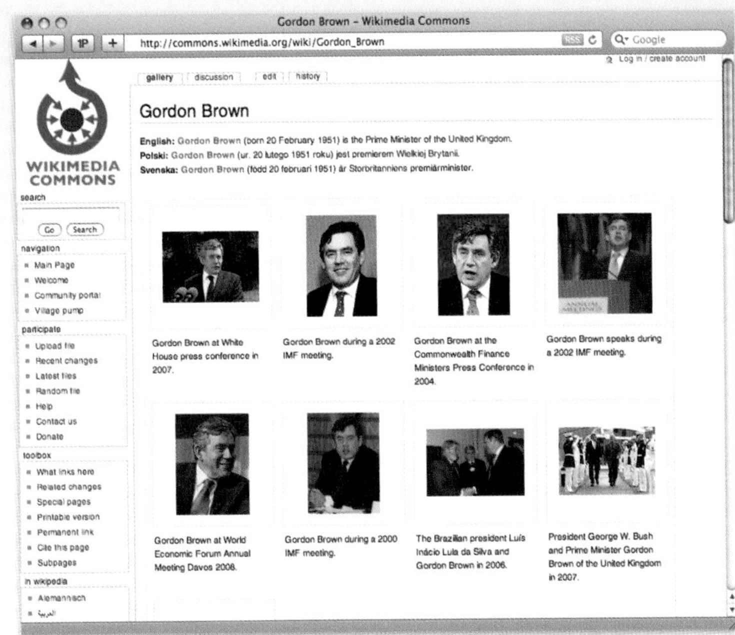

▲ **UK politicians can be a little harder to track down, so it's worth checking out Wikimedia Commons for the best free-to-use selection.**

can be used for any purpose whatsoever. Amazing, but true.

This opens the floodgates to a huge range of free images on a variety of environmental, scientific and political topics. Visit the Department of Defense (***defenselink.mil/photos***) for politicians, both American and foreign, military leaders, and all kinds of conflict-related imagery. For shots of rockets, moon landings, space scenes, planes and miscellaneous technology, you should try Nasa (***nix.nasa.gov***). If you're looking for underwater and weather images, check out the National Oceanic and Atmospheric Administration site (***photolib.noaa.gov***). These sites will often link with other government agencies, all with their own media libraries: try the California Department of Corrections and Rehabilitations, for instance, for an extraordinary collection of high resolution shots of their execution facilities (***www.cdcr.ca.gov/News/DeathRow***). For the image magpie, it's an enticing treasure chest.

Here in the UK, we're more guarded about giving permission. So while the Foreign and Commonwealth Office (FCO) does provide a large range of images of politicians on its Flickr page (***flickr.com/photos/foreignoffice***), they come with the condition that while some may be used, the FCO must be credited and no derivative works may be made from them. This means you can't download a picture of David Miliband with Morgan Tsvangirai and replace Miliband's head with a clown face.

For general purpose backgrounds, as well as large collections of images of just about every variety, there are two free image libraries that stand out: Stock Exchange (***sxc.hu***) and morgueFile (***morguefile.com***). These both have quick, well designed search engines and are a useful source of miscellaneous pictures. Many of the photographs, though, are licensed for non-commercial use only. You have to contact the photographer to request permission to use the image in a commercial project. This is rarely refused, but if you're a designer on a deadline, the time lag between request and approval can be a deal breaker.

There are several image libraries providing free texture content for 3D artists, who constantly need detailed textures to wrap around their models. These tend to hold mainly low resolution, tiling textures, which are of little use to the Photoshop artist. One notable exception is Mayang's Free Textures (***mayang.com/textures***), which currently holds nearly 4000 high-resolution images of walls, stone, roads, tiles, cloth, leaves, metal, wood, peeling paint and much more – as well as a fair selection of cars, buildings and skies. It's an excellent collection and is the first stop for many budget-conscious designers.

Finding company logos is always a tricky business, and they must be used with care if you don't want to get sued. The best source is the company's own website: head to the Investor Relations section, and download a pdf of their annual report. This should contain a vector, scalable version of the logo: zoom in as large as you like, and take a screen grab. Alternatively, visit the Russian site Logotypes (***logotypes.ru/default_e.asp***) for a huge range of logos from companies around the world.

▲ **The US Department of Defense is a good choice for public domain images of US politicians and generals.**

F: Free Transform

Don't confine your size and orientation adjustments to numbers tapped in a box – use free transform to free up your creativity.

Free Transform (Command-T) is the editing mode you use to stretch, rotate and distort layers or selections in Photoshop. Once you've entered Free Transform, you can then use the Image Warp controls, which allow you to apply preset shapes and custom envelope distortions to your layers – and we'll come back to this rather intriguing and powerful feature in a future article.

Once in Free Transform mode, you can resize a layer by dragging one of the corner handles; holding down Shift will constrain the proportions so you can scale it without distorting it. If you simply want to change a layer's width or height, dragging one of the handles on the midpoint of a side will scale in one dimension only.

Most scaling operations operate about the side or corner opposite to the one you drag. So if you drag a corner handle, the opposite corner will remain fixed. You can change this behaviour so that you stretch around the centre marker instead, by holding down the Alt key. This is useful on many occasions – when you're scaling a large object to fit a small space, for instance, you can scale twice as fast if you scale to the centre rather than a corner.

To rotate a layer, you position the cursor outside the Free Transform bounding box and its shape will change to show a rotation icon. The further from the object you click and drag, the more you have to drag the cursor to achieve the same degree of rotation, and so the more control you get. If you hold down the Alt key as you drag, you can rotate the object in 15° increments, which makes it easy to rotate to angles such as 45°, 60° and 90°.

For both scaling and rotation, you can move the centre point marker to anywhere on (or off) your artwork by simply picking it up and dragging it. There are many good reasons to do

▲ A magazine cover with a low resolution photograph used as a rough.

▲ To position the high resolution image accurately, align the eye, enter Free Transform and move the marker point over the iris.

▲ Next, hold down Alt to scale from the centre as you drag a corner handle towards this point.

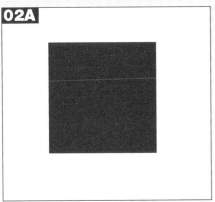

▲ To draw the compass points, begin with a square and enter Free Transform.

▲ Hold down Alt as you rotate to constrain to 15% increments and turn to 45°.

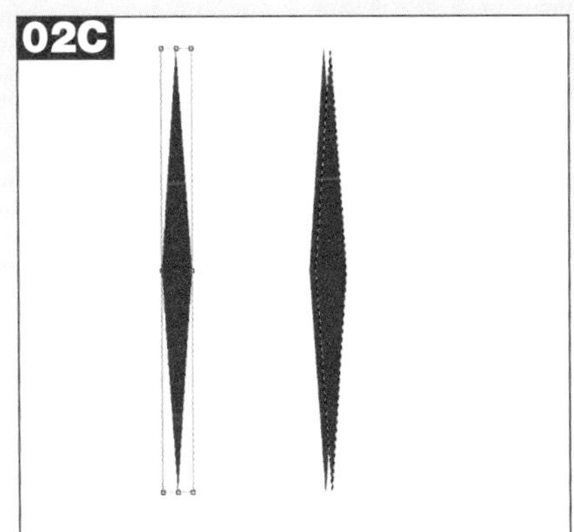

▲ Enter Free Transform once again and drag a side handle to squeeze the diamond (left). Select All and hold Alt-Shift as you nudge a copy of the diamond to the side (right).

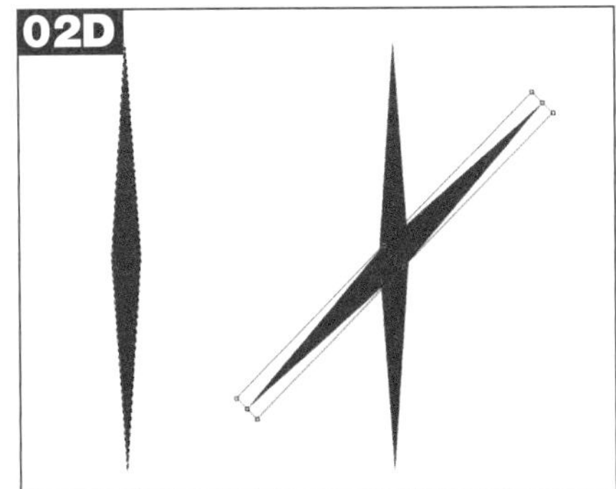

▲ Release Alt and hold down Shift as the copy is nudged back in place (left). Hold Alt as you rotate the shape 45° (right).

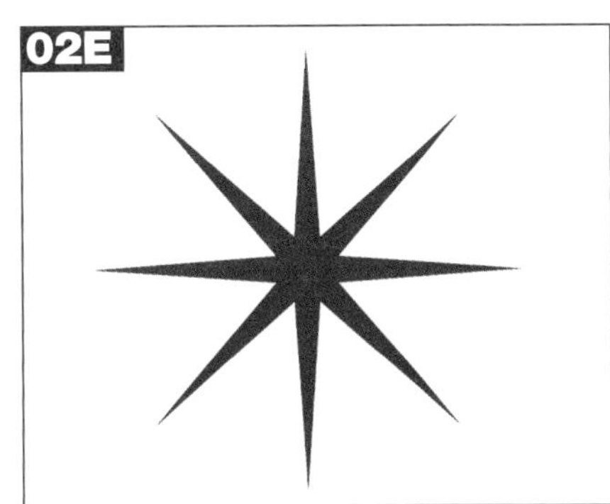

▲ Use Command-Shift-T to duplicate the previous transformation.

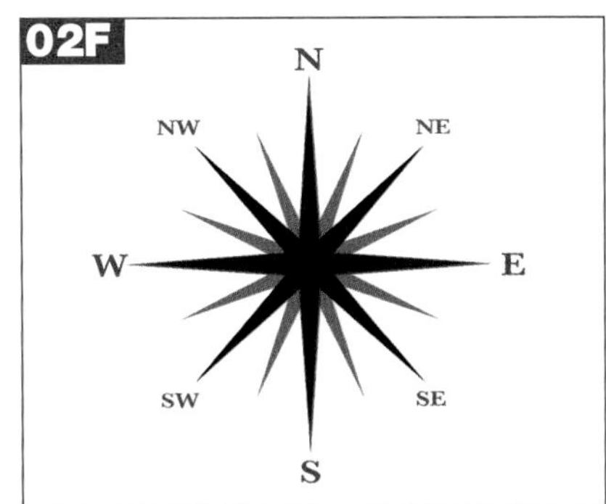

▲ The rest of the compass can easily be built from these components.

this. For example, you might want to scale a high resolution portrait to match an enlarged low resolution version on a magazine cover rough, which you would have used for comping. It can be difficult to judge precisely, but there are simple workarounds. Reduce the opacity of the high resolution version to, say, 50%, and align one of the eyes with the underlying version. Next, moving the centre point marker to this eye, and holding down Alt to scale towards the centre will allow you to reproduce the exact size with ease.

You can combine several of these techniques to automate a repetitive task with the Transform Again menu command, which is found in Edit > Transform (and which uses the shortcut Command-Shift-T). Let's say you need to draw a compass, in which the design is composed of a radial array of triangles. Here's a simple technique that will avoid a lot of repetition and guesswork.

First, draw the initial triangle vertically. The quickest way to do this is to hold down Shift while tracing with the Marquee tool to draw a square selection, and then fill this with a colour on a new layer. Enter Free Transform and hold down Alt as you drag to rotate it by 45°, to make a quick diamond shape. Press Enter to apply the transformation, then enter Free Transform once more and this time drag one of the edge handles to squeeze the diamond into a long, thin shape. This can be either chopped off to make a triangle, or left as an elongated diamond that represents two triangles joined at the base.

You now want to duplicate this elongated shape, but you don't want to make new layers from it. Use Edit > Select All to select the shape on a pixel level. If you were to rotate it now, you'd lose the original orientation, so you need to duplicate it first. Hold down Alt-Shift and press the right cursor key to make a duplicate 10 pixels away, and then release the Alt key and press the left cursor key to nudge the duplicate back directly on top of the original. You're now ready to perform the transformation.

Enter Free Transform once again and hold down the Alt key to rotate the copy by, for example, 45°. Since holding down Alt forces 15° increments, that's three clicks round. Press Enter to accept the transformation. If you now press Command-Shift-T, it will repeat that transformation, producing a version rotated at 90° from the original; you can continue pressing Command-Shift-T to create the final 135° rotation.

This technique would work equally well when creating a lot of fiddly rotations, such as seconds markers on a clock face. In this case, you first draw a short vertical line the size of the marker you want, and then Select All and duplicate it as before. This time, however, you want to rotate the marker not around its own centre, but around the centre of the clock face. So you drag the centre marker directly downwards (holding down the Shift key as you drag to get a pure vertical movement).

You now want to rotate this by 6°, since there are 60 seconds in a minute and 6 x 60 = 360. However, you can't rely on the 15° incremental clicks for this particular task. Instead, enter Free Transform and type 6 in the numerical field in the Options bar, specifying this as the angle of rotation, and then press Enter.

Repeated use of Command-Shift-T will now create an additional second marker, each one rotated by 6° around the midpoint of the clock. Of course, this method still requires the key combination to be pressed 58 times. A quicker method still would be to duplicate the first tick by, say, 30°, make a circle of 30° ticks, select the whole lot, and rotate the entire assembly 6° five times.

G: Gradients

Gradients are key to giving your work subtlety and merging one element into another. They can also be used to control the strength of effects when applied to layers.

As graphics applications have become more powerful, the possibilities of gradient construction – the smooth blending of shades in both mono and colour – have got ever more sophisticated. One such advance has been the gradient editor, which enables users to control every aspect of the blending process.

These days it is a powerful tool that creates complex, photorealistic images within vector software such as Illustrator and FreeHand. It also adds smooth transitional backgrounds in page layout applications, the most popular of which are InDesign and QuarkXPress.

All the major graphics programs use a fairly similar gradient editor, which allows you to set the colours at the start and finish, as well as adding additional hues in between. You can also set the direction of a gradient for a specific object to which it has been applied by dragging with the Gradient tool within the object or, in some applications, by turning a wheel to determine the desired angle.

To change the colour of an end-point of a gradient in Illustrator and InDesign, double-click on the one you want to change and set the RGB or CMYK make-up of that colour.

The marker between the start and end of the gradient marks the mid-point – drag this to the left or right to skew the gradient, determining the rate at which one shade blends into the next.

You can add additional colours within the gradient editor by holding down the Alt key and dragging an end colour to another point in the gradient. You can then change the colour of this by double-clicking it; or by adding multiple instances of the same pair of start and end colours, you can create a simple metallic effect that you can apply to any object in an instant.

In Photoshop, we have the additional option of using transparency within a gradient as if it were a colour in its own right. This enables you to create smooth gradients that blend from a solid colour to nothing, which is perfect for adding shading to an image.

When applied to a separate layer you get a movable vignette that can be turned on and off. For good measure it can be reduced in strength by lowering the layer opacity and moved around at will.

At their most basic, gradients can be applied in either linear or radial form – that is, in a straight line or radiating in a circle. But in Photoshop you get a far greater degree of control, with the added ability to set different shapes for our gradients. Diamond, for example, produces a rotated square gradient burst that's good for jewellery effects in small areas, while Angled creates a gradient that

▲ **When we first apply a gradient to multiple objects in Illustrator, it treats each object individually. Selecting them all and dragging across them with the Gradient tool sets the gradient correctly.**

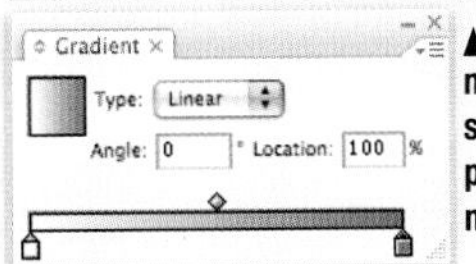

▲ We can make a simple metallic effect by first setting our start and end points to pale yellow and mid brown.

▲ Duplicate the right-hand brown swatch by dragging it to multiple positions, while holding Alt to make copies.

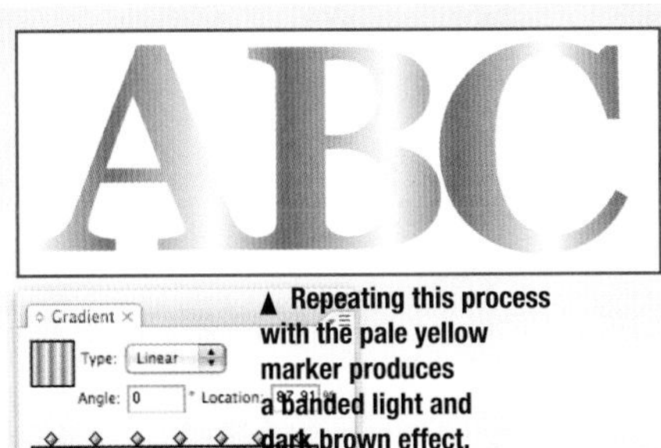

▲ Repeating this process with the pale yellow marker produces a banded light and dark brown effect.

▲ Drag with the Gradient tool to change the angle for a better effect – for some reason the stripes look artificial when they are displayed vertically.

▲ Here we've added a thick stroke and converted it to outlines, then filled it with the same gradient in a different direction to make a quick bevel effect.

▲ Changing the mode of the bevel from Linear to Radial makes for an interesting appearance. It's amazing just how many effects can be made with experimentation.

rotates – perfect for a radar-sweep effect. If you prefer, you can also choose reflected mode, in which gradients include a mirror image of themselves.

In addition Photoshop can create 'noise' gradients, in which random colours are placed together following the approximate RGB or CMYK make-up specified by dragging the appropriate sliders. This is useful for creating instant variegated backgrounds, without the bother of adding each colour individually.

A useful Randomize button here, by the way, allows you to try out variants of the colour combinations.

While you can set all these combinations, using the Gradient tool directly on a layer, you get far more power by using Layer Effects instead. The combinations are chosen from the pop-up menu at the bottom of the Layers palette – the dialog is opened by clicking on

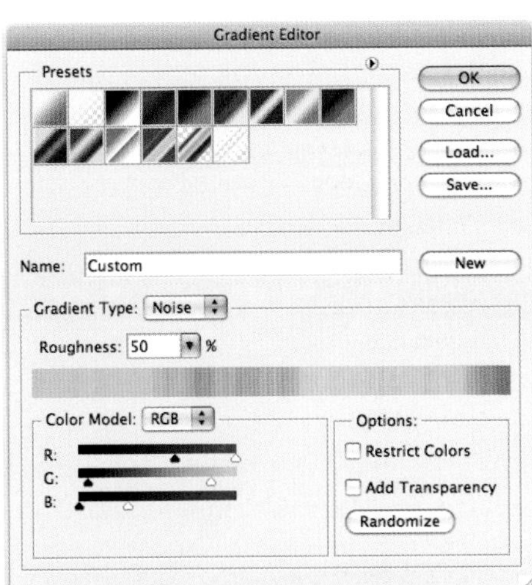

▲ The Noise feature in Photoshop's gradient editor automatically builds multiple colours at random – ideal for creating instant variegated backgrounds.

Gradient Overlay. This doesn't paint directly on to the layer but creates a gradient that matches the shape of the pixels present in the layer. The big advantage here is that you can set the angle, size and type of the gradient through the dialog, and change it at any time.

It's fully editable later, so you can just double-click the Layer Effect icon in the Layers palette for the layer in question to bring up the dialog once more and adjust it as you so wish.

A further option here, which is buried away rather, is to apply a gradient to a Stroke rather than the Fill. To do this, first select the Stroke button at the bottom left of the Layer Effects dialog to switch to that pane, then choose Gradient as the fill type from the pop-up menu.

You can set the gradient to be wholly inside, wholly outside or centred on the outline of our layer; you can also set the size of the stroke in pixels.

What's most interesting here though is the additional gradient type that appears only within the Stroke section of Layer Effects named Shape Burst. When you choose this option, the Angle and Scale controls are ignored, and the gradient wraps itself around

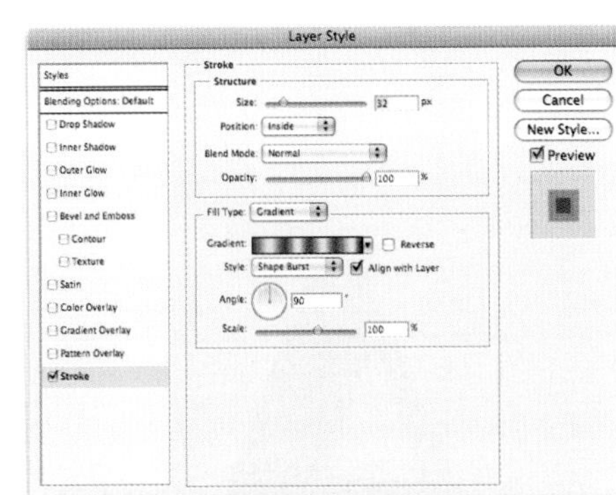

▲ By adding a Shape Burst to the Stroke of a Photoshop layer, a gradient is produced that wraps around the perimeter of our layer like a pipeline.

the perimeter of the layer so that the gradient is always at a 90° angle to this edge.

It's a powerful variant on the tool, as it's able to produce pipeline effects that follow the direction of any shape. This is ideal for creating neon tubing, for example.

The fact that the sophistication of Photoshop's gradient editor is not yet replicated in Illustrator where it would be of tremendous use is lamentable. Therefore, it can only be hoped that Adobe will address the issue in future releases of the application.

G: Graphics tablets

For times when you feel that the mouse is too restrictive, switch to a graphics tablet, which puts the screen on your lap and the pointer in a pen.

As a point-and-click tool, the mouse is great for browsing websites, making menu selections and blasting aliens in 3D shoot-'em-ups. However, as a drawing implement it has many shortcomings: it's clumsy, inaccurate and awkward to use.

Instead, most professional designers invest in a graphics tablet, which typically ships with three components: the tablet itself, in a variety of sizes; a pressure-sensitive stylus with configurable buttons; and a cordless mouse, generally including two buttons and a scroll wheel. The stylus isn't a pencil, though, and it's a mistake to assume that it feels like one in use. The first obstacle to overcome is that, unlike a mouse, the stylus has a 1:1 mapping with the monitor. Which means that the top left corner of the tablet will always map to the top left corner of the screen, for instance. It's a different mode of working to a mouse, other than just its form factor.

Because the stylus is a wholly different tool to either a mouse or a pen, many users have a bit of trouble getting to grips with it. At first, it seems difficult to control. Although it's easy to add shading to an image right from the start, it takes practice before most people feel comfortable using it to manipulate anchor points on Bézier curves.

The first choice to make when buying a stylus/tablet combination is which brand to go for. This is easy: only Wacom has comprehensively addressed the technology by offering a wide range of tablets in a variety of sizes and configurations.

The second choice is the size of the tablet. In our experience, the smallest mainstream tablet, with an A6 working area, is easily large enough to control even the biggest monitor resolutions with accuracy. Starting at about £60, this is a good size to begin with and may well suit all your future needs. Much larger tablets are available, but these are of benefit mainly for those wishing to trace CAD diagrams. There are also different ranges available, with the more expensive tablets offering a greater degree of sensitivity.

Wacom also makes the innovative Cintiq tablet, which is built into a pressure-sensitive monitor. The advantage here is that you can draw or paint directly onto the artwork, which brings an immediacy and fluidity to illustration work. Apart from its price, though, the Cintiq has several drawbacks. First, drawing on a monitor is tiring in the long term unless you rest the heavy device on your lap. If you do work in this way, you then face the problem of where to put the keyboard: if it's moved to

◄ **Graphics tablets are available in a large variety of sizes and styles. German company Wacom makes the best tablets on the market.**

one side, the process of choosing keyboard shortcuts becomes that much clumsier. However, the main issue is that, unlike a regular tablet or mouse, your hand is constantly in the way of the image when you draw.

A control panel sets basic behaviours for the stylus and mouse, both globally and on a per-application basis. This offers the flexibility of being able to set the scroll wheel to move one line per click in a word processing application, and 10 lines per click in Safari; or you could choose to have the right mouse button open a link in a new tab in Safari, and so on. For some applications, the mouse is better than the stylus, which is why it's shipped with it.

Some applications are fully tablet-aware, so you can set up behaviour patterns for each tool directly within the application. So in Photoshop you can define a set of soft-edged brushes for which greater pressure produces a greater opacity. This is the standard mode of operation and enables such tasks as adding shadows to be accomplished with ease: the harder you press, the darker the result.

You might also choose to set up a hard-edged brush for which higher pressure produces a larger diameter, with a constant opacity. This would be useful when using the Healing tool or the History Brush, for example, where 100% opacity is generally required. In these cases, you'd press softly for a small brush when working in fine detail areas, and hard for a large brush for covering larger areas at a stroke. When defining custom brushes in Photoshop, you can make the pressure of the stylus determine just about any aspect of the brush. It could determine the angle, for example, or the roundness, or the colour.

There's also a range of extra tools to simulate airbrushes, marker pens, oil paint brushes and other natural media. Some tools can recognise the angle of the tool relative to the tablet, as well as its pressure. This provides an extra parameter to control custom brushes, and also enables such tasks as painting on 3D surfaces to be accomplished with a more intuitive feel.

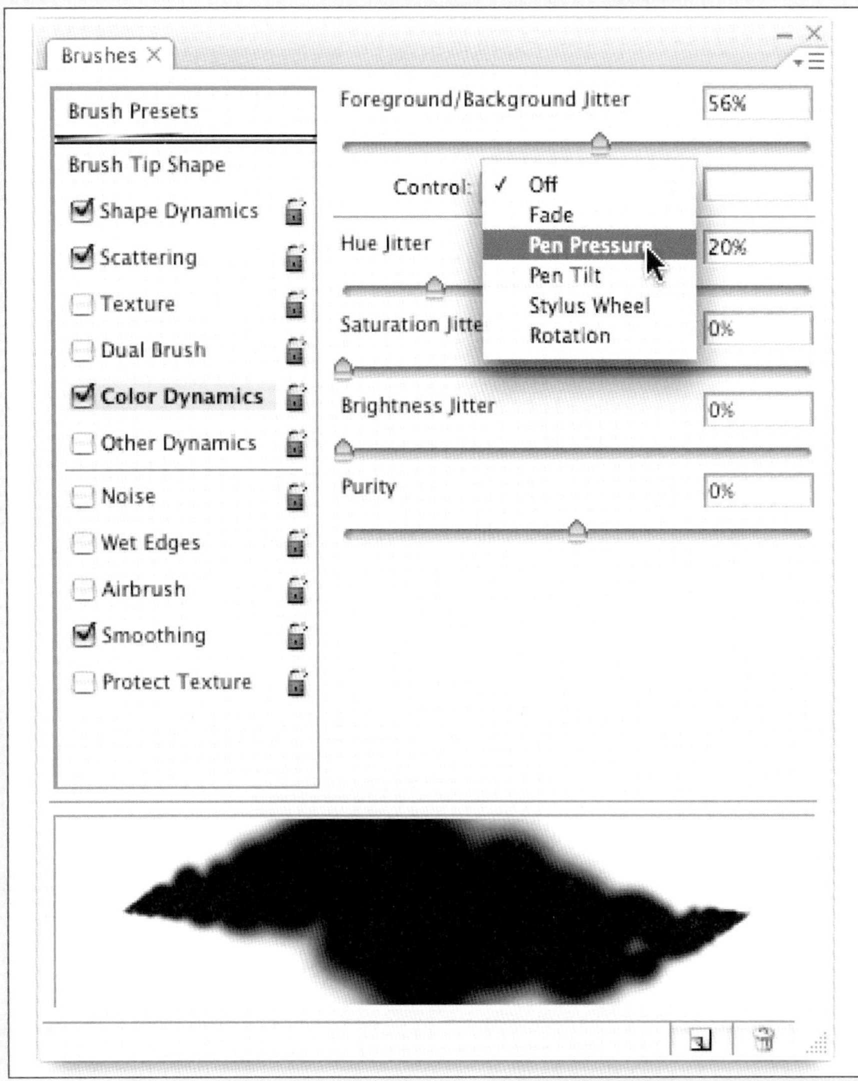

▲ Photoshop's brushes panel allows custom brushes to be built from scratch – with tablet support in virtually every category.

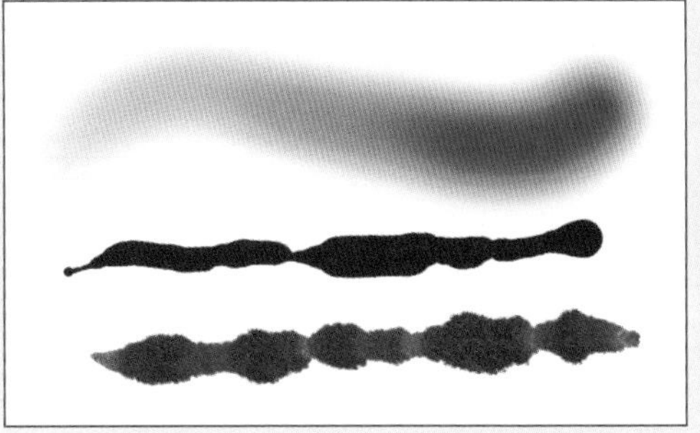

◄ You can use the stylus to vary painting opacity with pressure (top), or increase size (middle). It can also be set to change other parameters, such as the painting colour and scatter amount (bottom).

Applications such as Painter, in which simulating natural media is the key purpose, benefit hugely from the stylus and tablet approach; 3D modelling applications, including Cinema 4D, Maya, Bodypaint and ZBrush, also make good use of tilt capabilities. The handwriting recognition built into Mac OS X, known as Inkwell, is far easier to use with a stylus, of course.

Just about every graphics, audio, video, CAD and 3D application on the Mac has a range of settings specifically for tablet owners. It's not difficult to see why: with so many advantages, and a learning curve that means you can be an expert in a matter of days, ownership of a tablet is now essential for any serious designer. However, don't expect to take to it right out of the box: it frequently takes several days of pain before using the tools becomes second nature. ⊗

G: Graphs in Illustrator

It's not only Excel that can create graphs. By representing changes and values in Illustrator, you can give them a 3D finish and incorporate them into other projects.

The graphing function of Adobe Illustrator has remained essentially unchanged since it first appeared in Illustrator 3, way back in 1990. But despite the fact that the tool is now old enough to drink and vote, it remains a powerful, if rather under-used, part of Illustrator's impressive graphics arsenal.

Illustrator is capable of creating a variety of graph types: columns; stacked columns, in which multiple values are piled on top of each other; and bars and stacked bars, essentially, column graphs on their side. It can also produce area graphs, scatter graphs, and rudimentary pie charts.

The graph type you choose depends on the type of data you want to display. For showing, say, the number of times members of two families turn on a cooker, a kettle and a bath tap over a specific weekend, you'd want three concurrent column graphs showing the values for each occurrence side by side. But if you wanted to show how much each family spent on electricity, gas and water over a year, you'd probably want to use stacked columns, because the interesting statistic here is the comparison of the cumulative totals of all three.

To create a graph, pick the type you want from the pop-up icon set nested in the Graph icon, and drag it to the size you require, just like using the Rectangle tool, or simply click and a dialog box will appear, which allows you to set the size numerically. As soon as the graph appears on the page, another dialog box will pop up in which data values can be entered. Icons along the top of this floating panel allow data to be imported from Excel and other spreadsheets, and permit various operations to be carried out on the data such as swapping X and Y axes, transposing rows and columns, and setting cell styles.

So far, so good. The graph will, however, appear in various shades of grey, and look rather dull. To change the colour of column or bar segments, use the Direct Selection tool (A) and hold down the Alt key as you click inside one of them. As is standard, this will select the whole segment. But if you keep the Alt key held down and click in the same segment again, all matching segments will be selected (in the case of multiple-data column or bar graphs), allowing you to change the colour using the standard Colour panel. By changing

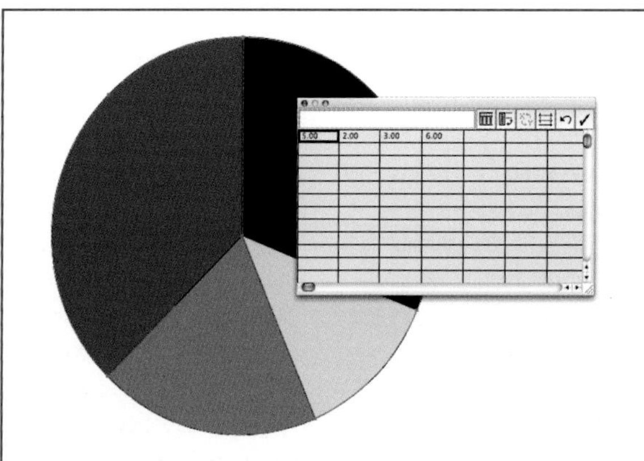

▲ **To create a pie chart, drag to set the chart size and enter your data in the floating panel. The graph will appear in shades of grey.**

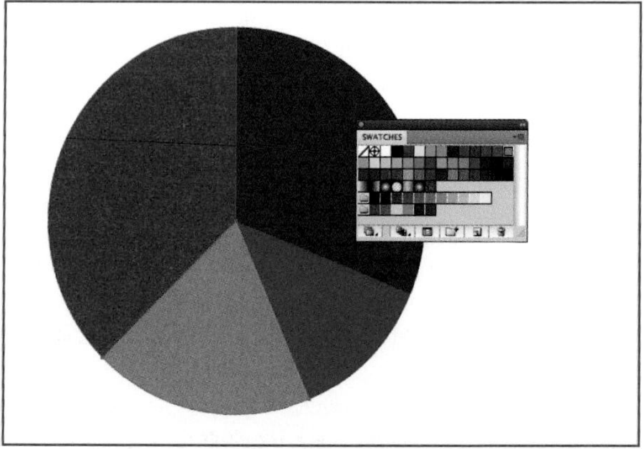

▲ **Select each segment with the Direct Selection tool to recolour the graph, and make sure to remove the stroke from the whole thing.**

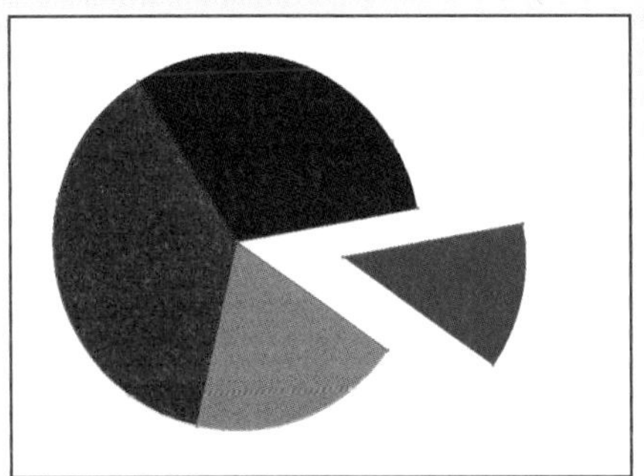
▲ If you like, you can rotate the graph and even pull whole segments out for emphasis.

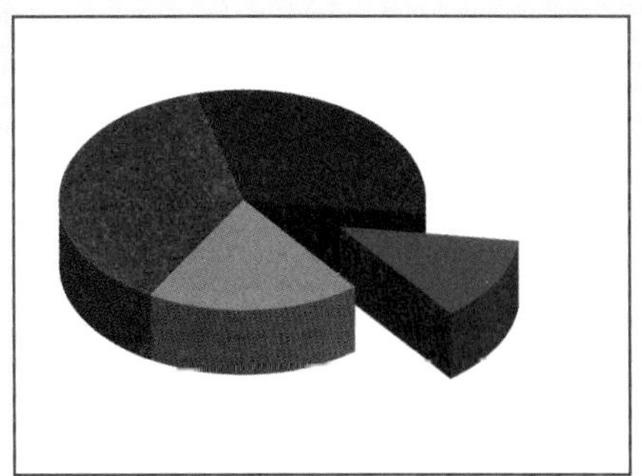
▲ Use Illustrator's 3D Extrude feature to turn the flat and uninspiring artwork into a 3D pie chart.

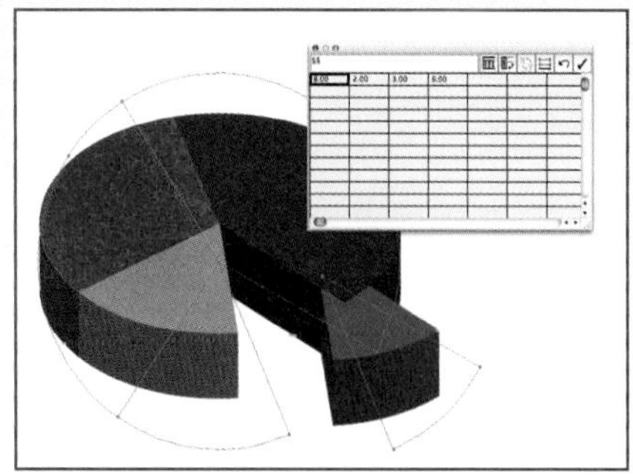
▲ If you edit the values, you may find that you have to adjust any segments you moved earlier.

▲ Displaying values using scaled bottles is one approach, but very large values will overwhelm the smaller ones.

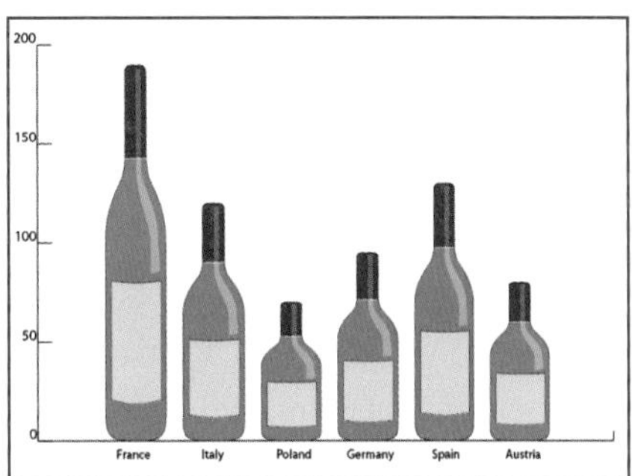

▲ Scaling each element vertically is another option, but the bottles look ungainly when distorted in this way.

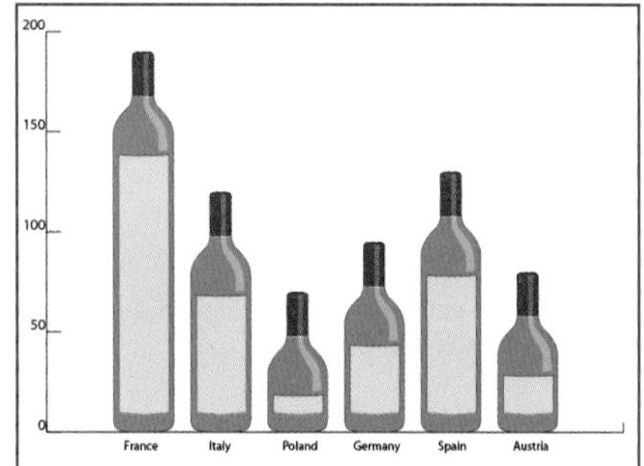

▲ Using a sliding graph design produces better results: a guide sets the point at which the graph extends.

colours in this way, the graph remains linked to its original data; change the data, and the graph will change to match. If the data panel has been closed, use Object > Graph > Data to reopen it.

The real interest in creating graphs comes when we make our own custom designs. Any object can be used as a graph element and can be scaled automatically to suit the data. A chart of wine consumption in different countries could be represented by wine bottles of differing sizes, with the size linked to the volume of alcohol consumed.

To create the graph element, draw the bottle (or whatever design you choose), select it and choose Object > Graph > Design, and give your bottle a name in the resulting dialog box. Then, with the graph selected, choose Object > Graph > Column, select your design in the dialog, and choose Uniformly Scaled in the menu.

While this approach might work for a small number of countries, there's clearly a problem when there are big discrepancies: a comparison of France and vodka-loving Poland, for instance, might show a huge bottle for France that completely overwhelms the tiny Polish equivalent. And so we might choose to modify the graph display, by using Repeating as the display method. In this case, we specify how many units are represented by each bottle, and the graph is displayed as a set of bottles piled on top of each other. When choosing Repeating as the method, we can select whether fractions of a unit are scaled or chopped to represent the smaller portion.

Yet another method of working with custom columns is to scale our designs vertically, again chosen using the pop-up menu in the Column dialog box. This has the advantage that, with all our columns the same width, we can display our data much more neatly. The downside is that with a design which features a recognisable shape, such as our bottle, the result will look ugly when distorted: a bottle that's three times the height, but no wider, will simply look stretched in an ungainly manner.

There is a neat solution to this problem, and that's to use the fourth custom graph display method – Sliding. In this method, the column element is stretched only at a horizontal level we specify. So for the bottle design, you can stretch the section that includes the body of the bottle and the label: because you're leaving the neck and the base unaltered, the bottles no longer have that distorted appearance. To create a Sliding graph design, you need to draw a horizontal rule at the level at which the design can comfortably be stretched. In our example, this is at any height within the label area. Select this rule, and use View > Guides > Make to turn this rule into a horizontal guide. Now, when the bottle design is selected together with this guide and defined as a graph design, the guide will indicate the sliding point.

Although Illustrator is unable to create 3D pie charts directly from the Graphing tools, it's easy enough to generate one using the 3D feature. First, create your pie chart and set the colours of each segment, making sure that all segments have a fill, but no stroke.

If you wish, you can select a segment with the Direct Selection tool and pull it to one side for emphasis. Next, select Effect > 3D > Extrude & Bevel, and click on the Preview box in the resulting dialog to view your pie chart as a 3D object. You can now rotate and view it from any angle. It's even possible to edit the data, as the 3D version is still linked to the original chart: select it and choose Object > Graph > Data to change it as you would any other graph.

G: Grep styles in InDesign CS4

Described as 'find and replace with superhuman powers', InDesign's Grep styles are capable of much more sophisticated styles than Style Sheets.

Grep is an advanced pattern search tool used for text – a sort of find and replace with superhuman powers. Don't be surprised if you haven't heard of it before, as its origins in the Unix programming environment mean it originally had an esoteric and very narrow appeal. Even the origin of the acronym is in doubt: those who use it regularly say it stands for General Regular Expression Parser, while Wikipedia reckons it derives from Global | Regular Expression | Print. Whatever its ancestry, it's a powerful tool that all InDesign users should have in their arsenal.

Using InDesign CS4's Style Sheets, you can create paragraph styles that allow you to apply fonts, sizes, justification, line spacing and every other descriptor with a single click. You can also create nested style sheets whereby you can set a different character style for a set chunk of text. So you might choose to have the first three words in red, or whole of the first sentence in bold, and so on.

However, even nested styles have their limitations. They can't include conditionals or multiple instances of a style to be applied, and their formatting is easily broken by a miskeyed entry from an inexperienced operator. Using the Grep system, however, you can apply specific character styles to any text you like, and you can even use wildcards to extend the range of application.

Let's say you want to pick out key words in a block of text and apply special highlighting to them. In a typical block of type [01], you might want to pick out each instance of the word 'text' and display it in bold, like a hyperlink: the implication is that this is a key concept. Assuming you've already defined a Paragraph Style for the text, you can open the style definition and switch to the Grep Style pane. Here, you have a simple choice: the Character Style to apply, and the text to apply it to. Beginning with the Character Style, you can either pick an existing style from the pop-up list or define a new one from here.

You can, for example, choose a sans serif font such as Myriad Bold to contrast with the serif body text. In the 'To Text' field, you only need to type the word 'text' to apply your Character Style to all instances of that word [02]. Assuming the Preview box is checked, you'll now see the results instantly on all text to which this style has been applied [03].

Say you want to take it a step further and apply this bold style to more key words, such as 'font', 'paragraph' and 'character'. Once again, you open the Paragraph Style dialog and switch to the Grep pane. You can edit the 'To Text' field to include all the words we want, using a vertical slash | between each word (Shift-\). Alternatively, click the @ sign to the right of the To Text field and choose the vertical slash character from the Match section of the pop-up menu – it's labelled as 'or'. All the Grep special characters are listed in subsections here, and it's a handy reference point [04]. So the text you need is:

Apply Style: bold
To Text: text|font|paragraph|character

Make sure there are no spaces between the vertical slash and the words on either side, and the bold style will be applied to all the words in the list [05]. You can see a problem immediately. Although each instance of the word 'character' has been picked out in bold, the word 'characters' – which, logically, should also have been in bold – has the final 's' in the default font. In addition, the word 'characteristics' displays the 'character' section of the word in bold, when this word

01

When setting text, we can define all the parameters for that text using Paragraph Styles (1). These allow us to adjust the font, leading and size, as well as other characteristics of the text in question (2). If we want a chunk of text at the beginning of a paragraph to be in a different font or style, we can use Nested Styles (3) to apply different character attributes for a set number of characters, so the text is differentiated more clearly.

02

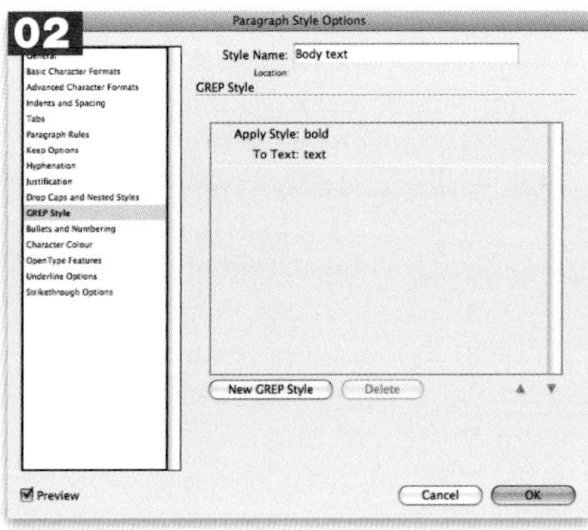

03

When setting **text**, we can define all the parameters for that **text** using Paragraph Styles (1). These allow us to adjust the font, leading and size, as well as other characteristics of the **text** in question (2). If we want a chunk of **text** at the beginning of a paragraph to be in a different font or style, we can use Nested Styles (3) to apply different character attributes for a set number of characters, so the **text** is differentiated more clearly.

04

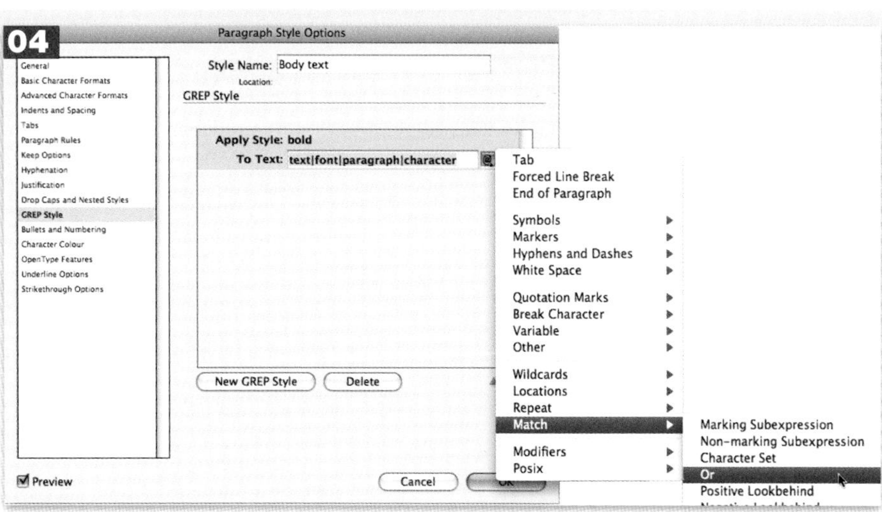

05

When setting **text**, we can define all the parameters for that **text** using Paragraph Styles (1). These allow us to adjust the **font**, leading and size, as well as other **character**istics of the **text** in question (2).
If we want a chunk of **text** at the beginning of a **paragraph** to be in a different **font** or style, we can use Nested Styles (3) to apply different **character** attributes for a set number of **character**s, so the **text** is differentiated more clearly.

06

When setting **text**, we can define all the parameters for that **text** using Paragraph Styles (1). These allow us to adjust the **font**, leading and size, as well as other **characteri**stics of the **text** in question (2).
If we want a chunk of **text** at the beginning of a **paragraph** to be in a different **font** or style, we can use Nested Styles (3) to apply different **character** attributes for a set number of **characters**, so the **text** is differentiated more clearly.

07

When setting **text**, we can define all the parameters for that **text** using Paragraph Styles (1). These allow us to adjust the **font**, leading and size, as well as other characteristics of the **text** in question (2).
If we want a chunk of **text** at the beginning of a **paragraph** to be in a different **font** or style, we can use Nested Styles (3) to apply different character attributes for a set number of **characters**, so the **text** is differentiated more clearly.

shouldn't be highlighted at all. You can fix the plurals problem easily, and that's by adding a wildcard to indicate any letter after the word 'character'. Choose this from the pop-up list, or just type the default shortcut – a full stop:

Apply Style: bold
To Text: text|font|paragraph|character.

Now, the 's' at the end of the word 'character' is in the correct font; but so is the 'i' after 'character' in 'characteristics' [**06**].

You must define the Grep instruction that will include the word 'character', but not the longer form 'characteristics'. One way to do this is to tell it to include the specified letters in its search only if they appear at the end of the word. You do this by typing a backslash after the word 'character' to indicate a Grep instruction, followed by the Greater Than symbol; this stands for 'end of word':

Apply Style: bold
To Text: text|font|paragraph|character.\>

You're getting close. The word 'characteristics' is now no longer in bold, because the 'character' section no longer appears at the end of the word. The trouble is, while 'characters' is still in bold, the singular form 'character' now isn't [**07**]. That's because the full stop indicates a wildcard letter, which means 'character' is no longer at the end of its own word; it's waiting for another character. You can fix this fairly easily using the formulation {0,1} before the full stop. This is Grep code for 'at least 0, but not more than 1', and applies to the wildcard letter:

Apply Style: bold
To Text: text|font|paragraph|character{0,1}.\>

Your text is now set correctly [**08**].

You can work with wildcards in several ways, and even compound multiple Grep instructions within the same paragraph. Say you want each of the bracketed numbers to appear in italics. Defining a new Grep style that chooses the 'red italic' Character Style, you can simply type */d* to make all digits appear in this style. To include the brackets, you need to type */(* at the beginning and */)* at the end. This is to show that the brackets are searchable characters, and not parentheses within an expression. So the full formulation is:

Apply Style: red italic
To Text: /(/d/)

You'll find that this creates the formatted text exactly as you want it [**09**].

08

When setting **text**, we can define all the parameters for that **text** using Paragraph Styles (1). These allow us to adjust the **font**, leading and size, as well as other characteristics of the **text** in question (2).
If we want a chunk of **text** at the beginning of a **paragraph** to be in a different **font** or style, we can use Nested Styles (3) to apply different **character** attributes for a set number of **characters**, so the **text** is differentiated more clearly.

09

When setting **text**, we can define all the parameters for that **text** using Paragraph Styles *(1)*. These allow us to adjust the **font**, leading and size, as well as other characteristics of the **text** in question *(2)*.
If we want a chunk of **text** at the beginning of a **paragraph** to be in a different **font** or style, we can use Nested Styles *(3)* to apply different **character** attributes for a set number of **characters**, so the **text** is differentiated more clearly.

H: Hard Light mode

The most versatile of blending modes, Hard Light can be used to improve contrast, sharpness and much more.

At the top of the Layers palette in Photoshop is a pop-up menu showing 25 different modes to which layers can be set – including Multiply, which darkens the layers beneath; Screen, which brightens them; and Difference, which inverts the view through the current layer. We looked briefly at some of these layer modes earlier in this section; here, we'll take a closer look at perhaps the most useful of them all, Hard Light.

In Multiply mode, black is invisible; while in Screen mode, white is invisible. But in Hard Light mode, the invisible colour is a mid-tone grey, exactly halfway between black and white. When you create a new layer using Command-Shift-N, so that the New Layer dialog appears, you can choose Hard Light from the pop-up menu – there's also a checkbox to fill the layer with the Hard Light neutral colour. If this is checked, you won't see anything – after all, it's invisible – but if you were to change the mode of the layer to Normal, you'd be able to see the grey fill.

The advantage of Hard Light mode is that the grey fill can be used as a neutral base on which to apply filters, shading and so on – all the colours that you paint on it will show up, as will all the highlights and shadows that are added.

But why do you need this underlying layer at all? Can't you just paint on an empty layer instead? There are many instances in which you need the underlying layer – and here are just a few of them.

One of the best ways of creating liquid effects is to use the Plastic Wrap filter. When applied to a layer that has some soft shading on it, the filter produces strong highlights and shadows that simulate an instant water effect. If the original layer is mid-grey, you can make it

► This beard has been made by painting on a new layer in mid-grey, then applying some Gaussian Noise and a Radial Blur filter. As it stands, it looks wholly artificial; but when we change the layer's mode to Hard Light the grey disappears, leaving us with just the black and white stubble effect.

◄ The water in this gutter was first painted in grey on a new layer, then shaded using Dodge and Burn, before the Plastic Wrap filter was applied to it. When we change the mode to Hard Light, the grey becomes translucent and we can see the cobbles through it, making it look much more like real water.

disappear entirely, leaving just the shading visible. You can also create a beard effect by adding some Gaussian Noise and a slight Radial Blur to a mid-grey layer; again, if you turn the layer into Hard Light mode, the underlying structure disappears, leaving just the shading.

There are many instances in which you may want to add shading to multiple layers in Photoshop. You may, for example, have an image consisting of multiple objects in a box, and want to add shadow onto all of them. While you could paint the shadow directly onto the objects, this would be irrevocable. You could also make a new shadow layer above each object in turn, and paint the shadow on that, but this would be time-consuming.

A far better solution is to hold the Command key and click on the object's thumbnail in the Layers palette to load up its pixels as a selection. Then hold Shift-Command and click on each additional thumbnail in turn to add the pixels of those layers to the selection.

With all the layers loaded up in this way, you can create a new layer, specifying Hard Light mode with a 50% grey fill. Then, when the new layer is created, inverse the selection (so everything outside the objects' region is selected) and Delete to remove the unwanted area. You can now use the Dodge and Burn tools to add light and shade to the Hard Light layer, which will give the effect of adding shading to the layers themselves – but without painting directly onto them. If you lock the transparency of the Hard Light layer, you will be able to paint on it in colour. This will produce the effect of coloured lighting on your objects, or – if you use dark colours – rich, colourful shadows.

Sometimes when you show a screen capture of a Photoshop image, you may want to show a 'marching ants' selection as part of that screen. But when printed small, the marching ants are just too small to see. One solution is to create a new layer set to Hard Light mode and filled with 50% grey – then hide this layer. Make the selection as normal, then turn the Hard Light layer on – you'll now see black and white 'ants' on a grey background. If you reduce your view to 50% of the original size, the image will get smaller but the ants won't.

So if you now take a screen capture of the reduced view, you'll get the selection outline at double the size. When you paste that screen capture into your Photoshop document and use Free Transform to double its size, the selection edges will appear twice the size they did before. All you need to do now is to change the mode of this pasted capture to Hard Light to make the grey disappear, leaving just the black and white marching ants visible.

Let's say you've constructed a poster-type image, and want to make it look old and tattered. To do this, simply photograph a tattered sheet of paper or cardboard, and then desaturate the result so it's just in monochrome. When you darken this image, so that the bulk of it is 50% grey, only the highlights and shadow will remain – perfect for changing to Hard Light mode and overlaying on our image.

Hard Light layers can also be used to add colour or shading to an image, and to store selection areas from multiple layers. You can duplicate this Hard Light layer to make the effect stronger, or reduce the opacity to make it weaker; and, of course, if you want to remove part of a painted effect selectively, you can always paint over it with 50% grey to hide it. It's a great way to add textures, as they can be applied to Hard Light layers and then overlaid on top of any image. They're a well-kept secret, and deserve experimentation.

▲ We've loaded up the selection areas of all these toys by holding Shift and Command, and clicking on their thumbnails in the Layers palette.

▲ We can make a new layer from this selection, filled with 50% grey. The transparency is locked, so that we can't paint over the edges of the selection area.

▲ Changing the layer's mode to Hard Light hides the grey. We can now paint in colour, or use Dodge and Burn to create shadows and highlights that show through onto the layers beneath.

H: History

Don't let limited Undo stifle your creativity. With Photoshop's History feature you can let your imagination run wild and wind things back if you take them a step too far.

For years, a multiple undo feature held top place in Photoshop users' wish lists. When it was finally unveiled in Photoshop 5, it far exceeded expectations: the History palette, and its associated History Brush, provides a powerful way to apply earlier – or even later – versions of your image in a selective manner.

The History palette stores each action you take as a discrete step, whether it's a brush stroke, a filter, a change of size or image mode, or any other task or process. By default, the History palette keeps track of the 20 most recent steps, although you can increase this number in the Preferences pane. With every step clearly listed with the name of the tool or process that created it, it's easy to step back and forth through your most recent actions, and even to jump to particular points.

When you open a document, the History palette creates a 'snapshot' of the state of the file at that point. Whatever actions you then take, it's always possible to return to this state by clicking on its thumbnail in the palette. Unlike choosing Revert from the File menu, this is a near-instant process, and it's possible to switch back and forth between the file and the reverted version with ease.

You can choose to take a new snapshot at any point by selecting it from the pop-up menu in the palette. This will capture the entire state of the document, represented by a thumbnail at the top of the palette. In practice, you can take as many snapshots as you like, providing an easy way to flip between different states of the artwork. It's a hugely powerful technology, enabling you to experiment at will without ever having to commit to a series of actions. However, snapshots aren't maintained when a file is

▲ Erasing the sky has had the unfortunate effect of removing the two clock faces, which happened to be almost exactly the same colour.

▲ Removing the sky from this image should be straightforward with the Background Eraser tool. First, we'll pin the History state.

▲ When we switch to the History Brush, we can paint back the state of the document as it was when we first opened it, restoring the clockfaces.

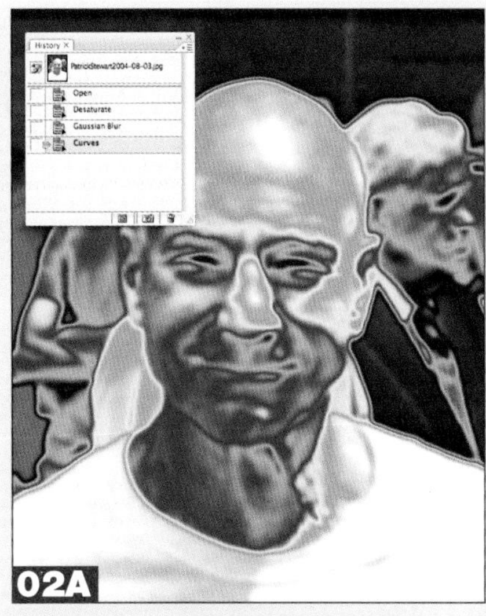

▲ 02A This photograph of Patrick Stewart, aka Captain Jean-Luc Picard, has been desaturated and blurred, with a metallic Curves effect applied to it.

▲► 02B We'll pin the history state after the final operation, and then click on the initial state of the document to revert it. The subsequent operations, though, have been stored in the History.

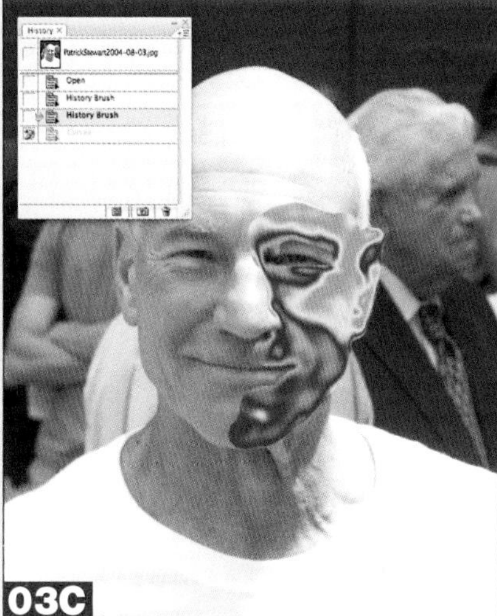

► 02C This lets us use the History Brush to paint in the effect we'd built, but which we'd then reverted from. This could be the first step to full Borg transformation.

closed and reopened: they only operate for the duration of the current session.

By default, a new snapshot is created whenever a file is opened. The Options dialog for the palette also enables a new snapshot to be created automatically each time the file is saved, although this can result in a huge number of snapshots. There's also the option to create a new document based on a chosen History state.

By the side of each snapshot, and each item listed in the History palette, is a separate column that can be clicked to 'pin' the History at that point. This allows the document to be reverted to that state selectively: make a selection and press shift-delete to open the Fill dialog. Choosing History from the pop-up menu in this dialog box will revert just the selected area on the current layer.

Where the History palette really comes into its own, though, is through the use of the History Brush. This allows the document to be reverted to an earlier state – chosen by pinning it in the palette – by painting on the current layer. You could, for example, apply a series of transformations or filters to a layer, and then paint back the original layer selectively. The 20-item default limit doesn't apply when a History state is pinned in the palette: that position will be maintained however many steps are subsequently taken, as long as the state to which you want to revert remains pinned in the palette.

This is particularly useful with processes such as using the Background Eraser tool to delete the sky behind buildings, or a background from behind a portrait. What frequently happens here is that if the Tolerance on the Background Eraser tool is sufficiently high to remove all of the background, you'll erase part of the face, or windows in a building that happen to be a similar colour to the sky. Since using the Background Eraser tool involves making a large number of small brushstrokes, your 20-item History limit can quickly be used up. However, if you pin the History state before you begin to erase, the state of the image at that moment will be retained. When all the background has been removed, you can switch to the History Brush and paint back any details that have been removed in error. Without the History Brush, the Background Eraser would be a significant more cumbersome tool to use.

As well as reverting to earlier states in a document, the History palette also enables you to return to 'future' states. Let's say we want to add noise to a layer, but we only want it to show up in certain areas. We can run the filter and then pin the History state after all the processes have been completed. We can now return to the original state of the document by clicking on its position in the palette; now, when we use the History Brush, we can paint in the state of the file after the filters have been run, exactly where we want them.

The History palette adds each new event to the bottom of its list. If you undo a series of actions, they'll be cleared from the list, which will continue to be added to from that point on. A special variation on this is available through the Options dialog for the palette, called Allow Non-Linear History. In this mode, reverting to an earlier state won't remove subsequent actions from the palette. Instead, any further operations will be listed below them. It's a useful option, but can be confusing in use: it's generally preferable to have this option turned off, unless there's a specific series of actions that requires it.

The History palette, especially when using snapshots, involves the writing of huge temporary files to your hard disk. Reading and writing these files can slow down Photoshop considerably: it's good practice to Purge your History every now and again to ensure smooth running of the application. This is best achieved through the Purge All command in the Edit menu, which will also clear the clipboard and standard Undo capability.

I: Image size

Get to grips with image size and you'll know in an instant how many pixels you need to end up with, whatever your output medium.

Understanding image size is a conundrum that puzzles most designers when they're starting out. Just what is the difference between dots per inch and lines per inch, and how do either relate to the megapixel sizes quoted by the manufacturers of digital cameras? What resolution is required when working for print?

Image size is measured in dots per inch (dpi), even if you're accustomed to working in centimeters. You can, of course, work in dots per centimeter, but we'll stick to dpi here to be in tune with the convention.

Computer monitors typically display images at 72dpi. This means 72 pixels across and 72 down, which amounts to 5184 physical pixels in each square inch of screen space. This is the resolution you should work at when designing for the web. In Photoshop, when you view an image at '100%', you're seeing it at 72dpi: in other words, each pixel in the image precisely matches one pixel on the screen. Viewing images at a smaller size – say, 50% – entails each pixel on the screen displaying an average of the colour of four pixels in the original document. If you zoom in you can see each pixel with much greater clarity; they will clearly appear as squares.

How colour is displayed depends on the medium on which it appears, and the mechanism that gets it there. On a computer screen, each pixel is a discrete colour. You'll generally work in '8-bit' mode in Photoshop and other imaging applications: this means 2 to the power of 8 (which is 256) shades of each colour. 256 reds x 256 greens x 256 blues = 16,777,216 colours in total.

Commercial printing uses only four basic colours: cyan, magenta, yellow and black. All other colours are simulated by overprinting these four. The bigger the printed dot, the more of that colour is seen; so if in one region there are equal sized cyan and yellow dots, you'll see green. If the cyan dots are twice the size of the yellow, the result will be turquoise. Clearly, these dots need to be tiny if we're not going to notice them; and the smoother the paper, the smaller the dots can be. Newspapers print at around 100dpi; glossy magazines at around 250dpi, occasionally more.

When printing on an inkjet printer, however, the colour is made up from arrays of tiny dots of equal size. The more dots that are

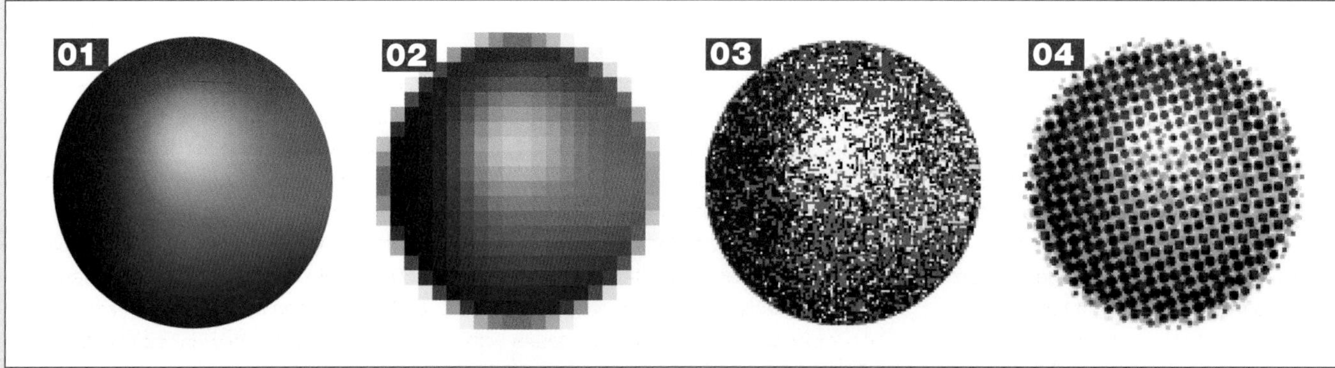

▲ This smooth image of a ball [01] is converted to pixels of discrete colour when shown on a computer monitor [02]. An inkjet printer reproduces the image using a random array of identically sized dots [03]; commercial printing uses dots of different sizes to create it [04].

▲ An image captured with a 3.2 megapixel camera would be large enough to be reproduced at half a page size in a newspaper, or half an A4 page in a glossy magazine; the same image would also fill an Apple 30in Cinema Display.

clustered together, the stronger the density of that colour. Inkjet printers typically print at 1200dpi, which produces a smooth tonal range with a dot that's barely perceptible.

When working for commercial printing, you need to ensure that the number of dots in your document exceeds the number of dots with which the file will be printed by a factor of around 1.5. So when working for a newspaper, creating your image at 150dpi will generally suffice; for glossy magazine printing, working at 375dpi is standard.

Digital cameras capture pixels on a CCD chip: the better the camera, the more pixels on the chip, and so the higher the resolution at which the image can be recorded. If a camera is quoted as having an image size of 3.2 megapixels, it will produce images that measure 2048 pixels wide by 1536 pixels high. Multiplying these values together – the total number of pixels in the image – produces 3,145,728 pixels overall: and that's what the 3.2 megapixel name refers to.

If printed in a newspaper, a 3.2 megapixel camera could produce a high quality image at up to about 10 x 8 inches. The same image in a glossy magazine could be used at up to around half an A4 page; if printed any larger than this, the pixels in the image would be larger than the printed dot size, and we'd start to see ungainly pixellation in the finished result. When shown on a web page, however, the same image would easily fill the entire area of an Apple 30in Cinema Display screen.

A lot of designers are confused when producing work for billboard posters, which may run to 10ft high by 20ft wide. How on earth do we work at a resolution suitable for that huge size? The answer lies in the fact that these posters are generally seen from a distance, and so don't need anything like the resolution required for magazine work. In practice, the posters tend to be printed at less than 25dpi. This means that our 3.2 megapixel image could be printed at nearly 7ft wide on a poster. When creating poster artwork, it's standard practice to work on an A3 sized document at 300dpi, which will create a high enough resolution for good quality results.

The software that accompanies most flatbed scanners tends, confusingly, to offer the ability to adjust both the size and the resolution of scans. In fact, these both amount to the same thing; it's the number of pixels captured in total that counts, not the relative dimensions. The easy solution is to scan an image at the size you're going to want to use it, at a resolution appropriate for the medium on which it's going to end up – in a newspaper, a magazine, or on the screen. Err on the high side: you can always reduce an image's size in Photoshop, but you can't increase it without loss of quality.

The Image Size dialog box has the ability to resample images to any size and resolution you choose, but if you uncheck the 'Resample Image' button, it will adjust the size and resolution together. This is a useful method for turning, say, digital camera captures – which typically have a resolution of 180dpi – into print-ready files with a resolution of 300dpi. When the resulting image is placed on the page, you know you can always reduce or crop it, but you can't expand it without losing quality.

I: Image Stacks

Taking images at a range of exposures with a tripod will capture all the detail you need to compose a perfect image using Image Stacks.

In 1856, pioneering French photographer Gustave le Gray tried to capture the image of a seascape. He realised that the only way to accommodate the different aperture requirements of the bright sky and the dark sea was to take two separate photographs at different exposures and merge the results together in the darkroom. This is the first known instance of the technique that is now referred to as high dynamic range imaging (HDRI, or often just HDR).

In recent years, we've seen a lot of HDR images showing up on Flickr and other photo-sharing sites. They work by combining the best of a range of exposures of the same scene, producing a result that's frequently almost surreal in its hyperrealism: every detail, from the deepest shadow to the brightest highlight, can be rendered with crystal clarity.

Although Photoshop can create HDR images automatically, the process is very hit-and-miss and difficult to control. It requires a rock-steady tripod, a remote firing mechanism that will avoid shaking the camera, and a good deal of luck. HDR composites can only be made from individual files, preferably Raw images, and the built-in auto-alignment feature is rarely up to the task.

However, there's a better solution: Image Stacks. This method takes images at a range of exposures that have been saved as separate layers within a single Photoshop document, and combines them by adding layer masks to produce high-quality results.

▼ One of Gustave le Gray's seascape composites, which used different exposures for the sea and the sky.

The example here shows a view of candles on a piano, with a window behind. As a glance at the original images will show, it's impossible to capture this scene in a single photograph: if we set the exposure to accommodate the bright scene outside the window, the delicate candle light and the reflection of the keys in the piano lid will be lost in shadow. By taking a range of photographs at different exposures, however, we can capture all the detail we need – and then trust Photoshop to put it all together for us.

Taking the initial photographs requires a tripod. Although

▲ **01-05 These five originals all show different areas of the image well, but none of them captures the full essence of the scene. To get all the detail in all the images, you can use Photoshop's Image Stacks. In the final composite image [06], you can see both the detail in the highlights (the view through the window) and in the shadows (the keyboard reflected in the piano lid), while retaining such delicate areas as the candle flames.**

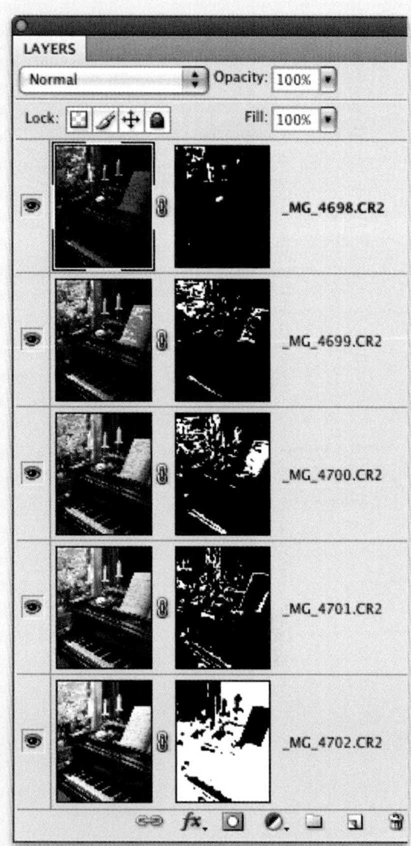

▲ **The Layers panel shows what's going on: what you can see is that each layer has a mask that permits only relevant areas to show through.**

Photoshop's Alignment tool can cope with some slight variation in camera position, the lengthy exposures needed to capture the deepest shadows means hand-held camera work isn't viable.

Many cameras have a setting for 'auto bracketing', in which several images are taken in rapid succession at different exposure settings. This isn't really sufficient for the purposes of this tutorial, as you need to take images with manual variations.

There are two ways of admitting more light into a camera: you can vary the exposure time or the aperture. In this instance, you should vary only the exposure time, as changing the aperture will also change the depth of field, which will introduce a variation in focus between successive images. You want the images to be as similar as possible, with only the brightness changing.

Take at least five images of the scene, ideally a couple more, increasing the shutter speed from very slow (to capture the deepest shadows) to very fast (in order for the highlights not to be blown out). The difference in exposure between images should be roughly equivalent to one or two f-stops.

Open all of the images in Photoshop and drag each one in turn into the same document. If you hold Shift as you drag with the Move tool, the layer will be placed in exactly the same position in the new document, which will make alignment easier later. Although the photographs may all have been taken on a tripod, there's likely still to be some slight variation in position between the captures. Select all the layers in the document, and use Edit > Auto-Align Layers to open the Alignment dialog. This dialog is designed to create panoramic images as well as straightforward alignments, so you could choose Reposition as the alignment method. However, it's possible that some slight rotation will be needed as well, so it's best to pick the Auto method, which will allow Photoshop to use the alignment combination that's most appropriate for the current conditions.

Once this is done, and with all the layers still selected, choose Edit > Auto-Blend Layers. This will open a new dialog, offering the choice between Panorama and Stack Images. Choose the latter, press OK and Photoshop will examine the images, salvaging the best exposure from each one to produce as perfect a composite as possible.

The result is a single image that incorporates the best of all the exposures you started with, resulting in a rich, deep image in which everything in the scene is clearly visible. You can at last capture with the camera what you can see with the naked eye.

Interestingly, Photoshop doesn't simply create a single, merged layer. Instead, it creates Layer Masks for each of the individual exposure layers, allowing only the best areas of each layer to be visible as the rest is masked off. This allows you to see the process in detail, which is interesting in itself. More significantly, it also allows you to correct the automated process, as it means you can edit each layer mask to allow more or less of that specific exposure to show through. In general, though, the results Photoshop comes up with tend to be as good as you need them to be.

You can even simulate this technique using a single Camera Raw image. Photoshop's Raw dialog enables you to create several files using different exposure settings from a single original. To achieve this, choose Open as Smart Object from the File menu, which will enable you to open the Raw file and continue to modify it within Photoshop. Create a Merged Copy each time by using Select All, Edit > Copy Merged, and Edit > Paste. After creating separate layers that accentuate the highlights, midtones and shadows, run the Image Stack process as before.

I: Isometric projection

Understanding isometric projection is key to creating 3D environments with less stress as well as giving your images greater depth.

Isometric projection is a form of false perspective drawing in which objects remain the same size as they recede into the distance. Initially devised by technical draughtsmen, the technique has been put to good use in computer games and, more recently, in the computer drawing style known as Pixel Art.

Isometric drawings are always viewed from the same angle: rather than seeing any object or scene head-on, we're always looking at a corner. In this view, the Y axis is truly vertical, while the X and Z axes go off in different directions at an angle of 60° to the horizontal. Unlike in true perspective drawing, objects drawn along the X and Z axis are not scaled down – all the measurements, in each of the three axes, remain in exactly the same scale.

This lack of perspective scale means that isometric projection is ideally suited to creating technical drawings, since all the elements can be shown clearly and at a comparable size. The fact that the scale doesn't reduce further back into the image, and that the scale is identical on all three axes, also means that we can measure components directly from a diagram. In some cases, components can be shown at actual size for ease of reference – Lego instruction manuals, for example, frequently use this technique.

Early computer games used isometric projection, including adventure and strategy games such as Q*bert (1982) and Populous (1989). In these games, moving characters were not 3D models, but animated sprites – sequences of drawings which, when cycled, gave the impression of motion. Because there's no distance scaling, isometric projection enabled the designers to have the sprites running all over the arena in apparent 3D, with no need to make them appear smaller in the distance.

The most notable isometric computer game is SimCity. When it first appeared in 1989 it used a top-down view, as if looking at a plan of the city. While the gameplay may have been good, the look was poor; the release of SimCity 2000 four years later jumped to the isometric perspective that was to become a trademark of the game's appearance. The lack of true perspective meant that players could see their entire city at a glance, and (more significantly) meant that the impression of 3D could be given with minimal computing power.

In 1998, a group of artists founded the Pixel Art group eBoy (*eboy.com*), which specialises in isometric pixel-based artwork. The group's commitment to producing individual components that can then be repurposed has enabled them to build vast, complex city scenes – the isometric projection means that items can be positioned anywhere within the scene without looking out of scale.

Drawing in isometric projection requires that you're zoomed in to a magnified view in Photoshop, since you're placing lines and dots at the pixel level. You also need to modify the tools that you use. Anti-aliasing, the technique that produces smooth edges in selections, needs to be turned off for the lasso and the marquee tools; while the Brush tool and Eraser tools need to be set to Pencil and Block mode respectively, to create hard-edged, pixel perfect drawings.

It's easy enough to draw lines in the Y axis (straight up), since these are pure verticals. When drawing horizontal lines in the X and Z axes, you need to adopt a stepping technique. If you placed your pixels corner to corner, the result would be a 45° line. But you need 60°, so your lines must be made of two pixels across and one up.

The simplest way to draw X and Z axis horizontal lines is by selecting a single pixel,

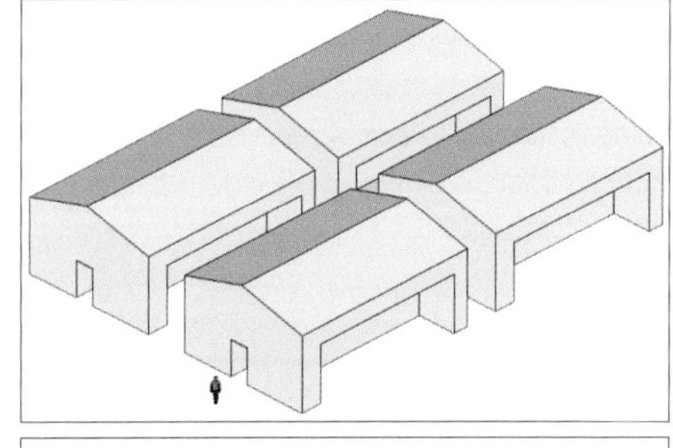

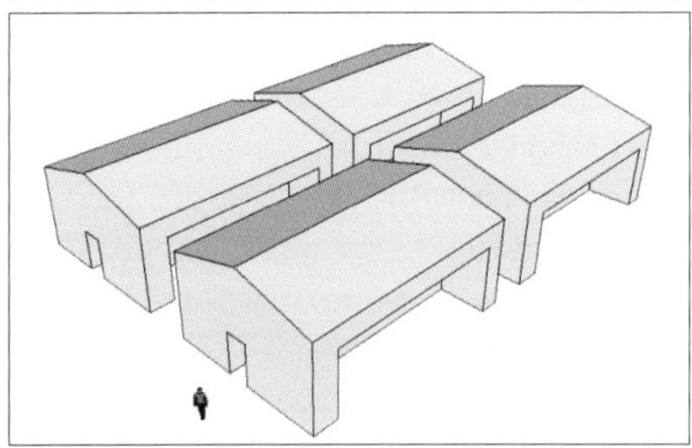

▲ **Two views, both of which have been drawn in Google SketchUp. The first example (top) shows isometric projection, in which objects remain the same size as they recede into the background; the second is the same view with true perspective.**

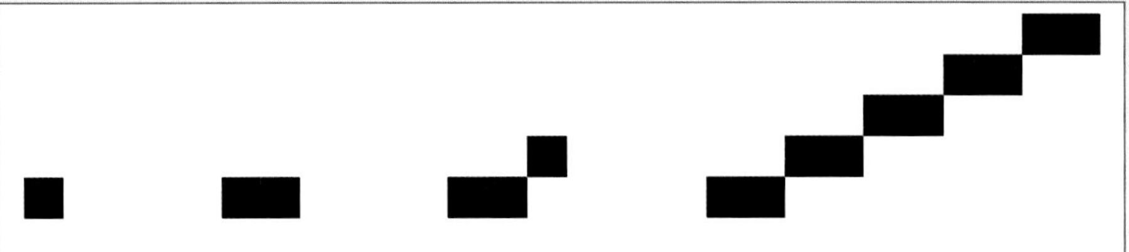

▲ **The 'stepping' technique used to draw 60° lines in Photoshop. Select a single pixel, and copy it one step to the right; then nudge a copy right and up one square. Repeat to make a 60° line.**

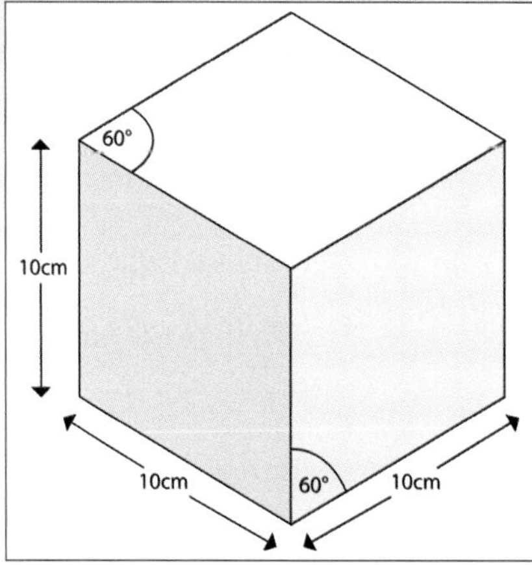

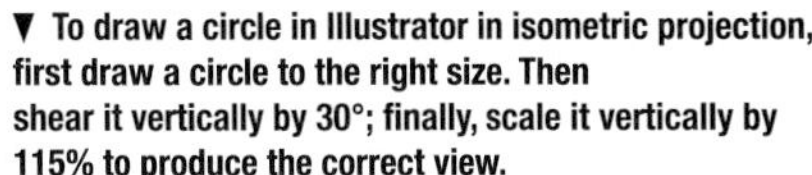

▼ **To draw a circle in Illustrator in isometric projection, first draw a circle to the right size. Then shear it vertically by 30°; finally, scale it vertically by 115% to produce the correct view.**

► **In isometric projection, measurements are the same along all axes – they don't reduce in proportion when viewed at an angle. This is a fundamental part of isometric drawing.**

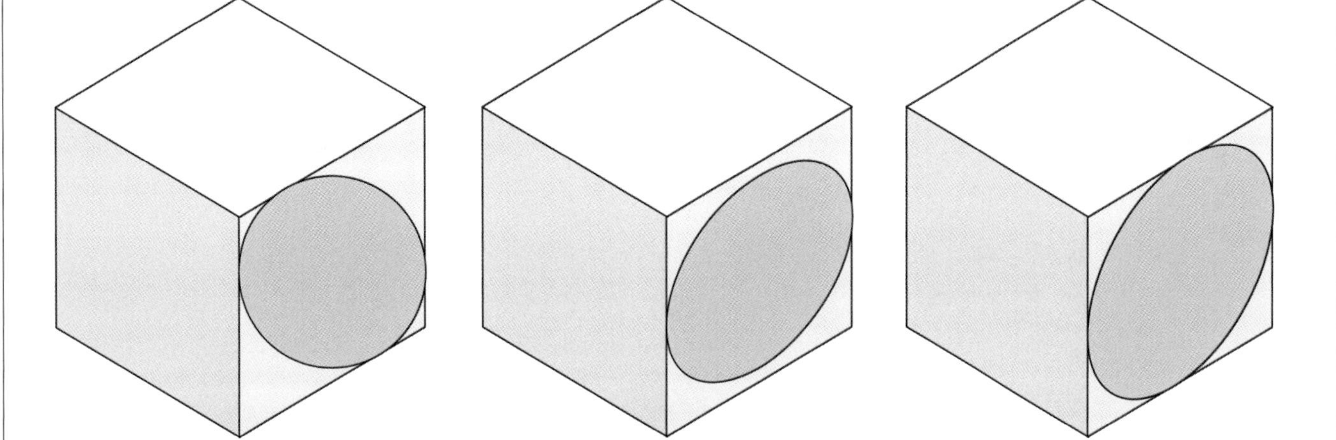

▲ **SimCity 2000 uses perhaps the most well-known implementation of isometric projection. Buildings in the distance are drawn at the same scale as buildings close to us, so greatly easing the processing power required.**

and using the cursor keys to create the sequence. The top-left figure shows how you would draw a line in the X axis – one that goes up and to the right. With a single pixel selected, switch to the Move tool and then hold the Alt key and nudge the selected pixel one square to the right. Repeat this procedure to nudge it one pixel further to the right, then release the Alt key, and nudge this pixel up one square. If you don't release the Alt key in this step, you would create an L-shaped array rather than the stepping effect we want. Although vertical and horizontal lines are simple once you get the hang of the stepping action, drawing lines at other angles is much more difficult. In particular, drawing circles in this projection requires mathematical precision.

When creating technical diagrams, you can use Illustrator for more control. Because you're not working in a pixel based environment, you don't need to concern yourself with the stepping technique described above; but you do need to ensure you draw at that important 60° angle. If you turn on Smart Guides, you can show these angles when you drag over a corresponding object or point in the diagram, which makes the process very much easier.

In addition, creating circles and squares is a very simple procedure – you can draw them head-on, then skew them upwards by 30° to create the perspective view. (Isometric drawing uses 60° from the vertical, which is 30° from the horizontal.) But this isn't yet right – you need to scale the object vertically by 115%, to account for the fact that measurements are taken along the diagonal – 115 is one divided by the sine of 30°. This technique can also be applied to hexagons, triangles and any other shape that need to be drawn in perspective.

Isometric projection has a highly stylised, distinctive appearance that's instantly recognisable. This, coupled with the fact that the approach makes it easy to repurpose drawing elements and move them around freely, makes it a compelling visual form. ⊗

J: Jargon

Use the right vocabulary when talking to a professional printer and you'll not only gain their respect – you might even bag yourself a discount.

At some point, every print designer will have to negotiate with commercial printers. It all starts innocuously enough, with the printer asking for details of the job in order for them to come up with a quote. It seems like a reasonable enough procedure: they have to know what you want so they can tell you how much it will cost.

But what might seem like a routine enquiry is actually a subtle character assessment. Printers, like plumbers' merchants, have evolved an arcane and specific vocabulary that's used to test your professionalism and competence. Most will begin by assuming that you're a complete novice, and so will inflate the quotation to cope with the work they'll have to do to rectify each of the problems they expect will crop up.

Every word of jargon you use when specifying the job will knock a couple of per cent off the quotation, as it's the language you use that reassures the printer of your competence. Learn the jargon and your printer will treat you like a professional – which means a better price for the job.

TRIM AND BLEED

If any part of your design extends to the edge of the page, then the artwork will need to 'bleed off'. This means that when you create the artwork, the images or background colour must extend by up to 5mm off the edge of the page. This is to allow for slight inaccuracies in the 'trimming' process: the job will be printed on oversized paper, and then cut down to the size you've specified.

A useful trick here is to ask the printer if a 3mm bleed is okay. This reinforces the fact that you know what you're talking about, while simultaneously challenging the printer's professionalism: you're asking him if he can ensure the accuracy of his trimming. He'll say yes, of course, and will then have to treat the job with more care and respect. If no elements appear within, say, a centimeter of the edge of the paper, you can specify 'no trim' to the printer, which will reduce costs, since they won't have to cut the paper after the job is printed.

FOLDING AND STITCHING

If your print job consists of more than four pages, it will need to be stapled. Don't ask for this by name, though. Staplers are stationery machines used by secretaries in offices. Instead, ask for the job to be 'wire stitched'. In most cases, the printed publication will be placed in a machine that folds it right down the middle, and staples it at the same time. This is called having it 'saddle stitched' [**01**] and is a good thing to ask for.

You could check that there's no additional charge for 'gathering' – putting the pages in order before they're saddle stitched. Books, too thick for a single staple, are perfect bound. If you're designing a single-sheet leaflet that's folded in half, ask for 'A4 folded to A5' – if those are the sizes you're using. If it's folded in three, ask for it to be either 'z-folded' or 'gatefolded' [**02** and **03**].

PAPER WEIGHT AND TYPE

One of the hardest decisions to make is the thickness and quality of the paper to be used. For starters, call it 'stock' instead of paper. There are several types, including 'matte', which is similar to standard typing paper; and 'art', which is a higher-quality paper that can come in either 'matte' or 'gloss' varieties.

To really show that you mean business, ask for a quote for 'blade coated'. This is a high-quality paper that has a slight sheen to

it. Ask to see a sample and scrape the back of your thumbnail across it: this will reveal a shiny track where you scrape, and shows that you mean business. Paper thickness is specified by its weight in gsm (grams per square metre), but never ask for this by name. Instead, refer to it as 'grams'.

For magazines, '80 gram' is a common weight, while for a standalone, folded leaflet, you'll need to go up to at least '150 gram' to avoid it looking too flimsy. If your paper is too thin, you might get 'show through', where the ink on one side can be seen from the other.

HEAVIER WEIGHTS

Once paper becomes thick enough to be used for a business card or greetings card, it's referred to as 'board'. Ask for '300 gram board' as a typical weight for a card. For greetings cards, if you want a shiny front but a matte inside (so you can write in it more easily), ask for 'single-sided gloss art'.

Magazines and brochures generally use a thicker paper for the cover, which needs to be specified separately. If your publication uses the same paper for the cover as for the inside, ask for 'self cover'.

COLOUR INKS

Printers will automatically assume that you'll want black as one of the ink colours in your job. Remember that if a job is in black and white, that's only one colour – the white is there already. Black-and-white print jobs are referred to as 'mono'. For standard four-colour printing using cyan, magenta, yellow and black, ask for 'CMYK'. These are known as 'process' colours.

If you want additional colours – for example where a company logo has to be a specific shade – ask for it by a Pantone name. All of the major design applications will show you an approximation of Pantone colours. These are referred to as 'specials' or 'spot' colours.

Sometimes you'll want a job that's printed in four colours on one side and black only on the other side. This is referred to as 'four back one'. If you want to see the job in colour before it's printed, ask for a 'cromalin' – a glossy proof. For long run jobs, you can ask for a 'pull proof', which is a sample from the actual press on the actual paper to be used, although this can be costly.

SPECIAL EFFECTS

A design printed on the cover in gold leaf is known as 'blocking' [**04**]. Fancy letterheads use 'thermographic' inks for raised text [**05**], while a raised section of text or illustration with no ink is called 'blind embossing' [**06**].

There are several ways to add selective gloss to a cover. Generally, the process is referred to as 'spot varnish', and you should supply your artwork to the printer with a separate channel detailing where the varnish goes. If you want a high gloss over the whole cover – for a cookery book, so its surface can easily be wiped clean – ask for a 'gloss laminate' for a plastic covering, or a 'UV varnish' for a less-durable version.

LONG AND SHORT RUNS

For runs of up to a couple of thousand copies, you'll want a 'sheet fed' press – one in which the paper is fed in one piece at a time. For lower runs, a 'digital print' is like a glorified inkjet printer. For longer runs, such as commercial magazines, you'll be looking at 'web offset', a high-speed process better suited to volume printing.

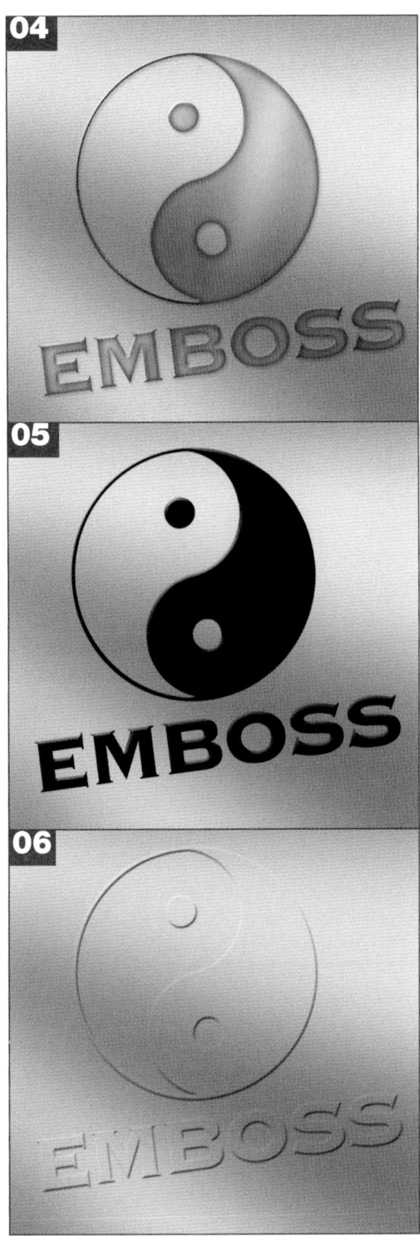

▲ **Simulations of gold blocking, blind embossing and thermographic printing.**

J: Joining and splitting paths in Illustrator

Paths are your most valuable resource in Illustrator, so a good understanding of how to control their length, size and scope is important to getting the results you want.

Ask an adult to build a model railway layout and they'll always join the tracks in a loop so the train can go round and round. Ask a child to do the same thing and they'll make the track as long as possible, stretching from one end of the room to the other. The adult will argue that the child has done it wrong, but the child knows better: after all, this is how train tracks are constructed in real life.

Paths in Illustrator work along a similar principle. They can be closed or open – that is, the start and end can meet at the same point, so that the path forms a continuous loop, or the two can remain separate, leaving start and end points unjoined. Paths have two components: fill (the colour, pattern or gradient within the object) and stroke (the stroke is the colour, texture or gradient around the edge).

When applied to an open path, a stroke will run along it like a train, starting at the beginning and finishing at the end. If we apply a fill to an open path, however, the two end points will be joined by a straight line at the edge of the fill.

The problem mainly arises when you draw an object using multiple paths. It all looks fine until you apply the fill, after which you see that each path is filled from its starting point to its end point, creating a horrible mess of triangular portions that destroy the effect. To fix the problem, you need to join the paths so that the fill goes where you want it, rather than between arbitrary end points.

While you're drawing a path, whether it's in Illustrator, Photoshop or InDesign, closing it is simply a matter of moving the cursor over the starting point. The cursor icon will change from the regular pen icon to display a tiny circle at the bottom right, indicating that you're about to join the start and end together.

If you want to close an existing path, you can join the two end points automatically in one of two ways. You can use the Direct Selection tool to select both end points, and then choose Object > Path > Join (the shortcut is Command-J). This will draw a straight line between the two end points.

However, it's easy to miss the two points when selecting with this tool. You might select another point as well by accident, or select a point from a different path that happens to be nearby, or select a segment of the path rather than an end. In the latter case, you'll get the following warning message:

'To join, you must select the two open endpoints. If they are not on the same path, they cannot be on text paths nor inside graphs, and if both of them are grouped, they must be in the same group.'

It's not a message that's going to win any awards for clarity. It's also one that Illustrator users get sick of seeing, as it pops up

▼ **The stroke around a path follows the line of the path like a train on a track. But the fill will always join in a straight line between the end points.**

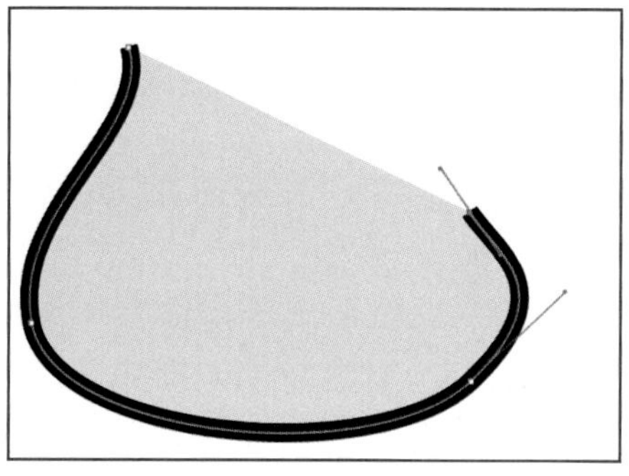

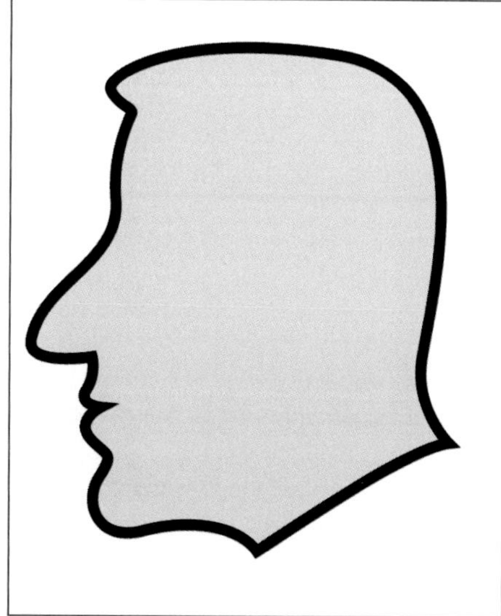

▲ **This outline shows a head in profile that's been filled with a flat colour, and stroked with a simple stroke. However, we want to make it a bit more interesting.**

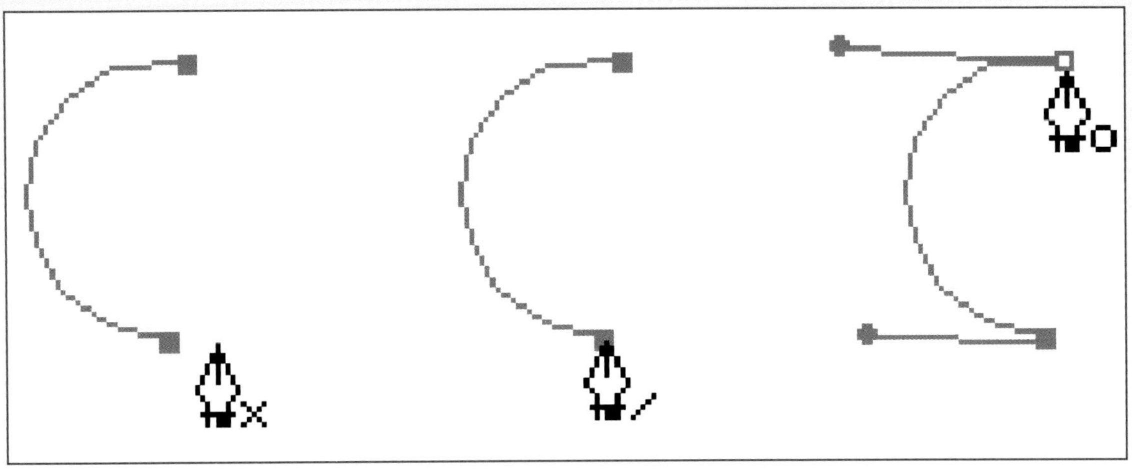

◄ **The Pen tool cursor changes to show how it will draw. An X in the corner indicates starting a new path (left). A / in the corner indicates joining an existing path (centre). When it displays an O, it shows you're about to close an open path.**

each time they inadvertently click close to an existing point.

An alternative way of closing a path is to click on it with the regular (filled) Selection Tool, or to Alt-click with the Direct Selection Tool so that the whole path is selected. Now, when you press Command-J, the two end points will be joined automatically.

The problem with the two previous methods is that the end points are always joined with a straight line. You can also join them manually using the Pen tool, and visual feedback again shows you how the tool will behave.

When you're about to start a new path, the Pen tool cursor displays a tiny X in the corner. If you're hovering over the end point of an existing path, the cursor shows a slash (/) instead of an X, indicating that you're about to continue from the current endpoint of this path rather than starting a new one. After clicking on one end point, you can hover over the other one until the cursor changes to show the closing circle. At that point you know that clicking now will close the path.

When you click on the first end point, though, the path will mirror any Bézier curve on the other side of that point. To cut the curve short and draw a straight line, Alt-click on that end point. You can also click and drag to start a new curve, so creating a corner point at the old one.

Although it's generally best to draw individual objects as a single, continuous path, there are times when you need to split the path into multiple segments. If you're applying a naturalistic Art Brush stroke, for example, you'll get better results if the path is in short segments.

However, splitting the original path will also cause the fills to go haywire. The solution to this problem is to duplicate the path first, and then remove the stroke from the first and the fill from the second. You can now split the copy of the path – the one that only holds the stroke – while leaving the filled version intact. You can split paths by clicking on them with the Scissors tool (the shortcut is to hit the C key). Unless a custom stroke is applied, you generally won't see any difference when you do so, but by selecting one of the new anchor points, you'll see it can be moved independently.

You can split a path either along a segment or at an end point. Splitting at an end point can be tricky, as it's easy to hit the end point of an existing path by accident, in which case you'll see the second infuriating Illustrator message: 'Please use the scissors on an segment or an anchor point (but not an endpoint) of a path.'

Again, this is a dialog box Illustrator users see far too often. It may help to nudge the object out of the way using the cursor keys first, so that the point at which you cut is free from obstruction.

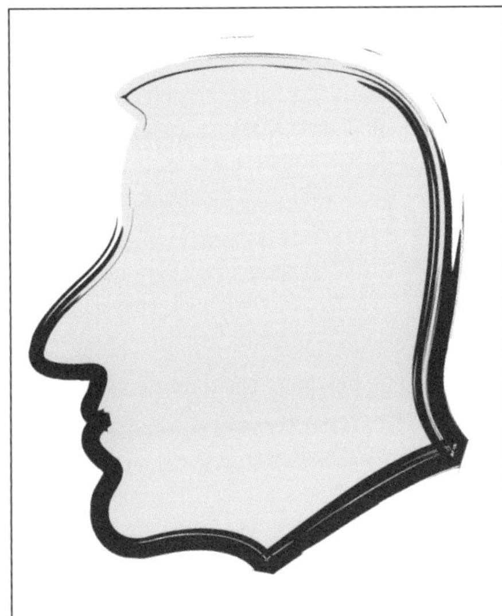

▲ **When you apply an Art Brush style, the brush stroke runs all the way around the path. It would be better if the path was in several segments.**

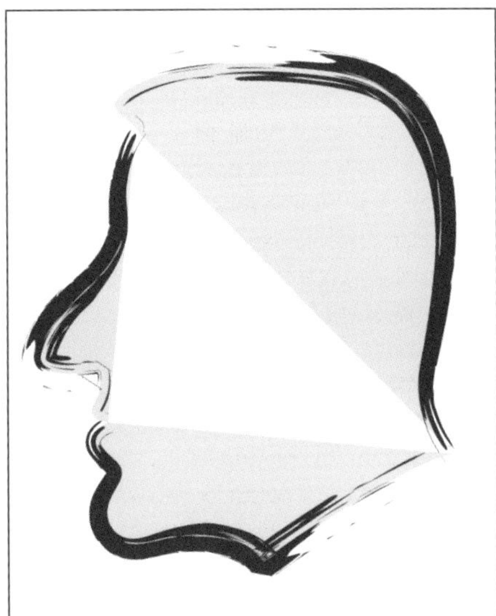

▲ **Cutting the path to make the stroke work better results in the end points of each segment being joined by the fill – an ugly result.**

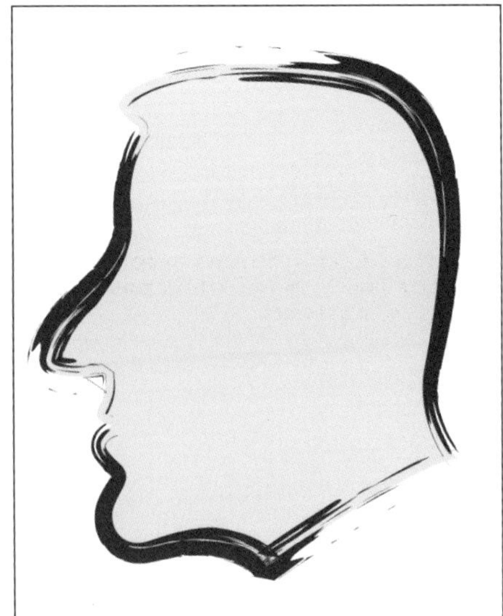

▲ **The answer is to duplicate the object. Use the whole version, with a fill and no stroke, in the back; place a version with stroke and no fill on top; and cut to suit.**

J: Jpeg

The most popular format in digital cameras needs careful handling if you aren't going to end up with noisy pictures lacking detail.

Jpeg (pronounced jay-peg) stands for Joint Photographic Experts Group, the name of the committee that originally devised the standard. Even the abbreviation is questionable: Jpeg is one character too long to be a PC file extension, so it's frequently shortened to JPG.

The Jpeg format has the distinct advantage of being able to reduce the size of image files by a significant amount. This makes it ideal for preparing images to be viewed on websites, as they can be delivered in a fraction of the time. It's also common practice to save files as Jpegs for archiving; most image libraries, both online and on CD, deliver their files in Jpeg format.

Jpeg compression is a 'lossy' format, which means that the more an image is compressed, the more degraded it becomes. At high-quality settings, this degradation is imperceptible to the eye, but the resulting file sizes are larger. Achieving smaller sizes involves a trade-off between speed of delivery (smaller file size) and image quality.

Digital cameras routinely save files as Jpegs to memory cards, which increases the number of images that can be stored. Most cameras offer a choice of compression ratios. Again, the larger the file size, the better the image quality. At first glance, you would be hard pressed to notice the difference between different compression standards on a digital camera. However, when the image is adjusted in Photoshop, the compression will become more evident.

Operations such as brightening shadows will tend to reveal ugly blocking in the image. For this reason, many professional photographers choose to save their images in either Tiff or Raw format, both of which use lossless compression when saving. The downside, of course, is that far fewer images can fit on a memory card this way.

HOW JPEG COMPRESSION WORKS

The human eye is good at seeing differences in brightness over a large area and at recognising transitions between areas of different contrast. However, it's not so good at spotting minor variations in colour or high-frequency brightness. It's this limitation that Jpeg files exploit by separating the brightness and colour components of the image. It then examines images for areas of fine and coarse detail: fine detail, too small to be seen easily with the naked eye, is discarded. At high-quality settings, we don't notice the difference, but since it's fine detail that increases file sizes more than anything else, losing just a small amount of this detail greatly reduces the size.

When a file is saved in Jpeg format, several processes ensue. The file is divided into blocks of 8 x 8 pixels, and a series of algorithms is used to reduce the fine detail to a degree determined by the amount of compression specified in the Jpeg quality value. An RGB file is interpreted in the YCC colour space, separating the luminosity from the colour component so that the colour can be compressed more than the brightness. Further processes involve quantizing the spatial frequency matrix and other complex mathematical procedures. It's all far too complex to go into here, but, rest assured, you really don't need to know about this side of things.

JPEG COMPRESSION IN PRACTICE

The standard way of saving a Jpeg file from Photoshop is to choose Jpeg from the pop-up menu in the Save As dialog. Choosing an image quality of 10 or higher (the maximum is 12) will produce files that are small in size, but that show no apparent damage. Files saved at this quality will be good enough for high-end print purposes. When saving for web delivery, file size is of paramount importance. So rather than choosing Save As, instead use the Save for Web dialog. This opens a new window that shows the result of saving the image with the quality setting you choose, together with an indication of the resulting file size. This way, it's possible to see the trade-off between file size and image quality clearly – you can even choose to view multiple versions of your image with different Jpeg quality settings so you can visually compare the results.

While saving an image as a Jpeg file will produce imperceptible loss of quality at high settings, repeated saving of the same file will build up the degradation over time. Therefore, if you have an image you're working on repeatedly, it's best practice to save it as a lossless native Photoshop file until you're sure you've finished editing it, and only then save it as a Jpeg.

TAKING JPEGS FURTHER

Saved at maximum quality, Jpeg files are an economical way of storing images. The standard Jpeg file format can include clipping paths, so cutout data can be stored within the file for later retrieval. A bonus for Photoshop users is that 3D grids set up in the Vanishing Point filter are also stored within the file when it's saved.

Jpegs can't hold multiple layers or additional channels the way that Tiff images can. But there's a second Jpeg format, called Jpeg 2000, which uses wavelet compression for less lossy results. It's also capable of containing alpha channels for storing soft-edged and semi-transparent selections. This format must be loaded and saved using a separate plug-in in Photoshop; as of Photoshop CS3, it's built into the Save As dialog. The only problem here is that, at present, Jpeg 2000 isn't supported by web browsers, so it's a format that can be used for archive only, rather than Internet delivery. In rare circumstances, you might want a Jpeg file that's more compressed in some areas than others. For example, if you're preparing an image that you're going to zoom into using After Effects, loss of detail around the edge is unimportant, while high detail in the centre is vital. This is achieved by creating a new channel in the original document and painting on it in white where the image is required at high quality, leaving it black elsewhere. Then, choosing Save for Web in Photoshop, click the Channel Mask icon next to the Quality setting to load that channel. In the resulting dialog, you can set the maximum and minimum quality settings for the image. ⊗

▲ **Our original image (top left), greatly magnified, shows a lot of detail on this Christmas tree. Even at a high-quality Jpeg setting (top right), some fine detail is clearly lost in the leaves and ornaments. At a low setting (bottom left), we can start to see the 8 x 8 pixel blocks the Jpeg algorithm uses for compressing the image. At the lowest quality (bottom right) these blocks overpower the image.**

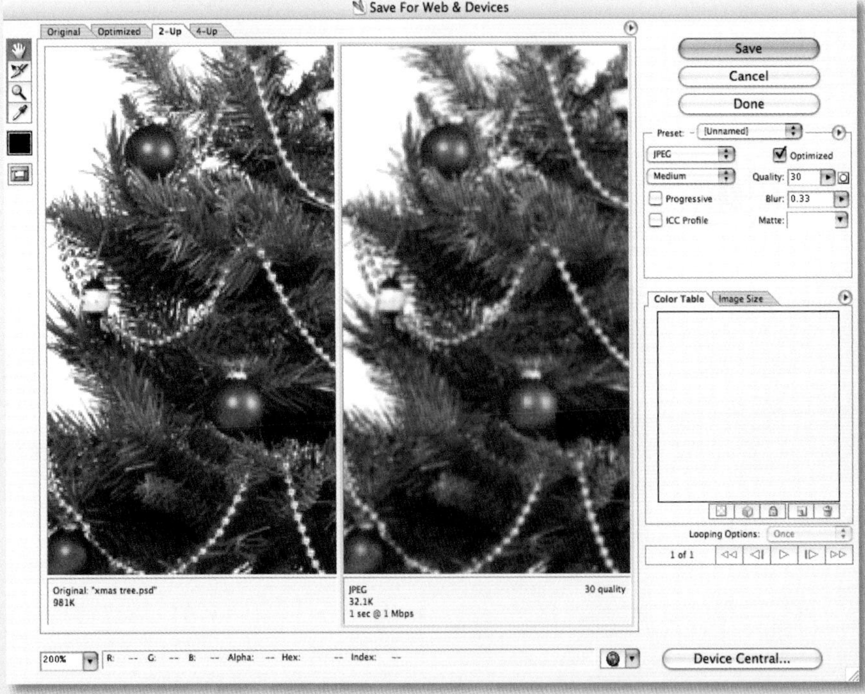

▲ **Photoshop's Save for Web dialog enables you to compare different Jpeg quality settings: it also shows you the resulting file size for the settings you choose.**

K: Kerning and tracking

Do you know your kerning from your tracking? Our guide to these two essential concepts will help you produce beautifully typeset text.

Kerning and tracking are typographical terms used to describe the process of adding or removing space between letters. Although they're often confused, the terms refer to different aspects of space adjustment: tracking, often called 'letter-spacing' in traditional typography, refers to the wholesale adding or removing of space to a whole group of letters, whereas kerning denotes closing up space between a single pair of characters in order to make them fit together better.

Both kerning and tracking are controlled using the Character palette in Photoshop, Illustrator and InDesign. Of more use are the keyboard shortcuts: place the cursor between a pair of characters and use Alt and the left and right cursor keys to reduce or add space between them, changing the kerning value; select the whole word and use the same keys to adjust the tracking amount.

WATER

▲ When each letter occupies its own vertical space, we get ugly gaps between certain pairs due to the letter shapes.

WATER

▲ We can kern these letters to tighten them up, but bringing them too close together produces a different ugliness.

WATER

▲ To give characters room to breathe, aim for roughly equal amounts of white space between each one.

KERNING

In the days when type was assembled as individual wooden or metal blocks, each character was embossed on a rectangular block so they could be pressed together by the compositor. When certain pairs of letters were put together – W and A, for example – an unnatural amount of space appeared between the two, due to the shapes of the letters themselves. And so the compositors took to 'kerning' or 'cornering' the type blocks, which meant cutting off corners at an angle so they could be placed more closely.

In modern typography, the designer will create 'kerning pairs' as part of the definition of the font. For each tricky pair of letters, a value will be assigned to be added to the space between them; this is usually a negative value, of course, since space is removed rather than added. For example, in Helvetica the letter pair 'VA' has a kerning value of -80, so that the space between them is closed up. For some pairs, such as 'ry', a positive value is used in order to increase the space. The existence of kerning pairs is one of the key factors that distinguishes commercial fonts from their free or cheaper equivalents.

OpenType fonts support 'kerning classes', in which pairs of letter types are defined to have a set negative kerning. So W and V, for instance, would always have the same negative kerning when followed by a, e, o or u, but not i (because of the dot on the letter).

In practice, we tend to let our graphics applications take care of most of the letter spacing for us. However, when setting major text elements, such as cover headlines and

Headlines style sheet

▲ Because this text is optimised for body copy, the spacing is far too wide when used for headlines.

Headlines style sheet

▲ We can apply negative tracking to tighten up all the letter spacing. But some character pairs still look clumsy.

Headlines style sheet

▲ For important headlines, kerning character pairs by eye is the only way to produce an attractive result.

When setting text, particularly in the rushed environment such of a newspaper office, editing copy to make lines fit is time consuming. One solution is for us to adjust the tracking instead.

▲ Standard tracking is applied to this paragraph, but it's one line too long for the space we have available.

When setting text, particularly in the rushed environment such of a newspaper office, editing copy to make lines fit is time consuming. One solution is for us to adjust the tracking instead.

▲ Applying negative tracking to the last line tightens it up enough to pull that stray word back a line.

mastheads, a good designer will always adjust the kerning.

The aim of kerning by hand isn't to make the letters fit as tightly as possible, since this produces an ugly result; the idea is that we should arrange the type so that there's a roughly equal amount of white space held in the gaps between each pair of letters.

TRACKING

When fonts are designed, the letter spacing will be set within the definition of each character. In the days of hand-set typography, type was available at set sizes. Today, we have the ability to set type in any size we want. This causes problems for the type designer, who needs to ensure that type is legible both at body text sizes (typically, 7–10pt) and at headline sizes (48pt or higher). In order to maintain legibility at small sizes, tracking is kept loose – that is, there's a fair amount of space between characters so that we can distinguish them clearly.

When we blow up these to headline size, the extra space looks awkward. It's common practice when defining style sheets for page layout applications to build negative tracking into headline styles: that is, headlines are tightened up to remove space between letters. This has two advantages: first, the headline will look better on the page with tighter spacing; and second, the tighter the spacing, the larger the headline can be set. A standard rule of thumb is 'close but not touching'– that is, tracking should be adjusted so that the characters are as close as they can be without physically interfering with each other.

Tracking can also be adjusted on an ad-hoc basis when the need arises. It's a technique commonly used in newspaper production, when tight deadlines mean there often isn't time to edit text: a little negative tracking can often pull a paragraph together so it's one line shorter, and positive tracking can make a short paragraph fill out an extra line. Usually, these adjustments are so slight as to be virtually imperceptible, and will certainly go unnoticed by the vast majority of readers.

We can add large amounts of tracking to page elements for special effects, to turn type into a graphic element – as seen in the examples (right). When we do this, however, the tracking will affect all of the characters, including the final one; this will add unwanted space at the end of the line. It's better to select all except the final character for a more consistent effect. We can also tighten tracking greatly for a bunched-up, contemporary typographic appearance.

tight spacing

tight spacing

▲ We can tighten up tracking considerably for dramatic special effects. However, it's important to make sure that the words are still legible: some manual adjustment is usually required.

A typographic feature that's been appearing in movie credits recently is to expand tracking as type is increased in size. This gives the impression of the type splitting apart as it comes towards us. It's a relatively easy technique to achieve in Premiere, Final Cut and After Effects, but isn't yet possible in iMovie.

K: Key commands 1

Save time and effort by switching from the mouse and menus to your keyboard. Learn a few shortcuts and you'll be racing through your work.

Efficiency in Photoshop is all about economical use of your time. The less time you spend dragging the cursor between menus, palettes and tool bars, the more time you will have to concentrate on your work. There's only one real solution to this: mastering Photoshop's keyboard shortcuts. Here are some of the essentials.

TOOL SHORTCUTS

Many of the shortcuts for switching tools are intuitive: B for Brush, M for Marquee, L for Lasso, P for Pen, E for Eraser, I for the Eyedropper, G for Gradient, W for the Magic Wand. But you'll need to learn R for Smudge, Blur and Sharpen, O for Dodge and Burn, U for Shapes and V for Move.

Several of these tools have variants, and you can cycle through them by holding Shift as you press the keystroke for that tool: Shift-R, for example, will switch between Smudge, Blur and Sharpen. There's also a useful shortcut with the Dodge and Burn tools, since you frequently want to use them in combination with each other: holding Alt when either tool is selected will give you temporary access to the other one.

This notion of temporary access also applies to the Move tool: holding the Command key when any other tool is active will allow you to grab and move layers without having to switch tools. But you'll have to switch to the Move tool if you want to use it to select multiple layers (holding Shift as you click on them), or to 'drill down' to select any layer beneath the cursor (holding Control as you click, to get a pop-up menu showing all the layers).

When using any of the painting tools – the Brush, Dodge and Burn, Smudge and so on – you can change the pressure of the tool with the numeric keypad: press 3 for 30%, 5 for 50% and so on, up to 0 for 100%. You can also get intermediate values by pressing two keys in rapid succession: pressing 4 then 5 will give you 45%, for instance. When the Move tool or one of the selection tools are active, pressing these keys will change the opacity of the current layer.

With selection tools, use keyboard controls to set how the selections are drawn. So with the Marquee, hold Alt after you start to drag a selection to draw from the centre out, rather than corner to corner; hold Shift to constrain a rectangle to a square, and an ellipse to a circle. If you hold modifier keys before beginning to draw selections, you produce different behaviours. Holding Shift will add to an existing selection, and holding Alt will subtract from it; holding both Shift and Alt will produce an intersection of the old and new selections.

When painting with the Brush tool, holding Shift will constrain the movement to vertical and

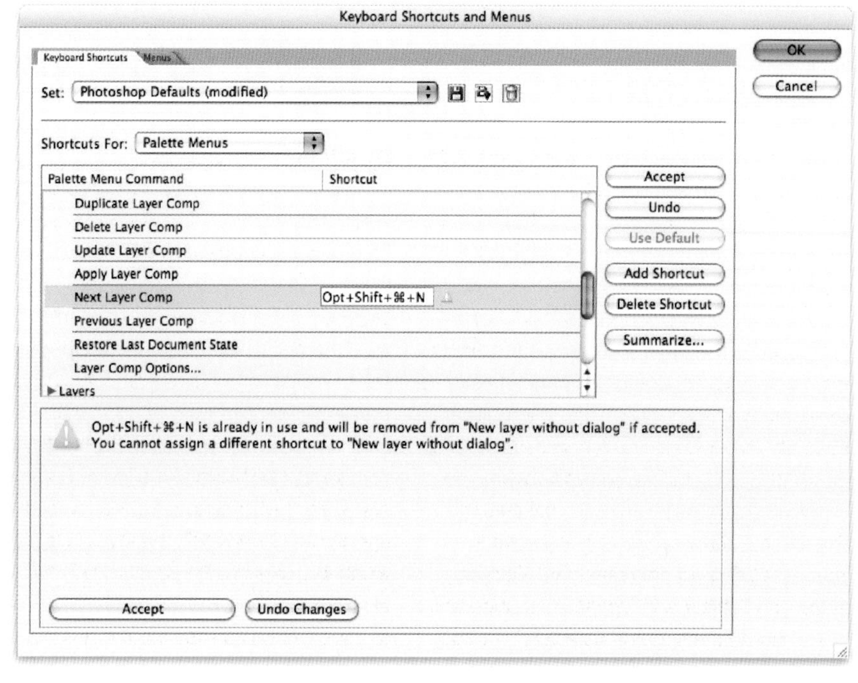

◄ **If you try to define a keyboard shortcut that's already in use, Photoshop will warn you of any possible conflicts.**

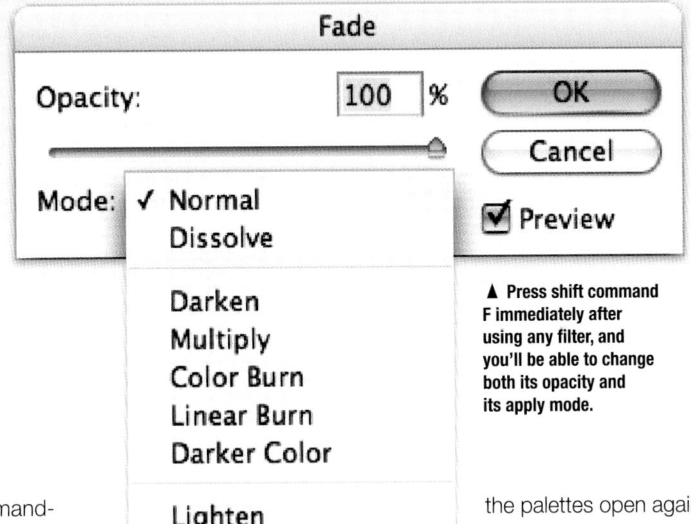

▲ Press shift command F immediately after using any filter, and you'll be able to change both its opacity and its apply mode.

horizontal. If you press Shift before painting, it will paint a straight line between the two click points. Pressing the control key with any tool will pop up a contextual menu relevant to that tool; with the Brush tool, control pops up a Brushes palette, and pressing Shift-Ctrl will pop up a menu allowing you to change brush mode.

WORKING WITH TEXT

Pressing T will switch to the Text tool. To change the font of a whole text block, don't click in it: with the text tool active, press the Return key, which takes you to the Font field in the Options bar. Here you can select a font by typing the first few characters of its name; press the up/down cursor keys to select the next and previous font. Pressing Tab will take you to the next field, where you can use the same technique to choose the weight – generally B for Bold, I for Italic, and so on. To change text size, select it and use Shift-Command with the > and < keys to make it bigger and smaller.

WORKING WITH LAYERS

Use Shift with the [and] keys to select lower and higher layers in the stack; use Command with these keys to move the layers up and down. Holding Command as you click on a layers thumbnail in the Layers palette will load up its pixels as a selection.

There are several shortcuts for changing layer modes, mostly intuitive. Hold Command and Shift and press H for Hard Light, M for Multiply, S for Screen, N for Normal. You can also cycle through all the layer modes by pressing Command-Shift + and -. With a selection active, Command-C will copy the contents of the current layer. Using Command-Shift-C, however, will copy a merged selection of all visible layers. And while Command-V will paste a clipboard selection, Command-Shift-V will paste it inside any active selection, creating a layer mask.

Use Command-Shift-N to make a new, empty layer. If you have a selection active, Command-J will copy that selection to a new layer; hold Command-Shift-J to cut the selection to a new layer. Hold Alt as well and a dialog will pop up, allowing you to give the layer a name.

OTHER SHORTCUTS

QuickMask, that useful selection mode, is easily accessed by pressing Q. Since you frequently need to switch between black and white here, you can press X to swap background and foreground colours – and press D to set them to their default black and white.

Holding different modifier keys can alter the behaviour of well known shortcuts. You probably know that Command-T will launch Free Transform mode; you may not be aware that pressing Shift-Command-T will repeat the last-used transformation, while Command-Alt-Shift-T will repeat it and duplicate the layer or selection upon which it was applied.

Pressing Tab will hide all the palettes in Photoshop, allowing you to see just your image. In CS3, you can press Shift-Tab to hide all but the Toolbar and Options bar; and sliding the cursor to the edge of the screen will pop the palettes open again. Pressing F will cycle through different backgrounds outside your image, isolating them from other images and applications.

When choosing any adjustment, holding the Alt key will launch the previously-used settings. So Alt-Command-M, for instance, will open the Curves dialog with the last settings intact. Similarly, while Command-F will repeat the last filter, Alt-Command-F will open its dialog with the last used settings. After using any filter you can press Alt-Command-F to open the Fade dialog: here you can change the opacity and mode of the effect.

BUILD YOUR OWN

You can assign your own keyboard shortcuts to just about any menu, palette or tool command using the Keyboard Shortcuts menu. This can be useful if, say, you regularly use the Shadows/Highlights adjustment, or if you find that pressing Alt-D to feather a selection conflicts with showing and hiding the Dock; you can also define shortcuts for such routine tasks as flipping a layer, and so on.

It's easy to navigate through the dialog and define your own shortcuts, but be careful not to use any key commands already in use. It's also worth knowing that the control key is not used in any existing shortcuts: add this to the mix, and you can be sure to have a unique shortcut. ⊗

K: Key commands 2

Navigating your way through menus can be frustratingly time consuming, so here are InDesign's essential shortcuts and ways to create your own.

We may wish that working in InDesign was all about creating beautiful layouts, but the reality is that as designers we spend much of our time placing items on the page, formatting text and resizing graphics. The donkey work is an essential part of the layout process, but we can ease the tedium by finding quicker ways to achieve our goals.

Here, we'll look at the essential keyboard shortcuts and show why it's important to be able to create your own. We'll also check out some useful solutions to avoiding the repetition in performing routine tasks.

KEYBOARD SHORTCUTS

All InDesign users should be familiar with the standard text formatting shortcuts: Command-R, -L and -C to align text right, left and centre; and Command-J to justify type. You can also use shortcuts to modify selected characters and spacing.

Command-Shift-> and -< will make selected text larger and smaller. You can also hold down Alt and press the left and right cursor keys to adjust tracking (letter spacing), and use the up and down cursor keys, again with the Alt key held down, to increase and decrease a paragraph's leading. Hold Alt-Shift and press the up/down cursor keys to change selected text's baseline shift. With all these shortcuts, you can hold the Command key as well to vary the amounts by 10 times the value – you can set the amount of the increment to suit your needs in InDesign's Preferences pane.

You can move objects around with the cursor keys, of course, nudging a default of 2pt with each click; holding down the Shift key as well will move them by 10 times the default distance. Less well known is the fact that you can make objects, including text boxes, larger and smaller by holding down Command and pressing the < and > keys.

There are two essential shortcuts for working with pictures: Command-Alt-C will fit a picture box to the size of the graphic; and Command-Alt-Shift-E will fit the graphic to the size of the box, maintaining its proportions – miss out Shift to allow its aspect ratio to change to that of the enclosing box.

QUICK APPLY

There's no need to go rooting through menus searching for a command: the Quick Apply box will do all the searching for you. Access it by clicking the lightning-bolt icon at the top right of the control panel, at the top of the window, or pressing Command-Return. Once the Quick Apply dialog pops up, you can start typing and it will search for menu items beginning with or containing those characters. Let's say you want to snap a block of text to the baseline grid. In InDesign CS3, there was a button on the control panel to do this; in CS4, it's hidden in the Paragraph panel, which means it isn't immediately on view. Open the Quick Apply panel and type 'bas'. The panel will show a list, in which the top item is 'Object Menu > Baseline Options'. That's not the one you want, but the second one down is: 'Text and Tables > Align to Baseline Grid'. So all you need to do is hit the down cursor key to select the second item and press Return, and the baseline grid will be turned on for the selected text. The item works both ways, so if the baseline grid is already on, this process will turn it off.

▼ **The Quick Apply panel produces a list of menu options that match the text you type. This can make menu selection quick and easy.**

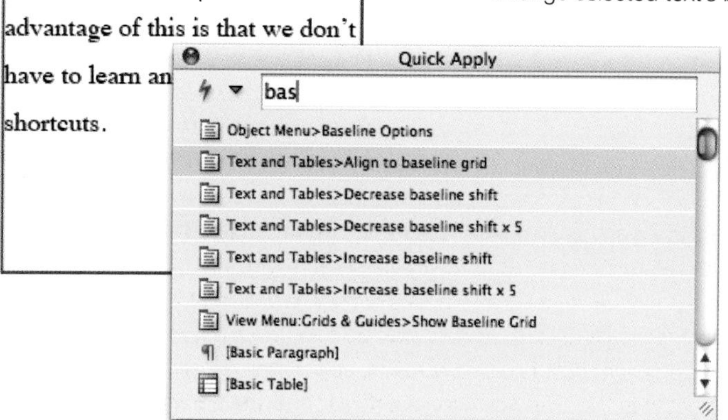

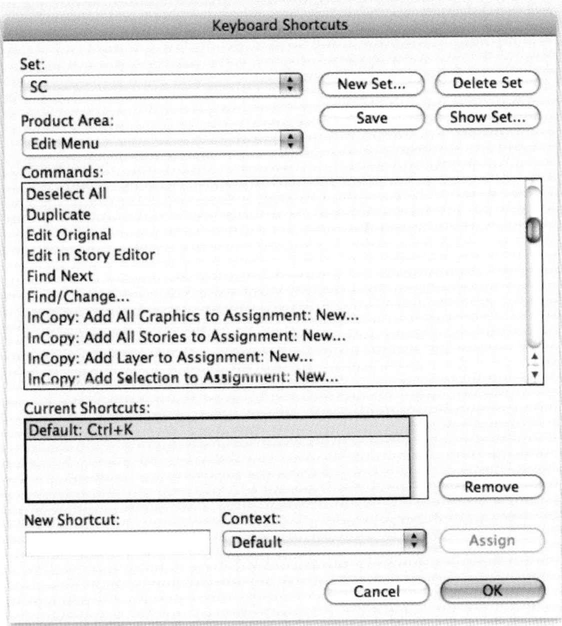

▲ **You can define your own keyboard shortcuts for commonly used operations, including all menus, panel and dialog options.**

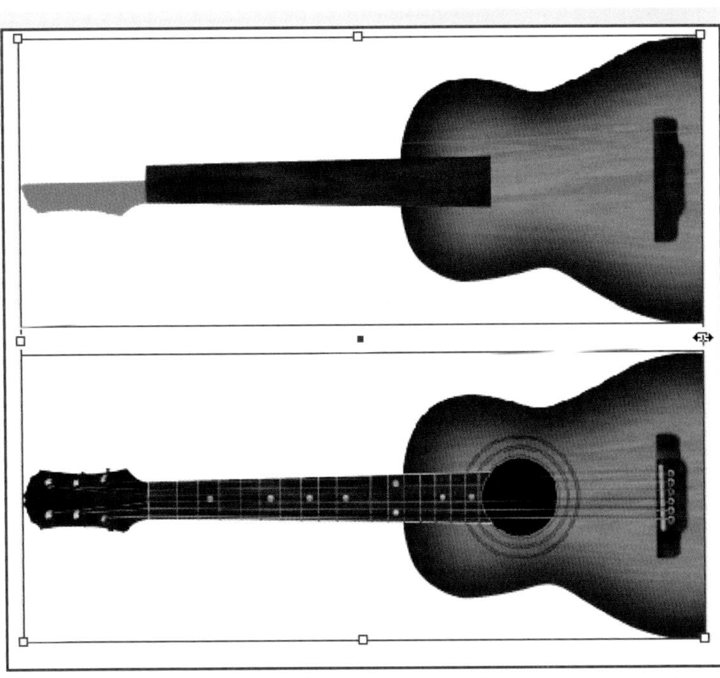

▲ **If you group two or more images together, you can crop them all by the same amount. Just ungroup them after the operation is completed.**

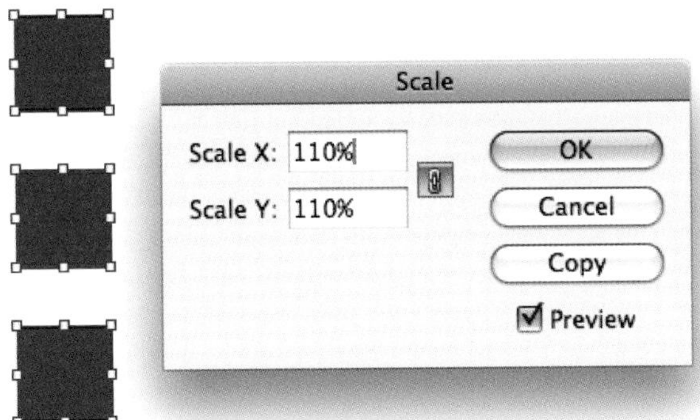

▲ **The Scale command scales all selected objects by the same amount. Remember to make sure the Preview box is checked so you can see the results before committing to them.**

► **The Cursor keys will nudge objects and can be used to adjust size, leading, baseline shift and tracking. You can set the amounts for each nudge in the Units and Increments section of InDesign's Preferences.**

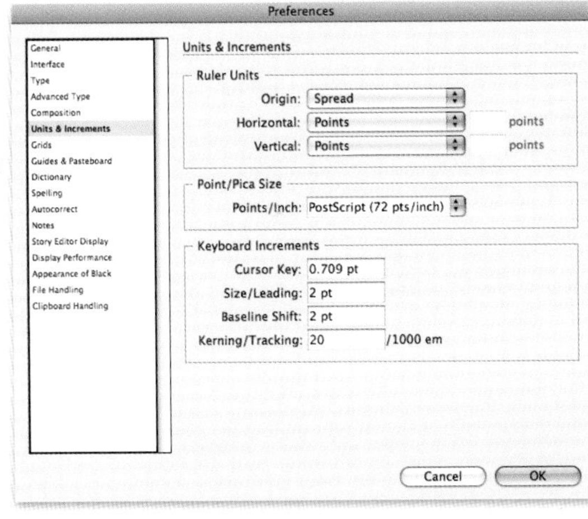

SCALING MULTIPLE OBJECTS

If you have several similar items on a page and want to make them all larger or smaller by the same amount, there are two quick ways to do this. The simplest is to use Object > Transform > Scale and type in a percentage. If the Preview box is checked, you'll see all the objects scaling immediately. Easier still is to use the up/down cursor keys to scale in 1% increments, holding down the Shift key to scale in 10% increments.

Another method is to select all the objects, and group them (Command-G). You can then scale the entire group, which will scale all the objects by the same amount. When you've finished, you can ungroup (Command-Shift-G) and reposition the objects as you choose.

Grouping objects is also a useful way to crop them in an identical manner. Make sure they're aligned, group them and then crop the group. When you Ungroup, you find that the objects have all been individually cropped.

DEFINING SHORTCUTS

In the above example, we used Object > Transform > Scale to transform a number of items at the same time, but why use the mouse to make this selection? You can use Edit > Keyboard Shortcuts to define your own key combination. The big advantage Mac users have over PC designers is that extra function key, the Ctrl key, which is hardly used otherwise. Defining Ctrl-S to trigger the Scale command takes just a few seconds.

You can define custom shortcuts for all your most commonly used menu items. It's worth saving your collection of shortcuts to disk, as InDesign can forget them if it crashes in the middle of an operation. The very first shortcut you should define, of course, is the one to trigger the Keyboard Shortcuts dialog.

MAKE USE OF TEXT STYLES

We tend to think of character and paragraph styles as being used only for documents that are going to be reworked again and again, such as magazine templates. However, you should define styles for even the simplest jobs, because you can make styles dependent on each other. If you have a document set in Myriad, for instance, with headlines in bold and text in light, defining these as styles allows you to change all the fonts by simply redefining the style. Better still, you can do so without having to make a text selection, so you can experiment with different fonts entirely using the Paragraph Style panel.

L: Layer blending

Successful montage rests on fooling the viewer into believing that every element in your scene goes together, often through careful layer blending.

Working in Photoshop is all about making layers interact with each other. In the next section, we'll look at how to use Layer Masks to control the visibility of a layer selectively, but you can achieve a lot without touching any of the painting tools. The two main ways to control a layer's visibility is to use different layer blending modes and to use the so-called 'advanced blending' controls, and it's these we'll look at here.

At the top of the Layers palette, you'll see a pop-up menu, set by default to Normal. This is where you can choose from all of the blending modes Photoshop has to offer. It's a long list, and many of the modes here have specialist uses that you'll rarely touch. However, it's worth getting to grips with the basic modes, as they can have a radical effect on your ability to work with layers.

Two modes that produce a dark result are Multiply and Darken, but these work in subtly different ways. Both will remove pure white from a layer, which is ideal when you're working with a logo on a white background: change to either of these modes and the background will vanish. The difference, however, is that the part of the layer that remains visible in Multiply mode will always make the layers beneath look darker, as if you're looking through a layer made of translucent glass.

Darken, however, produces a subtly different result: here, the layer to which the mode is applied will darken underlying layers only if they're darker than the target layer. If the underlying layers are already darker, they won't be affected. There are fewer uses for this mode: one might be if you're trying to remove burnt-out white patches from a portrait. Painting in a light fleshtone on a layer set to Darken will conceal the white, but won't affect areas of the portrait darker than the current colour.

Screen and Lighten modes are the counterparts of Multiply and Darken, and they brighten the layers beneath. Screen mode is useful when working with filters such as Lens Flare, which are hard to position as the underlying layers aren't visible in the preview. However, when they're applied to a separate layer filled with black, in Screen mode the black disappears and only the flare result is visible against the background, enabling it to be moved more easily to the right location. In Lighten mode, painting with a bright colour on a photo of a Union Flag, for instance, will affect the darker blue and red areas, but won't affect the white stripes.

▲ This plaque is set against a corrugated iron wall in Normal mode.

▲ In Multiply mode, the wall is darkened by the whole plaque, but we can still read the lettering.

▲ In Darken mode, the plaque is invisible where the wall is darker than it, making the text illegible.

▲ This image of the Gherkin building is placed in front of a foliage background.

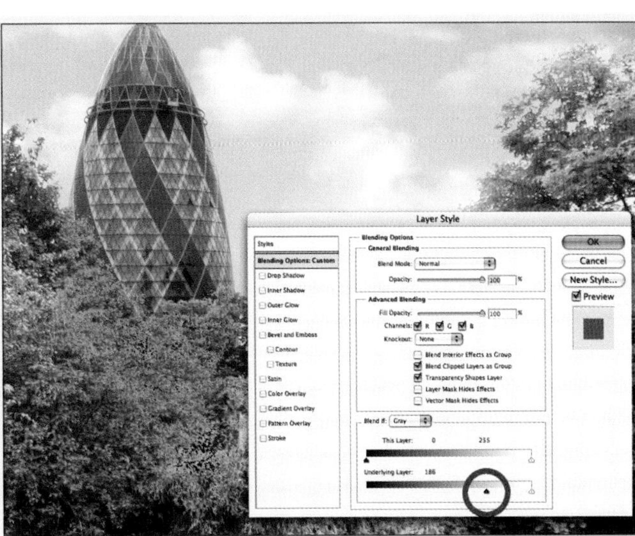

▲ By dragging the black slider in the Underlying Layer section to the right, we hide the Gherkin where the background is darker than this value, so it only shows up over the brighter sky.

One of the most useful layer modes of all is Hard Light. In this mode, midtone grey areas of the layer are hidden; the brighter or darker the layer becomes, the more visible it is. This makes it very useful for adding shading to multiple layers, as when a layer is filled with Hard Light neutral colour, it's initially invisible. Using the Dodge and Burn tools on this layer will add highlights and shadows, which will be clearly visible. Hard Light layers filled with this neutral grey also make a good 'base' for filters such as Noise and Plastic Wrap, producing translucent results in which only the filter's effect is seen.

All the other blending modes are worth experimenting with and produce variations on the effects described here. One worth further mention is Difference, which produces an inverted result on the layer beneath.
It's especially useful when comparing two images that are identical apart from small variations: in Difference mode, identical regions will appear as black, clearly highlighting the areas of difference. This mode is most useful for doctors comparing medical scans, but can also be a valuable aid to designers who want to check the differences between two PDFs of the same page: when imported into Photoshop and overlaid on each other, any differences will stand out.

There are keyboard shortcuts for all of these blending modes: hold down alt-shift and H for hard light, M for multiply and S for screen. Alternatively, hold down Alt-Shift and press the + and - keys to cycle through all the variations.

When you double-click a layer in the Layers palette, the Layer Styles dialog appears. Right at the bottom of the main pane is the advanced blending section, which determines the visibility of the layer based on its brightness.

Two sliders control the visibility of the current layer, marked by the This Layer section of the Blend If panel. Dragging the left slider to the right will hide any parts of the layer that are darker than the numerical value shown, so in the case of a night photograph, the black sky can be made to disappear entirely. Dragging the right-hand slider to the left will limit the visibility of the bright parts of an image – for example, making white clouds disappear.

Dragging these sliders produces a hard cut-off between what's visible and what's hidden, which can appear ragged and ugly. However, there's a further trick: Alt-selecting this slider will split it in two. Everything darker than the left-hand slider will be invisible, everything brighter than the right-hand slider will be visible and everything in between will fade smoothly into view.

The Blend If controls are enormously powerful, as they allow you to show and hide regions of a layer based entirely on the layer's brightness. Alternatively, use the Underlying Layer section to control a layer's visibility depending on the brightness of the layers beneath it. With these controls, you could, for example, place a photograph of a view on top of a shot of an overcast day taken through a window.

By hiding our view layer where the room layer is dark – that is, where it overlaps the interior of the room – we can make the view appear only where it overlaps the bright clouds outside, making it appear to be the other side of the window.

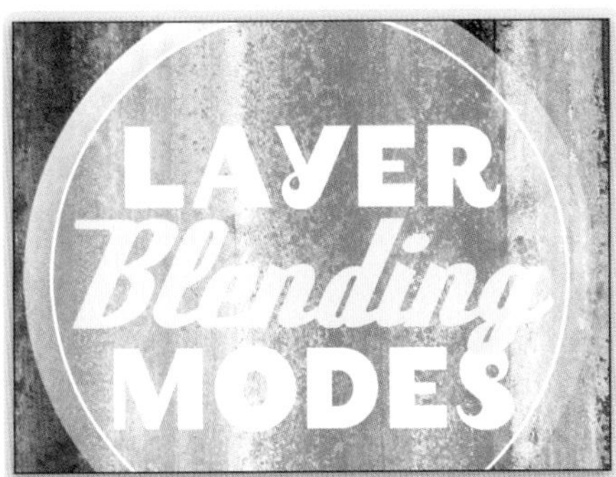

▲ In Screen mode, the wall is brightened by the whole plaque.

▲ In Lighten mode, the plaque can't be seen where the wall is already brighter than it.

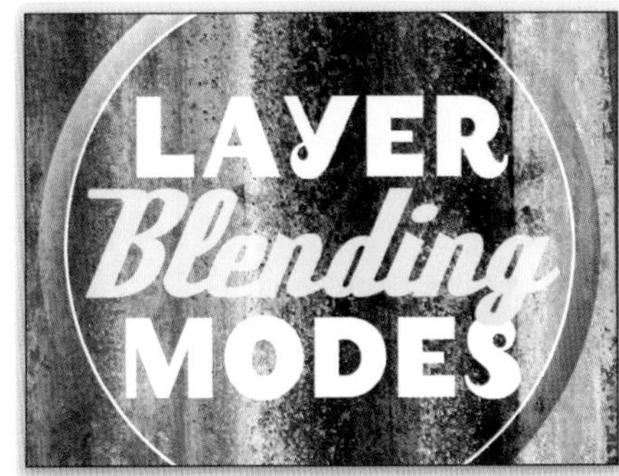

▲ In Hard Light mode, the midtone grey disappears entirely, leaving the highlights, shadows and text visible at full strength.

L: Layer Styles

As they don't alter the actual pixels, just the appearance of a layer, Layer Styles offer enormous flexibility. Here, we explore the options.

Layer Styles are a set of special effects that are attached to individual layers in Photoshop. They include bevels, shadows, glows, textures, colours and strokes. Unlike filters, which affect the individual pixels to which they're applied, Layer Styles affect the entire layer as it currently appears. If you were to apply a series of Layer Styles to make a layer appear to made of shiny metal, for instance, then any painting you then do on that layer will immediately and automatically take on the metallic appearance as you paint.

Layer Styles are add-ons that affect the appearance of the layer, but don't alter the pixels. This means you can reopen the Layer Style dialog at any time and adjust any of the settings, or even disable them. This gives you free rein to experiment without there being any danger of irrevocably damaging your artwork.

Layer Styles are accessed in two main ways. You can select the menu option Layer > Layer Style and choose the effect you want to apply, or you can click on the 'fx' button at the bottom of the Layers panel and choose the style you want from the pop-up menu. You can also choose preset combinations of Layer Styles from the Styles panel, where each has a thumbnail showing an indication of its effect.

You'll already be familiar with the Drop Shadow style, which adds a soft-edged shadow beneath the layer. You can adjust the size of the shadow, the spread (the amount by which the hard edge is larger than the layer itself), the opacity, the colour and the direction – all using the panel's sliders, which show the effects in real time. You can also drag on the image itself to set the direction and distance of the shadow.

COMBINING LAYER STYLES

The real interest comes when you start to combine multiple effects. As the sequence here shows, it's possible to build up a convincing metallic effect using a combination of bevels, satin and contours. Once created, this combination can be saved as a preset, and will then be available with a single click on the Styles panel. Because Layer Styles are added on top of the layer, they can be applied to text without having to rasterise it first. This means you can easily edit the text at any point, and it will retain its Layer Style.

▲ A simple stroke is easier to apply and more customisable than choosing Stroke from the Edit menu.

▲ This is the stroke changed to a Gradient – black at both ends, and white in the middle.

▲ Changing the stroke's mode from Linear to Shape Burst, it follows the contour of the object like a pipeline.

▲ The Pillow Emboss style applies its effect both inside and outside the object.

▲ This basic text is set in grey as a good neutral base colour.

▲ Adding a wide bevel gives the text a three-dimensional but plastic appearance.

▲ Changing the mode of the bevel from Smooth to Chisel Hard gives a carved look.

▲ Adding a Gloss Contour to the bevel is the beginning of adding some shine.

▲ The separate Contour subsection enables you to add a gloss element.

▲ The Satin effect offsets two extra versions of the outline, here adding depth.

▲ Adding a stroke outside the text gives it more body.

▲ Changing the mode of the stroke to Gradient add a shiny border around the text.

A number of Layer Styles make use of an angle indicator that sets both the direction and the height of the apparent light source for several of the effects: try dragging the marker around with a Bevel effect to see how changing the height alters the appearance of the bevelled edge. You'll notice a checkbox marked Use Global Light next to the angle indicator. This is to ensure the lighting is consistent across several effects. If you have a bevelled edge that's lit from the top left, say, any drop shadow will be placed bottom right so it appears to be cast from the same light source. Changing the angle of any effect when this box is checked will change the angle for all the Layer Styles in the document, not just in the current layer. If you want to change just one effect in isolation, uncheck this box first.

Many of the Layer Styles have variations that change their appearance. Bevels, for instance, can be inner or outer. They can be smooth or chiselled; both hard and soft chisel effects produce a carved appearance that works well for writing in stone. You can also choose such variants as Pillow Emboss, which produces an bevel both inside and outside the object, as if the outline had been stamped into the underlying surface.

A useful Layer Style is Stroke, which adds an outline to a layer. Unlike applying a stroke from the Edit menu, which physically paints the pixel border in place, the Layer Style version can be adjusted to any size and colour, and you can edit it later. As well as flat colours, strokes can include textures and even gradients.

You can make Layer Styles behave in ways Adobe never intended to create special effects. For example, Drop Shadows, Outer Glows and Inner Glows can all be made to appear as additional strokes by setting their size to zero and using the Spread control to make them larger. This means you can have multiple stroked objects. You can copy styles between layers by drag and drop. As of Photoshop CS3, dragging a Layer Style will move its effects from one layer to another; you now have to hold down the Alt key while dragging to move a copy of the styles.

Individual styles can be turned on and off directly in the Layers panel by clicking the eye icon to the left of the style's name. If you can't see all the individual styles attached to a layer, it's because the styles have been hidden away; click the tiny black triangle at the right of the layer's name to reveal them.

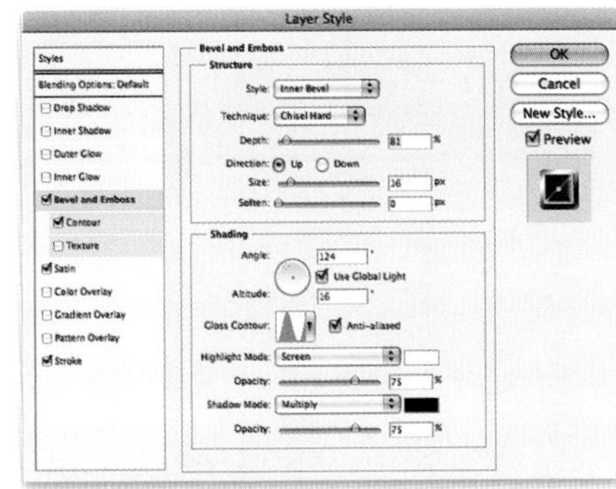

▲ **The best way to find out how Layer Styles work is to experiment with them. The preview is in real time; if you don't like the results, simply press Cancel.**

L: Light and shade

If you want to incorporate diverse elements in a single image you have to get your lighting right, or it will be obvious they weren't all shot together.

There are two tricks to creating realistic montages in Photoshop: making sure the lighting in the scene comes from a consistent direction and placing shadows behind and beneath objects in the scene. If you don't do this, the picture will feel wrong to even the least visually literate viewer.

Before adding lighting and shadows, you first need to balance photographic elements that already have a definite lighting direction. Some images from photo libraries are strongly lit from the side, making them hard to use unless you remove the shadows to produce a neutral image. The best tool to do this is the Shadows/Highlights adjustment, found under Photoshop's Image > Adjustments menu.

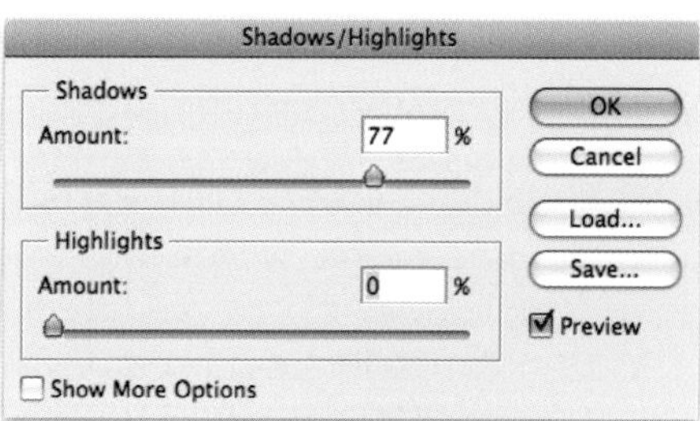

01A

▲ A strongly side-lit portrait from a photo library can look unnatural, so you need to balance this image.

01B

▲ Opening the Shadows/Highlights adjustment and increasing the Shadows level will boost dark regions.

In its basic mode, there are just two sliders: one for Shadows and another for Highlights. Firstly, drag the Shadows slider to bring more light into deeply shaded areas, then drag the Highlights slider to reduce over-bright regions of the photograph. Clicking the 'Show More Options' box at the bottom of the dialog will offer finer control over the process. As our example shows, the adjustment is capable of neutralising even a strong shadow to produce a well balanced image.

There are some cases when you may want to portray a light source within your image. One method of achieving this is to draw a white or yellow glow emanating from the object in question. While this is a reasonable approach and can produce dramatic results, it rarely looks realistic.

A more convincing solution is to add a shadow outside the affected area, darkening the area that isn't lit rather than brightening the area that is. The easiest way to do this is first to add a new Adjustment Layer to darken the whole scene. Use either Curves or Levels, whichever is your favourite method. You can then make use of the fact that all Adjustment Layers come with built-in masks, which can be painted on to hide the effect of the adjustment.

If you want to produce a directional light, use the Pen or Lasso tools to trace straight lines that define the shape of the light cone – hold the Alt key with the Lasso tool to draw straight lines between click points. Use Select > Modify > Feather to add softness to the edges of the selection, then fill this region with black on the Adjustment Layer's mask. This will hide the effect, limiting the shadow to just the region outside the selected area.

It can also help to add some colour to the lit area, using another Adjustment Layer. A

▲ This bright shot of an interior can be improved by bringing some light through that window.

▲ Make a new Curves Adjustment Layer, and drag down on the curve to darken the whole scene.

▲ Paint or select areas of the Adjustment Layer's mask to hide the effect in those regions.

touch of yellow will simulate incandescent light convincingly. By making the layer mask the precise inverse of that on the shadow Adjustment Layer, you can ensure that the colour only affects those areas not in shadow. To do this, hold the Command key and click on the Shadow Adjustment Layer's mask in the Layers palette, which will load the white (unmasked) area as a selection. Switch to the mask for the colour layer, and fill this area with black to produce an inverse.

You can add shadows to individual objects either on the object itself or behind it (on the floor or wall). There are two methods for adding a shadow directly to the object. First of all, you can create a new layer, using the object as a Clipping Mask (press Alt-Command-G after creating the new layer), so that you can paint the shadows here. This allows you to easily erase the shadows later.

An alternative approach is to create an Adjustment Layer, again using the object as a Clipping Mask, and darken the object here. Then, because the Adjustment Layer has a mask associated with it by default, you can paint on this mask the areas where you don't want the shadow to show up. This can be a preferable method, as it produces more realistic shading than simply painting in black on a new layer. It's directly comparable to the method for showing light glows, detailed above.

The simplest way to create a shadow behind an object is to duplicate the object, fill it with black, and then soften the edges using Gaussian Blur. By lowering the opacity and dragging the shadow to an appropriate location, you can create very convincing shadows. If the ground is visible, the shadow will need to be broken to bend across the floor to meet its base.

Most shadows on the floor, however, need to be painted by hand onto a new layer. Since floor shadows rarely follow the shape of the object that casts them, it's largely a matter of guesswork and intuition. Use a soft-edged brush, set to a low opacity, and build up the shadow in stages. The tendency is always to make shadows that are too strong this way; so when you've finished painting, try reducing the opacity of the entire layer for a more pleasing result.

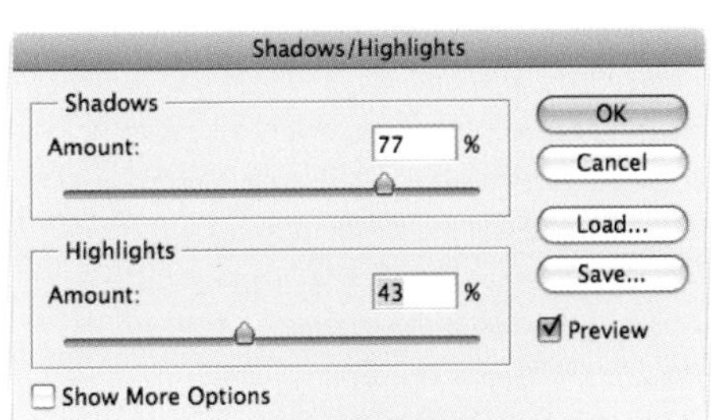

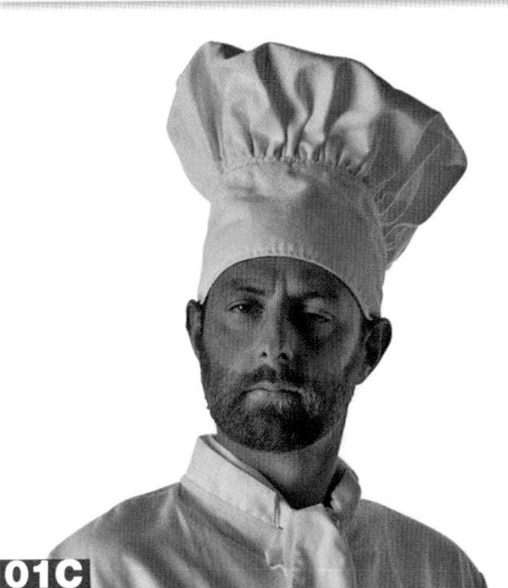

▲ Raising the Highlights amount darkens the brighter side of the face, bringing the two together.

▲ You will now be able to use Curves to brighten the whole of the image.

▲ This football looks as if it's floating above the surface, and hardly fits into the scene.

▲ Adding shading to the ball gives it lighting that matches the shadow direction of the rest of the scene.

▲ Painting a shadow beneath the ball places it firmly on the table, and it now matches the background.

L: Liquify filter

One of Adobe's most radical filters, Liquify lets you create some truly extraordinary results, and morph your photos into the realms of unreality.

The Liquify filter has been present in Photoshop since version 6, and provides a simple but powerful way to distort an image. Although it's listed under the Filter menu and even has its own keyboard shortcut (Command-Shift-X), Liquify is actually more a set of tools within a unified environment than a single filter.

Liquify is often used to apply cartoon-style distortions to faces, as it's easy to exaggerate a celebrity's features by simply dragging to shrink, enlarge and caricature them. However, Liquify has other, more intriguing uses that require more careful use of the tool set. Before beginning, always duplicate the layer you're working on. That way, if you take a distortion a step too far, you can always hide that area with a layer mask to reveal the original image beneath.

▲ You can make subtle changes to a character's expression by judicious use of the Liquify filter. Our new Barack Obama looks far more concerned about the credit crunch, for example.

One specific use of the Liquify filter is to apply a subtle change to a facial expression. If you're including a politician's image in a montage, for example, we frequently have to work with the mugshots you find online (and Wikipedia Commons is a great source of free-to-use images). However, if these are publicity photographs, as is generally the case, you'll find the subjects always grinning at the camera. And if you want to use a shot of, say, Barack Obama looking concerned about the credit crunch, the last thing you want is a cheery grin.

Tweaking expressions requires a light touch and a mirror: make the expression yourself and see how it affects the muscles of the face. Turn down the corners of the mouth, certainly, but don't forget to arch the eyebrows to accentuate the sense of concern. Small changes make a big difference: a slightly raised nostril can slightly unbalance a face, making the expression look more anxious.

Photographers will frequently turn to the Liquify filter to adjust a model's shape – softening curves, removing cellulite, enhancing, nipping and tucking without recourse to plastic surgery. This is a more delicate operation altogether, requiring patience and a necessarily slow approach. It's also likely that additional tools will be required, so we'll look at the range on offer.

The Forward Warp tool (shortcut: W) is the default tool, and works in a similar way to Photoshop's Smudge tool, pushing pixels around the window. It's best to work with a large brush to avoid unseemly wrinkles; change the size using the square bracket keys, holding the Shift key for larger-size jumps.

The Reconstruct tool (R) selectively reverts the image to its original form. There are special cases for this tool, which we'll discuss a little later. The Twirl Clockwise tool (C) twirls the image to

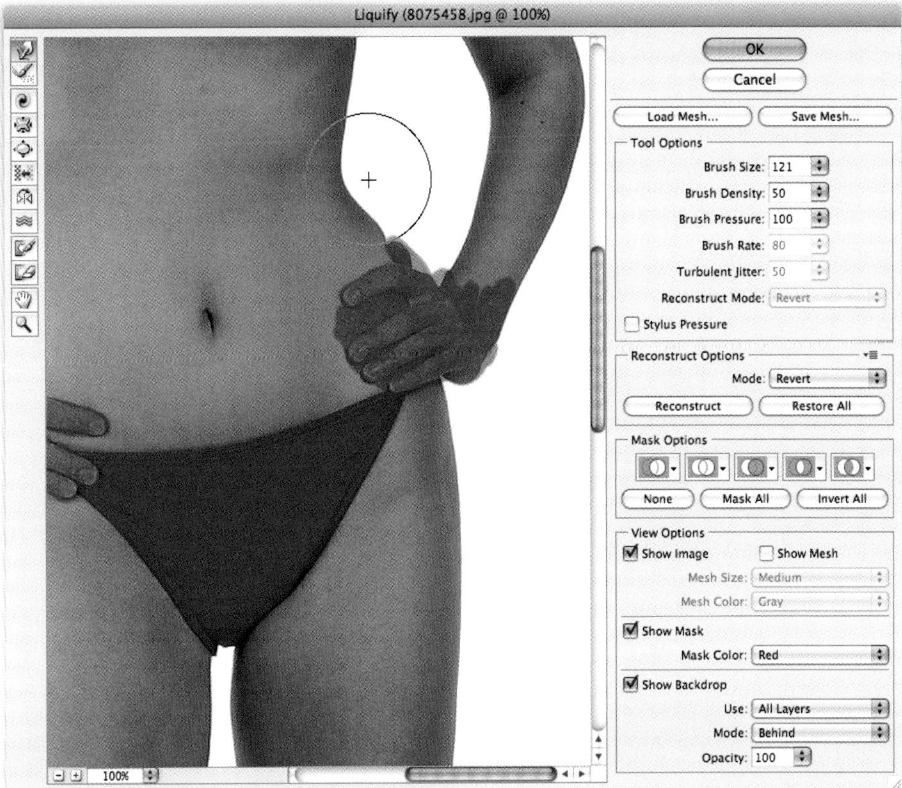

◄ **Freezing an area prevents it from being affected by the Liquify filter. Here, we don't want the model's hands reshaped as we adjust her body contours.**

the size of the brush, performing more distortion in the centre and none at the edges for a smooth result. The longer you hold down the mouse button, the more distorted the image will become. Hold down the Alt key to twirl anti-clockwise instead.

The Pucker tool (S) shrinks the area beneath the brush, while the Bloat tool (B) enlarges it. Bloat is good for making a model's eyes more appealing, Pucker is often used to reduce noses slightly; use both with moderation.

The Push Left tool (O) pushes pixels to the left as you drag up, and to the right as you drag down (you can reverse this with the Alt key). Although it may sound of little use, it's a great help for operations such as slimming a model's legs. Unless you're using a graphics tablet, you'll want to set a very low pressure for this tool to avoid chaotic results.

The Mirror tool (M) swaps pixels on either side as it's dragged and is best used in combination with the Freeze tool (see below) for such effects as creating water reflections.

The Turbulence tool (T) produces a smooth rippling effect, which is good for simulating natural textures such as bark and fire.

To protect areas you don't want distorted, use the Freeze tool (F). This paints a mask that freezes that area, and is best used for protecting eyeglasses, for instance, which look frankly absurd when they're distorted. Frozen areas can be inversed, unfrozen and added or subtracted. You can use the Thaw tool (D) to unfreeze areas selectively.

The Freeze tool can also be used to freeze a distorted area, enabling you to revert the area around it while leaving the distortion intact. In these cases, you can use the Reconstruct tool (R) to revert the unfrozen areas where you paint.

There are several reconstruction modes (Rigid, Stiff, Loose, Smooth and Revert) that determine how reconstructed areas blend into the frozen areas, affecting the smoothness of the joins.

You can choose to view the current layer in isolation or in combination with other layers in the document – either all of them or just one. You can also decide whether you want the other layers to appear in front of or behind the layer you're working on, and the opacity at which both the target layer and the background layers are shown. This can be vital when distorting a layer to fit a specific space: if you want to make a sheet of paper droop over the side of a table, for example, then you really need to be able to see the table.

When working with large images, you can see a noticeable slowdown in the Liquify operation, even on the fastest Macs. The sheer effort of having to move a huge number of pixels around can sometimes be overwhelming. Fortunately, there's a useful solution. Liquify works by modifying a mesh underlying the image, and you can choose to show or hide this mesh.

More significantly, though, you can save it for future use. So when you want to distort an image that's too big, the answer is first to create a lower-resolution version of the file. Apply all the Liquify distortions to it, then use the Save Mesh button to save the distortion to disk. All you have to do after that is to open the high resolution image, enter the Liquify dialog box, then load the saved mesh and it will be scaled and applied perfectly to the larger version.

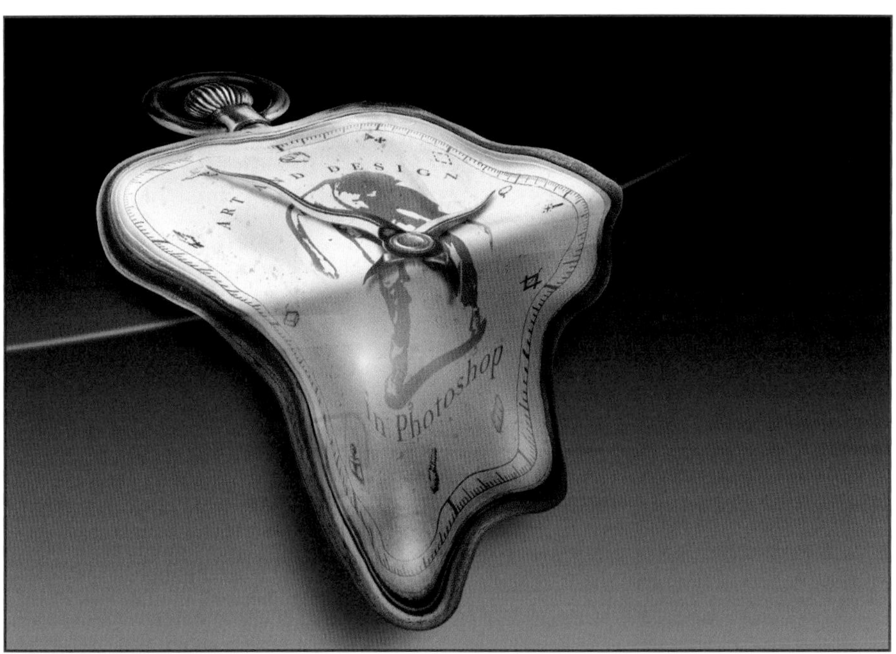

▲ **Viewing the background can help greatly, as in this cover for *Art & Design in Photoshop*, in which the Daliesque watch is distorted to look as if it's dripping off the edge of the table.**

M: Masks in Illustrator and Photoshop

Use masks to confine changes and adjustments to just specific areas of your image and you'll have far greater control over the results.

The easiest way to remove sections of a layer in Photoshop is simply to delete them. But this is an irreversible process: once something is deleted, it has gone forever. Far better to use a Layer Mask, which hides the unwanted region: the advantage is that hidden areas can always be shown again.

To make a new Layer Mask, select Layer > Layer Mask > Reveal All. This will create a new, empty mask with nothing hidden. Then choose any of the painting tools and paint in black on this mask. Wherever you paint, the layer will be hidden. Use either a hard or a soft-edged brush, depending on whether you want the unwanted parts to be removed cleanly or to fade smoothly out of view. If you want to reveal the hidden areas, swap the foreground colour from black to white and paint it back in. The X key swaps the foreground and background colours over. This is particularly handy when fine-tuning a mask, as it allows you to paint regions in and out without having to reach for the toolbar.

Any of the painting tools can be used on a Layer Mask, not just the Brush. So if you want to create a smooth fading transition over a large area, for example, use the Gradient tool set to black to white: this can be a simple way to add a new sky seamlessly to the top half of an image. For hiding large areas, use any of the selection tools – the Marquee, Lasso and so on – and then use Alt-Delete to fill that area to Mask with the foreground colour, or command-delete to fill with the background colour. If either of these is black, that area of the layer will be hidden more quickly than by painting it out. Filling an area with grey rather than black will lower its opacity without hiding it completely, and this can be useful for, say, giving the impression that the layer is behind a window or other transparent surface.

Other tools can be used for special effects. Let's say you want to place an object on a grass background, and need to make it look as if it's part hidden by the grass. The best method is to hold the command key as you click on the layer's thumbnail in the Layers palette, which will load up the layer's content as a selection. Then choose Layer > Add Layer Mask > Reveal Selection. This will fill the area outside the object with black on the layer mask: you won't see any difference, of course, as you'll only be hiding the parts that aren't visible anyway. But if you now use the Smudge tool to smear the mask in from outside the object, you'll create a natural-looking mask effect that is far more convincing (and easier to create) than painting blades with the Brush tool.

By default, a Layer Mask is linked to its layer, so when the layer is moved, the mask moves with it. There are times, however,

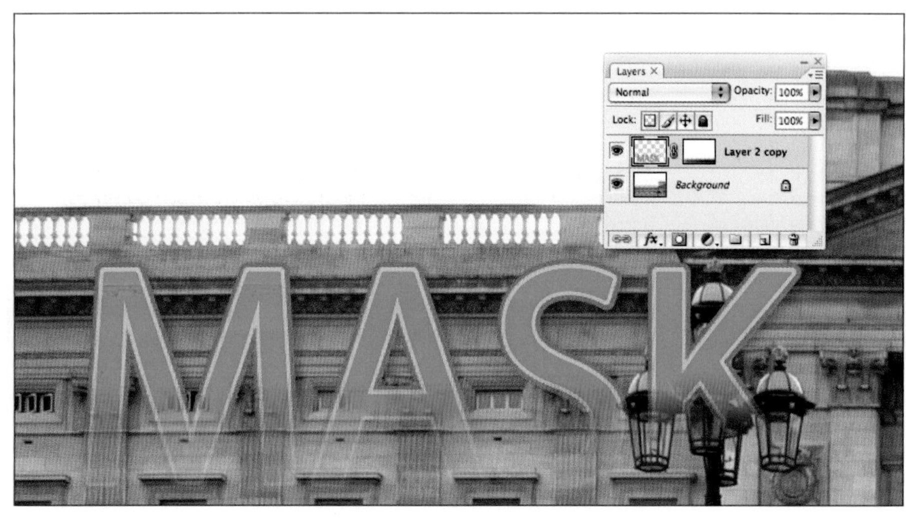

◄ **Painting on a Layer Mask with a soft-edged brush will produce a smooth fade-off between fully visible and hidden, as the layer is masked rather than deleted.**

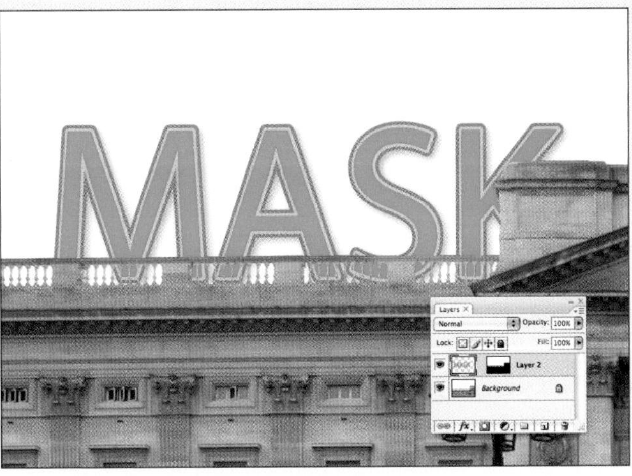
▲ **The mask on this lettering matches the white of the sky in this photograph of Buckingham Palace, so the lettering appears to be placed behind the building.**

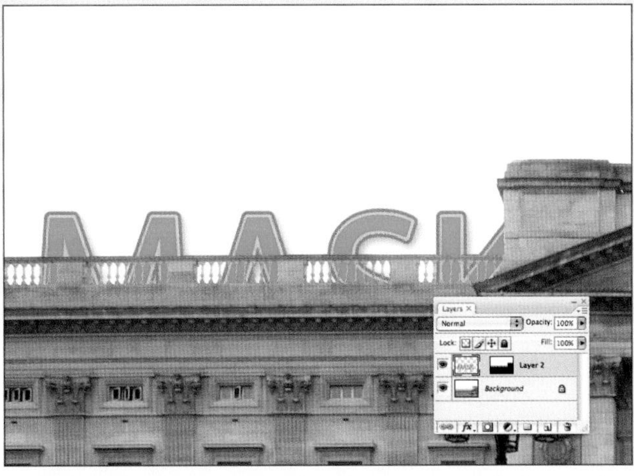
▲ **With the mask unchained from the lettering layer, we can move the text around and the mask remains in place.**

when you want the mask to stay in place – such as when you're placing an object behind an element in the background image. Click on the tiny chain that appears between the thumbnails of the layer and its mask in the Layers palette: the chain will disappear, meaning that the two are no longer linked. When you now select the layer rather than the mask by clicking on its thumbnail (you know which one is selected by the dashed thumbnail border), you'll be able to move the layer independently of the mask.

The alternative to a painted Layer Mask is a Vector Mask, in which the visible area of a layer is defined by a Pen path. These are created using Layer > Vector Mask > Reveal All, in a similar way to Layer Masks. The difference here is that when a path is drawn using the Pen tool, only the region bounded by the path is seen. This kind of mask can only support hard edges, rather than the appearance of feathering, but the smooth outlines and ease of editing that occurs as a result of using the Pen tool means that for many purposes Vector Masks are preferable. And, since a single layer can support both types of masks simultaneously, they can even be combined for greater ease of use.

Masks are supported in Illustrator as well, and can be used in two ways. The easiest way is to draw an outline of the area of an object or group that you want to remain visible, making sure it's the topmost object; select both it and the target object or group, and choose Object > Clipping Mask > Make. The area outside this masked region will now be invisible, but changing the shape of the masking object will bring it back into view. This is the equivalent of Vector Masks in Photoshop, producing hard-edged results.

It's possible to create masks in Illustrator that more closely match Photoshop's Layer Masks. Select an object or group, and open the Transparency palette. From the pop-up menu, choose Make Opacity Mask. Anything drawn on here will now mask the target object; solid black objects will hide it completely, and those filled with grey will hide it to a greater or lesser extent, depending on the darkness of the fill.

You can even create soft-edged masks in this way, by choosing Effect > Stylize > Feather; the greater the amount of feathering, the softer the edge of the mask will be. While the Mask is selected in the Transparency palette, any objects drawn will be added to the mask, so you can draw multiple objects on the same mask to create complex masking.

▼ **The area outside this lettering has been filled with black on the Layer Mask: we see no effect, as the hidden area is empty anyway.**

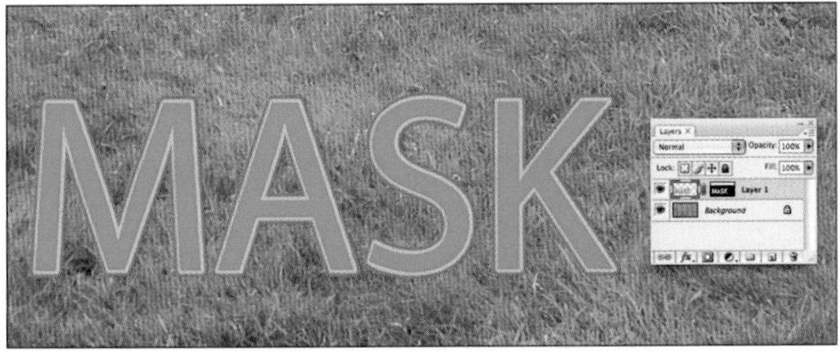

▼ **Using the Smudge tool to brush the mask into the object from below creates the illusion of it being partly hidden by the grass – a very quick solution indeed.**

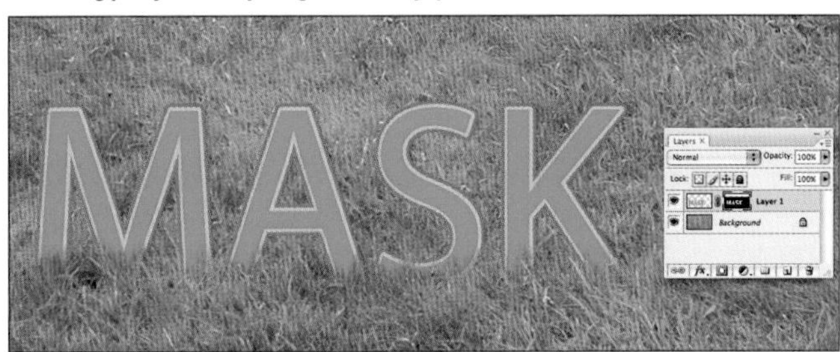

▼ **The topmost object in this Illustrator file has been turned into a Clipping Mask, and the underlying objects are visible only within the boundaries of the masking object.**

▼ **This mask has been softened by feathering its edges using the Effects menu. A rectangle filled with grey and placed over the letter S adds a semi-opaque mask to just that area.**

M: Measurements from a photo

Using one of Photoshop's lesser-known features, you can take measurements directly from a photograph. Here, we explain how to do just that.

Although it's used mainly for photo editing, Photoshop includes a range of tools for taking measurements directly from photographs. The Extended Edition has additional sophisticated measuring capabilities, but even the basic edition of Photoshop can read measurements out of an image, as long as you have some way of determining the basic scale.

In the first example, we're going to use the Vanishing Point filter to work out all the sizes in a kitchen. There's no need for tapes and rulers: a single snapshot will give us all the information we need.

We can begin by choosing Filter > Vanishing Point. As always, we need to start by defining the corners of a rectangle, and we can do this by clicking on the four corners of one of the cupboard fronts [**01A**]. Holding down the X key allows us to zoom in on the image, which is a great help when positioning the corners: it's important to be as accurate as possible.

Once the initial rectangle has been made, we can stretch the sides out to fit the width of the unit. We can then 'tear off' 90° planes by holding down the Command key as we drag a centre handle. Some further adjustment may be necessary when creating the first 90° plane, as Photoshop can have trouble reading the angle correctly in such a distorted view. Once this plane has had its corners adjusted to fit the scene though, we can go on to tear off planes at 90° to this one, until the whole kitchen has been mapped out [**01B**].

The next step is to set a measurement scale. We know that kitchen appliances come in standard 60cm widths, so we can make use of that fact. Zoom in and switch to the Measurement tool (the one that looks like a ruler at an angle), and drag it across the width of the dishwasher. Keep an eye on the angle indicator on the far left of the rule – this should read either 0 or 90°.

Once you've made sure that the line extends to the whole width of the machine, go to the Length field at the top of the dialog window. Here, type in 60 as the measurement [**01C**]. If you wish, you can also tick the Link Measurements to Grid checkbox, which will turn all the grids into 1cm increments – but as this is a tiny unit for such a large room, this might just end up being confusing.

Now, it's possible to use the Measurement tool to find the dimensions of any item in the room [**01D**]. Click and drag to measure cupboard fronts, tile height, the height of units from the ground, and so on – we can even use the tool to measure the size of the

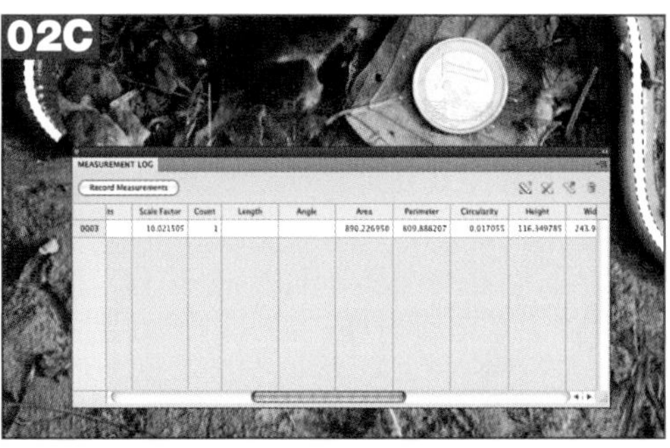

breadboards. This approach can also be used to measure elements on the outside of houses, such as the width of windows: all you need is one known measurement, and the rest can be read out of the scene.

Those with the Extended Edition of Photoshop can use a further set of measuring tools. The simplest is the Count tool, located beneath the Eyedropper in the toolbar. This is useful for keeping a count of the number of objects in a scene, marking each one with a unique number so as not to lose track. In this example, we've used it for a trivial purpose – to count the number of geese in a flock [**03**]. Clearly though, we could use the tool to count a far higher number of objects with ease.

The Ruler tool measures the distance between two points. But what if we want to measure a more complex length, such as the length of this earthworm [**02A**]? Once again, the Extended Edition of Photoshop has a clever solution.

We're fortunate that the photographer of this worm saw fit to include a 1 coin to set the scale. A quick check of Wikipedia tells us that this coin is exactly 23.25mm in diameter. If we choose Custom Scale from the Analysis menu, we can use the Ruler tool (it's activated automatically when the dialog is opened) to drag a straight line from side to side on the coin. The dialog tells us that the pixel length is, in this case, 233mm; all we have to do is to type in 23.25 as the Logical Length, setting the Logical Units value to 'mm' [**02B**]. Now, anything we measure in the image will be interpreted in terms of this scale.

But how does that help us measure the length of the worm? We can't make the ruler bend round curves. What we can do, though, is use the Pen tool to draw a path down the centre of the worm, from tip to tip. With the path still visible, make a new layer and switch to a hard-edged Brush, then hit the Enter button on the keyboard. This will stroke the path with the current brush size and foreground colour, producing a stroke that runs all the way down the worm. For greater accuracy, use the Eraser tool to square off the round ends of the stroke.

Load that stroke as a selection by Command-clicking on its thumbnail in the Layers Panel. Opening the Measurement Log panel will reveal an empty set of fields. Make sure the Ruler tool is not active (or the dialog will simply record the length of the last measurement with that tool), and hit the Record Measurements button. This shows a large amount of data about the measurement, including the Perimeter value [**02C**].

Here, the perimeter is shown to be 809.888207mm – note how the scale converts the pixels into units that relate to the size of the coin. This, of course, is the size of the entire perimeter. To get the length, we need to divide this in two, producing a figure of 405mm (rounding up slightly). This figure also includes the width of the stroke, though. We can measure that using the Ruler tool, and we find that its width is 2mm. Subtracting that from our previous measurement gives a length of 403mm. Certainly the most painless way to measure the length of an earthworm.

⊗

M: Moving objects

Whether you use the keyboard or the mouse, there's a right and a wrong way to move objects if you want to get neat results. Here's the right way.

Whatever graphics program you are working in – it may be Photoshop, Illustrator, InDesign or QuarkXPress – you need to move, align and arrange objects. Although it's easy enough to switch to the Move or Selection tool, and simply drag items to where you want them, there are methods of moving objects that are more precise, quicker and easier.

In Adobe applications, you can access the Move tool temporarily by holding down the Command key. In Photoshop, this allows you to move a layer around as you are painting on it, and in Illustrator it means you can move an anchor point in a path while still drawing it with the Pen tool. It's a serious time-saver, and one of the essential keyboard shortcuts.

The most common moving operation in many design applications is to change items' positions relative to each other. There are two methods for doing this: align and distribute. The difference between them is not always clearly understood, so it's well worth examining the way each method operates.

Aligning multiple objects means rearranging them so that chosen points line up along a horizontal or vertical line. These points can be either an extremity – the top, bottom, left or right side – or the centre. The notion of 'centre' here is taken to mean the centre of gravity. In other words, if the object were made of wood, this is the point at which you would drive a nail through so it could spin freely.

Aligning objects vertically will move them all, so that they line up with the topmost object. It's a slightly confusing term, in that vertical alignment means aligning along a horizontal line. Aligning objects horizontally, in contrast, will line them up along a single vertical line. When aligning objects in this way, you can choose whether to align their tops, bottoms or sides. Usually, the menu for alignment will be in the form of readily understood icons.

Distributing objects means spacing them to average out the space between them. Again, you can do this either vertically or horizontally, and you can set whether the space is measured from their tops, sides or centres.

Distributing is a far more useful technique than is at first apparent. Let's say, for example, that you're drawing a chart of moon phases in Illustrator. You've got all of your individual illustrations, and you need to space them to fit the width. Rather than moving each individually, you can put them in rough order, then precisely position the first and last. When you choose Distribute, the space between them will be automatically adjusted for perfect spacing – you can add a vertical Align command to tidy up the selection. The good thing about this technique is that if you want to space the moons over a wider grid you only have to move

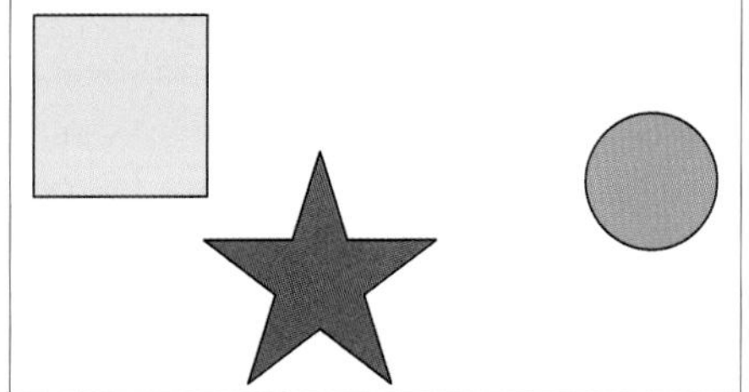

▲ **This simple array of objects can be aligned automatically, and in a variety of different ways.**

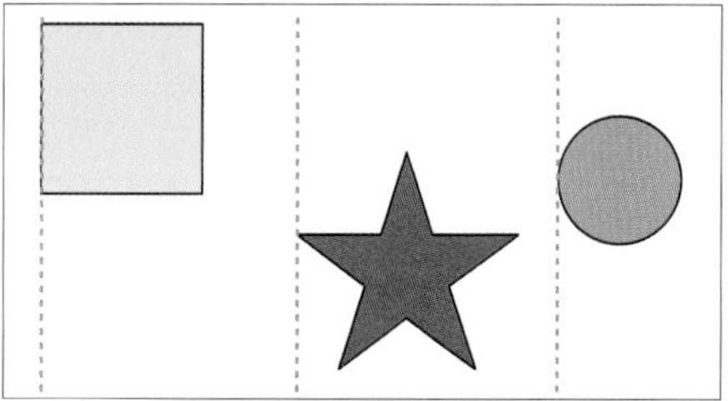

▲ **Distribute Left arranges the objects so that there's equal space between the left edges. Only the star moves here – the extreme left and right objects are untouched.**

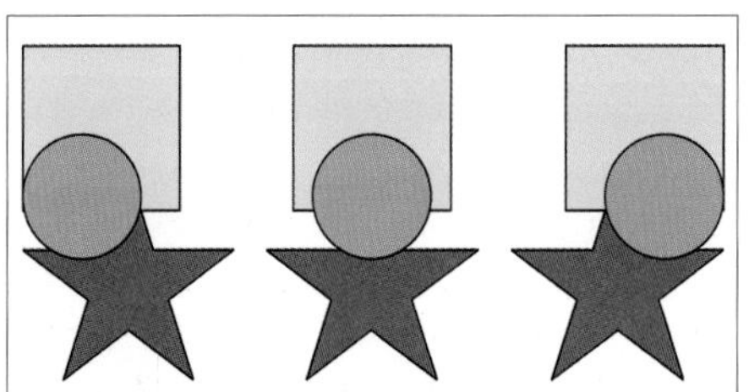

▲ **When aligning right, centre or left, it's the extremes of the objects that are lined up. Ensure that you're choosing the right method for the job in hand.**

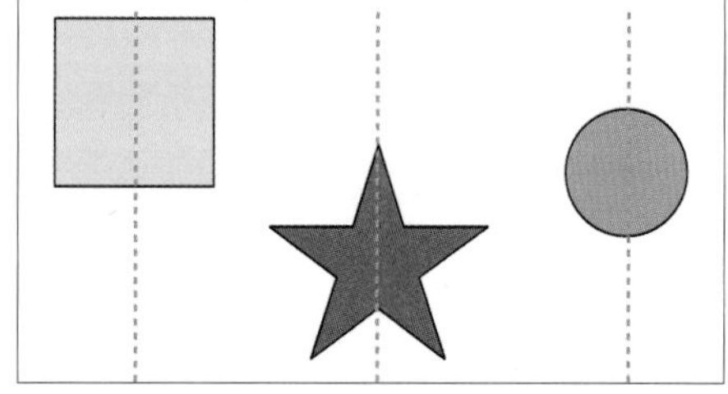

▲ **Distribute Centre places equal space between the centre lines of the objects, producing a markedly different result.**

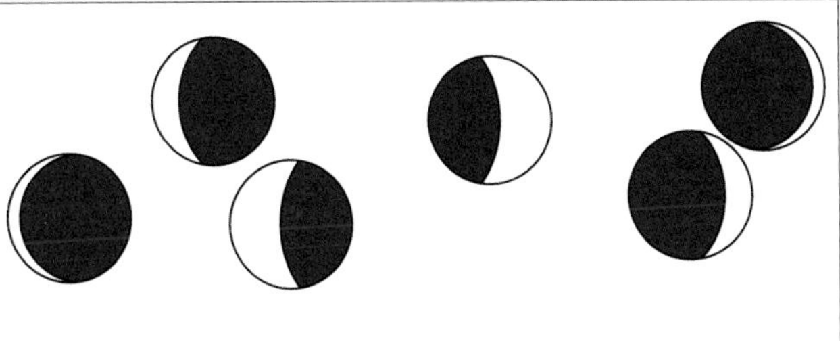

▲ **This set of moon phases can be aligned automatically. They first need to be in the right order, with the first and last objects placed at the extremes of the array.**

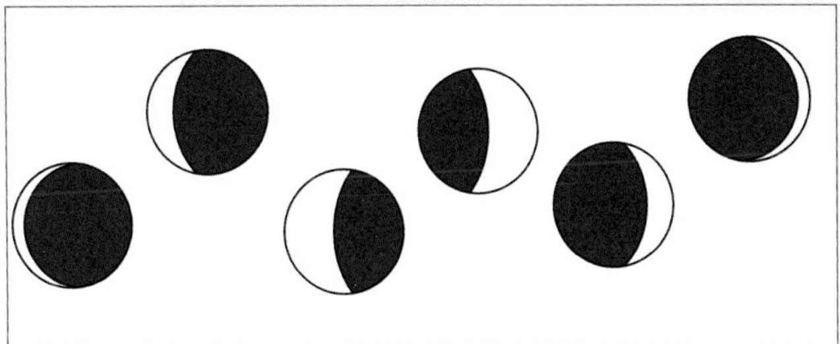

▲ **Distribute is used to equalise the horizontal spaces between all the objects. In this example, because they're all the same size, you could use distribute left, right or centre and you would get identical results.**

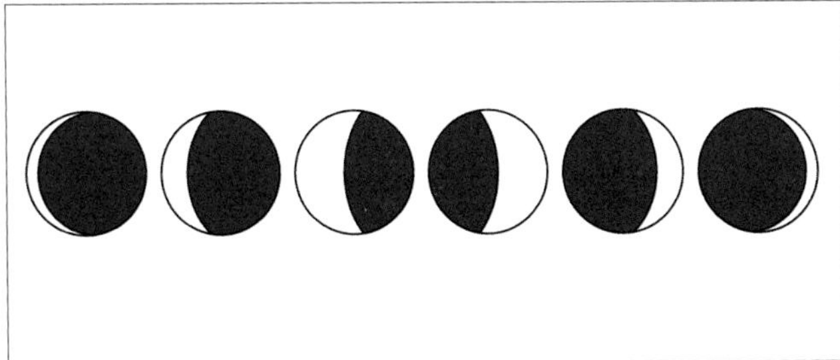

▲ **The Align command can now place them all on the same horizontal axis.**

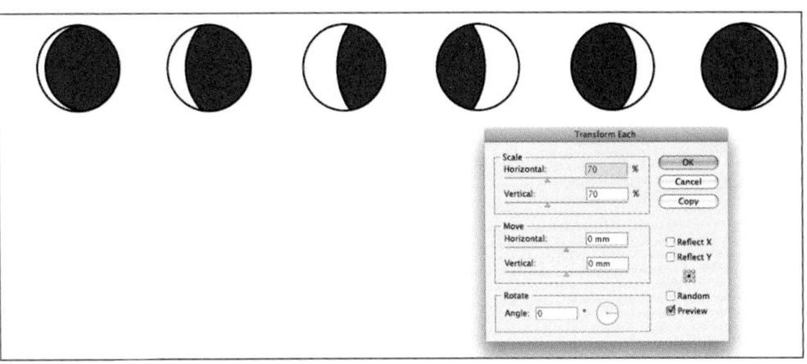

▲ **Use Transform Each to reduce the size of all the objects, without reducing the size of the space they occupy. Check the Preview button to see the effect of changing scale without having to apply the transformation.**

the final one, then use the Distribute command to move all the rest.

In Illustrator, you can move an object by a precise distance by hitting the Enter key. This brings up the Move dialog box, where you can specify the movement in one of two ways – either by the distance horizontally and vertically, or by the total linear distance and the angle of motion. You can also specify whether patterns should move with the objects that contain them.

Illustrator also includes a Transform Each dialog, found under the Object > Transform menu. After selecting a range of objects you can use this dialog to specify the movement, scaling and rotation of each object in the selection, as opposed to the selection as a whole. So if you've drawn an American flag, for instance, and made all of the stars slightly too big, there's no need to redraw them – you can use Transform Each to scale them all by the same amount, around their own centres. A Preview button shows the transformation as you drag the sliders, before you commit yourself to the operation.

The Random checkbox will move, scale or rotate each selected object by an amount up to that specified in the numerical fields in the dialog. You can use this to roughen up a drawing that's too precise. For example, if you've drawn an array of trees to signify a park on a map, you can use Transform Each to change the size and position of each in a random manner for a looser, more natural appearance.

You can specify movement in Photoshop more precisely by pressing Command-T to enter Free Transform mode. The Options bar at the top of the screen will show the distance to drag an object – you can also use this to enter the distance numerically, and the object will be moved by the amount specified.

When moving any object, holding the Shift key after you start to move will constrain the movement to 45° angles – including horizontal and vertical. This operation works in most design programs, and is used if you don't want to change the vertical position of an item, for instance, but only want to move it left and right.

Illustrator uses a system called Smart Guides to align objects with each other. The feature is turned on using Command-U, or by choosing Smart Guides from the View menu. When enabled, pale blue lines will appear when you move an object at 45° increments, and your motion will snap to those lines when you move close to them. More usefully, moving an object over one of its own anchor points will make it snap to that point, making it easy to create precise arrays.

Where Smart Guides really gets clever is when it interacts with other objects. When moving an object over another item on the page Smart Guides will activate for that item as well, showing guidelines when you're aligning with the object's anchor points, baselines and centre lines.

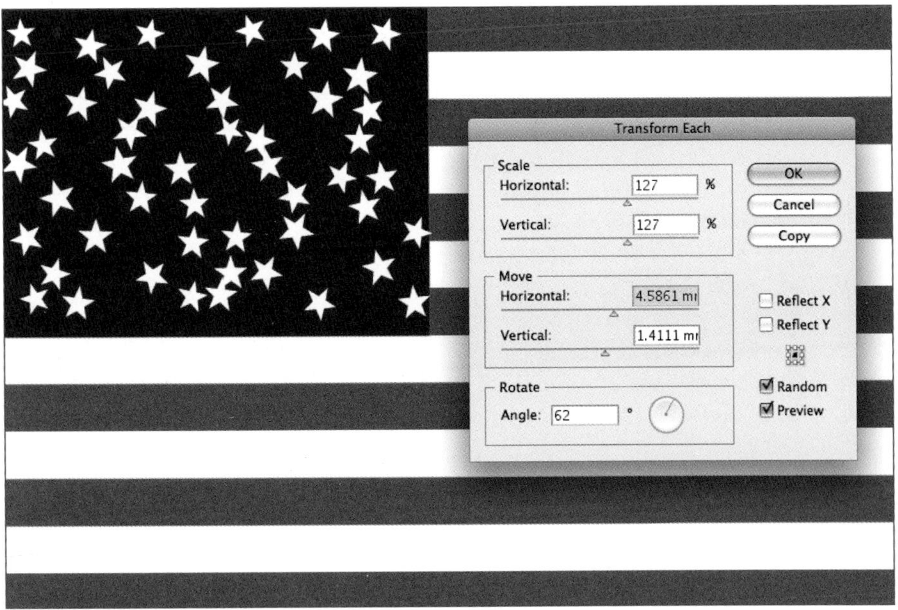

▲ **The Randomize feature of the Transform Each dialog can be used to break up rigid arrays.**

N: Noise reduction

Produce smoother results with less mess and noise by following this simple advice and you'll see the true potential of your photos.

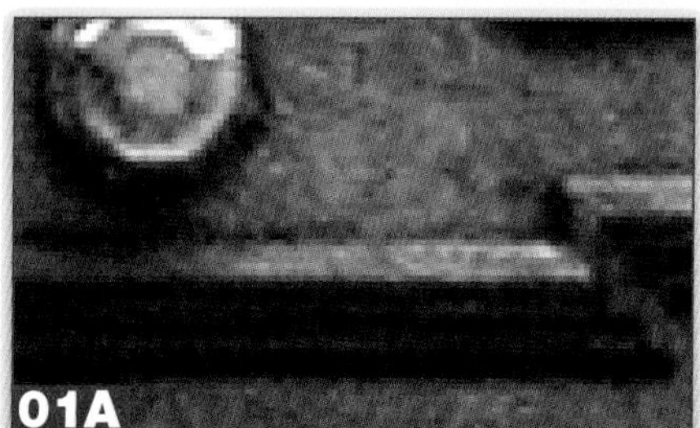

▲ A close-up of a photograph of a door. The colour noise is clearly visible here.

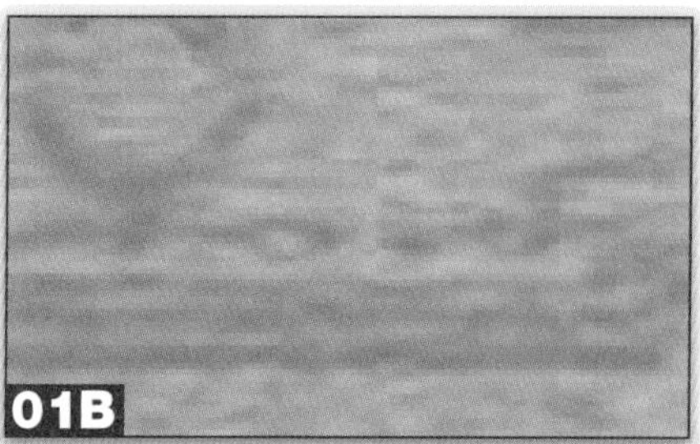

▲ Converted to Lab mode, this is the b channel: a fair amount of variation is visible.

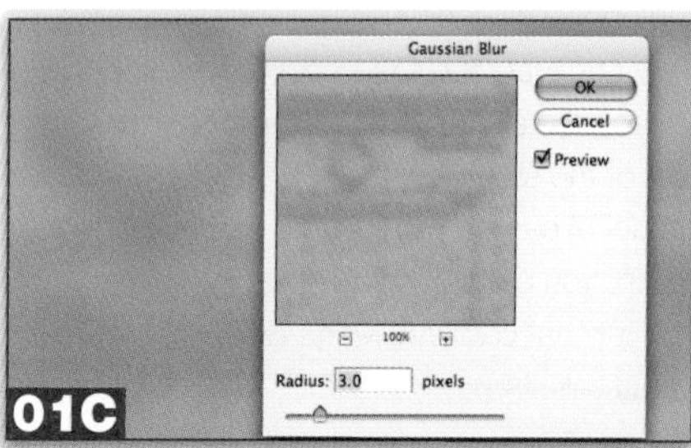

▲ Applying a 3.0 pixel Gaussian Blur to this channel smooths out all the colour variation.

▲ When we now view the composite image, the colour noise has gone.

Noise is one of the biggest problems with which designers and photographers have to contend. Easy to acquire and hard to get rid of, noise can render the best-composed images apparently unusable. However, there are ways of dealing with it, and the process involved depends on the kind of noise that's been produced.

Noise is caused by several factors. When taking photographs indoors without a flash, digital cameras have to work overtime in order to capture millions of pixels' worth of information in an under-lit scene. The most common result is colour noise – that is, the appearance of pixels of entirely the wrong colour cluttering up the scene. It could also be that the scene is simply too dark, and that noise appears as the equivalent of film grain in conventional cameras: using a high-ISO rated film may mean you'll be able to shoot with a fast shutter setting in dark conditions, but graininess will result. There's also moiré noise, which is generally caused by overlapping halftone screens when scanning printed images.

Here, we'll look at each noise type in turn and see how to deal with it.

COLOUR NOISE

Colour noise is seen as a kaleidoscope of stray colour pixels, which is most noticeable in areas of deep shadow or in large, blank areas such as walls. Most digital cameras produce colour noise, to a greater or lesser degree; the good news is that it's easy to fix.

Images are generally captured in RGB mode, and in this mode it's hard to remove colour noise directly. The solution is to convert the image to Lab mode in Photoshop using Image > Mode > Lab Color. This changes the familiar red, green and blue channels into three elements: Lightness (a greyscale version of the image); and the two colour channels, a (red/green) and b (blue/yellow). Pressing Command-1 will show the Lightness channel, while Command-2 and Command-3 will show a and b respectively.

The point of this conversion is that while in Lab mode, all the detail of the image is stored in the L channel, separate from the colour. This means you can apply loads of Gaussian Blur to the two colour channels, smearing all the stray colour pixels into each other without affecting the overall sharpness. Use Command-~ (the tilde key) to view the composite image when you're done.

A slightly less successful but quicker alternative is to remain in RGB mode. Use enough Gaussian Blur so the colour variation disappears and then press Command-Shift-F to bring up the Fade dialog box. Change the mode of the last-used filter to Color, and the sharpness will be retained.

IMAGE NOISE

Very noisy images, usually the result of high exposure settings, affect the grey component as well as the colour values – known as Speckle, or Salt and Pepper noise. The conversion to Lab colour space won't help here – more drastic measures are needed.

The most obvious way to remove noise is to blur the image using Gaussian Blur. This does work to an extent, but at a cost: the whole image will become fuzzy and out of focus. A better solution is to use the Median filter (Filters > Noise > Median), which operates in a similar way to Gaussian Blur, but with the added feature of recognising boundaries within the image and keeping them sharp. At high values, the Median filter will inevitably

02A
▲ A very noisy shot of a pub interior, taken in low light conditions.

02B
▲ Gaussian Blur removes the noise, but makes the whole image look out of focus.

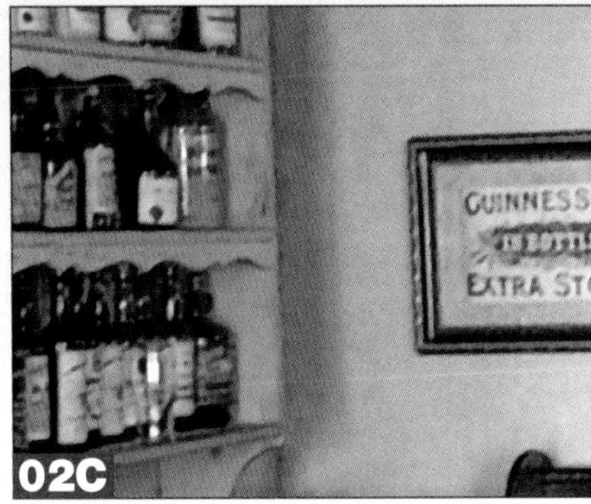
02C
▲ The Median filter removes the noise, while keeping the sharp edges within the image.

reduce sharpness in the image to some degree. For most cases, though, a value of just 1 or 2 is sufficient to create a dramatic improvement.

The best solution of all is to avoid noise in the first place. If you know you're going to be shooting images indoors without a flash, take a tripod and use your camera's manual override settings to allow for a longer exposure time, which will give the camera a better opportunity to capture the scene at a more leisurely pace.

MOIRÉ PATTERNS

Moiré noise is produced by two overlapping screens at different angles; the two arrays of dots combine to create strong patterns where the dots coincide. You'll generally see this noise when scanning photographs from a book or magazine, as a halftone screen will already have been applied to the image before being printed. When the regular grid of pixels is overlaid on this image, it will interfere with the printed dot to create an unwanted rosette effect.

It's almost impossible to get rid of moiré patterns, although the Median filter can help to some degree. However, it's possible to minimise the appearance of the patterns when scanning.

The angle at which a screened image is scanned will have a strong effect on the strength of the resulting pattern; the size of the halftone dot in relation to the pixel size will also make a difference. So in the first instance, try scanning at a different resolution. For images printed at high quality in glossy magazines, increasing the resolution can help a lot.

Second, try rotating the image in the scanner. Even changing the scanning angle by one or two degrees can help significantly, as the moiré pattern is most evident when the two screens are closest to each other. Experiment with different angles to see what produces the best results.

AUTOMATED NOISE REMOVAL

Recent versions of Photoshop have a filter dedicated to removing noise, which you can find in Filters > Noise > Reduce Noise. This will make a fair stab at removing both image and colour noise, and can also compensate to some degree towards removing Jpeg artefacts (the blockiness caused by over-enthusiastic Jpeg compression, usually produced by cheaper digital cameras). This filter won't produce perfect results, but it can make a significant improvement: choose Advanced settings to control each of the Lab colour channels independently.

A better solution still is to use third-party software. There are several products; our favourite is NeatImage (*neatimage.com*), which searches for a blank area of the image and analyses that, and then applies its findings to produce a significant noise reduction in the rest of the shot. If you know the make and model of camera with which the picture was taken, you can download specific settings files for that camera, which will produce even better results.

03A

03B

03C

03D

03E

▲ Two copies of an array of dots overlaid on top of each other (see figure 03A). When we change the angle to 1.5° (see figure 03B), 4° (see figure 03C), 10° (see figure 03D) and 22.5° (see figure 03E) we can see how the moiré pattern produced by coinciding dots varies tremendously with the angle.

N: Non-destructive editing

The benefit of working in a digital environment is that you can go back and change your mind. That's the benefit of working in a non-destructive application.

▼ Two versions of a chain – the pink one is a regular layer, the green one is a Smart Object (left). We've reduced these to a tiny size and rotated them slightly (centre). When we enlarge them again (right), the regular layer has degraded considerably – but the Smart Object version still looks as good as the original.

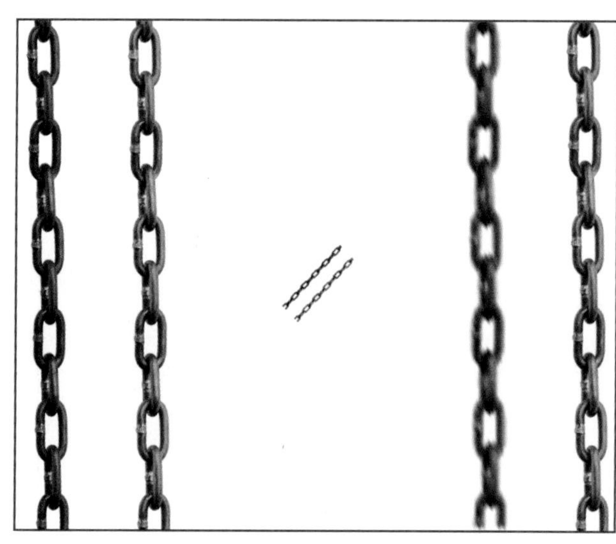

When you create artwork in a vector program, such as Illustrator, you can scale, rotate, distort and filter the image as much as you like – and you can always return to the original, unedited version if you need to. However, when working in Photoshop, it's all too easy to make changes to your work that are permanent. This is all very well as long as you're sure that's what you want. But if you change your mind further down the line, rebuilding an earlier version of the image can be a lengthy process.

Every version of Photoshop has introduced new methods of working around this problem, enabling you to work in such a way that you can undo operations at a later date. It's not just so mistakes can be repaired when you discover them, but to encourage users to experiment and to push the bounds of their creativity.

Rather than deleting part of a layer, use a Layer Mask to paint out the unwanted area. Painting in black on a layer mask hides the layer, but painting in white reveals it again – you can always return to the full, original layer should you need to. Choose Layer > Layer Mask > Reveal All to add a new mask to a layer.

Cropping an image will delete the pixels outside the crop area unless you change the Crop mode from Delete to Hide. This will keep all the pixel data intact, so that if the canvas is enlarged later, you'll be able to see the whole picture. Cropping in this way also means you can move layers whose edges project beyond the bounds of the image, and the hidden pixels will come back into view. To enlarge the canvas to show cropped layers in their entirety use Image > Reveal All.

When performing an operation, such as adding a different head to a body, you will often need to remove stray pieces of the original head that are still visible. This means you can't return to the original later – it's a destructive process. However, both the Clone tool and the Healing tools allow you to sample layers beneath the one you're working on, and that's the solution here. Make a new, empty layer above the one you wish to edit, then use the Clone tool to paint additional background where it's needed, in order to cover up offending areas. You then have the option of hiding or deleting this layer at a later date.

One of the most useful non-destructive techniques is the use of Adjustment layers. These behave exactly like regular adjustments, and are chosen from the pop-up menu at the bottom of the Layers palette. Curves, Brightness/Contrast, Levels, Hue/Saturation and Color Balance are among the available adjustments. Choose one of them, and the dialog will open as normal. However, after applying the change, the adjustment will appear as a special layer, which can be turned on and off. You can also double-click this layer at any point – even after the file has been saved – and change the settings.

Initially, the Adjustment Layer will affect all the layers beneath it, as if you're looking through a sheet of tinted glass. This differs from the way regular adjustments work, as they only affect the current layer. You can force Adjustment Layers to apply just to the layer directly beneath them by holding down the Alt key as you choose from the pop-up menu – this brings up a dialog that lets you use the previous layer as a Clipping Mask.

▲ This is a formal portrait of former US Secretary of State Condoleezza Rice in front of an American flag.

▲ After placing Nicole Kidman's head on top, parts of Condoleezza's hair are still visible from behind.

▲ You can set the Clone tool to Sample Current and Below, and clone from the background onto a new layer.

One of the biggest problems used to come from repeatedly rotating and scaling layers – every time you do so, a bit more quality is lost as Photoshop has to interpolate pixels with each operation. Thankfully, Photoshop CS2 introduced Smart Objects, which gives the flexibility you need. These are chosen from the pop-up menu at the top of the Layers palette, and can be made from single layers or whole groups of layers. The original file data is stored within the Smart Object layer, which can be edited by double-clicking on it.

The advantage here is that each time you rotate or scale the Smart Object, Photoshop refers to the original full-size file rather than the current pixel data, producing crisper, more editable results. As a bonus, any distortions applied to Smart Objects through Image Warp are shown in their grid state, just as when you applied them – you can edit the grid, or remove the distortions, with no loss of quality.

Photoshop CS3 added to Smart Objects' capabilities by introducing Smart Filters. These work like Adjustment Layers, in that they can be adjusted or hidden at any point – they allow you to experiment with different effects without damaging the original artwork. It's worth noting that adjustments such as Shadows/Highlights and Unsharp Mask can be applied as Smart Filters, as well as some of the wackier effects.

For maximum editability, it's best to shoot images as Raw files and adjust them using Camera Raw rather than the standard Photoshop adjustments. All the Camera Raw operations are recorded in a separate file, and can be removed later.

The trouble is that when opening the image in Photoshop, you lose that editing potential. However, if Camera Raw files are opened as Smart Objects, the Raw settings will be maintained and can still be edited later. The one thing you can't yet do non-destructively is to paint, smudge, dodge or burn onto a layer. But you can use a combination of layer masks and copying required areas to new layers, so that you can still keep the original intact. But the simplest method, of course, is to duplicate the layer and always to work on the copy.

▲ This is the clone layer on its own, patching the background while leaving it intact.

◄ Working in Camera Raw means you can edit files as much as you like, without ever changing the original file copy.

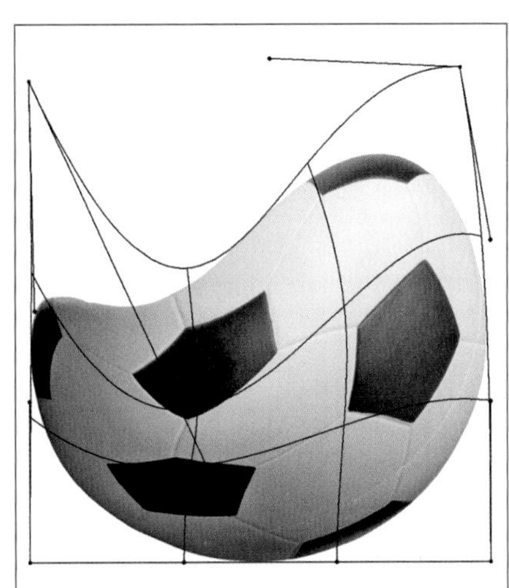

▲ When distorting a Smart Object layer, you can return to it at any time and find your grid position as you left it.

O: OpenType

Using OpenType fonts gives you a much wider range of characters to work with, ultimately producing neater text that's more pleasant to read.

OpenType is a font format developed by Adobe and Microsoft that takes typography to the next level. Building on PostScript and TrueType, it's cross-platform, which means that the same font will work on both a Mac and PC – there are no separate screen and outline files, as there are with PostScript, which makes them far more portable.

OpenType fonts have the ability to perform a range of automated tasks, such as converting numbers into fractions and changing character pairs to typographic ligatures – the process whereby pairs such as 'f' and 'i', which would clash when placed together, are replaced by a single typographical device that sidesteps the problem. Such devices are called glyphs – the word encompasses characters as well as other typographic elements. Some fonts include alternate decorative glyphs, such as swash capitals (those that include outsized flourishes) as well as added curlicues and twirls applied to regular letters. Fonts supporting this feature tend to be only those that are highly decorative to begin with, such as Bickham Script.

OpenType technology is supported by the three main Adobe CS3 and CS4 design applications – Photoshop, Illustrator and InDesign. Photoshop, however, has limited access to the feature, and can't, for example, choose between alternate glyphs. These applications do, however, ship with a wide range of OpenType fonts, including Caslon, Garamond, Bickham Script, Charlemagne, Lithos, Myriad, News Gothic and Tekton.

It's impressive that Adobe applications will see the letters 'f' and 'i' as distinct characters, even when they are represented by a single ligature – which means spell checkers and hyphenation dictionaries will continue to interpret them correctly.

Where PostScript and TrueType fonts were limited to 256 glyphs, OpenType can include up to 65,000. This means they can include character sets from other European languages, such as Russian and Greek – the fonts with 'Pro' after their name include this feature. Some OpenType fonts include different type cuts for different sizes, so headline sizes are optimised differently to body copy fonts.

Decorative fonts, which include multiple glyph variations, have the extraordinary and entertaining ability to adapt themselves as you type. Characters will change to their alternate versions, depending on the characters that precede and follow them – see above right to see a walkthrough of this particular process for the word 'Changeable'.

Most applications don't activate OpenType features by default – they have to be turned on manually. This is to prevent confusion among those who don't know about their capabilities. To see characters changing all by themselves can be unnerving, and it would be frustrating to end up with fractions when you don't want them and weren't expecting them. To turn OpenType features on, use the OpenType option from the pop-up menu on the Character

1/2 lb flat fish

½ lb ﬂat ﬁsh

▲ **In the top example, OpenType features are switched off. Notice the ugly fraction and the way the letter 'f' interferes with the 'l' and the 'i' that follow. In the second version, the fractions and ligatures are created as we type.**

▲ In the Bickham Script font, the characters adapt as we type. Here, the word begins with a swash capital, while the letter 'a' is at the end of the word (so far), so has a decorative flourish.

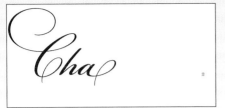

▲ When we type additional characters, the 'a' changes to a regular form. Note how the letter 'h' now produces an extended decorative vertical, as the swash on the 'a' has disappeared.

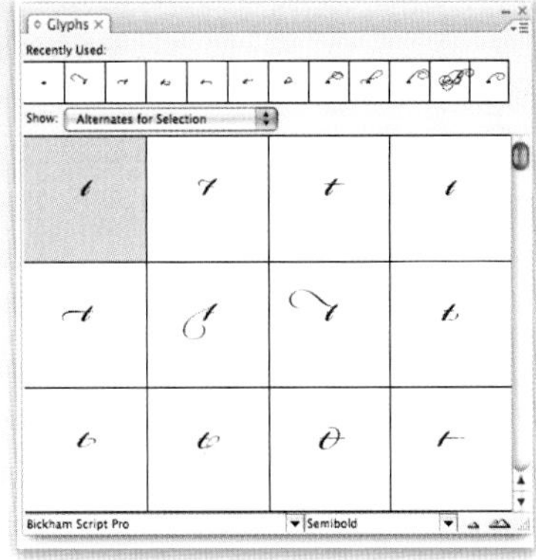

▲ The Glyph palette shows all the variations available for an individual character. Double-click one in the palette to apply it to your work.

▲ Continuing the word changes the 'g' to a swash version, which loops neatly under the first half of the word. See how the 'b' at the end is preparing to join to the next character.

▲ Because the next character is an 'l', the 'b' expects it to be followed by a character that will join to it – and so truncates itself automatically.

▲ Once the final character is added, the 'b' mutates again in order to join the 'l', which has itself changed in order to join onto the final 'e'.

palette in all Adobe applications. From here, you can choose which features you want to include.

In InDesign and Illustrator you can use the separate Glyph palette (chosen from the menu Window > Type & Tables) to choose your alternate characters. Choose Show Alternates for Selection from the pop-up menu at the top of the palette, and the palette will only show variants for the currently selected character. This is particularly useful when you want to handcraft an individual word.

When you use OpenType fonts in Photoshop, you should ensure 'fractional widths' is turned off in the Character palette. This will interfere with the precise letter spacing, producing ugly mismatched joins in those character pairs that are designed to run into each other.

With greater typographical precision and a library of over 2000 OpenType fonts available, the format is set to become the standard for type excellence. If, however, you don't have any CS3 or CS4 applications, you can still get a taste of the technology – in TextEdit, set a large type size and choose Zapfino as your font. When you type, the characters will mutate in context depending on their surroundings.

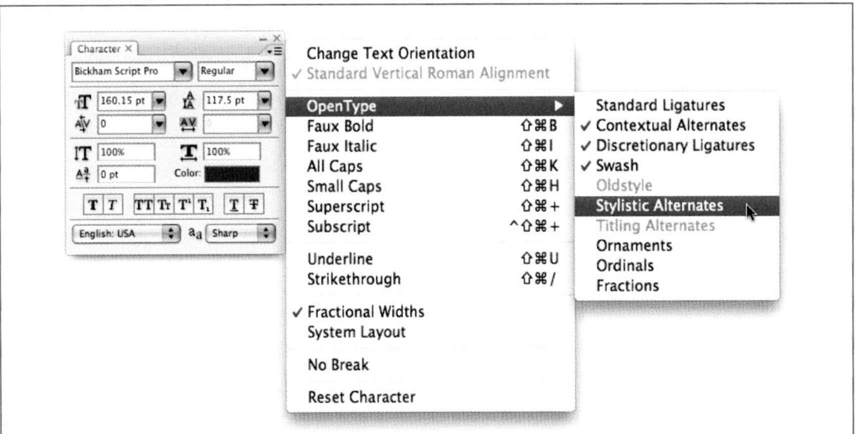

▲ OpenType features are selected from the pop-up menu in the Character palette (shown here in InDesign). Individual OpenType features can be turned on and off here. Not all features are available for all OpenType fonts.

▲ In Illustrator and InDesign, you can choose from several versions of each glyph. Here, the standard setting of the word 'Bath' has been replaced by a far more decorative version. But note the shape of the new 'a' among all the flourishes – this is a version without the leading tail that would join it to the preceding character.

O: Optimising Photoshop

Photoshop needs a lot of resources in terms of both memory and temporary disk space. You can help keep it running smoothly by optimising its settings.

Photoshop is probably the most memory-hungry application you own. It's not uncommon to hand over 75% of your total Ram allocation to Photoshop – and that's still not enough. For every file Photoshop opens, it needs the Ram equivalent to at least five times the file size in order to manipulate it. If you regularly have several files open at once, this means that Photoshop frequently requires more memory than is physically present in your Mac.

To cope with this, Photoshop writes huge temporary files to disk, storing the data required: every keystroke and process that can be reverted through the History palette, any item on the clipboard, every snapshot, they are all stored in the temporary 'scratch' file.

By default, Photoshop will choose your startup disk as its scratch disk (the place it stores its temporary files); but as these files are written and changed frequently, the amount of fragmentation that ensues will slow down not just Photoshop, but ultimately your whole system. Other than adding as much Ram as you can afford to your Mac or PC, the single best move you can make to speed up Photoshop is to allocate a separate hard disk for this purpose. External drives, connected by FireWire or USB2, are a reasonable option; internal drives will give better performance.

You don't need to allocate the entire drive as a scratch disk: a partition should be around five times the amount of physical Ram you have installed. By partitioning a new drive, you're allocating a permanent physical section of it purely for Photoshop's use. Drives can easily be partitioned using the Disk Utility application, but be aware that the process will wipe the drive first. You should use the first partition as the scratch disk.

You can still use the remainder of the drive for storage, as long as you keep the scratch disk clean. Once installed, go to the Performance section of the Photoshop Preferences dialog, and specify your new scratch disk in the top slot. You can add your other drives as secondary scratch disks as

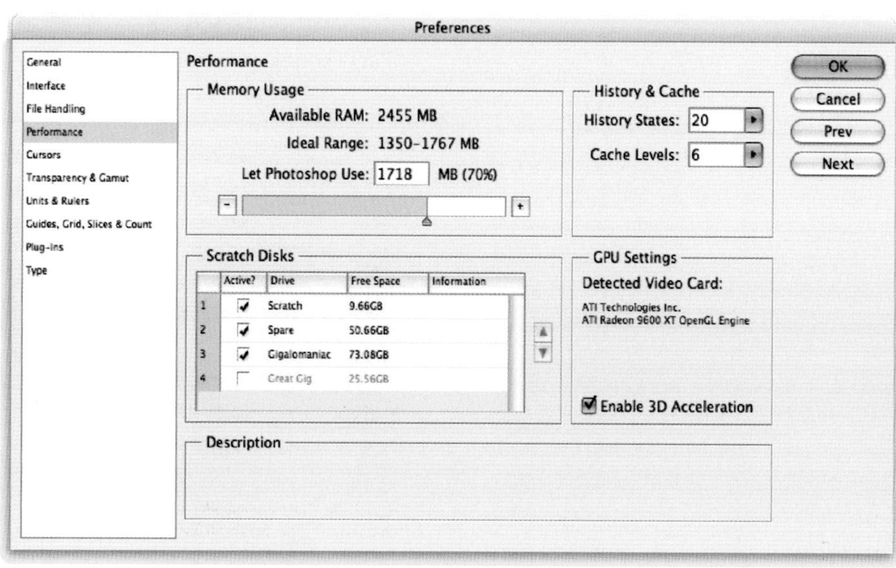

► The Performance section of the Preferences dialog is where you'll make the most difference. Set the amount of physical Ram available to Photoshop to at least 70%; this is also where you'll specify the scratch disk usage, number of History states and number of Cache levels.

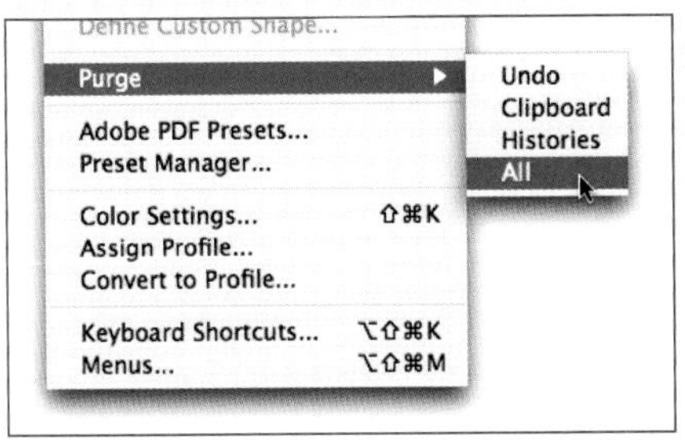

◄ **Purging Undo, Clipboard and Histories on a regular basis will free up large amounts of scratch disk space, improving Photoshop's performance considerably.**

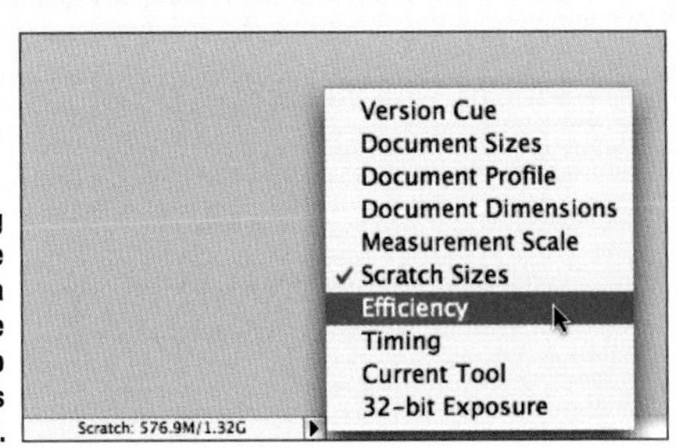

► **You can see how much Ram Photoshop is using via the pop-up menu at the bottom of the image window. Here, Photoshop is using 576.8 MB out of a total of 1.32 GB available. Check the Efficiency value as well: any figure below 100% means Photoshop has used all its available physical Ram, and is working on the scratch disk instead.**

well, but in practice they should rarely (if ever) be used. Photoshop can support up to 64 billion gigabytes of scratch disk space.

The Performance Preferences dialog is where you specify how much physical Ram Photoshop is allowed to appropriate. This is also where you set the number of Cache levels: these are downsampled versions of the image you're working on, and are used when you work with large images and frequently zoom out or pan around them.

The higher the Cache level, the more low-resolution versions of the file Photoshop will store, so the faster zooming out will become. The default value is 4; smaller values will free up more Ram (but entail longer screen redraw times), larger values will speed up redraw times – but the cost is that it will take longer for Photoshop to open each file, as it has to cache multiple resolutions when it does so.

The final option in Performance Preferences is setting the number of History states. The default here is 20, and setting a higher number will obviously mean that you can revert more steps should you need to – but, of course, all these extra steps will have to be written to the scratch disk, which will take more time. If you find you rarely use the History palette, then consider reducing the number of History states for improved performance.

The Options panel for the History palette allows you to specify how new snapshots are created, and you can also create snapshots of the document as you go along. Each one will add its toll to performance, though, so it's best to delete snapshots when you've finished using them.

We would recommend keeping the Automatically Create First Snapshot option, so you can always return to it if you have accidentally saved a version of the file when you didn't mean to. If you're really pushed for scratch space and have very little Ram, it's worth considering reducing the size of the thumbnails in the Layers, Paths and Channels palettes, or removing them altogether, using the palette's Options dialog box.

Older versions of Photoshop have an additional option in the Displays & Cursors Preferences, called Pixel Doubling: this works with pixels twice the size when moving items around, so speeding up the process. The option has now been dropped from the application.

In the General Preferences pane, you can specify whether Photoshop should export its clipboard. While this is frequently a useful ability, it does mean that the process of switching from Photoshop to another application is slowed by its having to format its clipboard into an exportable format; disable this option for faster application switching. In the File Handling Preferences pane, you can specify whether Photoshop includes both Mac and Windows thumbnails in its image previews, whether it saves full-size icons, and whether to maximize psd compatibility, which means saving files in such a way that they can be opened be earlier versions of Photoshop and other, older applications. Disabling these options will reduce file sizes and, more significantly, the time it takes to save files: saving composite images can slow down the saving process to a large extent.

Photoshop now allows users to work in 16-bit mode, which means 65,000 colours per channel, rather than the 256 found in 8-bit. While photographers may value the extra tonal range this produces, be aware that it means working with files of a vastly larger size: the performance trade-off is considerable.

If you want to shave a few seconds off the time Photoshop takes to start up, consider deleting presets you never use – brushes, layer styles, gradients, swatches and so on. Use the Preset Manager (edit menu) to avoid having to open each palette's settings individually, and do remember to save copies of the originals.

The single most effective performance enhancer while working in Photoshop is to purge unwanted elements in the scratch file, using the Purge item at the bottom of the Edit menu. Here, you can purge Undo, the Clipboard and History states: the final item in the list is Purge All.

If you're sure you won't need to undo recent actions, then choosing Purge All will massively reduce the size of the scratch file. It's worth creating an Action to do this with a keystroke, and to perform the Action frequently during your working day.

◄ **If you have little Ram installed, consider reducing the thumbnail size in the Layers, Paths and Channels palettes – or turn them off entirely.**

P: Paragraph rules

Take the tedium out of setting lines above, below or over parts of your paragraphs by using paragraph rules in your DTP application of choice.

Both the heavyweight page layout applications, InDesign and QuarkXPress, enable you to place horizontal rules above and below paragraphs. You can specify the thickness of the rule, its colour and style, which may include dotted lines, fancy borders and more.

However, there's a lot more to this operation than you might expect from the simple dialog box. Because you can specify the precise positioning of the rules, both vertically and horizontally, you can use the feature to create automatic WOB subheads. The term is an abbreviation for 'white on black' and refers to white text on a black rectangular background, of the sort commonly seen dividing each section in newspaper classified ads.

The dummy classified ads here show a typical example [**01**] of how they might appear in most newspapers. Click anywhere in the subhead – there's no need to select the whole line, as the rules will apply to the entire paragraph. In InDesign, choose Paragraph Rules from the pop-up menu at the top of the Paragraph panel, or use the shortcut Alt-Command-J. In XPress, use Style > Rules, or use the shortcut Command-Shift-N.

In either application, check the Rule Above box. In XPress, you need to press the Apply button after making each change to see the effect on the page. In InDesign, check the Preview button to see each change live, as you make it. The remainder of the operations are almost identical in both programs; the examples here are from InDesign because they're clearer in print [**02**].

You need to make the rule thicker so it overlaps the text top and bottom. The trouble is, when using a default black rule with black text, you can't see the text above it, making precise positioning impossible. A good trick is to change the colour of the rule temporarily, so you can see where it lies [**03**]. Increase the thickness of the rule so it extends both above and below the text. A value of 10pt here is perhaps a little tight.

The problem now is that the rule is sitting too high within the text block – most of it is above the line, and we need some below. You can fix this type of problem with the Offset control in the dialog box: setting a value of -1pt shifts the rule just below the baseline, and increasing the thickness to 12pt gives a comfortable margin above

01

work. Box 36223.

FOR RENT

• Studio flat, complete with darkroom. Lights will be repaired in next fiscal quarter. Suit compulsive photophobe. Box 46222.

• Large cardboard box, handy

02

work. Box 36223.

FOR RENT

• Studio flat, complete with

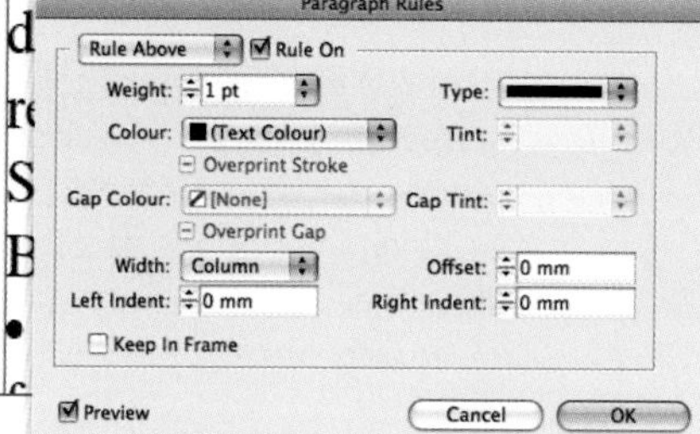

03

recent subsidence. Needs work. Box 36223.

FOR RENT

• Studio flat, complete with darkroom. Lights will be repaired in next fiscal quarter. Suit compulsive photophobe. Box 46222.

• Large cardboard box, handy

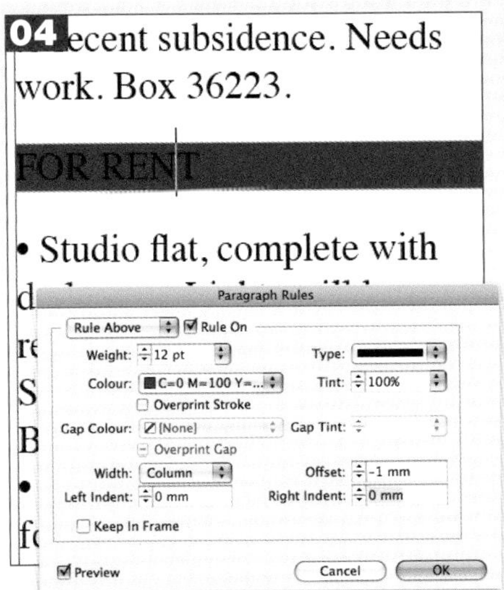

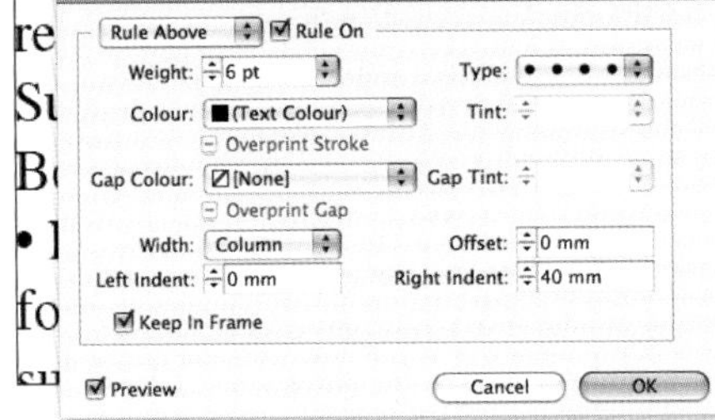

and below [**04**]. With the weight and position of the rule now set, you can change its colour back to black and set the text colour to white [**05**].

Here, we've set the text centred within the rule. You can leave it aligned left, of course, but you'll need to indent it by a millimetre or so in order for it not to be flush with the left edge of the rule. Once all is set, the text, complete with its alignment, colour and rule, can be defined as a paragraph style so it can be applied with a keystroke.

So far, we've been looking at the subheads that divide each section of our imaginary classified ads page. The ads themselves begin with a bullet point, and there are two ways of creating this. It can either be a standard Alt-8 bullet, which may be fine for creating lists but is really too small for our purposes. Or it could be a bullet created using Zapf Dingbats, but that means changing font at the start of each new paragraph. There is a better method: creating bullets using paragraph rules.

Before you add the bullet, you need to delete the existing one and replace it with an indent. Choose First Line indent, as it will add space just before the first character but not to each subsequent line.

Open the Rules dialog box again, and this time choose the dotted line rule variant [**06**]. There's a difference here in the way in which Rule Above is interpreted: in InDesign, the offset is specified as distance above the baseline; in XPress, it's placed above the text on the line. You'll need to adjust the offset to position the dots according to which program you're using. The dot size depends on the point size of the type to which it's attached. Here, a 6pt rule gives us a bullet point of the right size [**07**].

The problem now is that the rule extends the full width of the text. You need to limit it so that it's only a single bullet wide by changing the right indent, raising it to a level that's almost the full width of the text. In InDesign, you can do this by guessing a figure (say, 35mm) and then using the up/down cursor keys to adjust it. With the Preview button checked, you can see the change as you hit the keys. XPress doesn't use the cursor key feature, which means typing in the numbers and hitting the Apply button.

There's a further wrinkle when you get close to the right figure: rather than showing just a single bullet, both InDesign and XPress double up the final two, trying to fit them into the available space. InDesign shows two overlapping black dots, whereas XPress shows the outlines of the dots, with just the overlap area showing in black [**08**]. There's no alternative but to try different settings, using fractions of a millimetre, until the two dots overlap perfectly. In this instance, this is a value of 40.8mm, but it will vary with the column size of your publication [**09**].

It may be a fiddle but, when it's done, you can define it as a paragraph style for an instant large bullet when you need one, without having to worry about changing font or increasing point sizes.

P: Pathfinder panel

Illustrator's Pathfinder provides all the tools for merging, intersecting and cutting paths. Here, we show how to use it to make a twisting 3D form.

▲ Unite: merges all selected objects. The colour of the merged result will be taken from the front object and any stroke will be applied to the result as a whole.

▲ Minus Front: as its name suggests, removes the front objects and cuts the shape away from the back object, cookie-cutter fashion.

Merging two shapes into one in Illustrator used to be a complex business. First, you'd use the Scissors tool to cut the top shape where it overlapped the bottom one. Next, you'd have to cut the bottom shape with the same tool – except that you couldn't, because the Scissors tool would keep complaining that you were trying to cut an end point of a path. So you'd have to nudge the top shape out of the way, cut the bottom one, then nudge the top one back, delete the unwanted portions of both paths, then select each pair of endpoints and join them.

Illustrator's Pathfinder panel does the entire process for you. It's a comprehensive set of tools for merging, intersecting and cutting paths in a variety of useful ways. Curiously, the one thing it won't do is find paths for you.

Select the Pathfinder panel from Illustrator's Window menu to open it. The panel consists of 10 buttons, four on the top row and four along the bottom. To use them, select two or more objects and then press the button to get the results. The operation of each one is explained here with illustration (see right and below). You can use Pathfinder to create complex shapes that would be difficult, if not impossible, to draw by conventional means. In this workthrough, we'll see how Pathfinder can build a twisting 3D form with ease.

Begin by drawing a circle. Next, draw an ellipse that fits within this circle, touching the right edge. The shapes are shown here with a thick stroke to make it easier to see what's going on [01]. Duplicate the ellipse, moving a copy so it touches the left edge of the original circle [02]. Next, duplicate both ellipses and rotate them by 90°, so that they touch the circle at the top and the bottom [03].

Select all four ellipses and the circle, and press the Divide button on the Pathfinder panel. This will split the object into its constituent shapes so you can work on each independently [04]. You probably won't see any difference at this stage. Each object is a separate entity, but the entire assembly is grouped together. In order to manipulate individual elements, you need to use the Direct

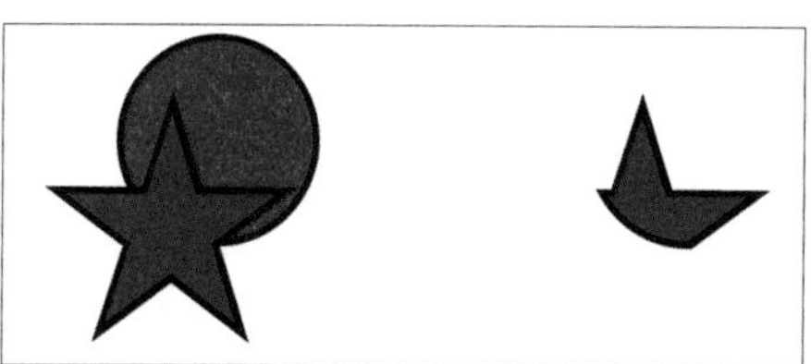

▲ Intersect: deletes everything except the region where the shapes overlap.

▲ Divide: breaks up the objects into individual pieces where they overlap. Nothing is deleted.

▲ Exclude: removes hidden areas, like Trim, but similar-coloured objects aren't merged.

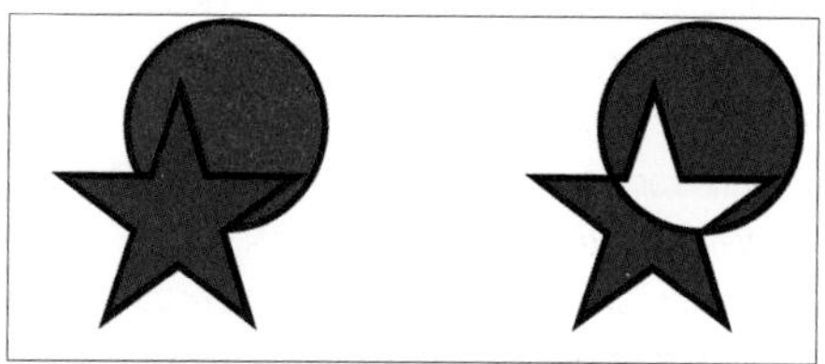

▲ Exclude: this is the opposite of Intersect, deleting the overlapping region while keeping everything else.

▲ Trim: removes hidden areas in overlapping shapes, so the visible portions are separate objects. Strokes are removed and similar-coloured objects are merged.

▲ Crop: deletes everything outside the area of the front object; the colour of the front object is lost.

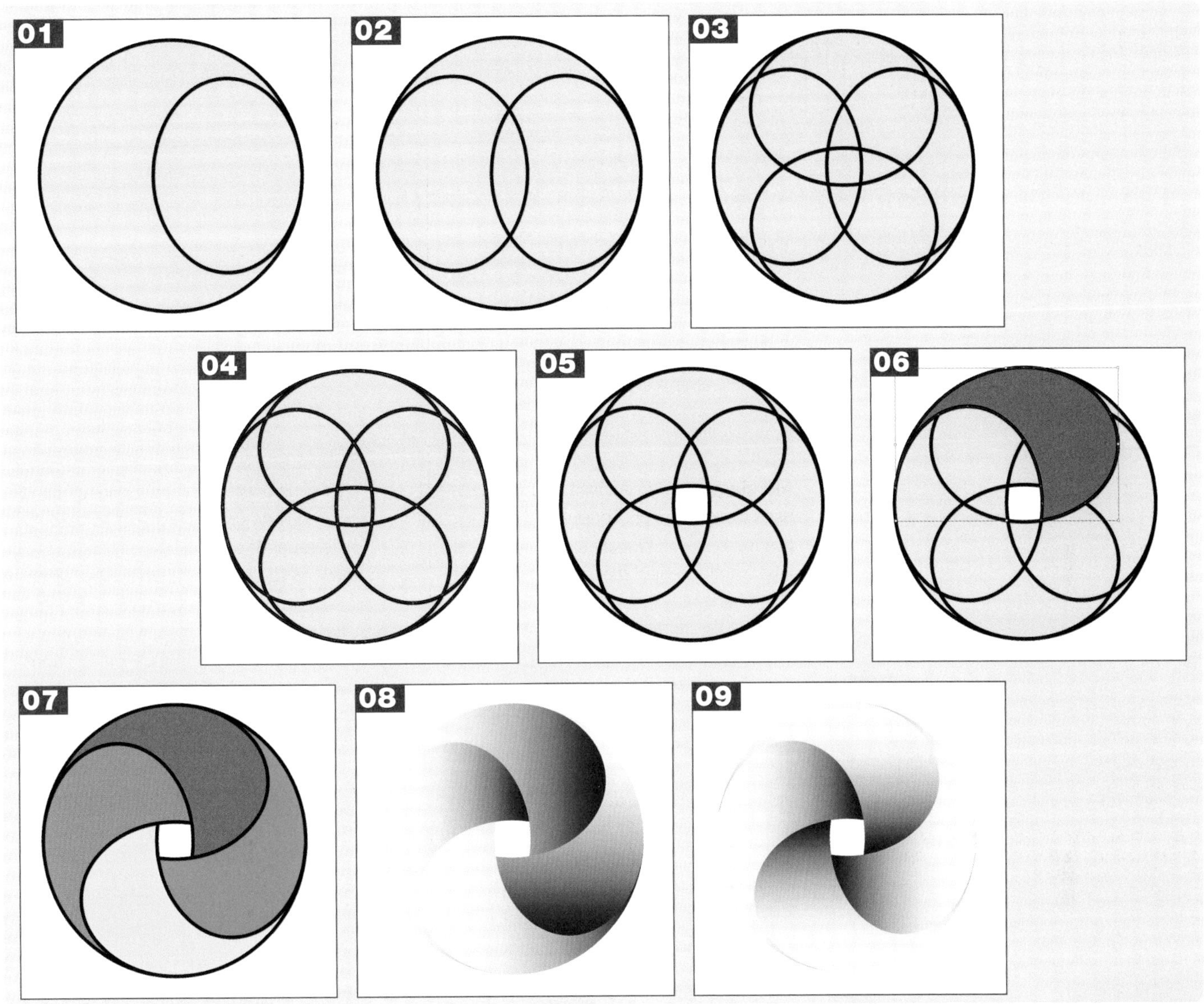

Selection Tool rather than the regular Selection Tool. For example, you can now select the centre shape and delete it [05]. There are four different shapes here, each repeated four times in rotation. You can select one group of shapes with the Direct Selection Tool, holding down Shift to add each new object to the selection. If you press the Unite button, you can merge the selection into a single unit, and re-colour it as a single item [06]. Repeating this process with the remainder of the objects creates a logo made of four curved shapes that interlock [07]. Changing the fill from a flat colour to a gradient adds depth to the logo [08]. Create a gradient for one of the component objects, remove the stroke and use the Eyedropper tool to sample this gradient and place it into the other objects. You can use the Gradient tool to change the direction of the gradients, so they all radiate from the centre, producing the effect of a three-dimensional twisting form [09].

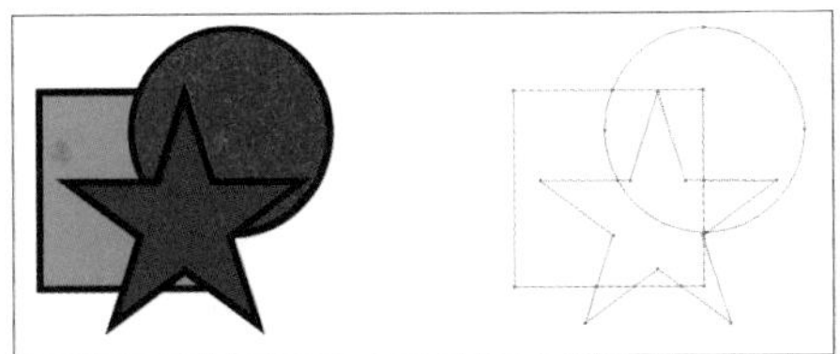

▲ Outline: similar to Divide, this command removes all colour and stroke, leaving just the outline shapes.

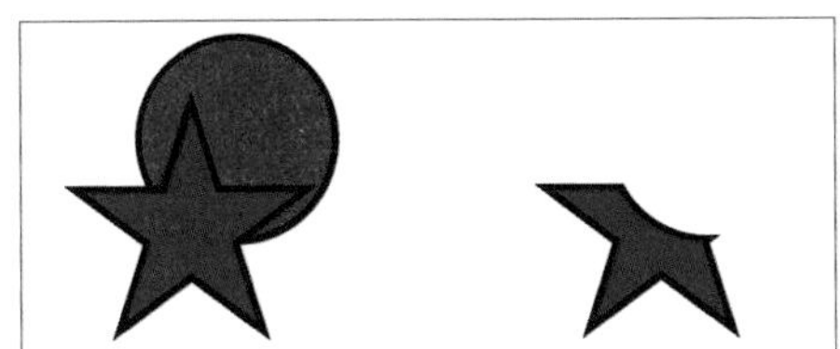

▲ Minus Back: removes the backmost object and cuts its shape away from the rest.

How Illustrator performs its operations depends on which version you have. Up to and including Illustrator CS3, selecting a Pathfinder operation will create a compound path rather than deleting any shapes. When the resulting object is selected, you'll be able to see the original outlines, although fill and stroke won't be applied to hidden areas. The advantage is that you can move objects around even after a Pathfinder effect has been applied, and the effect will be reapplied to the objects in their new position. The disadvantage is that further path editing is made more complicated by the presence of unwanted objects. Press the Expand button to turn the compound path into regular paths. This will remove the hidden areas. Alternatively, hold Alt while pressing the Pathfinder buttons to perform this task as the Pathfinder effect is first applied.

With Illustrator CS4, the situation is reversed: unwanted areas are deleted when a Pathfinder button is pressed. If you want to use the old method of creating complex paths, hold Alt while pressing the button.

P: PDFs

Automator lets you automate repetitive tasks and has extensive options for PDFs. Here, we show you how to set up actions for reducing file sizes.

Automator is one of the most frequently overlooked features of Mac OS X. As its name implies, it allows users to automate repetitive tasks, performing a variety of chores from simply renaming Finder items to building complex sequences of actions.

As well as providing excellent text handling, Automator has several tools specific for use on PDFs, enabling you to perform tasks that would be awkward if not downright impossible to reproduce by any other means. Here, you'll start with the basics of building an Automator workflow to reduce the size of PDF files.

Begin by opening Automator, which you'll find in your Applications folder. You're initially presented with the opening splash screen asking how you want to begin (**01**). Although you could choose Custom and build everything from scratch, choosing Photos & Images gives you a good starting point. You now have to make two choices: where the source files will come from (you can choose 'my Mac'), and when Automator will ask for them – choose 'Ask for image files when my workflow runs'. Click OK, and the first action will be placed in the list for you: Ask for Finder Items. You can specify here where Automator should open its Find dialog to, and whether it will handle files or folders.

You now need the action to compress the images in your PDF. From the first column on the left, choose PDFs as the action category and the column to the right will show only PDF appropriate actions. Choose 'Apply Quartz Filter to PDF Documents' and drag it into the workflow on the right, below the existing 'Ask for Finder Items' action. At this point, you'll see a warning that says that the action will change the file, asking if you want to add an action to copy the file in the Finder first (**02**). This is generally a good idea, so click Add. Now, the Quartz filter action will appear in the list, and a Copy Finder Items action will be listed above it. Each of the actions will be performed in the order shown, from top to bottom.

From the pop-up list in the Quartz filter action, choose Reduce File Size. And that's it: the workflow is now complete (**03**). Press the Run button at the top right and choose a PDF to compress. Automator will run through the series of actions, first duplicating and then compressing the images in the file. The amount of saving depends on the number of images in the original PDF, but typically you can reduce a file's size to about 20% of its original size, which is ideal for emailing.

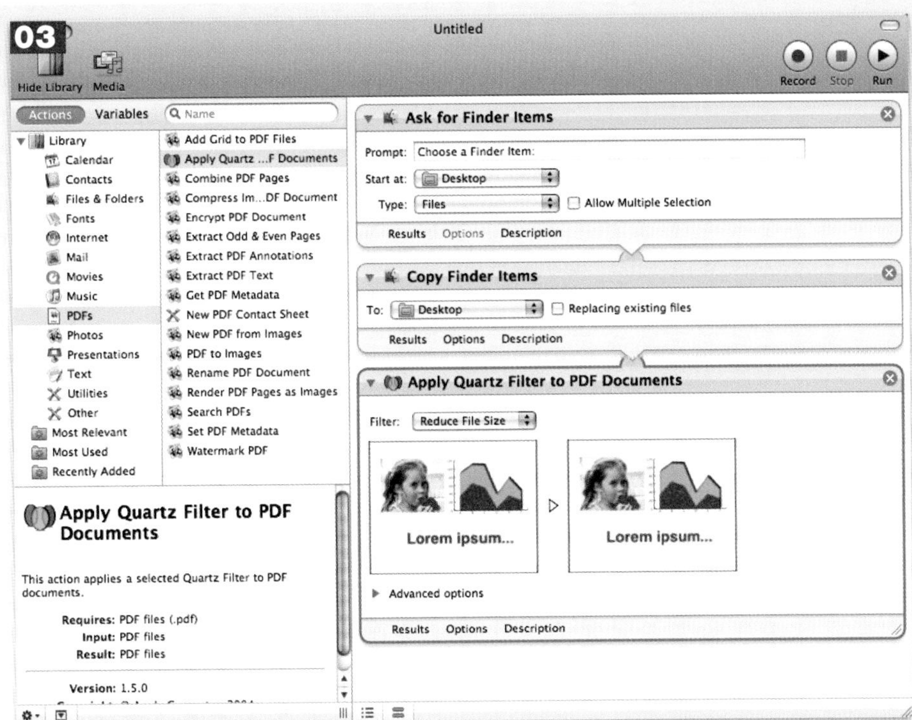

You can save the set of actions in one of several ways. First, you can save it as an Automator workflow, using File > Save. This is a good first step because it means you can retrieve it if you need to adapt it later. In order to run it again, you simply double-click the saved file and it will launch Automator with all the actions in place.

However, you don't need to launch Automator each time you want to run a workflow. You can save the workflow as a standalone application, enabling you to drag your PDF files onto it in the Finder in order to reduce their size immediately. Before you do this, however, you have to note that the first step in the workflow is to ask for a file to work on. You don't want to see this dialog every time you drag a file onto the mini application, so you need to delete this step first. Click the tiny 'x' in the top right corner to remove it from the workflow, and then choose Save As, selecting Application as the file format.

The File > Save As Plug-In menu item allows you to save the workflow as a Finder plug-in (**04**). Now, when you select your PDF file in the Finder, you can hold down the Ctrl key to access the contextual pop-up menu, and you can choose the workflow from the Automator section of the menu. Alternatively, you can save it as a plug-in for the Script menu and it will appear in your AppleScript menu. You'll need to open the AppleScript Utility in Applications/AppleScript to make this menu visible.

Let's try another sequence of actions. In this example, a friend has scanned a printed manual for you, saving the cover and each spread as a Jpeg file. It's far easier to read all the files in a single PDF, so you can create a workflow to build this PDF for you.

Begin by creating a new workflow. This time, you can choose Custom as the starting point, so you begin with a blank canvas. Your friend scanned the A5 document a spread at a time, and the images are all rotated to vertical

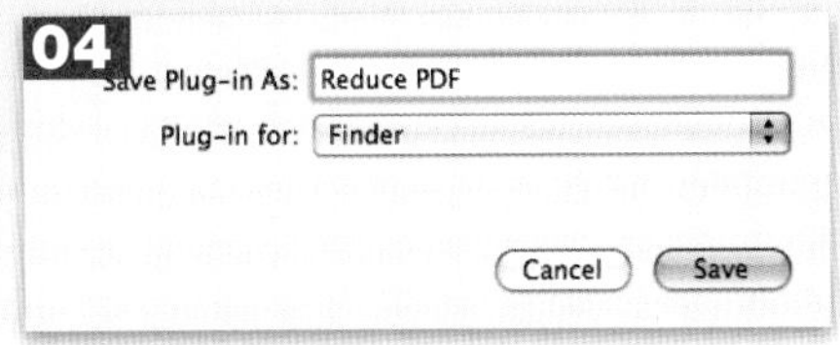

A4 format; the first step is to rotate each image by 90°. Select Photos from the library list, and then choose Rotate Images from the Photos category and drag it into the empty workflow. Again, you'll be asked if you want to add an action to duplicate the files first; you can say Don't Add in this instance. Once the action is in place, you can choose whether to rotate the images clockwise or anticlockwise.

Switch to the PDFs category, and choose New PDF from Images. Drag this into the workflow and it will appear below the Rotate Images action. A useful option is the 'Make All Pages the Same Size' checkbox: if your friend has scanned the cover as a single page, this action will pad it so it's the same width as all the other images in the PDF. You have to give the resulting PDF a name and a location in which it's saved. The workflow is complete, and you can run it on your image files (**05**).

You can perform many more tasks on PDF files, such as combining multiple PDFs into a single file, extracting text from PDFs and adding watermarks. You can even create PDF contact sheets from multiple images. All of the options are listed and clearly described, so it's just a matter of choosing the sequence of actions that fits the job in hand.

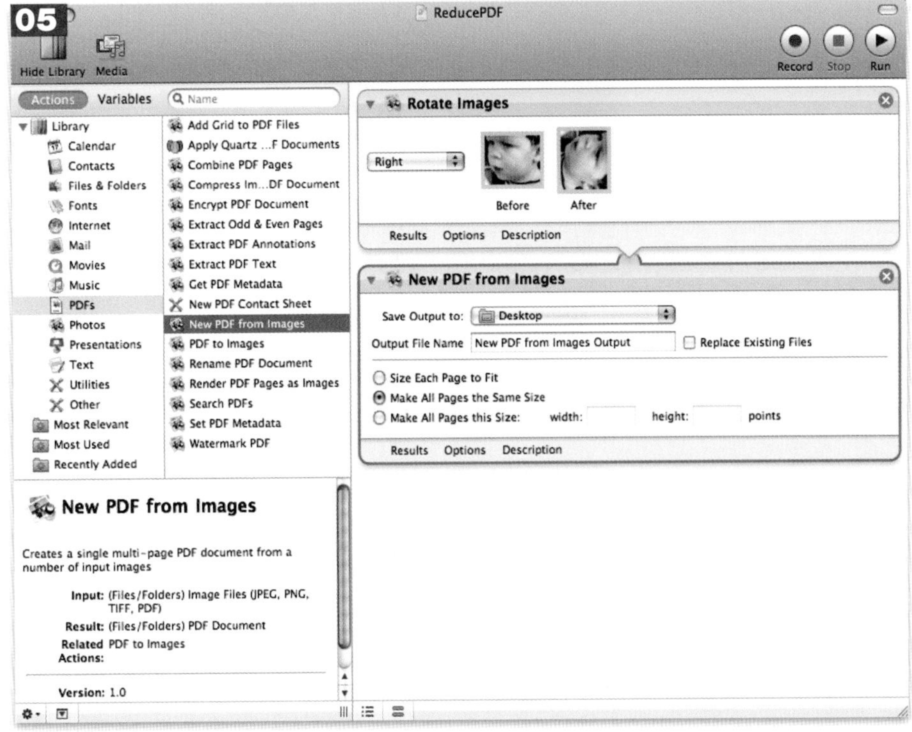

P: Perspective

It's all in the eyes… understand how perspective works and you can successfully incorporate people into any environment every time.

Whether you're drawing illustrations from scratch in Illustrator or Freehand, or creating montages in Photoshop, you need an understanding of how perspective works in order to make your creations look convincing. Incorrect perspective is the single factor that, more than any other, makes illustrations look wrong: and yet it's easy enough to get it right, as long as you follow a few basic rules.

There's one essential rule that always holds: the horizon is always at the same level as the viewer's eyes. No matter whether you're sitting or standing, lying on the beach or gazing out of a high window, you'll always look straight ahead to see the horizon. It's perhaps a surprising rule, and you may need to try it for yourself before you believe it. But it's the bedrock upon which the whole of perspective depends. What the horizon means, in practice, is that if you're populating a landscape or a room with figures drawn from a variety of sources, then one way of guaranteeing that they all look as if they occupy the same space is to ensure that the eye height of all the characters also lines up with the horizon. The distance the people are from the viewer is then determined by the position of their feet, rather than their heads.

Clearly, there are exceptions: children will be below this line, as will Oompa Loompas and other people of diminutive stature; the eight-foot swamp monster from the planet Zog will tower above it. We can also change the emphasis by placing our subjects above the horizon line, which will mean we're looking up to them (a technique favoured by Mussolini, for example) or below the horizon, so we're looking down from a height (Princess Diana was often photographed this way to make her appear shorter and more feminine).

We can establish the horizon line in an existing photograph, even if no horizon is on view. All you need is an image that shows clear horizontals receding in the z-axis – that is, lines which are parallel to the ground, but which recede into the distance. In Photoshop, make a new layer; with the Shapes tool set to draw straight lines, drag a line that follows any of the lines along this axis, but which continues past it into the distance.

Repeat this procedure with another line in the picture, preferably one far away from the original. Where these two lines meet is the vanishing point, which always sits on the horizon. If you now continue this procedure with other z-axis lines in the image, you'll find that they all meet at the vanishing point. Draw

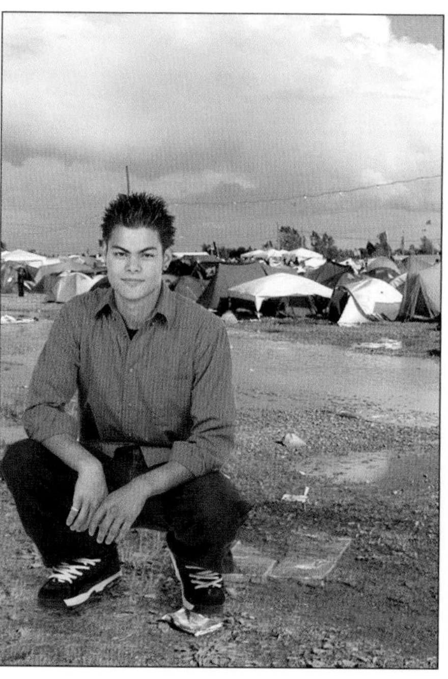

◄ **Whether we're standing or sitting, the horizon is always on our eyeline. This is true even when we're on the top of a tall building.**

► **By drawing vanishing point lines attached to an already-photographed object, we can position it correctly within our scene by coinciding the two vanishing points.**

a new horizontal line through this point, and your horizon will be clearly defined.

Now, when you place people into the scene, arrange them so their eyelines are on the horizon, and they'll look as if they fit within the scene. This is the simplest way to position people, whether indoors or outside: it makes the business of getting the scale correct much easier.

We can also use the vanishing point for drawing new objects in our scene. To make a simple box, draw lines from the vanishing point first, to give you a readymade perspective onto which to place your top and sides. We can also use the vanishing point when placing already-photographed items into the scene. One way of doing this is to draw vanishing lines from the object in question on a new layer and linked to it; then drag the whole assembly until the vanishing point on the object meets that of the scene, and the object will be in perfect perspective.

So far, we've been looking at one-point perspective, where all the vanishing lines meet at a point. This is mainly used for interior views, when the rear wall is head-on and directly facing the viewer. The perspective lines on the side walls will all meet at the vanishing point.

If we're looking at the outside of a building, then the two walls adjacent to the corner facing us will point in different directions. Each wall will tend to a different vanishing point: this is known as two-point perspective, and is by far the most common in everyday use. There's an excellent Java model showing how two-point perspective works at *tinyurl.com/bjr74*. When verticals in the scene aren't directly vertical in the picture, you'll need to look at three point-perspective – which further complicates the process.

When drawing perspective lines to the vanishing point, you'll frequently find that it's out of the side of the frame. There are two solutions to this: the first is to increase the canvas size of the image, so the vanishing point is included. The second method is to use the Shapes tool set to drawing Paths, and to zoom out so that the grey background outside the current image area is visible in Photoshop. The paths will show up on the background, allowing you to set the vanishing point without increasing the image size.

A lot of perspective in Photoshop and Illustrator can be faked, using the Free Transform tool. When holding the Command key to drag a corner handle, and so freely distort a layer or selection, the contents will automatically be distorted as if they were being viewed in perspective. So to add black and white tiles to a floor, for example, first make a black and white pattern. Then enter Free Transform, and hold Command as you drag each corner to its correct position within the scene: the tiles will be distorted to follow the perspective of the scene with almost no effort on your part.

▼ **01 We can read the perspective out of this scene by drawing lines along the z-axis – the top of the left wall, the sides of the table. Where they meet is the vanishing point; the horizon line (in red) passes through this.**

▼ **02 We can use the horizon to correctly position figures within the scene. Because their eyelines match the horizon, they all fit the scale and perspective of the image.**

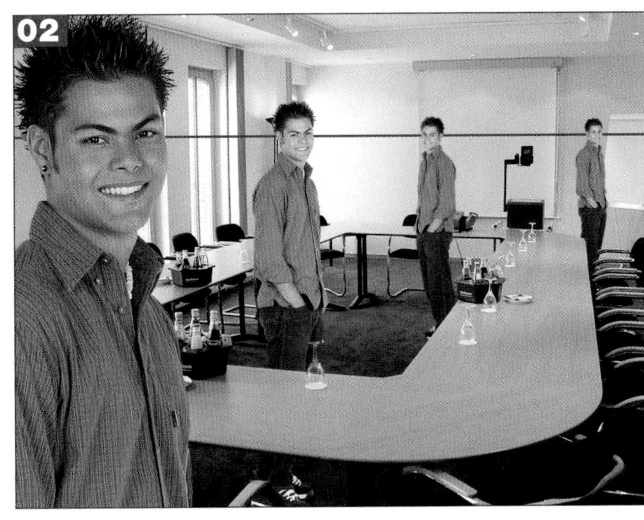

P: Plug-ins

Just because your graphics application shipped with one set of filters doesn't mean you have to stick with them. Using plug-ins lets you expand its skillset.

Photoshop comes with a wide selection of filters that allow users to perform tasks ranging from the mundane to the extraordinary. We're able to rescue out-of-focus images, turn images into works of art and distort our pictures in a variety of mind-boggling ways. But that's just the beginning – thanks to its architecture, Photoshop is opened up for third-party developers to create plug-in filters that extend the range of what's possible.

Some of the most useful plug-ins come in sets. Alien Skin (*alienskin.com*) sells three bundles of plug-ins in its Eye Candy collection, under the umbrella titles Nature, Impact and Texture. Impact, the most dramatic of the three, offers bevels, glass, starbursts and a useful motion trail effect, as well as a dazzlingly effective filter for creating chrome and other metals from flat shapes. Nature includes realistic fire, smoke, water drops and ripples; while the Textures suite lets users render convincing furs, stone, wood and reptile skins. Each bundle costs $99 (about £44.50), or you can buy all three for $199 (about £99.50). Alien Skin filters are known for their effectiveness, slick interface and ease of use.

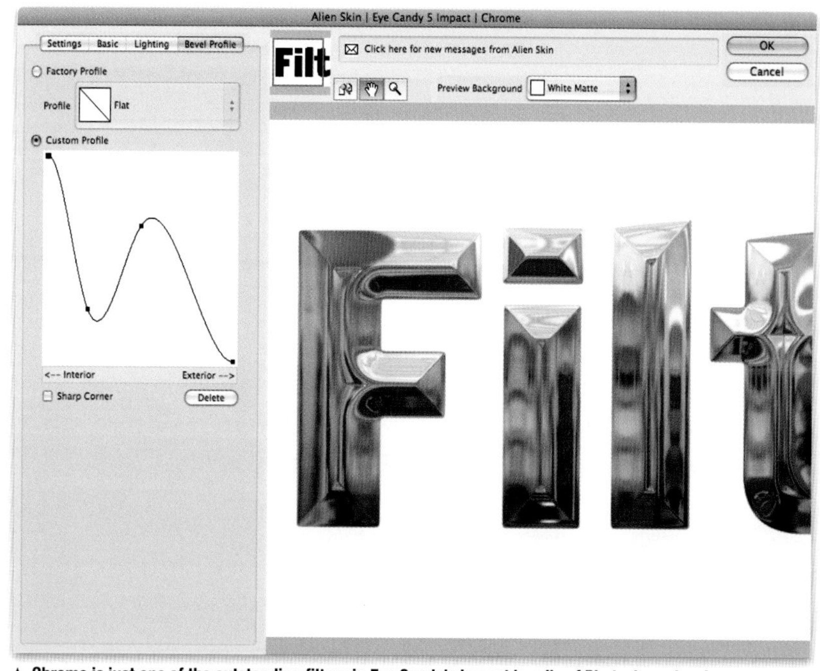

▲ **Chrome is just one of the outstanding filters in Eye Candy's Impact bundle of Photoshop plug-ins.**

The one-man-band operation that sells plug-ins as Flaming Pear (*flamingpear.com*) includes an esoteric selection of tools to replicate natural phenomena, including Lunar Cell, for creating moons and planets; Solar Cell, for building glowing suns and stars; and Glitterato, for making star fields. Of special interest is Flood, which can be used to half-fill any image with water – the refined user interface enables full control over the waviness, distortion and rippling of the water surface.

Flaming Pear also offers a selection of other plug-ins including SuperBladePro, a surface texture generator for creating jewel-like images; Melancholytron, which adds moody glows; and Polymerge, which builds bizarre concoctions by distorting and rearranging image parts. Prices range from free to $20 (about £10) per filter, with multi-buy packs available.

Two novel distortion filters come from AVBros (*avbros.com*), providing specialised solutions to niche problems. Puzzle Pro creates jigsaws in a huge variety of patterns and styles, with a tremendous degree of user control and customisation. More spectacular by far, however, is the extraordinary Page Curl Pro, which allows users to take flat artwork and display it as if on a rippling paper surface.

With full control over curl amount, direction, creasing and angles of view, it adds shadows to create a dramatic sense of realism. Users can even choose separate artwork to be placed on the back of the curled page, for added effect. The filters are £34.95 each, or you can buy them both for £55.95.

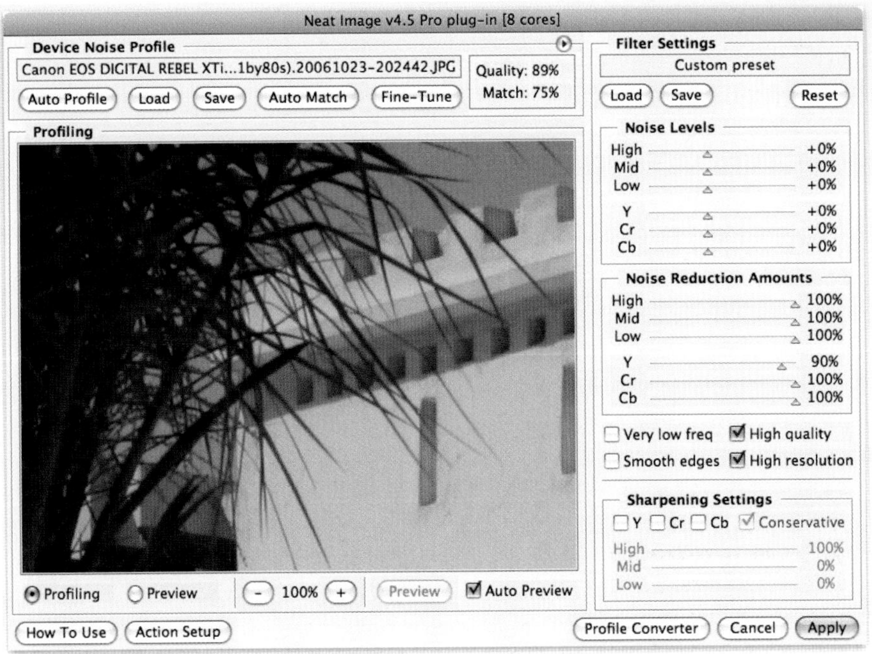

◄ **Neat Image is the quickest and most effective way to get rid of digital noise – without losing any fine detail.**

A range of filters from AutoFX (*autofx.com*) create special painting effects – these include Mystical Lighting and DreamSuite. Priced at between $129 (about £64.50) and $199 (about £99.50) per bundle, they're capable of turning everyday images into dramatic, powerful works of art. The problem is that the interface is sluggish, with lengthy waits for previews that discourages experimentation.

Akvis (*akvis.com*) produces a catholic selection of filters including Sketch, for turning images into pencil drawings, and the innovative Coloriage, which makes the process of colouring black and white photos much easier. Its site also includes many more filters for decorating, enhancing and adding special effect to artwork. Filters cost between $49 (about £24.50) and $120 (about $60), and are available in bundles. The problem is the slow interface. Although some of the filters are capable of dramatic results, the time you have to spend waiting for them to complete preview operations makes using them a frustrating business.

So far, we've looked mainly at filters for creating special effects. But there are filters for enhancing images without adding extra decoration. Our favourite is Neat Image (*neatimage.com*), which offers the best noise-reduction available. It works in two ways. Firstly, by examining your image, finding a clear area on which to work, and then producing a custom algorithm to remove digital noise from the file; or by allowing users to download profiles specific to their model of camera for even better results. In practice, Neat Image is the single most useful Photoshop plug-in we know of, with the ability to remove all visible noise without damaging fine detail. It costs between $34.90 (about £17.50) and $59.90 (about £30), depending on whether you opt for the Home or Pro version.

There are several plug-ins for enlarging images, using a variety of technologies, in an attempt to better Photoshop's built-in bicubic interpolation method. These include Blow Up from Alien Skin ($199, about £99.50), Genuine Fractals from onOne Software (*ononesoftware.com*, $159.95, about £80) and Magnifier from Akvis ($129, about £65). They all do a good job, but don't expect miracles – you can't put detail back that wasn't there originally. These tools are best for working with simple artwork – try them on images of people though, and you'll find the results unconvincing.

For those with the Extended version of Photoshop CS3 or CS4, the Design 3D[in] plug-ins from Strata (*strata.com*) take the potential in the built-in 3D engine and extend it tremendously. There are three plug-ins in the suite that, together, allow you to model, texture, light and render top-quality 3D images, and then to have those images returned to Photoshop as multi-layered groups providing full control over the final image. It's a great set of tools, with extra modules to allow images photographed from multiple angles to be turned into 3D models automatically. The plug-ins cost $149 (about £75) for each module.

Most of the plug-ins listed here provide demo versions, so you can try out their effects before buying them. With all suites, the chances are that you won't want several of the components, but look at it as the price for the single filter you really need, and view all the others as a bonus.

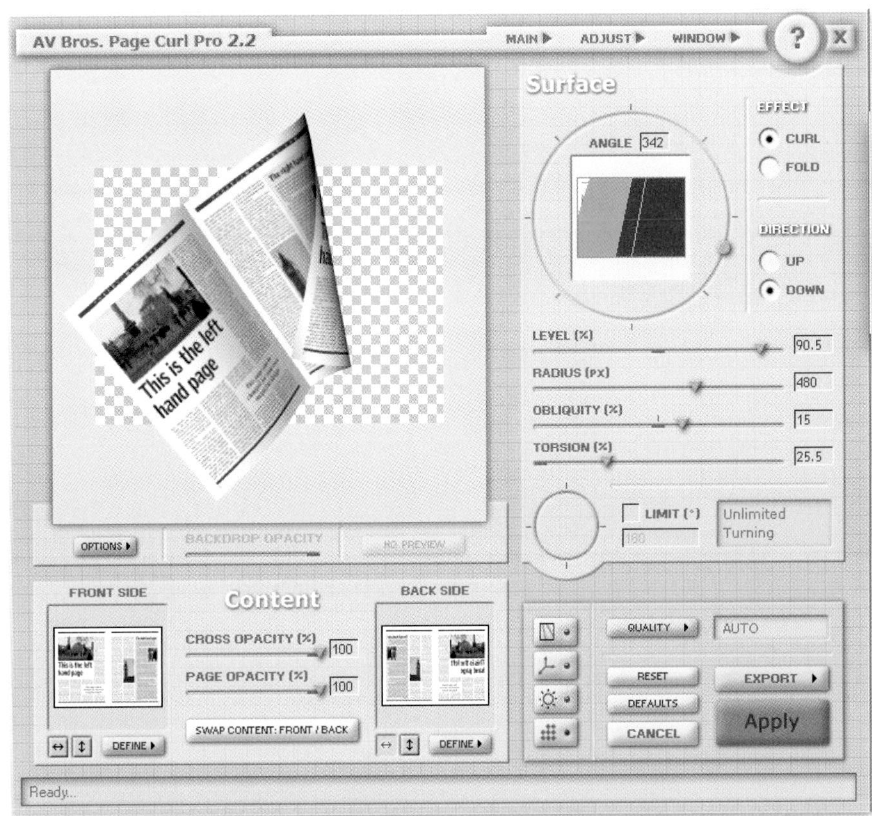

▲ **Page Curl can turn flat artwork into a 3D, shaded image that looks just like the real thing.** ⊗

Q: QuicKeys

This handy utility is not only a time-saver: it can also add shortcuts for obscure features in Photoshop and combine several tasks into one.

QuicKeys is an automation tool ($79.95, about £40, from *quickeys.com*) that can reproduce just about any series of actions on your Mac with a single keystroke. It's of particular benefit to digital artists, as it allows you to create memorable, one-step shortcuts that help to increase your speed and productivity.

At its most basic level, you can use QuicKeys to build shortcuts for menu items. Most applications allow you to define your own shortcuts, of course, but these tend to impose restrictions such as always having to use the Command key as one of the modifiers.

Say you want to create a shortcut for Flip Vertical in Photoshop; you can't specify Command-V, of course, since that's used for Paste; but you can't go for Shift-Command-V either, which performs Paste Into, or Shift-Alt-Command-V, as this opens the Vanishing Point filter. However, with QuicKeys, you can tell it to implement the little-used Ctrl key instead – and use Ctrl-V, which is memorable and simple.

QuicKeys also offers the concept of 'sticky' keys, which wait for a second keypress before performing a task. You can use this approach to create a shortcut for a general feature, followed by a single key for a specific item. For instance, you might define your most frequently used Photoshop filters by setting Ctrl-F as the initial trigger, followed by U for Unsharp Mask, G for Gaussian Blur, P for Plastic Wrap and so on. Anyone can remember a single key, and it's far quicker than hunting through hierarchical menus.

As well as selecting menu items, QuicKeys can replicate keystrokes. This is of great

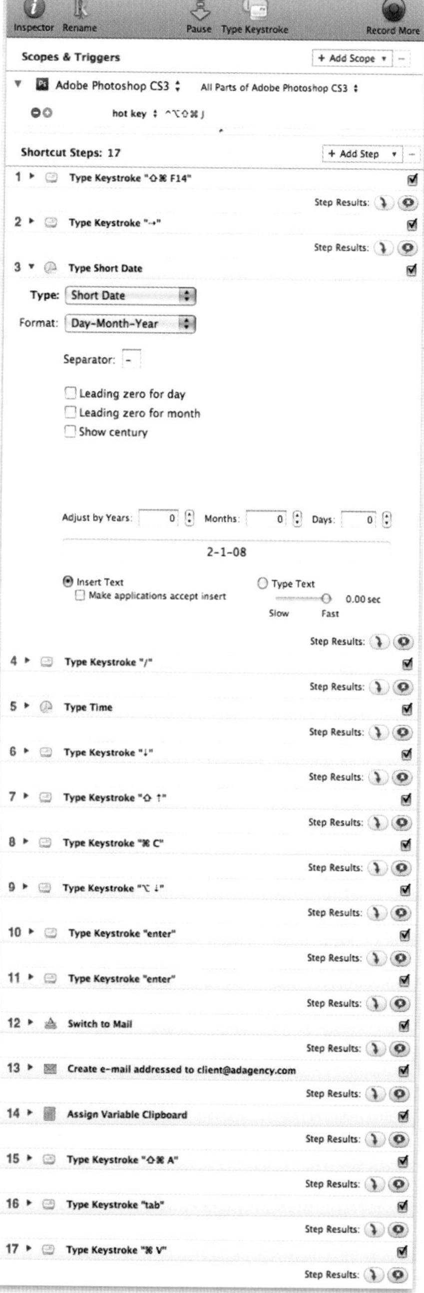

► The steps in a shortcut that saves a file as a Jpeg, adds the date and time, switches to Mail, creates a new email to the client and attaches the file to the message. Only the Date section is shown expanded here, giving an idea of the sort of detail you can apply.

benefit when working with Photoshop Actions, since they absolutely require the use of Function keys. It might be tricky to remember Shift-Command-F8, which will save a file as a Jpeg copy, but Ctrl-J is an obvious trigger.

There are two ways of creating shortcuts in QuicKeys: the simplest is to use the Start Recording button and perform the series of actions you want recorded. When you've finished, the Stop Recording button will open the QuicKeys Editor, where each step is detailed and can be edited. Alternatively, recordings can be built up step-by-step from the menus within the Editor window.

The ability to edit your recordings gives you far more flexibility. In the example above, you used Ctrl-J to create a shortcut to save a file as a Jpeg. But saving in this way from a multi-layered document will add the word 'copy' to the end of the file – which you don't need, since the extension '.jpg' is enough to tell you it's a flattened version of the image you've been working on. So you can edit the recording and instruct QuicKeys to go to the end of the file name, step back four characters (to skip over the extension) and then delete the preceding five characters (the word 'copy' and the space which precedes it).

You can build far more complex sequences through QuicKeys' ability to perform a wide range of system tasks. To continue the Jpeg example, let's say you're working on an image for a client, while talking to them on the phone about it. They want to see regular updates: there has to be a way you can use QuicKeys to help the process of sending them images. Some ingenuity is often required to make the automation process work, and this is one such example. You can create a shortcut that saves the file as a Jpeg, as you've already seen.

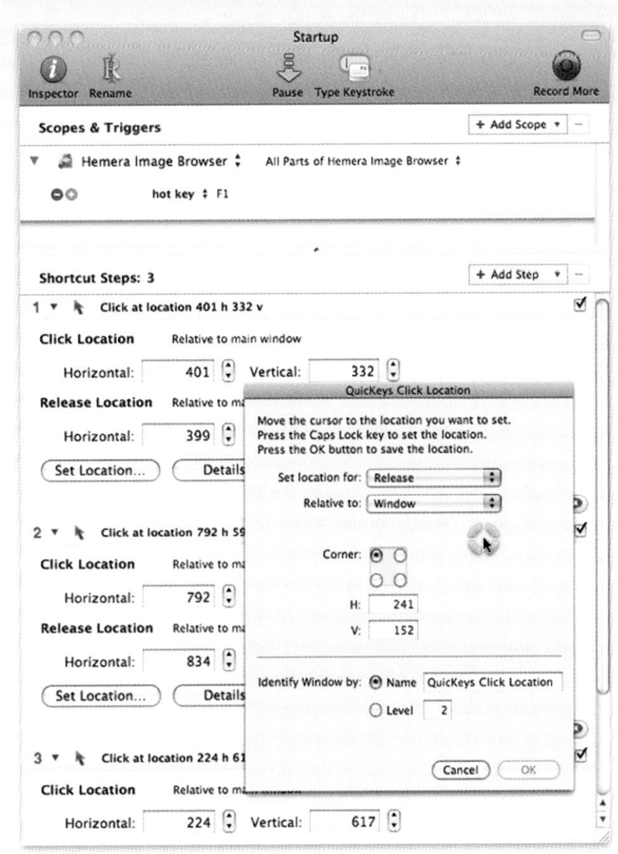

◄ **The shortcut for opening Hemera Image Browser. You can position the cursor for drag/click operations where you want and press Caps Lock to mark that position relative to the screen or individual window.**

But let's take this a few steps further. You can add the current date and time to the file name as a unique identifier (there are QuicKeys tools to do this), and then copy the whole name to the clipboard before saving the file in a specified folder. You can then switch to Mail, and create a new message addressed to your client. Using Shift-Command-A to add an attachment, you can then tab to move to the Search field and search for the file you just saved by pasting its name.

You could then instruct QuicKeys to add the found file to the email and fire it off, but it may be better to stop at this point so you can check it's the correct file. Assuming it is, it's straightforward for you to press Enter to attach the found file, then F1 to send the email. (Assuming, of course, you've already used QuicKeys to set up F1 to trigger the Send button in Mail.)

This may sound like a long series of actions, but you only have to perform it once: thereafter, you can use a single keystroke to complete the whole sequence in just a few seconds, leaving you free to continue working on your artwork.

You can use QuicKeys to drag items on screen, as well. Here's an example: when you first launch the Hemera Image Browser application, the default is for the window to show all searchable libraries, a tiny display of thumbnails, and a small window size.

However, this is precisely our advantage: the application always displays exactly the same configuration. This means that it's easy to record a sequence that will reduce the size of the library list to zero, grab the bottom right corner and resize the window to fill our monitor, and then move to the Search field.

The Hemera application is also lacking implementation of the Page Up/Page Down keys. No problem: you can tell QuicKeys to click at the top or bottom within the scroll bar, pinpointing the click position relative to the window and assign these keys to perform the task that should have been built into the program in the first place.

QuicKeys is a tremendous productivity booster, that's capable of reproducing almost any series of repetitive tasks. With a large range of advanced features – such as the ability to perform mathematical functions on clipboard contents, make decisions and perform loops – it's a hugely powerful tool for the designer, or just about anyone else. ⊗

Q: Quick Mask

Make selections the easy way: by painting. Quick Mask removes the pain from accurately picking out the parts of an image you want to work on.

▼ Be sure to change your Quick Mask settings from Masked Areas to Selected Areas, so you can more easily use it for making selections.

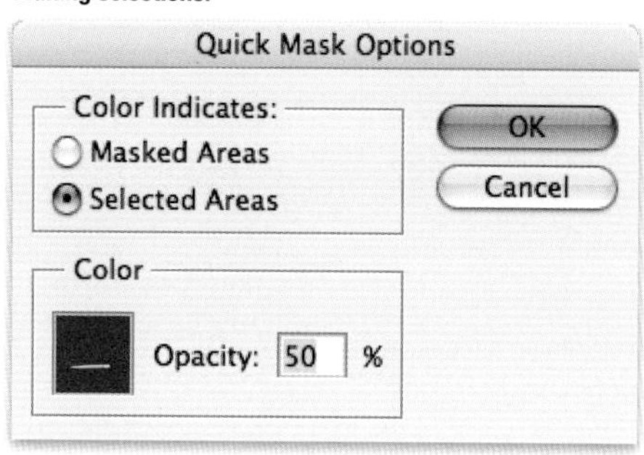

Quick Mask is one of the most versatile selection tools in the Photoshop arsenal. But it's under-used by the vast majority of users. In part, this is due to the name: it was originally designed as a digital equivalent of the rubylith film airbrush that artists use to mask off areas that they don't want to work on. This explains both the red colour, and the fact that, by default, areas highlighted are 'masked' – unselected areas.

But by double-clicking on the Quick Mask icon (the second from bottom icon in the Photoshop toolbar) you can change the mode from Masked to Selected areas: now, when you paint in Quick Mask, you'll be painting areas that will become your selection when you exit Quick Mask mode. A useful keyboard shortcut is Q, which takes you in and out of Quick Mask mode.

All the standard painting tools can be used within Quick Mask, and this is part of its versatility. The concept is simple: paint in black to show the red overlay, adding to your selection; paint in white to remove the overlay, so removing that area from your selection. You could select a person's outline by laboriously tracing with the Pen tool; but it's far easier to use a small, hard-edged brush in Quick Mask to paint it instead. Use a brush the width of a finger to paint in the selection of a hand; switch to a larger, soft-edged brush to paint in the hair, and then use the Smudge tool to tweak out the mask to follow the strands of hair.

Since you'll be changing brush size and hardness frequently while using Quick Mask, it's worth learning a few shortcuts. Use the 'greater than' and 'less than' signs (> and <) to make the brush size larger and smaller; hold Shift with the same keys to make the brush harder or softer. Pressing D will set the foreground colour to black and the background colour to white; pressing X will swap these colours over.

As well as black and white, shades of grey can be used for a partially transparent selection. If there's an area you want to be consistently transparently selected, such as the wing of an insect, then use a mid grey to ensure that the wing is evenly selected. Alternatively, use black with the brush set to 50% opacity – but be aware that painting over existing strokes will build up the opacity. If you've selected a wing using the grey method and find, on exiting Quick Mask, that it's too transparent, then it's easy to fix without repainting. Return to Quick Mask mode, and use the Brightness/Contrast, Curves or Levels adjustments to lighten or darken the midtones of the mask.

You can enter Quick Mask after using any of the selection tools, and the selected area will be highlighted in red (as long as you've swapped the default setting). Not only that, but you can use any of the selection tools within Quick Mask. Say you want to select a regular array of rectangular sections from an image. Go into Quick Mask, make the first rectangular selection, and use Alt-Delete to fill with black (the foreground colour). This will fill in red within Quick Mask.

Now duplicate that selection, nudging it a single pixel by pressing the cursor keys while holding Alt to make a copy; remember, you can hold down the Shift key to move the selection by 10 pixels rather than one. Release Alt and nudge it to where you want it, then repeat again to make an array. When you exit Quick Mask, you'll have a perfectly lined-up and evenly spaced set of rectangular selections.

Making elliptical selections is always tricky in Photoshop, especially at an angle. It's far easier in Quick Mask. First make an elliptical or circular selection at any size; then enter Quick Mask to

▲ Selecting the elliptical top of this cup, at an angle, would be tricky by more conventional means.

▲ First, make a circular selection; then press Q to enter Quick Mask mode, and you'll see it highlighted in red.

▲ Use Free Transform to rotate and scale the selection to fill the space required...

▲ ...so that we can work with it when we leave Quick Mask.

show it as a red overlay. Use Free Transform to rotate, move and scale your ellipse to the required position, then exit Quick Mask. No need to make a further selection before entering Free Transform: simply press Command-T when within Quick Mask and the mask will be automatically selected.

The only difficulty comes when you've painted around an object to select it, and want to fill the 'hole' to select that as well. The Paint Bucket tool will fill any bounded area, but will tend to leave an unselected fringe within your border. A better method is to use the Magic Wand to select the interior, then use Select > Modify > Expand to make that selection a few pixels larger; then fill with the foreground colour using Alt-Delete to complete the selection. If this is a process you use frequently, it's worth assigning a simple Action to it automatically.

You can also use Quick Mask to smooth selections, in much the same way as the Refine Edges dialog does in Photoshop CS3 and CS4. After making a selection with the Magic Wand, say, you may find its edges are too rough. Enter Quick Mask, and apply some Gaussian Blur to soften the edges. Then open the Levels dialog, and drag the black and white triangles together so they're just touching the centre grey triangle, to tighten up the outline. The result will be a smooth tight selection.

▼ Selecting the background with the Magic Wand produces jagged edges, as the close-up shows.

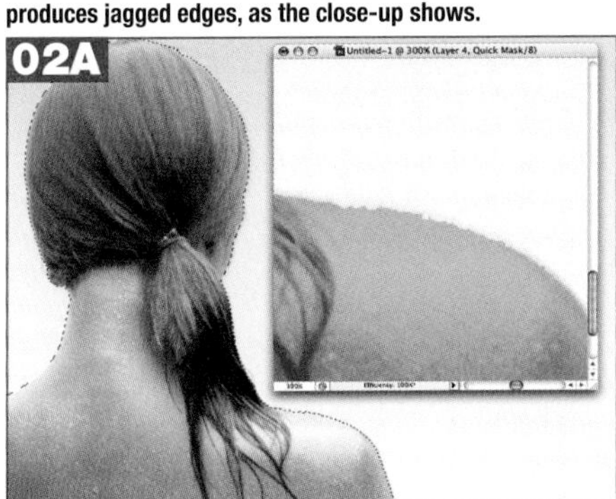

▼ By applying Gaussian Blur to the Quick Mask view, we can greatly soften that edge.

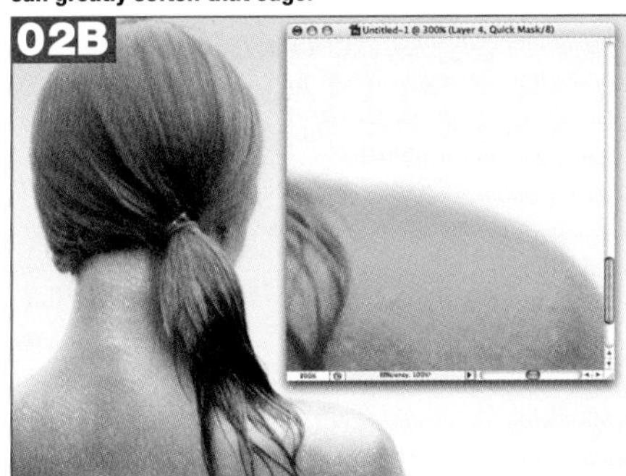

▼ We can now use the Levels adjustment to tighten that selection. Jaggies gone!

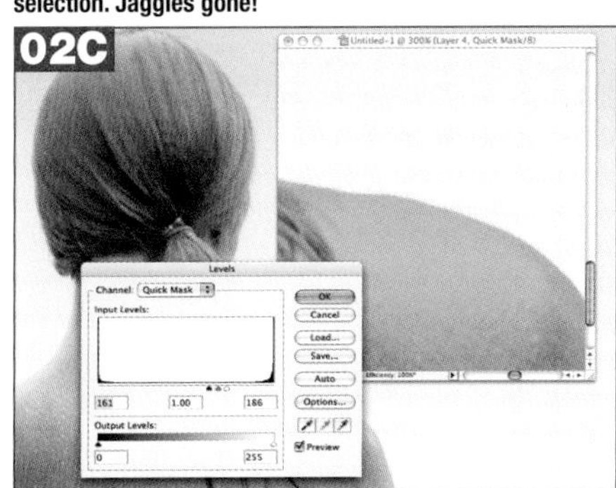

R: Raw images

Camera Raw unlocks the power of 12-bit Raw images, allowing you to safely tweak pictures in real time, taking shots from acceptable to perfect.

The charged-couple device (CCD) chips in digital cameras are capable of capturing a large amount of data. These Raw captures are large and unwieldy, taking up a lot of space as well as taking a long time to save onto memory cards. Traditionally, these cameras have then compressed this data into a more manageable form, resulting in the Jpeg or Tiff files with which we're familiar.

Raw files are usually captured at 12-bit, rather than the 8-bit mode in which Jpeg files are saved. Although it sounds like only a 50% difference, it's actually eight times the amount of data: rather than capturing 256 colours per pixel (2 to the power of 8), they record 4,096 (2 to the power of 12). In traditional digital cameras, most of this extra data is discarded as the image is squeezed into a colour space such as sRGB and saved to disk.

For standard snapshots, the greatly reduced colour space isn't a major issue. Cameras do a good job of optimising the image before saving it, and you're generally left with an image that's crisp and clear, with strong, vibrant colours and a good balance between light and dark.

► **Adobe Camera Raw has a useful defringing mode, which can be used to get rid of the colour fringe in this image by using simple sliders to correct the blue/yellow and red/cyan ghosting often found in areas of high contrast.**

The problems start when you try to manipulate the images in Photoshop. As you tinker with the tones – lightening the shadows, correcting the exposure, compensating for wrong white balance choices – you find that you're trying to expand a range of tones where there's nothing to expand. It's like trying to let out a pair of trousers where there simply isn't enough spare material to work with: the image has already been pared back to its most basic essentials.

In recent years, however, the more sophisticated cameras have allowed you to access the Raw files themselves. Often referred to as digital negatives, these files aren't complete, usable images yet – just as negatives are not usable images from film cameras – but they contain all the captured data, allowing you to create the perfect result from the huge amount of data available.

Raw isn't a single-file format, however, but a generic term covering the range of formats different camera manufacturers use to capture images. Almost every manufacturer uses a different format: Canon uses .cr2 and .crw, Nikon prefers .nef and .nrw, Sony prefers to use .srf and .sr2, and so on. Without specialist software, you would be completely unable to read all these file formats.

Fortunately, Photoshop comes with Camera Raw, Adobe's answer to the Raw format minefield. When you open a Raw file, it will automatically open in Camera Raw, which acts like an intermediary between the file on disk and Photoshop itself. It's a self-contained, modal dialog that allows us to manipulate every aspect of the image you're working on.

You can get confused by the fact that Camera Raw includes most of Photoshop's standard image enhancement tools – hue and saturation control, sharpening, shadows and

▲ Camera Raw is able to rescue this dark, muddy image and turn it into the bright example shown – and it can even get rid of that distracting wall plaque.

highlights – but in a different format, with different controls and in an unfamiliar layout. That's because Camera Raw is one dialog, allowing you to make a vast number of tweaks and amendments to an image at the same time. Until you press OK, you haven't committed to any one effect: if you performed the same series of steps in standard Photoshop, you'd have to commit to each one before moving on to the next.

Even then, Camera Raw doesn't force you to make irrevocable choices. The original Raw file isn't altered by the process: instead, the alterations made in Camera Raw are written into it as a set of instructions, rather like a recipe for creating the perfect image from raw ingredients. You can change the make-up of that recipe at any time, adjusting the results as you like. This is part of the huge power of Camera Raw: nothing you do is destructive, and you can always return to the original file.

When you start to make changes in Camera Raw, you really notice the difference that 12-bit capture mode makes. Lightening shadows, for instance, reveals a wealth of image detail that was previously completely hidden. All the data is there, ready for us to expand some areas and compress others as we adjust the tone and contrast.

You can also perform a number of functions in Camera Raw that can't be replicated in Photoshop. In the Lens Correction section, you can compensate for the chromatic fringes sometimes seen in areas of high contrast, especially in the corners of images – the blue/yellow or red/cyan ghosting that mars an image. Both are easily corrected using a simple slider. Another slider lets you control the white balance of the original image and another pair let you reduce the amount of digital noise, with separate controls for the colour (the most common digital noise problem) and the luminance (the brightness of the image).

Sharpening in Camera Raw is more subtle and less destructive than using Unsharp Mask. You can also use the Vibrancy slider to accentuate edge contrast without additional sharpening, which can bring a lot of detail back into a soft image.

Photoshop CS4 brings a range of enhancements to Camera Raw. These include the ability to treat two halves of an image independently, using the equivalent of a gradient mask to differentiate between the two regions. Typically, this would be used to enhance the contrast in a sky without affecting the rest of the image. You can also spot heal image blemishes, make paint-on adjustment areas, remove red-eye and correct crooked horizons – all without leaving Camera Raw.

The difference between working on Raw images and working on Tiff or Jpeg files is immense. For anyone who's serious about images, the first check when buying a new camera must be to ensure that it has a Raw capture mode. All modern DSLR cameras do and some of the pricier compacts now include this option. Raw mode makes the difference between acceptable and perfect. ⊗

R: Refine Edge

If you want your selections and cut-outs to be accurate, you're going to have to spend time working at the very periphery with Photoshop's Refine Edge.

The Quick Selection tool, introduced in Photoshop CS3, brought you the ability to isolate complex objects from detailed backgrounds quickly and easily. But, like the Magic Wand before it, the tool inevitably produces rough edges, as there's a sharp divide between those pixels that are selected and those that aren't.

The Refine Edge dialog box was designed to smooth out those edges in an entirely new way. Rather than simply blurring the roughness by adding feathering to the selection, Refine Edge allows you to combine feathering with a contrast mask that tightens up the smoothed selection afterwards.

As well as enabling you to create better selections, the Refine Edge dialog box brings some unexpected extra bonuses: you can use extreme values to bring rounded corners to hard-edged shapes, a task that was previously a very complex process in Photoshop.

You can activate Refine Edge in three ways: if a selection tool is active, you can press its button on the Options bar which is located at the top of the screen; you can choose it from the Select menu; or you can activate it using its keyboard shortcut, Command-Alt-R.

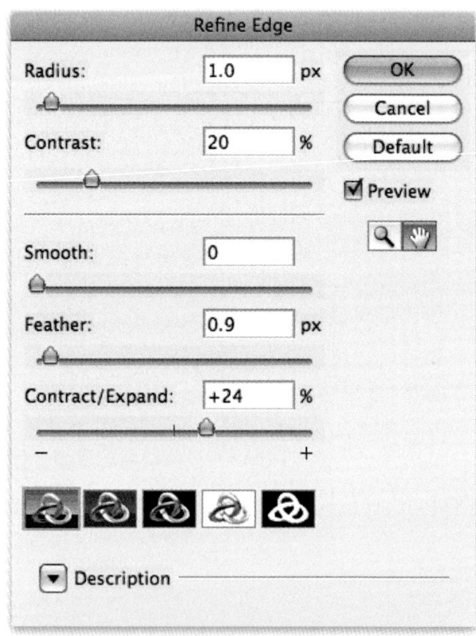

▲ **The Refine Edge dialog allows you to smooth, contract, expand and round your selections with live feedback.**

At its default settings, Refine Edge adds a small amount of smoothness and feathering to a selection. Assuming the selection has been made with the Quick Selection tool, this is often sufficient: rough edges will be removed, and the moderate feathering adds a softness

▼ **You can view your cutouts in a variety of ways, so you can check for fringing and completeness.**

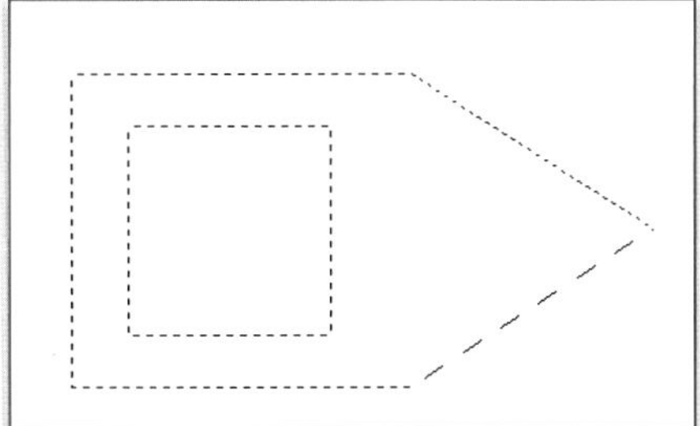

▲ **To round selections, begin by using the Marquee or Lasso tools to make the initial selection.**

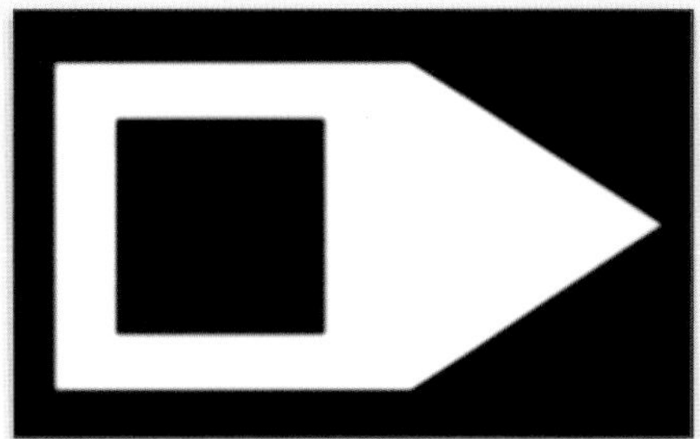

▲ **Open Refine Edge and choose the last icon to show the selection as white on black.**

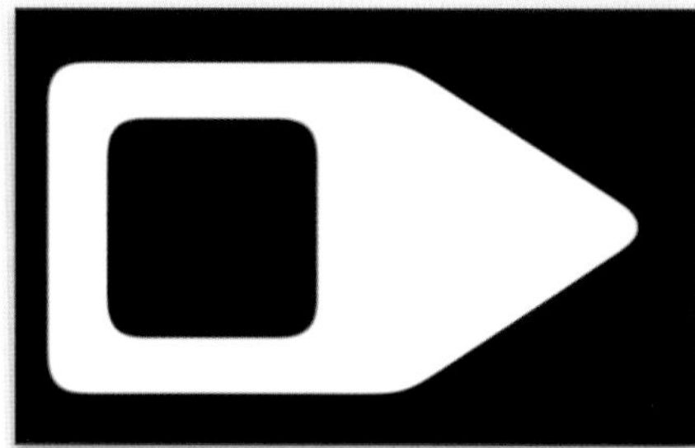

▲ **Increase the Contrast and Feather amounts to round the edges smoothly.**

to the edge that will help the cutout object to blend in with a new background.

If the object is to be placed on a white background, however, the feathering will look unnaturally soft: the fuzziness will simply look like a poor quality cutout. You could reduce the feathering amount, but this will bring back the very roughness you wanted to get rid of. Instead, a better option is to raise the Contrast setting. This tightens the feathered edge, creating a result that's both crisp and smooth.

If you've isolated your object using the Magic Wand tool to select the background, you'll find you have a different problem. The chances are that the anti-aliasing (the smoothing transparency at the edges) will have allowed some of the background colour to seep through, producing a noticeable fringe around our cutout.

This is most noticeable when an object has been photographed against a white background: it's often hard to get rid of the white fringe that results. In this case, you can look at the Contract/Expand slider at the bottom of the dialog box. By dragging this, you can reduce the size of your selection in order to remove the fringe entirely.

It can sometimes be difficult to see the fringing or rough edges clearly, particularly if the fringe is the same colour as your background. And so Refine Edge enables you to change the background within the dialog box: using the buttons at the bottom of the window you can view your cutouts against white or black, as well as in QuickMask and with the 'marching ants' selection views turned on.

Refine Edge also enables you to view your cutouts as a selection mask, hiding the image itself but showing the selected area in white against a black background. This is useful for checking on the overall shape and looking for holes in the selection, but it has a further benefit: you can use the technique to create the round-cornered selections mentioned above.

To begin with this technique, first make your selection using the Lasso, Marquee or other selection tool. Remember, you can hold down Shift before drawing to add to a previous selection and Alt to subtract from it; remember, also, that holding down the Spacebar as you work with a selection allows you to move it around while you're still drawing it.

Once the selection has been made, open the Refine Edge dialog box and click on the final icon on the bottom row to view the selection as white against black. Increase the Contrast setting to about 90% – you can raise this later if you need to. Then drag the Feather setting to the right to raise it, and as you do so you'll see the sharp corners gradually smoothing off.

Raising the Feather value too high will inevitably produce a softness that even a maximum Contrast setting can't deal with. While this is a problem for standard selections, it can be a positive benefit when working with text. Any font can be turned into a blur version, with full user control. First, 'load up' the text as a selection by holding the Command key and clicking on the layer's thumbnail in the Layers palette. Then use the Refine Edge dialog box to round the edges, varying both Feather and Contrast amounts until you get the effect you want.

THE BLUR/LEVELS ALTERNATIVE

If you don't have Photoshop CS3 and CS4, there is a way of producing similar results, albeit in a somewhat more laborious fashion. With an active selection, choose Save Selection from the Select menu. This will create a new channel: use the Channels palette to

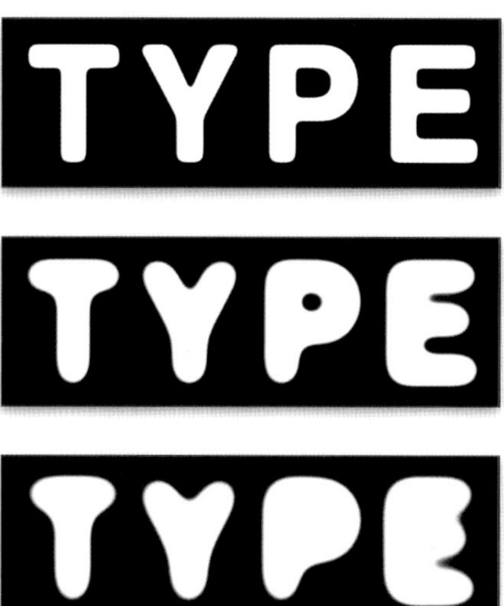

▲ **You can use the technique on type outlines to turn even plain old Helvetica into a Tate Modern style logo.**

switch to it, and you'll see the selection as a white shape on a black background.

To smooth the edges, first use the Gaussian Blur filter. Choose a value high enough so that there's no roughness visible in the edge: or, if you're rounding corners, start with a value of about 5 pixels.

You now need to tighten that blurred edge. Open the Levels dialog box and drag the black and white triangles beneath the Input Levels pane towards the centre grey slider, so they're almost but not quite touching it. This will turn the blurred outline into a smooth, crisp edge. Move the whole black/grey/white triangle assembly left and right to enlarge or reduce the selection.

Once you're happy with the result, press OK to apply the Levels action and use Load Selection from the Select menu to load the selection into your document. The method can be a little hit and miss and you may have to experiment with different Blur values before you get the results as exactly as you want them. ⊗

R: Reflections

Not just a matter of flipping an object and fading it out, reflections are tricky to master when you're working at angles or with irregular surfaces.

Creating reflections in Photoshop can be the easiest, or hardest, job in the world. It depends on the object you're reflecting and the surface on which it stands.

The simplest type of reflection is a head-on view of an object – you flip a copy of the image vertically then lower the opacity. As mirrors are the only surfaces that are perfectly reflective, you'll also need to fade out the reflection so that it's more transparent the further it is from the base of the object.

The easiest way to do this is to add a layer mask to the reflected copy and use the Gradient tool to draw a white-to-black gradient vertically downwards from the object's base. This produces a smooth, gradual fade. Reflections of this kind are popular on websites at present, largely due to the effect being a style that is built-in to Apple's iWeb application.

If the object is flat but not head-on to the camera, the reflection becomes slightly more complicated. When a copy is flipped vertically it won't line up with the base of the original: you'll need to distort it to fit.

Usually, shearing the image is the simplest way to match the original. Enter Free Transform mode using Command-T: then hold Command and Shift as you drag a side handle vertically. The Command key allows that side to move independently; the Shift key limits its movement to up or down. Finally, apply the Gradient to a layer mask, as described above, to create a soft fade.

The third type of reflection occurs when we can see two faces of the object – such as a box viewed from an angle. No amount of shearing or distortion will make a vertically flipped copy match the original, since fitting one side will throw off the other. The solution is to split the faces into separate layers by selecting a face and using Layer > New via Cut (Command-Shift-J). Now all the sides can be sheared independently.

But what of lowering the opacity and fading with layer masks? It would be tricky to make two separate gradients align on our two layer masks. We could merge them but there's a better solution. Select both layers and press Command-G to make a new group. You can now change the opacity of the group as a whole and apply a Gradient to a layer mask for the group. Combining multiple layers into groups will make even complicated reflections behave as you want. And it's good practice, too.

The fourth type of reflection is when there are multiple planes in the object, such as a box whose lid we can just see. When reflected, the lid would be visible, but not in the position it appears in the original. Again, the solution is to split the object into multiple layers, distorting the sides, and sliding the top

▼ A head-on subject, such as this wardrobe, is the easiest sort of reflection to make. First, flip a copy vertically and move it below the original, then lower the opacity and use the Gradient tool on a layer mask to fade it away smoothly.

▲ **An angled view of the same wardrobe is more problematic. When flipped, the reflection clearly won't fit the object. But by shearing it in sections, we can make it line up with the base of the original.**

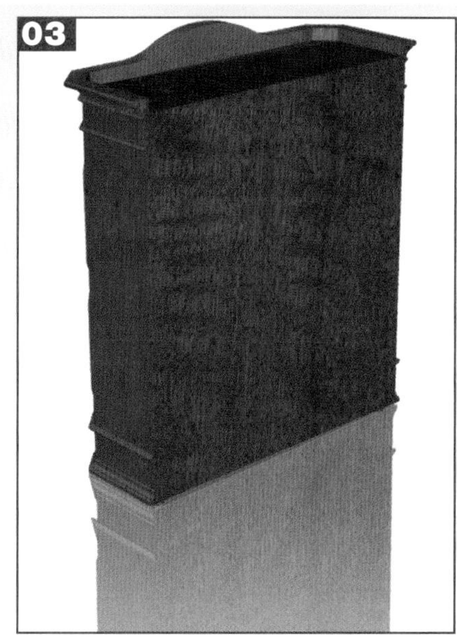

▲ **When we spin this wardrobe around and raise our point of view, we have a different problem: that curved top won't be so visible. Separating it into back, side and top allows us to transform each individually.**

down so it appears lower in the mix. This process gets more complicated with non-boxy objects, such as cars. The only way of dealing with these most complex of reflections is to split the reflected object into as many constituent layers as is necessary to make it work. Again, unifying all the layers as a single group will help you to deal with them afterwards; and if the opacity of the group is sufficiently lowered, any minor inconsistencies can be easily concealed.

There's another, rather different approach that feels a bit like cheating. Let's say you have a photograph of an object with a large top and narrow sides, such as a notebook, and you want to make a reflection beneath it. You could cut the sides in two, as before, but there's a simpler method.

Make a copy of the notebook layer and move it behind the original. Now lower its opacity and drag the whole thing vertically downwards. Assuming the sides are more or less symmetrical, you'll get the impression of a reflection without having to do any reflecting: you may need to shear the sides slightly, and perhaps flip any off-centre features or writing, but you'll end up with a far more convincing result this way.

This last approach can also be used when reflecting objects such as candlesticks, which have a large curved base. Flipping vertically and distorting the base into an opposite curve will prove almost impossible. It's far easier to make a copy of the base alone, slide it downwards and flip a copy of the whole candlestick behind it.

▲ **To make the reflection for this MacBook, the bottom section is simply duplicated and slid down behind the original. It's then a straightforward matter to flip elements such as the thumb recess, and place the screen behind it.**

Finally, we need to consider reflections on surfaces that aren't perfectly smooth, such as water. We need to distort the reflection so that it appears to ripple on the surface. You can use a Photoshop filter such as Ocean Ripple to create your distortion but it's more effective to use a Displacement Map.

Duplicate the reflection and, if it's a group, merge the group into a single layer. Copy the water in a greyscale document and blur it slightly to remove the hard edges. Save it to disk and use Filter > Distort > Displace on the flipped reflection. Choose the saved file when asked for a displacement map and you'll find that the displacement will precisely match the surface of the water. You may need to experiment with the displacement amounts to get the best results, so be prepared to run this filter a couple of times in order to get it right.

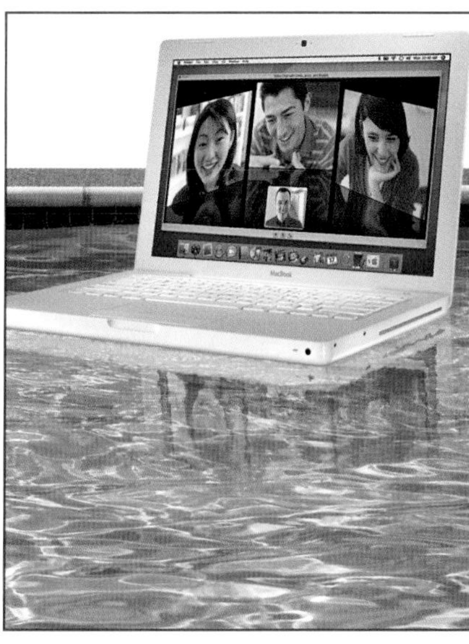

▲ **When reflecting in a non-flat surface, we need to add some distortion to make the effect convincing. Here, a simple Ocean Ripple filter is sufficient.**

R: Rule of thirds

It has been around for hundreds of years, but to this day the rule of thirds continues to turn average images into powerful ones…

Every episode of *The Simpsons* opens with an introductory sequence showing America's first family returning to their home in Springfield, where they collapse onto a sofa in front of the TV. Above the sofa is a painting of a sailboat. Sometimes it's a red boat with white sails, sometimes an orange boat with red sails. Whatever the colour, the boat is always right in the middle of the painting, both horizontally and vertically. The question is: what's wrong with this picture?

As long ago as 1797, the artist J T Smith wrote a book about landscape painting in which he outlined his 'rule of thirds'. For a visually pleasing effect, Smith argued, the horizon should always appear at the bottom third of the picture, so that one third of the painting was land or sea and the remainder was sky.

The rule of thirds has become a mantra for painters, photographers and Photoshop artists alike, as it helps us to create more powerful images by aligning our main picture elements with the vertical and horizontal divisions. Imagine a noughts and crosses grid overlaid on your image, dividing it into nine equal regions. The horizontal lines mark the optimal position for the horizon, the vertical lines indicate the best place to align vertical elements. The four inner points where they cross define the 'power points' in the image [**01**], the positions that have the most emphatic pull: placing the focus of the image at one of these points instantly makes for a stronger, more dynamic result.

However, does a rule formulated in the 18th Century really have any relevance today? Indeed it does, and we see examples of the rule of thirds throughout the commercial, artistic and broadcast media. The studio layout for the BBC's *News at Ten*, for instance, places the presenter's head directly at the upper right power point; the dividing line between the desk at which he's sitting and the screen behind aligns with the lower horizontal rule [**02**].

This rule is so important because, strangely, the centre of any picture is a weak place to position a key element. In the example of a surfer coasting across the image. When he's placed dead centre, the image is static [**03A**]. He's simply standing there, with no sense of motion. When we move him towards the left, we can see the distance he still has to travel [**03B**]; toward the right, and we can see how far he has already surfed [**03C**]. We can also change the emphasis by moving the image up or down. We can choose to emphasise either the close-up sea in front or the distant sea behind, by giving each element a larger proportion of the picture. Lining the surfer up with one of the power points guarantees a stronger, more dynamic shot.

When working with portraits, we can use the rule of thirds to align the eyes and the mouth. The face may be right in the middle of the frame, but by positioning the eyes on the upper hotspots and the mouth on the lower horizontal third, we bring a greater strength to the image. It may operate on a subconscious level on the viewer – after all, it's unlikely anyone would take

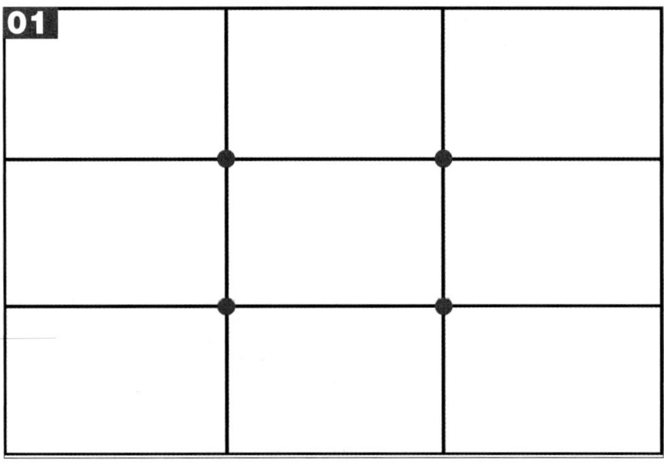

◄ The grid for the rule of thirds, showing the power points at the intersections.

▲ The studio layout for BBC's *News at Ten* shows the two thirds rule in action, with the presenter's head lining up with a power point and the desk occupying the bottom third of the shot.

▲ Placing the surfer dead centre in the frame kills the shot – even though it should be full of action.

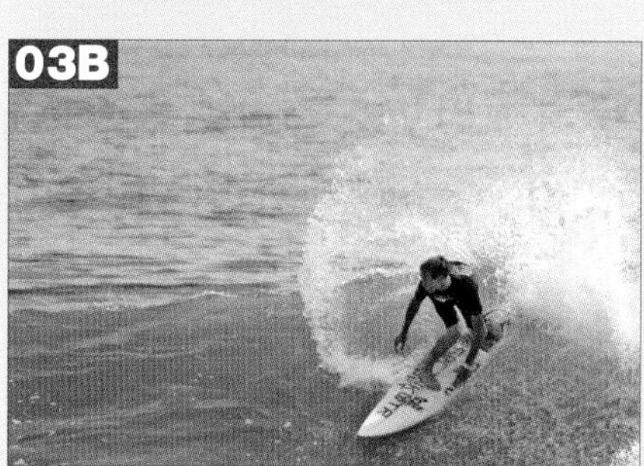

▲ Moving him to the bottom right power point emphasises the distance he still has to travel, showing the expanse of sea beyond.

▲ Moving the surfer to the top left power point shows the turbulence of the nearby water in greater detail, making for a dynamic shot.

a ruler to the photograph to measure the position of the eyes – but the placement still has its effect. We may rarely want to crop an image so tightly, but even if we ignore the power points, placing the eyeline on the upper third rule will generally lead to a more balanced portrait.

Landscape photographers regularly use the rule of thirds to divide the shot into three separate components – foreground, middle ground and background. In this case, the different fields appear in separate sections of the image. It may well be that nothing is placed directly on the rules, but each component will appear firmly rooted within its own one-third section. The rule is perhaps most often used when composing a landscape, as a guide to aligning the horizon. Placing the horizon directly through the centre of the image divides the picture in half, producing an artificial and awkward composition; by moving it to either the upper or lower third position, we can choose whether we want to emphasise the land or the sky, so creating a more powerful image.

When a scene contains two objects, such as this shot of a bird approaching its nest [**04**], we can add extra dynamism by cropping the scene so the bird appears at one power point, and the nest occupies the opposite third of the image. This kind of shot is almost impossible to frame when taking the shot, but is easy to crop later.

Some digital cameras now have a composition overlay mode, in which lines corresponding to the rule of thirds appear in the viewfinder, enabling photographers to align elements as they take the shot. Some photographers prefer to crop their image after they've taken the shot, using the rule to force picture details to appear in the optimal location. Photoshop artists, on the other hand, can create their images from scratch, and will frequently bear the rule in mind when composing a scene.

We don't need to be too rigorous in our adherence to the rule: it's a suggestion, not an absolute diktat. There are many occasions when the dead centre of the image really is the best location, or where the composition of a shot forbids the precise application of the rule. But as long as we're aware of it when we take a photograph, create a montage or even paint a landscape, we can be sure that our labours will have much more punch and visual appeal.

► This is a perfect composition made easy using the rule of thirds. The bird is at the upper left power point while the nest occupies the bottom right third of the image.

S: Smart Objects

By using Smart Objects, you have greater flexibility in resizing your work, and in changing several instances of each one at once.

Introduced in Photoshop CS2, Smart Objects give designers the power to experiment with scaling and distorting images without the loss of quality normally associated with repeated transformations. But there's much more to the technology than this: the contents of a Smart Object can be replaced with different artwork at any stage, which means that a complex distortion can be endlessly repurposed with different content.

Here's how it works. A layer, or set of layers, is first processed by choosing Layer > Smart Objects > Convert to Smart Object. This will turn all the selected layers into, apparently, a single layer, which can then be distorted, rotated and transformed at will: you can even use Image Warp distortions to bend the layer around curves.

The difference is that the contents of the Smart Object are saved in their original state in the Photoshop document, and when further transformations are applied, it's this original document that's referred to. So if you scale a Smart Object down to, say, 5% of its original size, when you return to it later and scale it back up again the original layers will be used to perform the scaling operation. Try this with a regular Photoshop layer, and you'll see the degradation that would normally occur in this extreme instance. Smart Objects also work with placed Illustrator files, meaning that imported vector artwork can now be scaled in Photoshop as true vectors, with resolution-independent adjustment.

It gets really clever when you double-click a Smart Object in Photoshop's Layers palette. The contents will open in a new window as a .psb file (the format Photoshop uses for storing large documents), with all the layers intact. It's now possible to edit each of the layers within the Smart Object: when the .psb file is saved, the changes made will be returned to the transformed version in the original Photoshop document. If it contains a placed Illustrator object, this can be opened in Illustrator and edited, then returned to Photoshop and transformed automatically back in place.

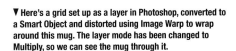

▼ Here's a grid set up as a layer in Photoshop, converted to a Smart Object and distorted using Image Warp to wrap around this mug. The layer mode has been changed to Multiply, so we can see the mug through it.

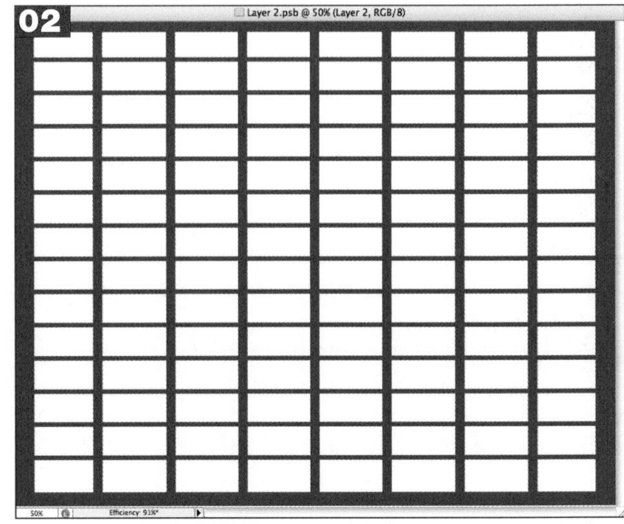

▲ Double clicking the Smart Object layer opens it as a .psb document, showing – in this case – the original grid we used to wrap around the surface.

▲ We can replace this grid with any artwork we choose – even with multiple layers, as shown here. Each element remains a separate, editable layer.

▲When we save the .psb file, the new artwork is immediately wrapped around the mug, following our initial distortion.

▲ We can even drag the artwork off to the side, so it's clipped by the bounds of the Smart Object document.

▲ Now, because the Smart Object used the mug as a clipping layer, we can see the effect of printing the logo in different positions around the surface.

So why is this so useful? Well, here's an example. Let's say we take a photograph of a ceramic mug. We can set up a grid pattern and make that into a Smart Object, then distort it using Image Warp so that the grid appears to wrap around the mug. If we change the mode of the Smart Object layer to Multiply, then we're able to see the original mug shading through it. Now, we can double-click the Smart Object to open the document: we can replace the contents with any artwork we choose and, when we save the file, that artwork will be wrapped around the mug, with the original shading showing through it. And, of course, we can repeat this process as many times as we choose with different artwork.

The possibilities here are endless. If you photograph a rippling white flag and distort a grid to fit it, you can impose an Illustrator drawing of any country's flag on it in a couple of seconds. You can photograph a wine bottle in a still-life situation, and replace the label; or photograph a blank magazine spread, and impose your flat artwork on it to make it appear to have been photographed in place.

A Smart Object can be duplicated in a document, and each duplication then transformed and distorted individually. When any of the Smart Object instances are edited, each version in the document will be changed to match the edit. For designers, this works in much the same way as using Symbols in Illustrator. Complex layouts can be produced using a company logo, for example: if the logo then changes, it's a simple matter to change one instance and the same effect is applied to all the versions of the logo in the artwork.

By turning text into a Smart Object we can then apply effects to it that wouldn't otherwise be possible, such as filters and warp distortions. Previously, we'd have had to rasterise the type first, to turn it into a regular pixel layer; now, we can leave it as live text, opening the Smart Object when we want to edit it or change the font.

Smart Objects give us the ability to use 'placeholder' artwork in Photoshop, then to change it to the final artwork in a couple of seconds. Here's a real-life example: I was recently asked to produce a cover for *The Guardian* magazine *G2*, in which the whole cover, complete with headlines, was to be distorted to look like a sheet of crumpled newspaper, with fish and chips placed on top. Naturally, the headline and other cover lines were decided at the last moment. But, using Smart Objects, I was able to create the entire artwork using dummy text, only replacing the contents with the real headlines shortly before going to press. And then to do so again, when the editor changed his mind. Without Smart Objects, it would have meant painstakingly recreating the distortions – a combination of Image Warp and the Wave filter – from scratch, each time the headlines changed.

Photoshop CS3 and CS4 brings us the ability to apply filters to Smart Objects. This means we can apply ripples, paint effects, blurs and more to groups of layers and then edit the contents, instantly seeing the same set of filters reapplied to the new artwork. Smart Filters also come with masks, just like Adjustment Layers, so the effect can be selectively hidden and faded.

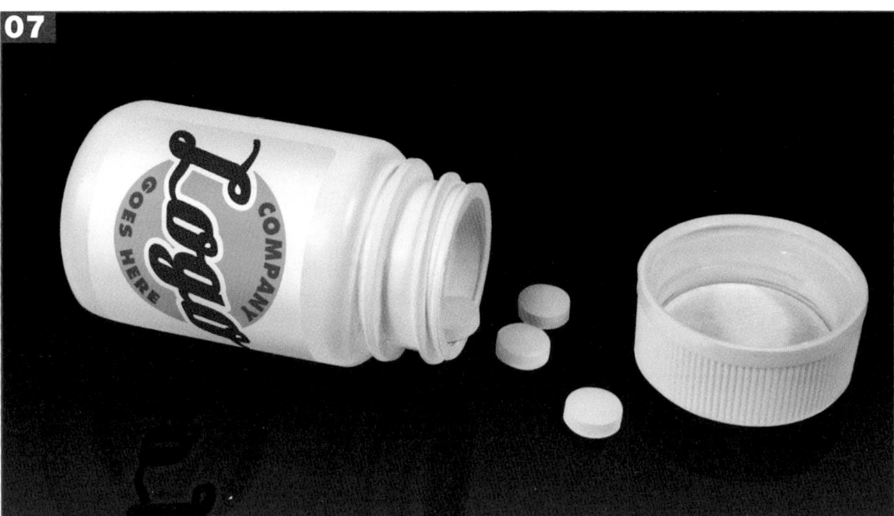

▲ If a Smart Object is duplicated within the artwork, both instances will be updated when one is changed – so the reflected version of this pill bottle matches the label on the bottle.

S: Smart Guides

Using Adobe's Smart Guides feature can take the tedium out of precision layout tasks, so here's how to use them in Illustrator and InDesign.

Smart Guides in Illustrator and InDesign can be a huge time-saver when it comes to aligning objects on a page, but the implementations of the feature are subtly different between the two applications.

SMART GUIDES IN ILLUSTRATOR

Introduced into Illustrator a few versions back, Smart Guides are a convenient way to show when an object being moved aligns with other objects already on the artboard. Guidelines also pop up when an object is moved close to horizontally or vertically, or at a preset angle of your choice. In Illustrator, you can turn Smart Guides on and off from the View menu, or by using the Command-U keyboard shortcut.

When you move an object vertically, a guide line will pop up (the default colour is green) showing a precise vertical movement – and the object will snap to that line as you move it [**01**]. The original square is shown in blue, and the version being moved appears in outline. In addition, you see a text readout showing the distance and the angle moved. Of course, you could simply hold down the Shift key to effect a purely vertical movement, but Smart Guides has more tricks up its sleeve.

It can also alert you when various parts of the object align with other parts. So, for example, you can see when the centre point of an item being moved aligns with the edge of its original position [**02**]. There are times when this kind of feedback is invaluable. For instance, if you're trying to create a checkerboard pattern, you can do so more easily when Smart Guides show that you're moving to a precise corner alignment [**03**].

The strength of Smart Guides lies in the fact that it shows when objects align with other items on the page. In this example [**04**], the blue square is being moved, and so shows in outline: we're alerted when its centre aligns with the centre of the red square.

You may not always want to align edges and centres: sometimes you want to align an arbitrary location, such as the top of a capital letter. You can do this by Command-dragging an object. This will make the Smart Guides show up when they align with the cursor, rather than a fixed point on the object.

You can use Smart Guides to show multiple alignments, which is particularly useful when transforming objects. In this example [**05**], we're transforming the blue square by dragging its bottom-right corner: the guides show that we're aligning both with the right edge of the blue square itself, and the base of the red square next to it.

As well as vertical and horizontal alignment, you can use the Smart Guides preferences to set additional behaviour [**06**]. You can choose to have Smart Guides alert you when you're moving an object at a 45° angle, for example. For artists creating isometric drawings, you can set 60° and 30° angles instead, which is a huge benefit. Not just object movement, but paths drawn with the Pen tool will snap to these angles, greatly simplifying an otherwise

01

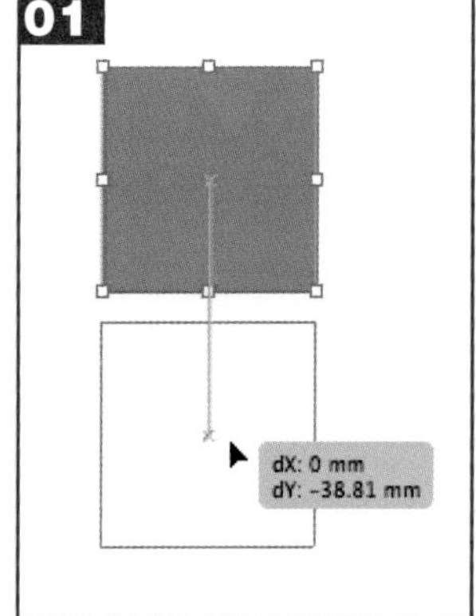

02

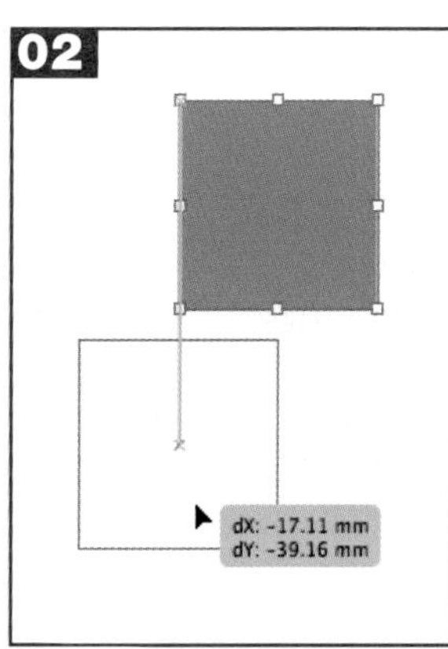

03

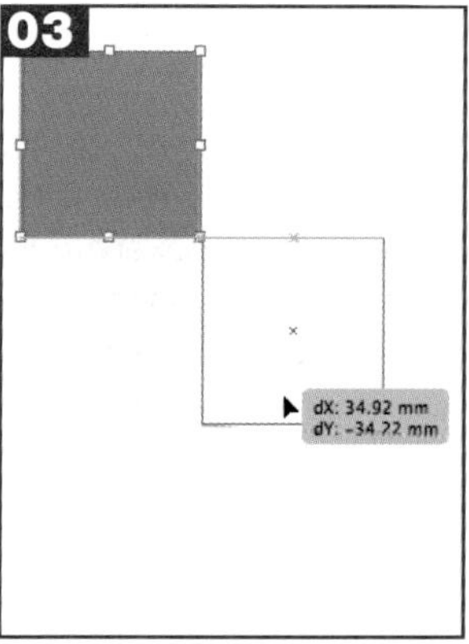

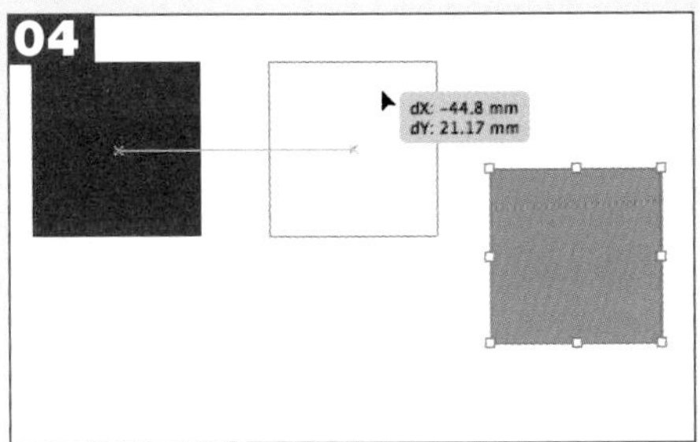

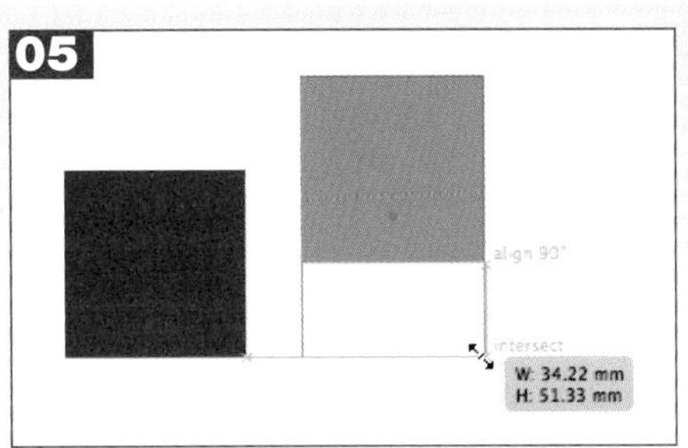

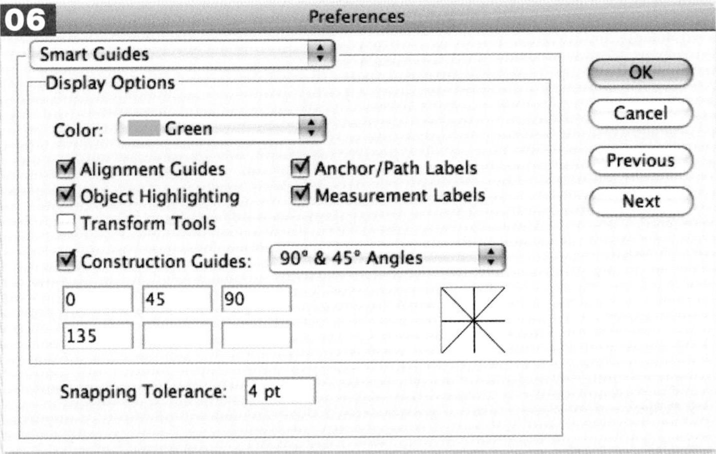

complex process. You can also choose whether transformations such as scaling and shearing will activate the guides: again, this is of particular benefit for isometric construction.

SMART GUIDES IN INDESIGN

When Smart Guides were introduced into InDesign, a few extra capabilities were added. Smart Guides are found under the View > Guides and Grids menu; use Command-U. When you move an object, guides indicate the top, bottom and centre line of alignment simultaneously [**07**]. When moving objects of identical size, all three guides will highlight for you. In InDesign, you're also treated to Smart Cursors, which show a numerical readout that displays scaling size or angles of rotation.

Smart Guides in InDesign have the ability to display equal space between objects. Moving an item such as a text box between two existing page elements will now show when the moved object is equidistant between the elements already in place, snapping to the mid point to ensure perfect alignment [**08**]. This is of huge benefit, especially when working off-grid, performing a task that otherwise would require use of the Distribute panel to equalise the spacing.

InDesign's Smart Guides can also match the angle of rotated objects on the page. If a piece of text such as a table header has been rotated to tighten a layout, then rotating any other object will pop up the familiar Smart Guide indicator when the angle approaches that of the first rotated item [**09**].

Because there may be many objects on a page, it would simply be confusing if Smart Guides were to attempt to snap to all of them. That's why InDesign's Smart Guides only snap to objects within the current viewing window. To exclude objects elsewhere on the page from the snapping process, simply zoom in so that they aren't in the current view and Smart Guides will ignore them.

Although they're undoubtably useful, InDesign's Smart Guides have some surprising shortcomings. If you rotate an item and then attempt to draw a line beneath it at the same angle, the Smart Guides won't match the angle for you, but will give you a range of extraneous information that's frequently of little use. In this example [**10**], we're attempting to draw a rule beneath a rotated text box. We have no help matching the angle, but the Smart Guides do show us when the rectangle that theoretically surrounds our straight line is the same width and height as the text box above. It's a pointless indication, as it doesn't relate to the object in any meaningful way. The best way to match a rotated angle in a case such as this is to draw the rule horizontally, then use the Rotate tool to turn it, at which point the Smart Guides system will come into play, showing the correct angle to match the rotated object.

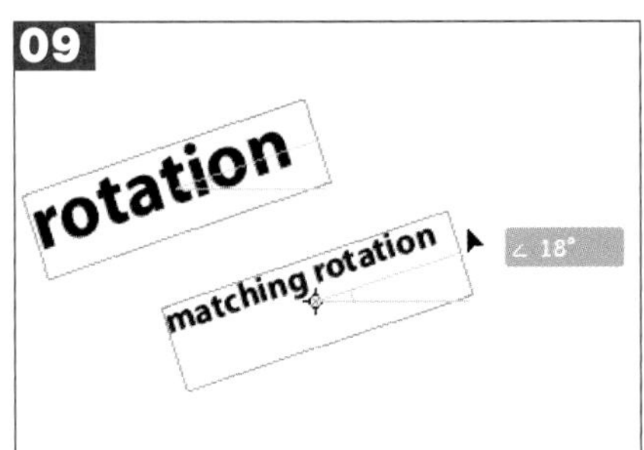

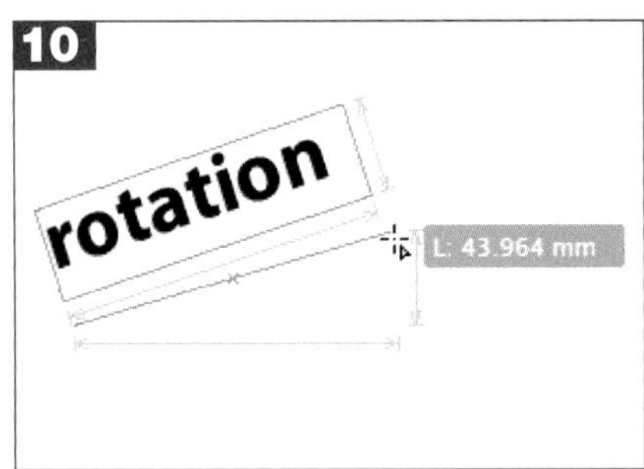

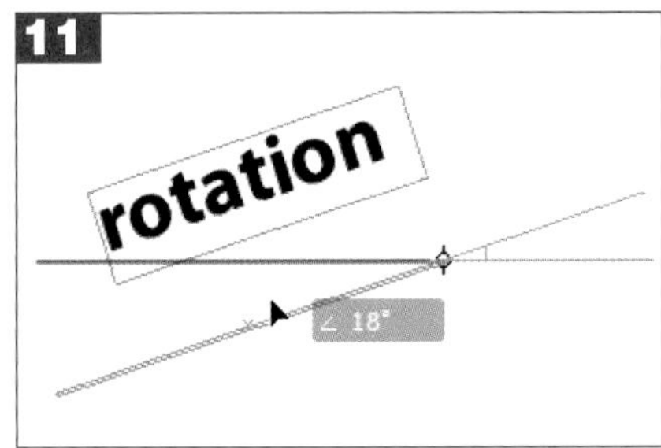

Like most help systems, you need to know when to ignore it. With Smart Guides, the snapping function can be counter-productive rather than beneficial: get used to using the Command-U shortcut to toggle Smart Guides on and off, so they're operational only when you need them.

S: Style sheets

Key to ensuring a standard look and feel to your work, every DTP professional should be using style sheets to control fonts, spacing, sizes and more.

Style sheets are a way of recording characteristics of a block of type – font, justification, spacing and so on – that can be retrieved with a keystroke and applied to the current text position. The system has become more and more sophisticated over the years, with greater functionality and ease of use built in. Style sheets are implemented in most page layout applications: here, we'll look at how they work in Adobe's InDesign.

There are three different kinds of style sheet in InDesign, operating on paragraph, character and object level. We'll begin with the paragraph version.

To create a new style sheet, first set up the current paragraph of text so it's formatted as you want it, with the correct font, leading, before and after spacing, hyphenation settings and so on. We'll make this the standard body text style, so set a first line indent of 3mm (or whatever you choose). This is so that the first word of each new paragraph is automatically indented for ease of reading, which is standard practice in books, magazines and newspapers.

To define the style, open the Paragraph Styles palette (Window > Type & Tables menu) and Alt-click the New Document icon at the bottom of the palette. This creates a new style based on the current selection: holding down the Alt key also opens the dialog. Here, you can set a name for the style (let's call it Body Text) and a keyboard shortcut to invoke it. Style shortcuts in InDesign use the numerical keypad: let's assign Command-2 to this style, for reasons that will become clear. Click on the Apply Style to Selection checkbox, and then click on OK to create the new style.

The first paragraph of any story needs to be 'full out' – that is, without an indented first line. You could do this manually each time, but it makes more sense to define a style for it. You could define it by example, as you did for the body text style. It's easier and neater, though, to create the style using the palette.

Select the Body Text style in the Paragraph Style palette and choose Duplicate Style from the pop-up menu at the top of the palette. In the dialog that appears, the new style will be given the default name Body Text copy: change this to First Para, or similar, and change the keyboard shortcut to Command-1.

The only difference between this style and the body text is the first line indent, so change the 'Based on' pop-up menu to Body Text. The

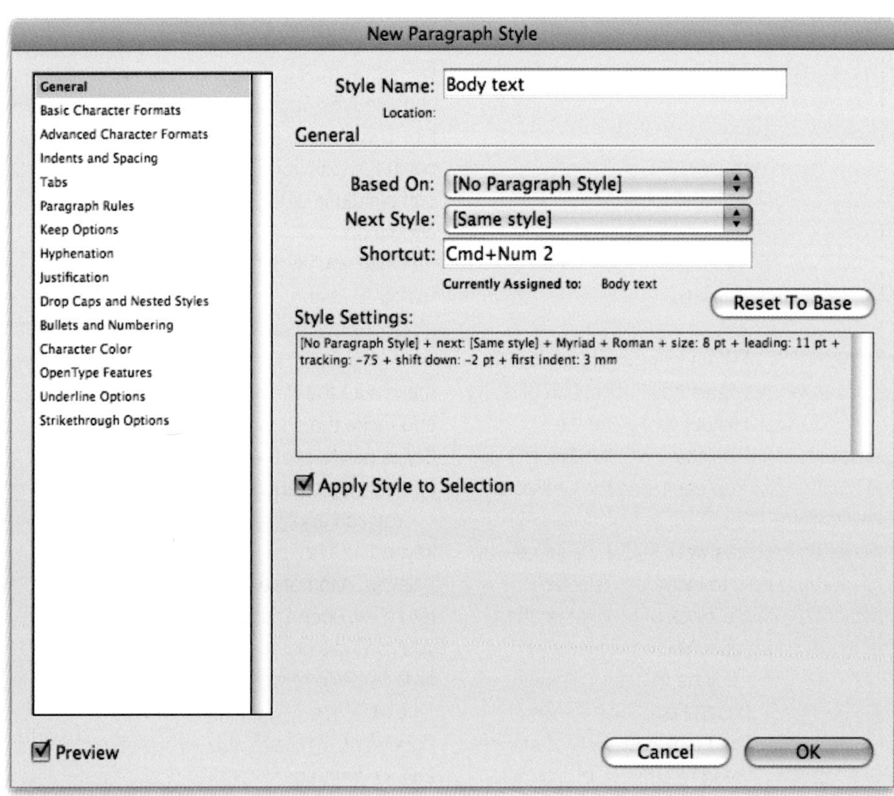

◄ **The easiest way to set up your paragraph styles is to format your paragraph as you want, then create a new style based on the current selection.**

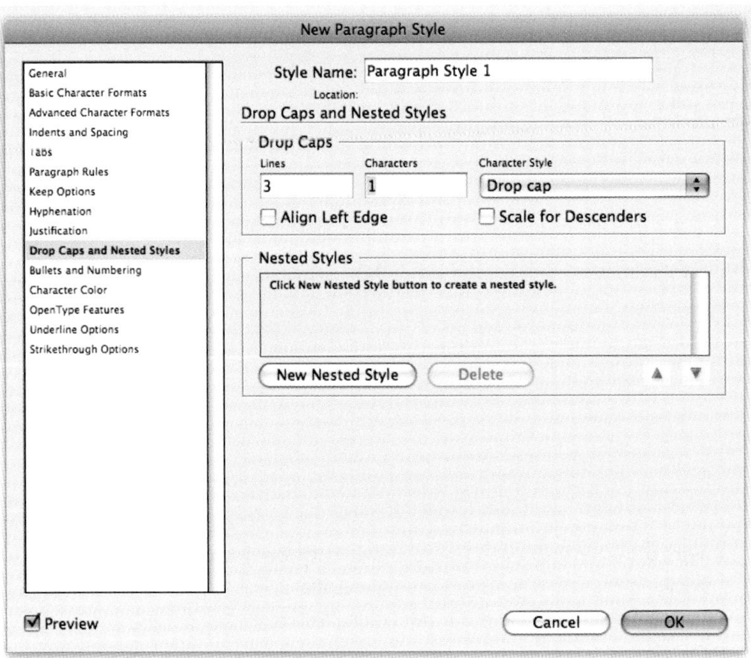

◄ **To create a drop capital at the beginning of a paragraph, simply define your drop cap style using the Character Styles palette and apply it using Paragraph Styles.**

New Paragraph Style

General
Basic Character Formats
Advanced Character Formats
Indents and Spacing
Tabs
Paragraph Rules
Keep Options
Hyphenation
Justification
Drop Caps and Nested Styles
Bullets and Numbering
Character Color
OpenType Features
Underline Options
Strikethrough Options

Style Name: Full out
Location:
Indents and Spacing
Alignment: Left
Balance Ragged Lines
Ignore Optical Margin
Left Indent: 0 mm
First Line Indent: 0 mm
Right Indent: 0 mm
Last Line Indent: 0 mm
Space Before: 0 mm
Space After: 0 mm
Align to Grid: None
Preview
Cancel
OK

◄ **To create a full-out paragraph style, simply duplicate your body text paragraph style and amend its indents from the palette. You can also specify what the next style will be so follow-on styles are applied automatically.**

new style will then replicate all the characteristics of the initial style. It's also possible to specify here what the next style is to be – that is, the style that will be applied when you hit a paragraph return while typing. You can change this to Body Text, as well, so follow-on styles will be applied automatically.

All you need to do now is fix that indent. The list on the left of the panel shows all the possible type feature categories. Click on Indents and Spacing, and change the First Line indent value to 0. Then click on OK to finish creating the style. Let's say you want to make the first paragraph stand out more: you might want to create it with a three-line drop capital, for instance, or at least have the option of doing so. You can set this up, too, using the Paragraph Styles palette. First, though, let's set the font for this drop cap using the Character Styles palette.

Character Styles work in just the same way, except they apply to individual selected characters within a block of text, rather than the whole paragraph. You can use the Character Styles palette to create a new style, called Drop Cap Font (for instance), and choosing a bold font such as Myriad Extra Bold. You don't need to define it by example, as you did earlier: all this can be done directly through the Character Styles palette. Because it's a drop capital, the size will be set automatically, so you only need to be concerned with the font.

With the Character Style created, return to the Paragraph Styles palette. Duplicate the First Para style, as you did before, and change its name to something memorable, such as Drop Cap and give it a new shortcut. As before, base the style on Body Text.

In the Drop Caps and Nested Styles section, fill in the Lines field with the number of lines you want the drop cap to take up (it's usually two or three) and the Characters field with the number of characters to be enlarged (generally one). Now, using the Character Style pop-up, choose Drop Cap Font as defined earlier.

You can also use this section to define 'nested styles'. You might, for instance, want the first three words to be in bold, or all the digits to be in a particular style – and that's the kind of effect we'd define here.

You can use the Character Styles palette for defining styles such as Regular Italic weights in multi-weight fonts, where simply choosing the 'italic' shortcut won't do the job. There's also a separate Object Styles palette, which you can use to store favourite combinations of fill, stroke, drop shadow, and so on.

Once you've defined a style, it's a simple matter to change all the characteristics globally. For instance, if you want to change the font, size or leading of your body text, make sure the Preview button is checked and make the changes in the Paragraph Styles palette: you'll see the changes immediately on the page.

You can apply styles using the numeric keypad, or choose them by name from the palettes. Alternatively, pressing Command-return will open the Quick Apply field, where you can type just the first few letters of a style name to select it.

Even if you're creating a single-use document, it's worth defining styles for ease of editing; for magazine work, it's essential. ⊗

T: TextEdit

The free word processor included with Mac OS X has some surprisingly advanced features under its belt… if you know where to look.

TextEdit is the basic, no-frills word processor that comes with every Mac. It has none of the zip and sparkle of more powerful applications such as Word or Nisus, and certainly none of the layout capabilities of InDesign or QuarkXPress.

Or does it? We'll see how to customise TextEdit so it can produce attractive layouts without you having to buy any extras. Let's look at 10 basic TextEdit misconceptions and show how to get around them.

1 TextEdit can't create multiple columns.

Yes, it can. As you'll know if you've ever opened a multi-column Word document

THE JOURNAL OF THE VINICULTURAL FROMAGERIE SOCIETY

Issue 2307 • October 2008 • Published weekly by the society for the benefit and elucidation of its members

A history of innovation

Lorem ipsum dolor sit amet, consectetuer adipiscing elit. Praesent semper. Cum sociis natoque penatibus et magnis dis parturient montes, nascetur ridiculus mus. Fusce sed elit. Vivamus dignissim.

Donec ut neque. Suspendisse quis ante. Maecenas rutrum vulputate massa. Fusce dictum, lacus vel ullamcorper hendrerit, erat justo consequat justo, at faucibus elit justo id magna. Curabitur eleifend, metus eu scelerisque volutpat, urna massa tempus nibh, quis elementum quam purus vel mi.

Cras sagittis porta sapien. Vivamus vehicula orci eget purus. Mauris blandit pellentesque libero.

A particularly runny Camembert

Vivamus nec elit. Etiam vulputate leo a massa. Proin in nunc vel felis venenatis euismod. Etiam eu velit at sapien. Etiam posuere bibendum diam. Curabitur molestie. Maecenas vitae mi in erat dignissim faucibus. Nulla lobortis, sapien venenatis sagittis blandit, arcu nunc volutpat neque, ut molestie lectus lacus sit amet tortor. Nam tempus mauris ut lectus.

A selection of prime vintages

Curabitur eleifend, metus eu scelerisque volutpat, urna massa tempus nibh, quis elementum quam purus vel mi.

Aenean non ipsum in arcu facilisis tincidunt. Suspendisse elit turpis, scelerisque ut, hendrerit et, pretium ut, libero. Proin varius, leo non dignissim ornare, tellus purus porttitor lorem, sed luctus sem risus vel risus. Nam eros. Class aptent taciti sociosqu ad litora torquent per conubia nostra, per inceptos himenaeos.

Cras sagittis porta sapien. Vivamus vehicula orci eget purus. Mauris blandit pellentesque libero. Vivamus nec elit. Etiam vulputate leo a massa. Proin in nunc vel felis venenatis euismod. Etiam eu velit at sapien aliquam consequat. Proin venenatis varius justo. Pellentesque eleifend velit vitae sapien. Etiam posuere bibendum diam. Curabitur molestie. Maecenas vitae mi in erat dignissim faucibus. Nulla lobortis, sapien venenatis sagittis blandit, arcu nunc volutpat neque.

More info

Curabitur eleifend, metus eu scelerisque volutpat, urna massa tempus nibh, quis elementum quam purus vel miniusque. Aenean non ipsum in arcu facilisis sed tincidunt. Suspendisse elit turpis, scelerisque ut, hendrerit et, pretium ut, libero. Proin varius.

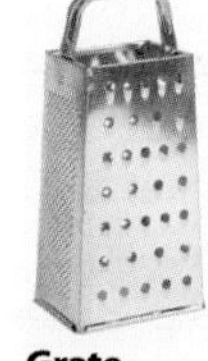

Grate stuff

Curabitur eleifend, metus eu scelerisque volutpat, urna massa tempus nibh, quis element.

► **This page was created entirely in TextEdit (with a little help from Photoshop to resize the images). The narrow column on the right includes an image by defining that column as a separate nested table.**

1. There are several ways to create a list.

2. We could type the numbers in manually, which is time-consuming but leaves us in charge.

3. Or we could use the List feature built into the TextEdit ruler.

4. But what if we want to change the style of all the numbers?

▲ **Hold down Alt when dragging to select vertical rectangular areas of type. This is particularly useful when you want to change the font of a whole column, such as these numbers.**

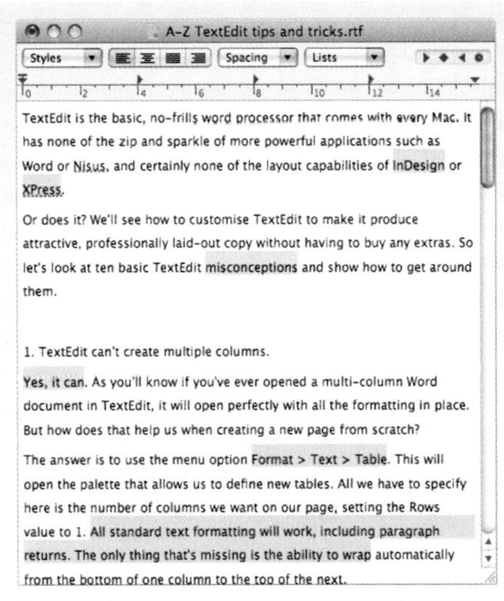
A–Z TextEdit tips and tricks.rtf

TextEdit is the basic, no-frills word processor that comes with every Mac. It has none of the zip and sparkle of more powerful applications such as Word or Nisus, and certainly none of the layout capabilities of InDesign or XPress.

Or does it? We'll see how to customise TextEdit to make it produce attractive, professionally laid-out copy without having to buy any extras. So let's look at ten basic TextEdit misconceptions and show how to get around them.

1. TextEdit can't create multiple columns.

Yes, it can. As you'll know if you've ever opened a multi-column Word document in TextEdit, it will open perfectly with all the formatting in place. But how does that help us when creating a new page from scratch?

The answer is to use the menu option Format > Text > Table. This will open the palette that allows us to define new tables. All we have to specify here is the number of columns we want on our page, setting the Rows value to 1. All standard text formatting will work, including paragraph returns. The only thing that's missing is the ability to wrap automatically from the bottom of one column to the top of the next.

▲ **Make selections of unconnected words and phrases by holding down Command as you select them. This is an easy way to apply styles to several words at once.**

in TextEdit, it will open perfectly with all the formatting in place. So how does that help us when creating a new page from scratch?

The answer is to use the menu option Format > Text > Table. This will open the palette that enables you to define new tables. All you have to specify here is the number of columns you want on your page, setting the Rows value to 1. All standard text formatting will work, including paragraph returns. The only thing missing is the ability to wrap automatically from the bottom of one column to the top of the next.

The default value is for side-by-side columns of text to be aligned around their midpoints – the way tables are usually laid out. The row of icons in the Alignment section of the Table palette has two sections, one each for horizontal alignment (left, right, centred and justified), and for vertical alignment. Here, you can set text to be aligned at the top instead of the centre. You can also choose to align baselines, which helps to prevent columns of type from becoming mismatched.

Once created, clicking on the dividers between columns will allow you to drag to change their width. This allows you to design pages with, say, two wide columns for main text and a narrow column for further information or captions. You'll probably also want to remove the default grey cell border. To do this, set its size to 0 in the Table palette.

2 TextEdit can't embed images within text.

It can, of course: you simply use Copy and Paste to take an image from another source, and place it on the page at the insertion point. However, TextEdit has no tools for resizing, panning or cropping images. Once the file has been saved to disk though, double-clicking the image will open it in Photoshop or any other default image editor. It will open with the name 'Pasted Graphic 1.tiff', and can be cropped or resized, and then copied and pasted back in place (although the image can't simply be saved).

What about if you want to position an image to the right or left of a chunk of text? TextEdit only allows an image to sit on a line by itself, with no wraparound facility. The solution, once again, is to create a new table to hold the image. You can now run the text in a column down the side of the image, resizing the table width to fit the width of your picture.

3 User-defined styles only apply to whole paragraphs.

Once you've set up a paragraph as you want it, choosing the font, colour, size indents and so on, you can define it as a new Style by choosing Other… from the Style pop-up menu. This is where you specify whether you want to include the font information, the ruler information (including tabs and so on) or both.

However, what if you come across a situation where you want to apply a style to just a few words? The answer is to use Alt-Command-C to copy the style of a selected word that's already in the style you want. You can then select the words you want to change, and press Alt-Command-V: this pastes the style you've just copied onto the new words.

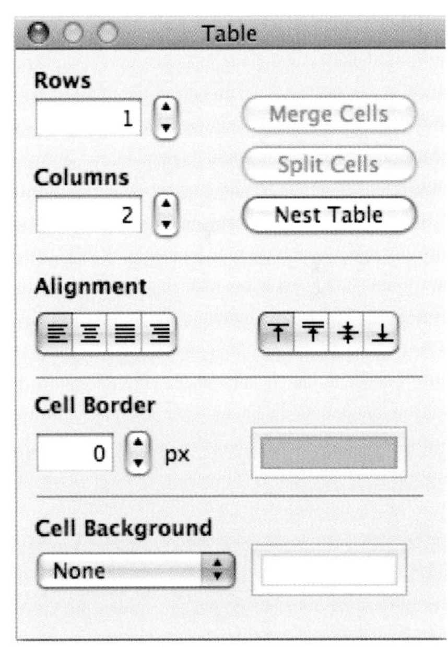

▲ **Create multiple columns of text by defining a table. Set the cell border to 0 and the alignment to Top.**

4 Changing multiple instances of a font or style is a clumsy process.

It's true that there's no way to select all instances of, say, Arial Bold, and change them to Helvetica Black, as you might expect to be able to do in a more sophisticated page layout application. Nevertheless, there are a few clever ways to select text in TextEdit.

TextEdit enables you to make type selections that aren't contiguous. Double-click or drag to select the first word or phrase. Next, hold down the Command key and double-click or drag to select the next word or phrase. Just as the Command key lets you add multiple selections in the Finder, so it also allows you to select multiple words in different locations within a TextEdit document. With all the words selected, it's then easy to change the font and style of all of them.

If you've set up a list with a hanging indent, you might want to select all the numbers and change them to a different font. You don't need to change them individually: simply hold down the Alt key to draw a rectangular vertical selection, enclosing just the numbers. This is also a particularly useful method for changing items between tab stops.

5 It's impossible to create white-on-black slugs in TextEdit.

Not if you use a table, it isn't. Select the text and choose Format > Text > Table. At the bottom of the dialog, you'll notice a Cell Background field: change the pop-up from None to Color Fill, and then click on the swatch next to it to choose the colour you want. When you've done that, open Format > Font > Show Fonts, and change the colour of the type from the default black to white (or whatever other pale colour you've decided to use).

You can also use TextEdit's arrow tables to create horizontal rules in any colour. Type a single space, and create a new table that contains one column and one row. Add a colour fill to the cell background. The next step is to open the Spacing dialog box (from the pop-up menu on the toolbar) and choose Other from the bottom of the list. Changing the Line Height Multiple will allow precise control over the height of the horizontal rule.

6 It's difficult to align type precisely in TextEdit.

Aligning type may not be as elegant a process as it can be in some applications, but it's possible – and it's also very precise.
Click the Spacing pop-up on the toolbar, and choose Other. This will open the dialog from which you can set the line, inter-line and paragraph spacing. Type in numerical values, or click the up/down arrows next to each field. You'll be able to see the difference immediately in the selected text.

Settings that are used in the current document will appear automatically in the list in the pop-up menu, so you can retrieve them without having to set up the values again. Of course, you can set your favourite combinations as paragraph styles so they're permanently available in all of your documents, which can be a real time-saver.

7 TextEdit won't format text automatically.

TextEdit can produce lists, complete with bullets, numbers, letters and figures in a variety of styles. Make sure that the ruler is showing by choosing Format > Text > Show Ruler. Choose the list type you want from the Lists menu and just start typing. TextEdit will place bullet points or numbers as required, adding numbers when you hit Return.

If you insert or delete items, choose the list type again from the pop-up menu to re-number it. To end the list, just press the Return key twice to return to normal text formatting.

▲ Use the Spacing palette to set inter-paragraph and line spacing. All the variations will be listed for one-click retrieval.

8 TextEdit insists on printing with 1in margins.

It's profoundly irritating that when you override the standard wide margin setting in the Page Setup dialog, it has no effect on printing, either to paper or to PDF. Happily, there is a solution.

First, save and close your document. Open TextEdit's Preferences dialog, and check the 'Ignore rich text commands in RTF files' box in the Open and Save section. When you open the document again, you'll see a paragraph of coding at the top of the file, including these words:

\margl1440\margr1440

This specifies left and right margins of 1440 (measured, for some arcane reason, in 'twips' – 20ths of a point). Change this value, save and close the document, and then uncheck the box in Preferences. When you reopen the document, it will have the margins you set.

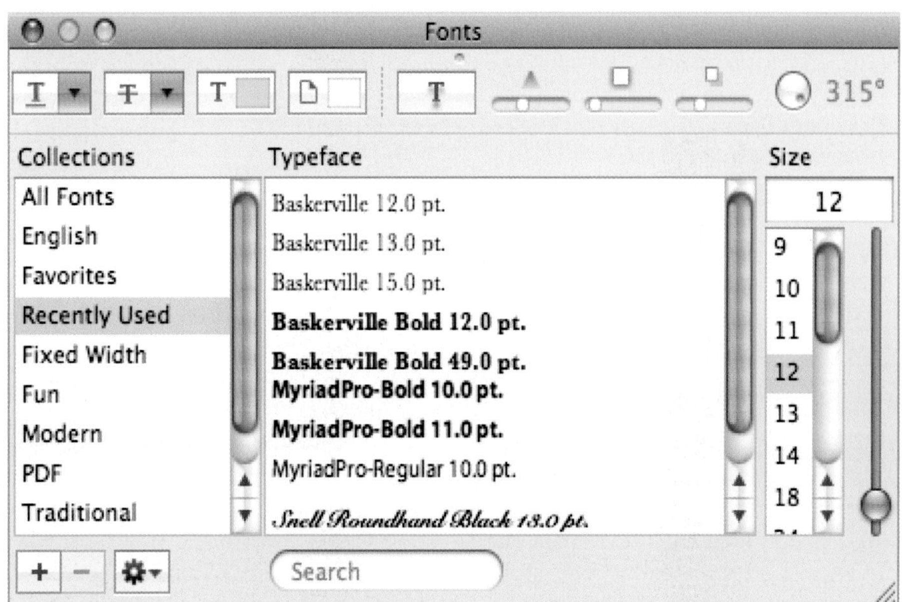

▲ There's no character style palette in TextEdit, but the Recently Used section of the Fonts palette shows both the fonts and the sizes at which you've used them.

9 TextEdit can't include hyperlinks.

Actually, it can, although it's a little hidden away. Choose Format > Text > Link and type in the URL, complete with *http://* at the beginning. It will appear in the text, underlined in blue. You can edit the type as it appears on the page to make it shorter and more readable, but when you click on it, you'll be taken straight to that page in Safari.

10 There's no word count facility in TextEdit.

True, but it's not difficult to find a suitable add-on. Among the best on offer is Word Counter, which is available from *supermagnus.com*. This useful, free utility will automatically count any text pasted into its window. Click the TextEdit button, and it will pop up a tiny floating window showing a live word and character count.

T: Typography

Not merely shapes on a page, letters can be works of art if handled the right way. Get to grips with typography for some smart, impressive results.

Typography is the art of choosing the right typeface with which to convey information, and of arranging the words on the page to their best effect. The modern designer has hundreds of typefaces to choose from, and selecting the right one for the job is of paramount importance.

Typefaces fall into two broad categories: serif and sans serif. The word 'serif' refers to the tiny lines at the ends of strokes, found in typefaces such as Times, Baskerville and Garamond. These originated with Roman stonemasons, who found that if they attempted to carve a thick character, such as the letter I, there was a danger of the stone splitting. To prevent this, they first carved thin lines at the top and bottom of the character to act as stoppers. These lines, the serifs, would stop the thick strokes they carved later continuing too far.

This isn't the only advantage of serifs, as it was found that these thin lines formed a kind of horizontal rule at the top and bottom of the letters, which helped to guide the eye along the printed page. The earliest examples of modern typography followed these Roman letter forms to aid legibility. Garamond, one of the earliest examples, is still in use today.

When the early Victorians started churning out posters to advertise plays and other events, they thickened the type to produce 'Egyptian' or slab serif letter forms. But the serifs took up too much space, reducing the size at which they could print the type. This led to the development of sans serif lettering (from the French for 'without'), which enabled printers to use larger sizes and increased legibility from a distance. Initially called 'Gothic' – in the sense of 'vandalistic' – these typefaces were initially considered too ugly for all but the most garish headlines.

Today, serif typefaces are used for extended passages in print: most books and newspapers, and almost all magazines, set their body copy in a serif face. Sans serif is often considered just too difficult to read in large chunks. The trouble is that serif type takes up more space and needs to be printed larger for legibility. When conveying information that is intended to

"The artist is not a
different kind of
person, but every
person is a differ-
ent kind of artist"

ERIC GILL (1882-1940)

▲ Typographic matter can be used to break up text in place of graphic elements – such as this quote from Eric Gill. But make sure hyphenation is turned off – it looks ugly and ungainly with small amounts of centred text.

"The artist is not a
different kind of
person, but every
person is a
different kind of
artist"

ERIC GILL (1882-1940)

▲ The appearance is improved with hyphenation turned off. But the top and bottom lines of the quote look unbalanced: the 'T' in the first line is above the 'd' in the line below, but the 'a' at the end of the first line awkwardly overhangs the next line.

"The artist is not a different kind of person, but every person is a different kind of artist"

Eric Gill (1882-1940)

▲ Using Hanging Punctuation places the quotation marks outside the body of the text. Now the type looks correctly centred. That single word 'of' at the end of the fifth line is hanging in space. With nothing above or below it, the effect is unbalanced.

"The artist is not a different kind of person, but every person is a different kind of artist"

Eric Gill (1882-1940)

▲ By changing to Adobe Every Line Composer, the line breaks are arranged to create a more even spread of words in each line. There are no instances where a whole word appears to be separated from the rest of the text.

In reading, for example, the enunciation of a proposition, we are apt to fancy, that for every word contained in it, there is an idea presented to the understanding; from the combination and comparison of which ideas, results that act of the mind called judgement.

So different is all this from the fact, that our words, when examined separately, are often as completely insignificant as the letters of which they are composed; deriving their meaning solely from the connection, or relation, in which they stand to others.

Dugald Stewart (1753-1828)

In reading, for example, the enunciation of a proposition, we are apt to fancy, that for every word contained in it, there is an idea presented to the understanding; from the combination and comparison of which ideas, results that act of the mind called judgement.

So different is all this from the fact, that our words, when examined separately, are often as completely insignificant as the letters of which they are composed; deriving their meaning solely from the connection, or relation, in which they stand to others.

Dugald Stewart (1753-1828)

▲ For long passages of text, sans serif type produces a result that's difficult to read. Setting the same text in a serif font makes it easier on the eye, because the serifs create the effect of rules above and below the characters, helping the reader to follow each line of text.

7.00 News and weather
7.30 The Simpsons
8.00 World's Greatest Disasters: an amusing look at how close we nearly came to Armageddon
8.30 All Aboard! Reality show set in a submarine beneath the arctic ocean, hosted by Graham Norton
9.00 Heavens Above! Reality show set in a hot air balloon, hosted by Graham Norton
10.00 News and weather
10.30 Local news
10.35 Hot Stuff! Disaster show set in an active volcano, hosted by Graham Norton

7.00 News and weather
7.30 The Simpsons
8.00 World's Greatest Disasters: an amusing look at how close we nearly came to Armageddon
8.30 All Aboard! Reality show set in a submarine beneath the arctic ocean, hosted by Graham Norton
9.00 Heavens Above! Reality show set in a hot air balloon, hosted by Graham Norton
10.00 News and weather
10.30 Local news
10.35 Hot Stuff! Disaster show set in an active volcano, hosted by Graham Norton

▲ When used to convey information, a serif typeface takes up too much space and can look awkward in narrow columns. The same text set in a sans serif face can be printed much smaller, with the same degree of legibility – which means more words will fit in.

The letters of the alphabet, the characters of a typeface, are building blocks. Besides being symbols to construct a written language, they can be used to compose any visual impression imaginable. To me, typography is the visual arrangement of letterforms and symbols. Its style creates identity. If the composition contains coherent content, this visual identity will convey the message in a distinct and original way. A new expression. A new impression. A new corner of the mind is opened. How exciting !

Max Kisman (1953-)

The letters of the alphabet, the characters of a typeface, are building blocks. Besides being symbols to construct a written language, they can be used to compose any visual impression imaginable. To me, typography is the visual arrangement of letterforms and symbols. Its style creates identity. If the composition contains coherent content, this visual identity will convey the message in a distinct and original way. A new expression. A new impression. A new corner of the mind is opened. How exciting !

Max Kisman (1953-)

▲ A common mistake is to increase the size of the type in an attempt to make it more legible. But when type is set too close, it's harder to read. A better solution is to reduce the size and increase the leading. This takes up the same amount of space but improves legibility.

be dipped into rather than read at length, sans serif faces are more suitable and enable designers to squeeze the information into a far smaller space. As a result newspapers use sans serif faces for financial information, TV listings, weather reports and so on.

One of the first truly modern sans serif faces was created by Edward Johnston in 1915 for the London Underground. The need was for a face that was legible and unambiguous from a distance – and London Underground still uses this typeface, Johnston, today. All road signs, which have much the same requirements, are in a similar face. To an extent, those in general use – from the regular, geometric Univers and Futura, to the more 'humanist', looser Gill and Optima – all owe their existence to Johnston.

Typefaces can be modern or old-fashioned, formal or relaxed; the choice depends on the context. When *The Guardian* launched its new design back in 1988, designer Dave Hillman took a radical step with its masthead, setting 'The' in Garamond Italic (serif), and 'Guardian' in Helvetica Black, a contemporary extra-bold sans. By mixing the old with the new, and the formal with the informal, The Guardian was making a definite statement about both its new approach and its heritage. Now, after the more recent redesign two years ago, both words are in lower case, run together and differentiated by different colours – a masthead for the Internet age.

The arrangement of type on the page is as important as the choice of typeface. In Illustrator and InDesign, Adobe provides a useful set of tools for balancing type. These include hanging punctuation (or 'optical margin alignment'), in which the punctuation is set outside the main block of text to create a greater visual balance. Also of interest is the Adobe Every Line Composer, a method of balancing spacing across multiple lines to create the best balance. Our visual examples on this page show how these techniques are used in practice.

One of the errors that novice designers often make is to set type too large in the mistaken belief that this increases legibility. It's generally far more effective to reduce the type size and to increase the leading – the space between the lines. (The name is taken from the strips of lead that compositors used to place between lines of type.) In part, the error is a result of designing wholly on screen: while 12pt Lucida Grande may be the most legible typeface for on-screen editing, it looks far too big and clumsy in print.

U: Unknown fonts

If you've seen a font you need but don't know what it is, don't despair: there are two tremendous online resources that will find it for you.

As designers, we frequently have to match a design's appearance to something that already exists. And while it's easy enough to match colours and layout, it can be much harder to match an existing font when you have no idea of the name of the original typeface.

Because this is a common problem, it's not surprising that a number of developers have brought their expertise to bear in trying to solve it. Two websites in particular – Identifont and WhatTheFont – perform an extraordinarily good job, taking very different approaches to solve the same conundrum.

As our example, we'll use a query that was sent in by a reader on the *How to Cheat in Photoshop* reader forum, who wanted to know the name of the font used for the words 'LOVE GUN' on the Kiss album of the same name. The font is quirky, highly distinctive and unusual, but if you don't happen to know it, how do you go about tracking it down? The quickest method is generally to try WhatTheFont. You can type that straight into your browser address bar, where it will redirect to ***new.myfonts.com/WhatTheFont***.

WhatTheFont works by examining an image of a string of characters and trying to find a match. You can choose an image that's already online, or upload your own. Whichever method you choose, you must make sure the text is as clear and – most importantly – as straight as possible. It helps to crop the image down to just the text area, so there isn't too much extraneous background noise to confuse the software. WhatTheFont will attempt to split the image into individual characters, prompting you to confirm the identity of each character it finds. For each one, it shows a cut-down version of the original scan, with that character clearly highlighted. This is the only area in which WhatTheFont needs our input. In our example, it failed to correctly identify most of the letters at all, assumed the final 'N' was an 'X', and so on. However, it takes just a few seconds to go through the list and key in the correct character.

Press the Continue button and in an instant, WhatTheFont will come back with suggestions for the name of the font. In the case of the Kiss album typeface, it got the answer spot on first time: the font is EF Dynamo, and WhatTheFont shows a display of the entire character set together with a link to buy the complete font. The technology is so slick it's astounding.

Identifont (***identifont.com***) approaches the problem in a different way. Rather than examining a scan of the lettering, it works by asking you a series of questions about the typography. Since the site recognises that you'll often be working from an example that contains only a small subset of the entire character set, it allows you to tell it which characters are available to you, and then will only ask about those characters.

▲ The task in hand is to identify the font used for the title of this Kiss album. The first step is to find the highest-quality image you can, and then crop it down to just the area on which you want to concentrate.

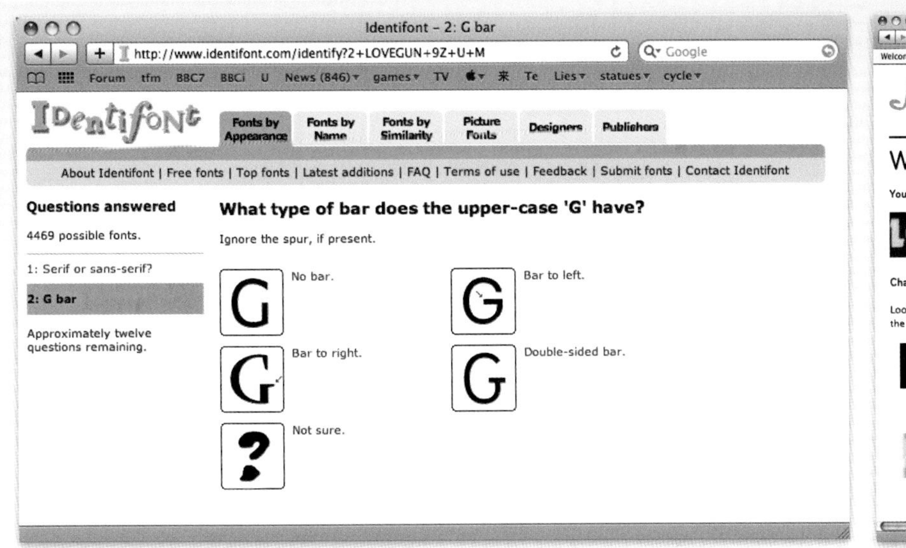

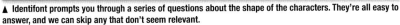

▲ Identifont prompts you through a series of questions about the shape of the characters. They're all easy to answer, and we can skip any that don't seem relevant.

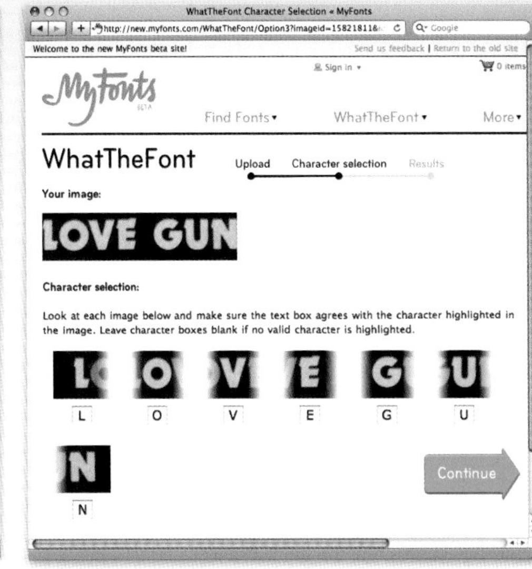

▲ You may need to tell WhatTheFont what some of the characters are, but it nearly always returns a perfect result in an instant.

The questions are all straightforward and easy to answer: is the font serif or sans serif? What type of bar does the upper-case G have? Is the font hollow or solid? Does the upper-case U have a stem? In each case, you're provided with a simple, explanatory graphic that shows exactly the feature that you're being quizzed about. As the questions continue, a counter shows the number of possible matching fonts remaining. If there are any questions you're unsure about – say, 'Is the font suitable for body text?' – you can simply click the 'not sure' button, and go on to the next question.

Identifont works best with a large character set, as that gives it the opportunity to ask more questions and so to narrow the field down further. Nevertheless, with the seven characters in 'LOVE GUN' we were able to talk about, Identifont came up with a list of more than 30 possible fonts that matched the criteria we'd set through the questioning. Number 4 on the list was, indeed, EF Dynamo, the font we were looking for. It's also interesting to see not just variations on this font – Linotype Dynamo and MN Dynamo are subtly different versions of the same font – but other typefaces that have similar characteristics and that we might consider using as alternatives.

Both Identifont and WhatTheFont limit themselves to displaying – and selling – commercially available typefaces. Which is fine, as long as the font you're looking for is a standard face in common use. But what if you're looking to parody, say, *The Simpsons*? Or the *Harry Potter* movies? Or *Star Trek*? The lettering for each of these shows or movies was custom-designed for the purpose and isn't based on a standard commercial typeface.

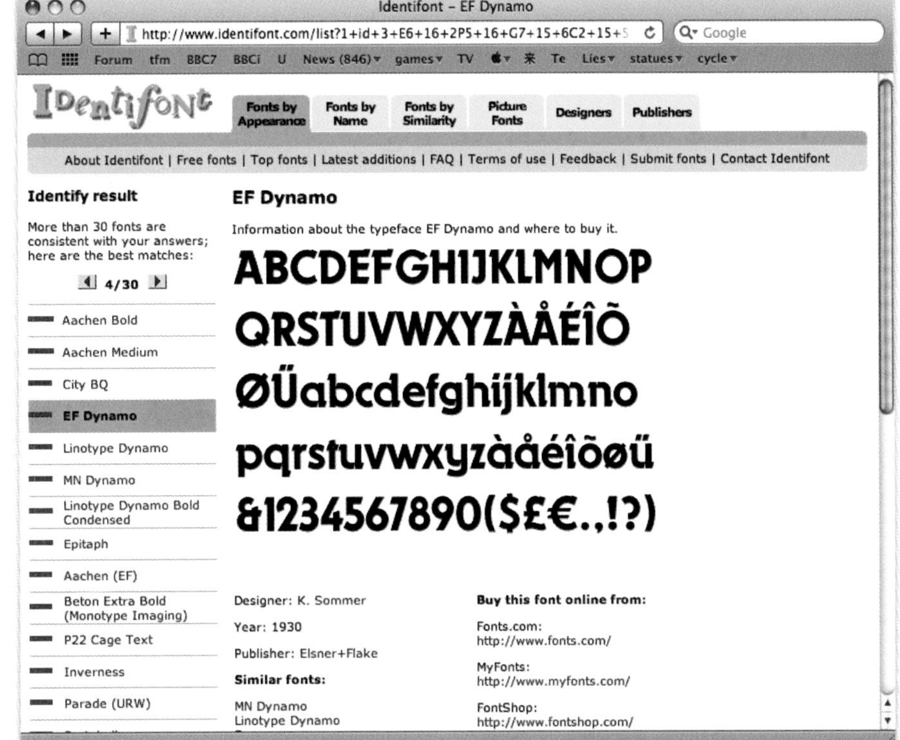

▲ Identifont returned more than 30 results, but the one we want, Dynamo, is up there in the top four matches.

One approach would be to attempt to build the characters you need from those already present in the sample you have, and it's relatively easy to extrapolate the appearance of some letters from others. For example, given the letters in 'LOVE GUN', we could fairly easily create a letter M from the N, an F from the E, a J from the U, and so on. But how could we imagine letters such as S, Q or B? These would be a tricky task from the character set we have. One solution would be to use a similar but undecorated font, such as Futura Bold, and add the quirky spikes from Dynamo to that.

A better solution, however, is to see if anyone else has attempted to make a version of this font. The first port of call is always DaFont (*dafont.com*), a vast repository of freeware fonts that anyone can download and use (although there are often restrictions for commercial use). There's an army of typographers out there who like nothing better than to spend their free time recreating fonts: you'll find just about every movie font lovingly rebuilt here, often to a high standard of accuracy. There are also freeware versions of many commercial fonts, as well, but their quality does vary considerably.

U: Unsharp Mask

It has an unusual name, but this refugee from the era of traditional photo printing is the most flexible way to sharpen up soft pictures.

Unsharp Mask is a filter that's routinely applied to images to increase the contrast between regions of differing luminosity. But despite the fact that the filter has only three controls, its use is confusing to many designers. Even the name is baffling: how can a technique used to sharpen images possibly be described as 'unsharpening'?

The answer to the name issue lies in the origins of the technique. It dates from the 1930s when photographers would overlay a blurred positive of an image on top of the original negative. This 'unsharpened mask' would hide some of the detail in the negative, combining with the original to create a sharper print.

The digital process works in much the same way. It first applies Gaussian Blur to a copy of the image, and examines the difference between the two. This difference is then subtracted from the original, so that the remaining area – in other words, the disparity between the sharp and blurred regions – can be strengthened. So much for the theory. In practice, the Unsharp Mask filter has three controls: Amount, Radius and Threshold. Each of these makes a difference to the way that an image is enhanced and since to some extent the Threshold slider appears to cancel out the operation of the other two, it's important to understand just how individually they affect the finished result.

The Amount slider is a percentage – which rather confusingly ranges between 0% and 500%. It adds contrast to edge regions, effectively strengthening the boundaries between light and dark areas, but exerts little or no effect on smooth, similar tones. Where a light region borders a dark one, the light side will be brightened and the dark side darkened.

The Radius slider varies from 0 to 250 pixels. This controls the width of the border around edge regions upon which the sharpening action has its effect. The size of the Radius setting determines the size of the detail in the image that receives the sharpening process. As the Radius is increased, a visible halo begins to appear around contrasted areas, and so it's usual to apply a Radius setting of about 1 pixel to begin with, increasing it as required. The Radius can be increased in steps of 0.1 pixels, giving a lot of user control.

The Threshold slider is the one that causes the most confusion. This determines how different contrasting borders have to be from each other for the filter to operate on them. The higher the value, the more difference is needed before any effect is seen. Although the Threshold slider appears to reduce the overall effect, it actually serves to limit the effect to those regions that need it the most – the true borders between light and dark areas. By raising the Threshold value by one or two levels we can avoid sharpening smoother areas and so prevent the speckling

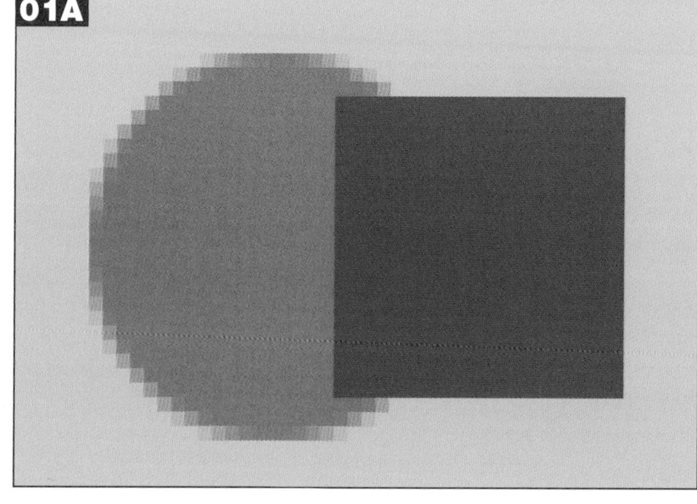

► **A greatly enlarged image before an Unsharp Mask filter is brought into play (sequence continues top right).**

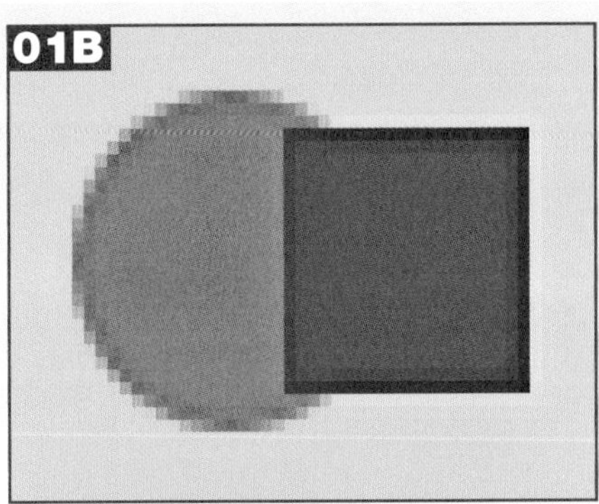

▲ When we add an Unsharp Mask filter, using an Amount of 100% and a Radius of 1 pixel, the two geometric shapes have darkened interior edges, and the background is correspondingly brightened outside them.

▲ Raising the Radius to 2 pixels doubles the width of these brightened and darkened areas, increasing the area used to display contrast between the shapes and the background.

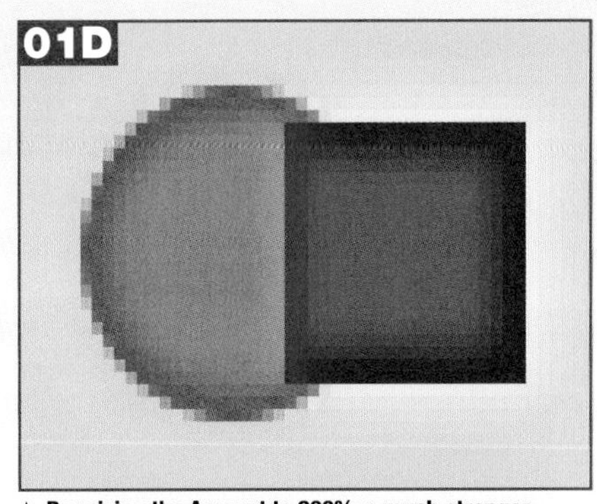

▲ By raising the Amount to 200%, a much stronger effect is produced. You'll note that this operation has increased the contrast, while leaving the Radius (the thickness of the rim) untouched.

effect seen when regions such as skin and sky are oversharpened.

In practice it's best to start with low values for all the sliders – an Amount of 50%, a Radius of 1 pixel, and a Threshold value of 0. Raise the Amount while looking at the preview image to see the effect it's having but for general purposes keep it below 200%. You should rarely need to raise the Radius value above 2 pixels as an absolute maximum. If noticeable noise is creeping into smooth, toned regions, raise the Threshold value to 1 or 2 until this disappears (see our example, right).

Although it's a very powerful and useful filter, Unsharp Mask is not without its pitfalls. Zealous over-sharpening can produce severe degradation in the image that's difficult to get rid of later: err on the conservative side when applying it.

If you're producing items for the Internet be aware that sharpened images will produce much larger file sizes, which will slow the delivery of your website. This is because Jpeg compression works best with soft images: the higher the amount of contrast between border regions, the less compression the Jpeg algorithm will be able to apply. When working for low-quality print such as newspapers, it's worth adding more sharpening than you'd normally use, to compensate for the lack of focus caused by printing ink bleeding into the coarse paper.

An unwanted side effect of applying Unsharp Mask is so-called colour fringing, in which halos of unnatural colour appear around the edges of objects. This tends to happen with high degrees of sharpening but can be visible even with low amounts on areas of differing colour contrast. A photo of a green tree against a blue sky, for example, may well produce such an unwanted haloing effect.

One solution is to convert the image to Lab colour mode, using Image > Mode menu. Lab space is a way of describing colour using a Luminosity channel (which holds a greyscale version of the image) and two colour channels, labelled a and b. By applying the Unsharp Mask filter to just the Luminosity channel we can produce a strong sharpening effect without the risk of the operation affecting the colour components. After applying the filter, you can return the image to its original RGB colour space.

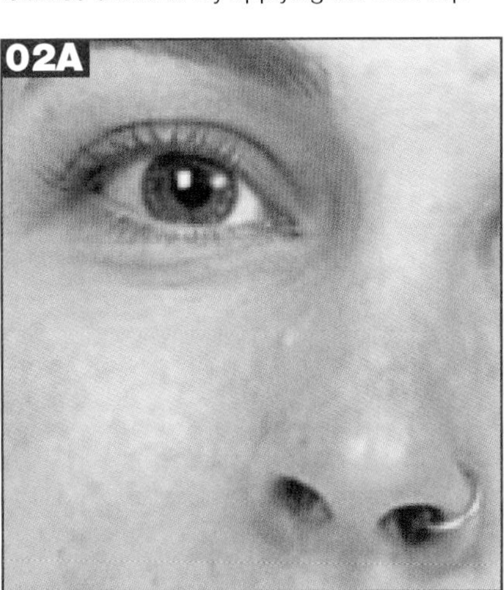

▲ In this real-life example, our enlarged close-up of an eye and nose shows a soft image that's sorely in need of sharpening.

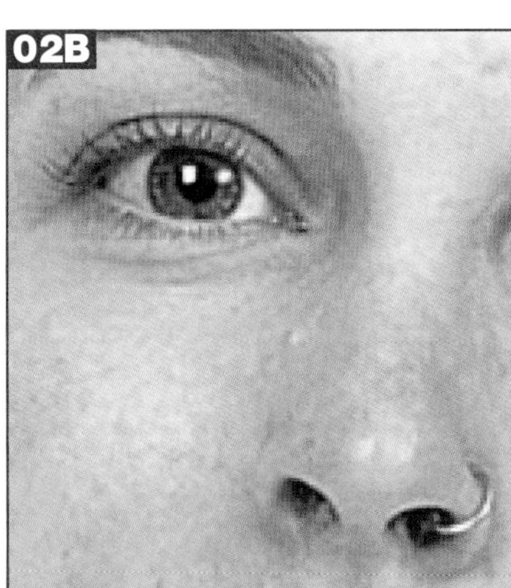

▲ Applying an Amount of 100% and a Radius of 1 pixel produces a clearer eye and nose ring, with well-defined lashes.

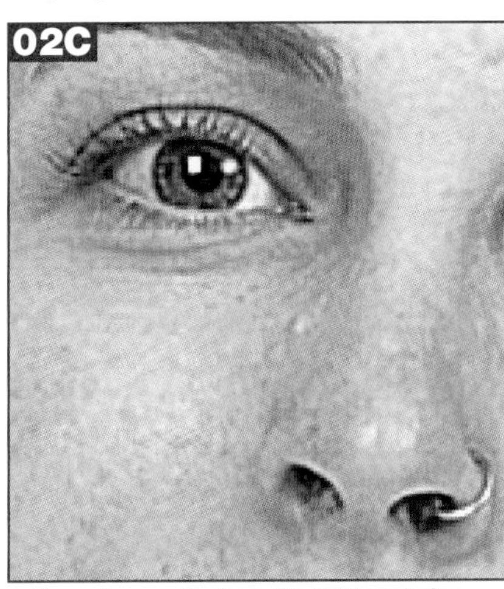

▲ We can increase the Amount to 150%, producing stronger contrast in the eye. But now the skin tones have taken on some unwanted sharpening, producing a strong speckling effect.

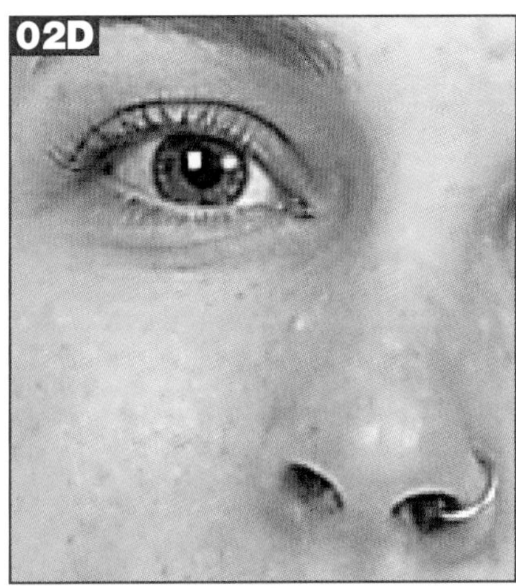

▲ By raising the Threshold value we can prevent the filter from having any effect on the skin region, while still producing strong sharpening where we want it – with the eye and nose ring.

U: Upscaling

We all have to contend with small pictures from time to time. With careful upscaling, though, you can increase them to almost any size you want.

We've all seen those movies in which a government agent takes an image from a CCTV camera and enlarges it until it's possible to read the destination on the plane ticket in the suspect's top pocket. It's a plot device we've seen so often that it has become part of the vernacular of movie making and is widely accepted as being not only possible but an everyday occurrence. The reality, however, is altogether different.

Making images larger is a task every designer has to deal with from time to time. This may be something as personal as blowing up a friend's wedding photograph to print as a poster, or as public as enlarging a camera phone image for the front page of a newspaper. Either way, you have to contend with the problem of inventing extra information that wasn't present in the original.

As a basic example, let's look at a 4 x 4 grid of colour [**01**]. The colours here move from light to dark as you move from left to right, and from blue to pink as we move from top to bottom. This is a tiny image of just 16 pixels in total, enlarged here so you can see the result more clearly. So what happens when you enlarge this image to 7 pixels wide?

The reality is that each of the 16 pixels in the original is being moved away from its neighbour by a distance of one pixel, leaving gaps that need to be filled [**02**]. And there are a lot of them: the original 16 pixels are now in a field of 49, leaving 33 spaces that have to be created afresh.

You could simply make each of the original pixels larger to fill the space. This is the 'nearest neighbour' approach [**03**]. However, as you can see, it's far from perfect. Some pixels are doubled up and others are not, due to the scaling percentage – the result is very blocky.

An alternative approach is to interpolate colours between the original pixels, producing intermediate blends of the pixels either side [**04**]. The result here is a far smoother image, and one that's far closer to the feel of the original. Interpolation is the key to successful enlargements, and it's a process that Photoshop performs automatically.

The basic method of sampling is called

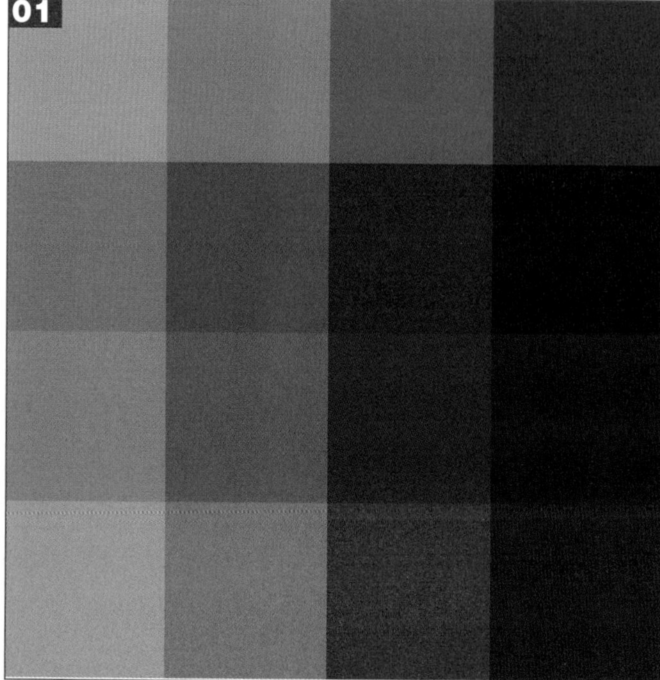

► **The original 4 x 4 pixel grid.**

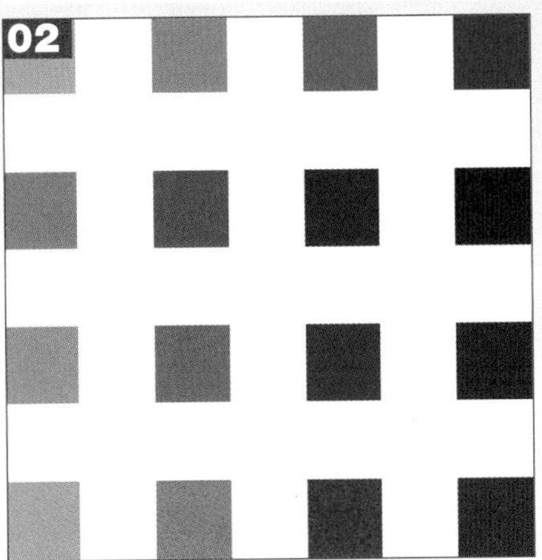

▲ When we enlarge the image, the original pixels are spaced out, so how do we deal with the gaps?

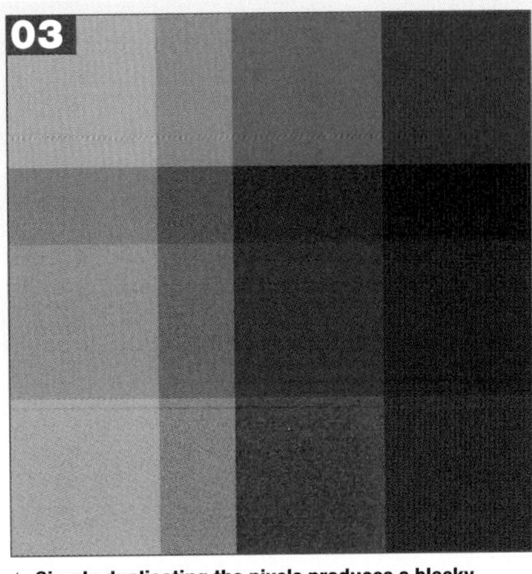

▲ Simply duplicating the pixels produces a blocky effect that does no justice to the original.

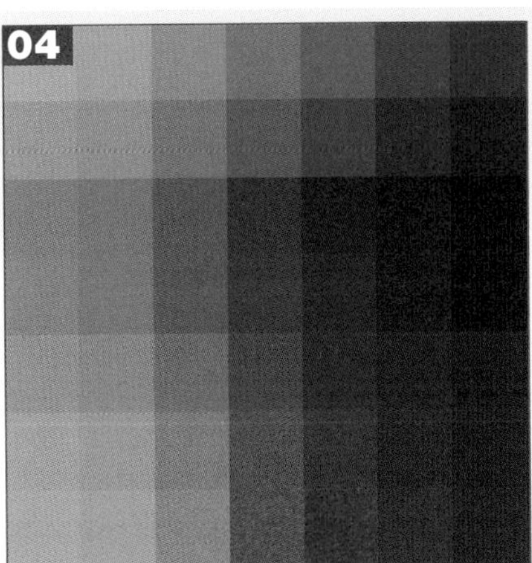

▲ Interpolating between the existing pixels produces a significantly smoother result.

Bilinear Interpolation, which takes samples from the four closest pixels and then interpolates their colour according to how far they are from the sample point. It's a fairly rudimentary approach: a better method is Bicubic Interpolation, which uses complex mathematical algorithms to compute the appearance of interpolated pixels. Fortunately, Photoshop will do all the maths for us. Photoshop offers several different interpolation methods, and these can be chosen from the pop-up menu at the bottom of the Image Size dialog box.

The real problem with enlarging images is that the interpolating process tends to produce results that are fuzzy and blurry. In a way, this is inevitable: you can't put back data that wasn't there in the original. If a string of text in a photograph occupies just four or five pixels in height, it will be impossible to blow that text up to make it more legible. The information just isn't there.

However, for regular photographic purposes, there are a couple of alternative solutions. In Photoshop, you can use dedicated plug-ins such as Alien Skin's BlowUp (*alienskin.com*) or onOne Software's Genuine Fractals (*ononesoftware.com*). These use rather more complex algorithms to enlarge the images, but then add a range of techniques designed to enhance the image further. Sharpening is an obvious step, which can tighten up a lot of fuzzy detail. Another technique is to add picture grain, which masks the unnatural smoothness caused by over-enlargement and fools the eye into thinking it's seeing more detail than it really is.

These plug-ins work particularly well with graphic images – logos, book covers, text and so on. Large expanses of flat colour separated by hard black lines are the easiest for them to work with. They're less successful with detailed photographs, although the results tend to be better than those that can be produced by straightforward enlargement.

But there's another method, which can be used directly in Photoshop. If you want to double the size of an image, rather than doing it in one go, try increasing its size by about 105%. Then do the same again. And again. (It will be a lot easier if you create a simple Photoshop Action to perform this task with a single keystroke.) By repeating many small enlargements, you can retain much of the crispness that would otherwise be lost. It's surprising, but it works.

The way in which an image is treated after enlargement depends very much on the nature of the image in question. When enlarging portraits of people, for instance, it's not a problem if the skin tone looks a little soft, but fuzzy eyes will always look wrong. If you duplicate the enlarged image as a separate layer, you can apply the Unsharp Mask filter to bring back lost detail. Then create a Layer Mask for the new layer, choosing Layer > Add Layer Mask > Hide All. This will hide the entire layer. When you paint on the mask in white, you reveal those parts of the sharpened layer. You can bring in detail selectively in this way – in the eyes, around the lips, on the eyebrows, for example. These are all areas where additional sharpening won't look artificial.

It's possible to enlarge photographs by a surprising amount while retaining apparent detail. However, the concept of revealing crisp text from a blurred image is pure fantasy: it's a technology that, along with gyrocopters and matter transporters, belongs more in movies than in reality.

▲ A section of a printed circuit board, blown up by 500% using the 'nearest neighbour' method: the pixels have simply been duplicated.

▲ Bilinear Interpolation produces somewhat smoother results, but there's still some ugly stepping visible.

▲ Bicubic Interpolation is smoother still, especially around the text: it now looks far more legible than in the previous methods.

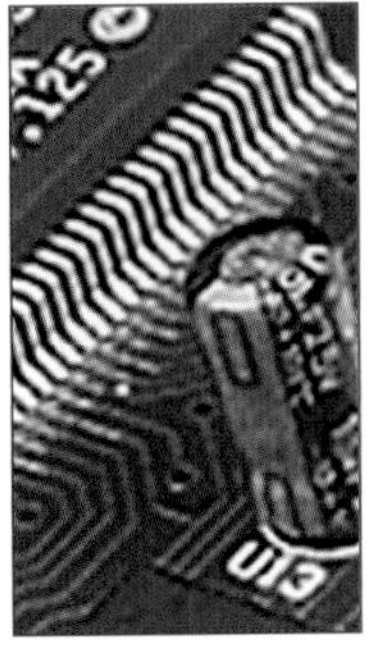
▲ Repeated enlargement of 105% gives us smoother edges, hiding the blockiness seen in the previous methods.

▲ Alien Skin's BlowUp filter produces crisp results, but perhaps with a slightly graphic, artificial flavour.

▲ The original image from which the enlarged sections (left) are shown.

V: Vector objects

Vector objects will always be sharp and true to their originals no matter how many times you resize or move them. Here's why.

Photoshop is the archetypal bitmap paint program. The image is made of pixels of varying colours and intensities, and zooming in enlarges those pixels until all we see is a mass of coloured squares. However, Photoshop also contains the ability to work with vector objects, which can be scaled to any size and endlessly edited and re-edited, without any loss of quality. Here, we'll look at how to make the most of this vector capability.

The easiest way to make vector objects is to use the Shapes tool (keyboard shortcut: U). This tool has three modes of operation, and it's important to choose the right one: they're selected using the set of three buttons immediately to the right of the tool icon on the Options bar. The first of these will create a Shape layer, which is an editable, filled object. The second will return a Pen path, which can then be used to make a selection. The third will simply paint the shape as a solid filled object directly onto the current layer. Make sure you check which one you're creating before starting to draw, although it's fairly obvious once you've started.

The Shape Options bar includes icons for a variety of different basic forms. You can draw a shape using the Pen tool if you're familiar with drawing Bézier curves; if not, you can use the Freeform Pen tool, which is like drawing with a pencil except that the curves you draw are turned into Pen paths when you've finished. The Rectangle and Ellipse tools draw plain rectangles and ellipses, whereas the Rounded Rectangle tool enables you to specify the corner radius (although you have to do this before you draw, as you can't adjust the radius afterwards).

The Polygon tool draws regular forms of any number of sides. Clicking on the small down arrow at the end of the tool row gives you access to an additional palette. This allows you to draw stars rather than polygons, with control over the amount of indentation and the roundness of the joins. By setting a large number of sides and a small indentation, you can create 'special offer'-type stars with plenty of room inside for wording.

The final icon is for the Custom Shape tool. Clicking on this will cause a new pop-up dialog box to appear, from which you can choose from a variety of preset shapes including hearts, ticks, speech bubbles and so on. You can also choose to add more libraries of shapes, or define your own from Pen paths or imported Illustrator paths.

When creating a Shape layer, what you're effectively doing is making a new solid colour layer, which has a vector layer mask attached. This layer mask is the vector shape you've just created. This means you can apply any adjustments to the layer that you could to a regular layer, including changing the colour and, more importantly, adding layer styles. You can also use the Stroke facility in the Layer Styles dialog box to add an outline to the layer.

You can edit Shape layers by transforming them using standard Free Transform commands, including rotation, scaling and Image Warp. Unlike regular layers, you can distort them as much as you like, endlessly enlarging and contracting, with no loss in quality whatsoever.

▼ The Shape tool can be set to draw Shape layers, pen paths or just to paint a fill on the current layer.

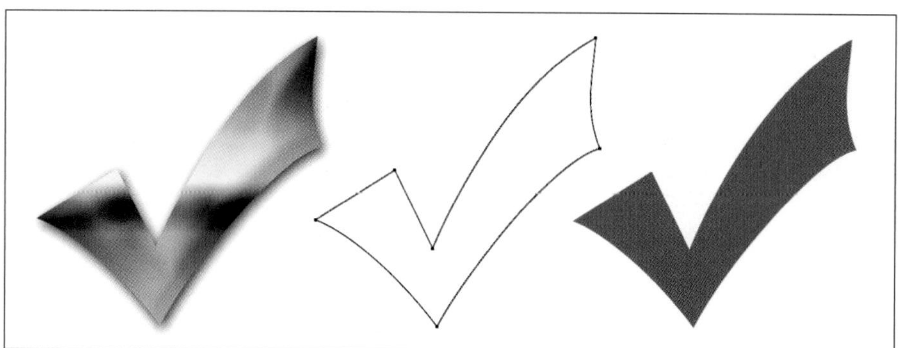

◄ The speech bubble is one of the basic preset Shapes. Drag it to roughly the shape you want.

► Double-click on the layer icon to open the colour picker, and fill with white.

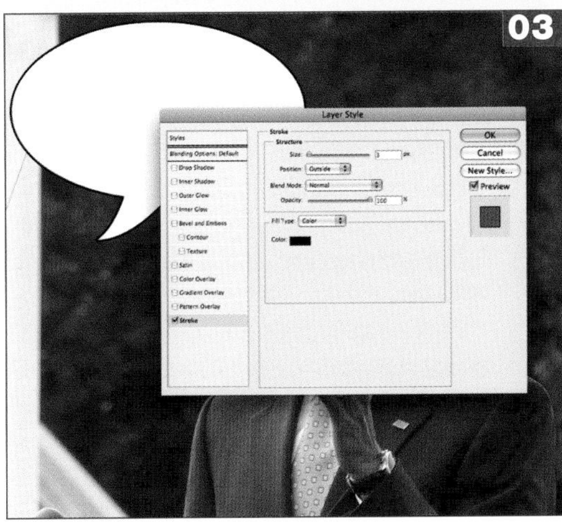

◄ Use the Layer Styles dialog box to add a black stroke to the layer.

► Use the Pen tool to adjust the shape of the tool, and add your chosen text.

Because Shape layers are no more than paths on vector layer masks, you can also use the Pen tool to edit those paths directly, moving individual anchor points and changing their curve descriptors. This is where much of the functionality comes in: it's easy to start with a basic preset shape and then adapt and modify it to fulfil your specific requirements.

Let's say you're mocking up a comic, or a birthday card, and you want to add speech bubbles. You can start with the basic bubble shape using the Custom Shape tool, dragging it to the size you want. It may well default to a solid colour layer, but it's easy to change that: double-click on the layer icon in the Layers palette to open the colour picker, and select white. Next, open the Layer Style dialog from the button at the bottom of the Layers palette, and move to the Stroke section. Choose a black stroke, with a weight of between 1 and 3 pixels depending on your preference.

What you'll probably find is that the tail of the speech bubble doesn't point towards your subject's mouth. Choose the Direct Selection tool (shortcut: A) and make sure you have this tool active (with the white head), rather than the Path Selection tool (with the black head), which selects entire paths. Click on the end of the tail, and you'll be able to drag it where you want it. You'll now need to adjust the Bézier handles so that the curves work well, moving each handle so it follows the direction of the tail.

To make further bubbles, simply duplicate this Shape layer and use Free Transform to flip, rotate and scale it to fit your chosen lettering and position, adjusting the tail once more as required.

If you want a stroke but no fill on a Shape layer, open the Layer Style dialog. On the main Blending Options pane, you'll see a section named Advanced Blending. Lower the Fill Opacity here to zero to remove the fill from the original layer. Note that if you add textures, gradients or colours as layer styles, they'll still show up, but the original colour fill will be removed.

The only slight problem is that there's no easy way to make open-ended stroked paths as Shape objects. Fills and strokes will always join the beginning and end of the path in a straight line. The best solution is to make a layer mask for the layer. Check the Layer Mask Hides Effects box in the Advanced Blending section of the Layer Style dialog box, and when you paint in black on the mask the layer (and its stroke) will be hidden from view.

▼ Use the Polygon Shape tool to draw regular geometric shapes or stars. By minimising the indent and increasing the number of sides, you can create badge flashes.

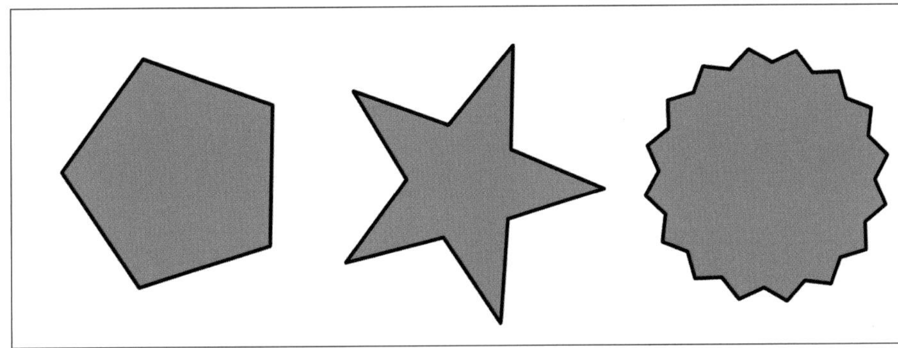

V: Vector vs bitmap

Confused by the differences between Photoshop and Illustrator? It's all to do with vectors and bitmaps. This handy guide explains when to use each type.

When I bought my first Mac back in 1987, the specification – as well as 512 kilobytes of Ram and an 800K floppy disk drive – included the choice of either MacPaint or MacDraw. Never having heard of either, I asked the salesman what the difference was. 'MacPaint is a bitmap program,' he explained curtly, 'whereas MacDraw is object orientated.' 'Do what?' I replied. 'It's a vector application.' I didn't have a clue what he was talking about.

Twenty years on, novice designers are still confused by the difference between the two. So, let's look at what both terms mean, how they work and how they can interact.

Bitmap programs are those that work with pixels, one 'bit' at a time. The resulting image is literally a map of the bits that make it up: each square in the grid could initially be either on or off, and so would appear either black or white. Later, with the introduction of greyscale monitors, these pixels could be one of any of 256 different shades of grey. As colour was introduced, they could be one of any of 256 shades of red, green and blue mixed together.

Bitmap programs include Photoshop, Painter, and the paint half of Canvas. They're often referred to as painting programs and the analogy is a good one: adding or moving sets of pixels is very similar to painting onto a canvas. We can push pixels around, paint over them and even erase them, but they remain part of the background or layer on which they appear.

If we make a bitmap image double the size, then we make each pixel occupy the space of four pixels on the screen. Because this would produce an unsightly blocky effect, most bitmap applications use sophisticated algorithms to interpolate between neighbouring colours, producing intermediate values that add new pixels intelligently.

Hard edges, though, as well as areas of high contrast within the image, tend to suffer from enlargement; the result is a clear degradation of the image, as interpolated pixels always produce a softer image that appears lacking in focus.

Vector or object-oriented applications work differently. Rather than colouring in the page pixel by pixel, each shape is defined as a set of linked and optionally filled points in 2D space, each point specified by its co-ordinates. In early programs, such as MacDraw, the range of shapes was limited to lines, rectangles, circles and polygons. Today, vector applications, such as Illustrator and Freehand, can use far more sophisticated shapes and fills.

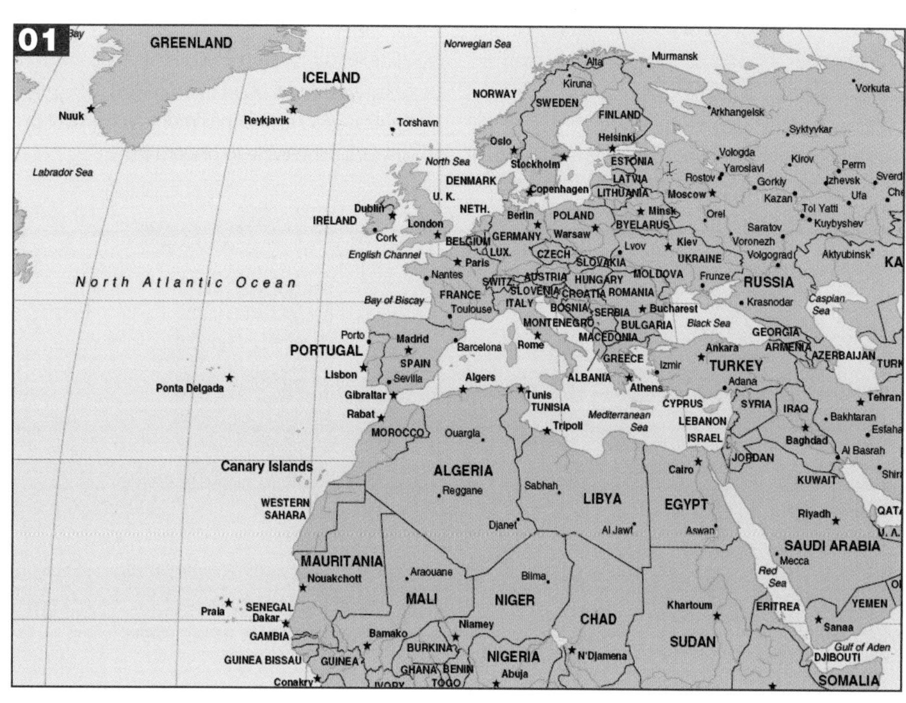

◄ **With the whole of Europe on view, it's hard to tell at a glance whether this map is in bitmap or vector format.**

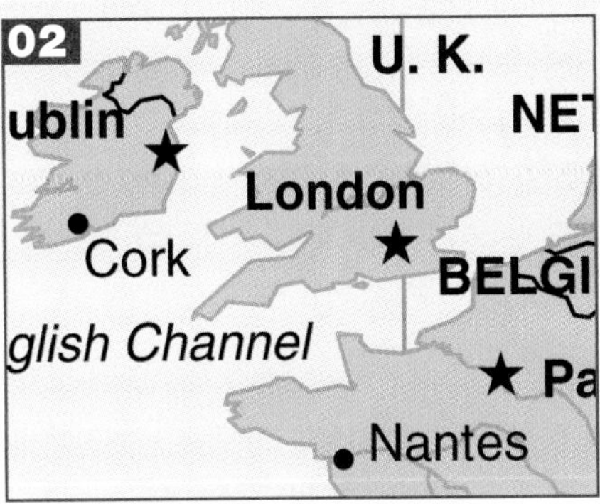

▲ When we zoom in, the vector version scales everything up smoothly, including the text.

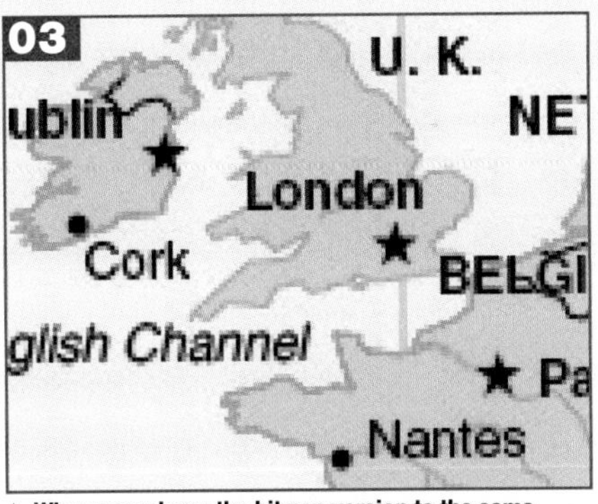

▲ When we enlarge the bitmap version to the same degree, we can see how the pixels are enlarged, producing an ugly result.

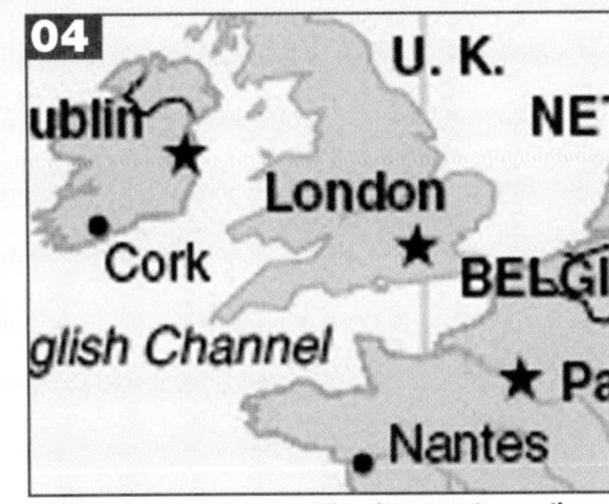

▲ Photoshop is able to smooth enlargements, creating a better image – but it's still nowhere near as crisp as the vector version.

In vector programs, each shape we draw is a separate object. It can be moved independently of all the others and scaled to any size. Because the vertices are mathematically defined, making it larger simply means performing the same multiplication on each of the co-ordinates. This means that we can scale vector artwork to any size with no loss of quality whatever. It's largely for this reason that company logos, for example, are always designed in Illustrator rather than Photoshop: the resulting vector artwork can be used on a letterhead, or covering the entire face of a building, without any quality issues as it's enlarged or reduced.

In high-end applications, such as Illustrator, InDesign and QuarkXPress, the mathematical curves are driven by the PostScript language, developed by Adobe in 1984. Most commercial fonts are written in PostScript and this gives them the scalability to be used at any size without degradation. Although Photoshop and Illustrator are the archetypal bitmap and vector applications respectively, neither program is purely one or the other. Mixing bitmap and vector capabilities is as old a technique as MacDraw itself, which had the ability to fill vector shapes with bitmap patterns: when the object was scaled, the pattern remained the same size.

Photoshop makes use of vector functionality in several ways. Clipping paths drawn with the Pen tool are vector objects, as are Shapes layers. The more recent versions of Photoshop make use of Smart Objects, which can be items such as logos drawn in Illustrator. Because they store the original object in vector form, this means that such Smart Objects can be scaled to any size without any loss of quality. Smart Objects can also store bitmap artwork created in Photoshop itself. When scaled down, the original is still used as the basis, so that when they're scaled up again no quality is lost up to the size of the original.

Illustrator has long had the ability to place and work with bitmap artwork, whether it was created in Photoshop or acquired directly from a scanner or a digital camera. Although they're being used in a primarily vector environment, these are still bitmap images which will suffer a loss of image quality when enlarged.

Part of the confusion between bitmap and vector elements in these applications comes from the way they're displayed on screen. Zooming in to Illustrator artwork will produce crisp, clean edges, regardless of the amount of magnification. But zooming in to vector elements in Photoshop – such as Shapes layers – will show enlarged pixels, just as if we were working with bitmap artwork. That's because Photoshop works on a pixel-by-pixel basis and will not display sub-pixel sizes at any magnification. The Shapes layers themselves can still be enlarged losslessly, but zooming in will give a false impression of their status.

When moving items around in Photoshop, we're limited to multiples of one pixel. By increasing the resolution of the image, we can effectively move items by smaller amounts relative to the overall picture, but we can never get away from that one pixel limit, however far we zoom in. In Illustrator, on the other hand, we're able to move an object or an anchor point by as little as one ten thousandth of a millimetre: even at the maximum zoom level of 6400%, it's impossible to discern this movement.

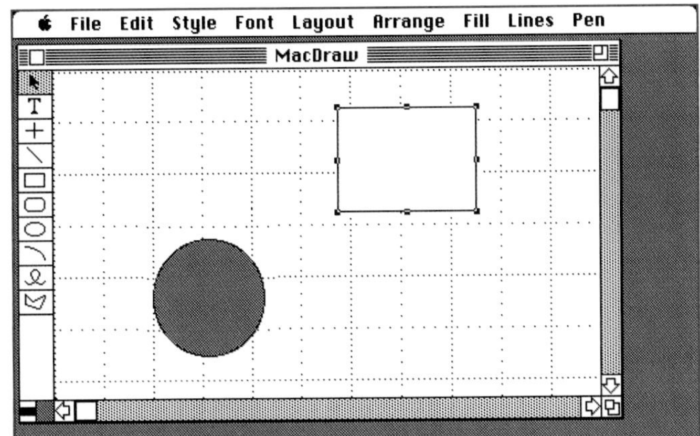

▲ The early vector application MacDraw used the same technique as Illustrator and FreeHand, where each object is a separate item that can be moved or scaled independently.

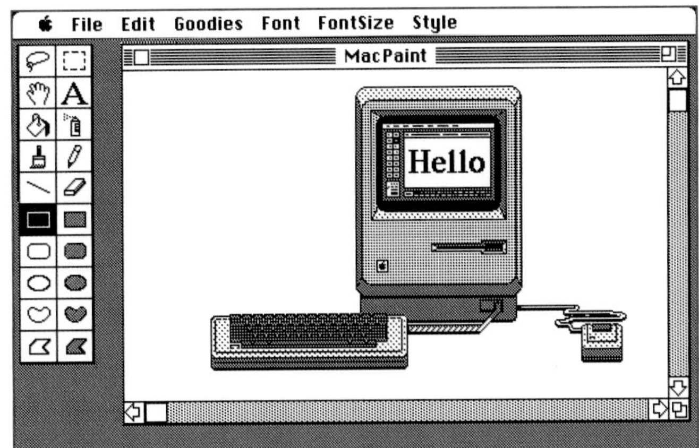

▲ The early bitmap application MacPaint painted pixel by pixel, in much the same way that Photoshop does today.

W: Workspaces

Make Adobe's Creative Suite applications work the way you want them to by setting the working environment to suit your own particular needs.

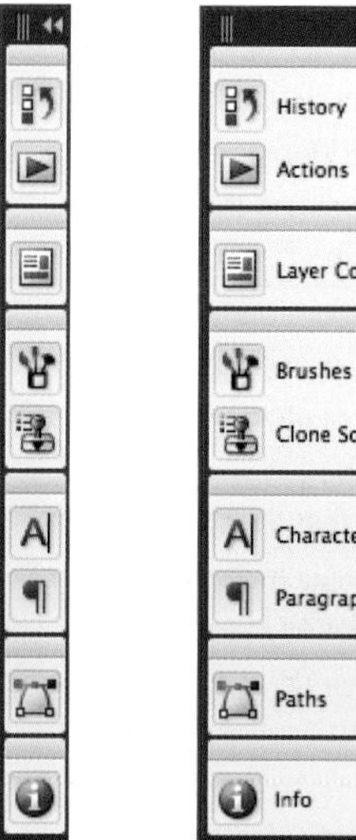

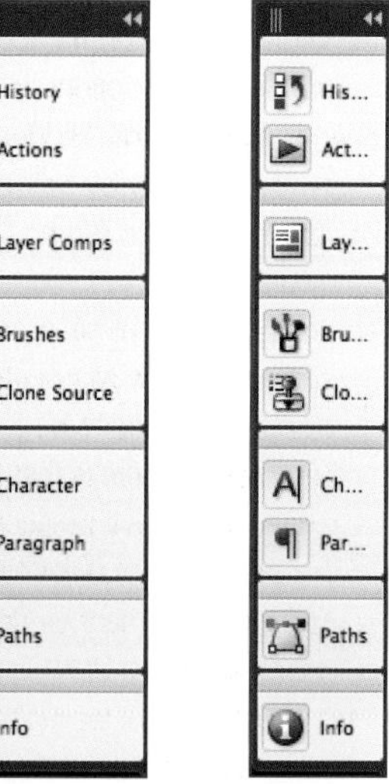

▲ **Docked palettes can be stored as icons only (left), or as icons and text (centre). If you have trouble recognising the icons, you can expand the view to show the first few letters of the palette name (right) to help you learn them.**

Whether using a 15in MacBook screen or a 30in Cinema Display, you'll always want to see the image you're working on at the largest possible size, which means dealing with the clutter of palettes and toolbars that eat into your viewing area.

In Photoshop CS2 and earlier, a Palette Well at the top of the screen is a convenient place to store infrequently-used palettes. These have the advantage of popping open when their tab is clicked on and neatly disappearing from view once you click elsewhere. In CS3, a unified interface for the entire suite approaches things differently: the Palette Well has gone, and instead we can store these infrequent palettes in a narrow strip on the right of the monitor.

On-screen palettes have three states: fully open, icon and name, or just the icon. Once you've learned which palette each icon represents, the icon-only view is the most convenient way to store a lot of palettes in the minimum possible space.

But while you're still learning, it's useful to be able to drag the button width to reveal the first word, or even the first few letters, of the palette's name. It takes up a little more space this way of course, but serves as an instant key to the palette's function.

Because palettes can be stacked next to each other in any of the three states you can choose which ones you want permanently on view and those that are reduced to icons or text.

The arrangement depends on your own working practices but a good starting method is to have the Layers palette fully open at all times since you'll need to refer to it frequently. You may use the Channels palette only occasionally but when you do, you'll want it to stay open. Nesting this behind the Layers palette makes it easy to switch to it when required, switching back to the Layers palette when you've finished. If you have a large monitor, then it can be handy to keep the Colour and Swatches palettes open on top of this. They don't take up much space and having the colour picker handy is a good use of the space.

The Layers palette can be customised to show small, medium or large thumbnails of the layers they represent. Choose the size from the Palette Options item at the bottom of the pop-up menu list at the top right of the palette.

Generally you'll want to work with small thumbnails since this enables you to get the maximum number of layers on view in the palette. You can also choose how each thumbnail is displayed – either in 'layer bounds' mode, in which each thumbnail will fill the space with a view of that layer, or in 'entire document' mode. In the latter the thumbnails are much smaller but they do show the layer's location within the file. This is probably the more convenient method as it makes it easier to identify which layer you're working on.

Keep your infrequently used palettes in button form, if you can remember the icon, attached to the side of the Layers palette. For easier recognition they can be grouped by kind – by dragging the icons together so that they link. By default, these palettes will stay open when selected; the Auto-Collapse Icon Palettes option in the Interface section of the Preferences dialog allows them to disappear once they've been used.

Not all palettes are best auto-collapsed, however. The Animation palette, for example, needs to be constantly on view while working with movies or animations; so if you use this only occasionally, don't dock it as an icon but select it from the Window menu each time it's needed. When you've finished with it, put it away manually. You may wish to have different

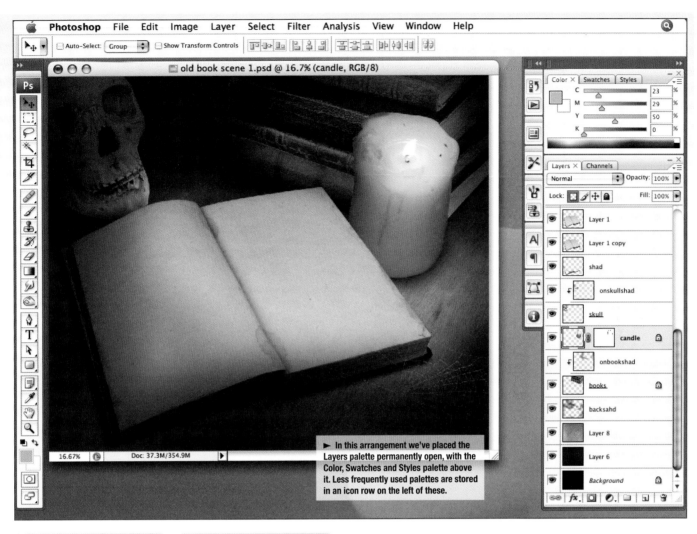

► In this arrangement we've placed the Layers palette permanently open, with the Color, Swatches and Styles palette above it. Less frequently used palettes are stored in an icon row on the left of these.

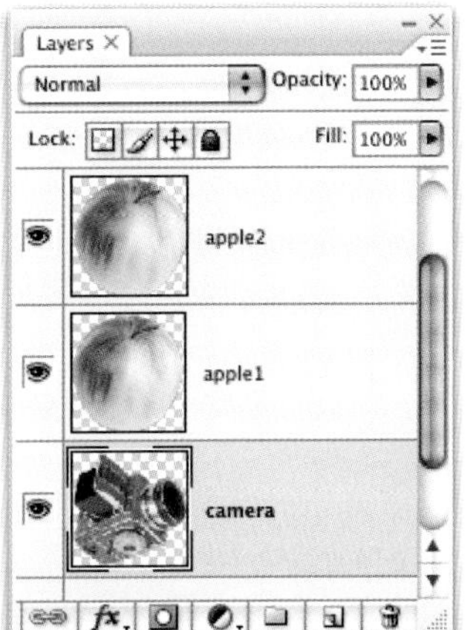

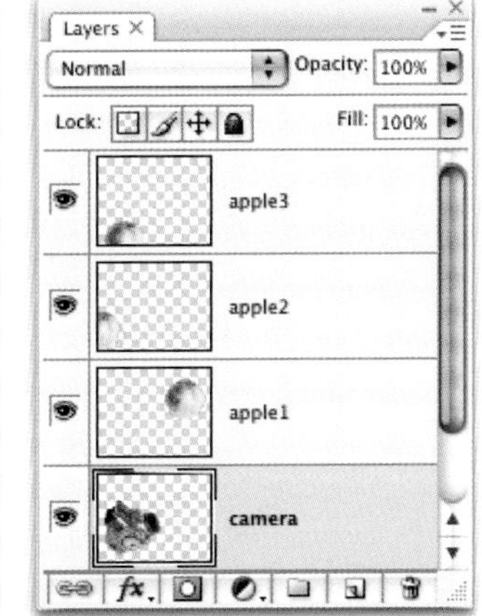

▲ In Layer Bounds mode (left), the Layers palette displays each layer as large as possible within the thumbnail. Although it's easy to see the contents of the layer this way, it's hard to tell their location; the preferred Entire Document view (right) shows the thumbnails smaller but in their correct location within the document.

set-ups for different kinds of jobs. For example, with general montage work, you'll want the Layers palette to have prominence; but for text-heavy design work you may need the Character and Paragraph palettes on view permanently.

You can save multiple workspaces in the Workspace section of the Window menu, making it easy to switch between them with a single click. Photoshop ships with a selection of pre-set workspaces customised for colour correction, image analysis, web design and more.

A novel addition is the What's new in CS3 workspace, which highlights all the changed menu items in a different colour, so you can explore them more easily. But be sure to save your preferred workspace arrangement here before changing to another, so you can return straight to it.

You can make individual menu items stand out, using the Menus dialog box (found in the Edit menu). Here it's possible to assign different colours to specific menu items, making it easy to spot those suitable for a particular task. This dialog box also allows you to hide certain items from view, which in turn shortens the menu list – but you should think carefully before doing this. It's likely to cause confusion and frustration when you can't find the item you're looking for.

This mode is best saved when designing a workspace for students, for whom you want to limit the range of options to just those they've been taught already. Hidden items can be shown temporarily by holding the Command key as you click on a menu.

If you need to see your image without any on-screen clutter at all, pressing the Tab key will hide and show all palettes – including the Tools and the Options bar.

The problem here is that the Options bar is extremely useful as it presents the key information from the palettes in a more compact, context-sensitive manner. So instead of just pressing Tab, press Shift-Tab – this will hide the floating palettes but leave the Tools and Options on view. In this mode, dragging the cursor to the right of the screen will pop the palettes back into view temporarily. These will hide themselves though once they've been used. ⊗

W: Wrapping text

Handling the way that text moves from one line to the other can make the difference between results that you do or don't want to read.

Wrapping text around images and other page items is a common task when designing pages. Unless your publication works to a particularly restrictive grid, you'll need some flexibility in the size, placement and type of text wrapping. Adobe InDesign provides a comprehensive tool for making text flow smoothly around any placed object, which may include additional text blocks, but as with most tasks, there are options and variations that need to be taken into account.

After placing your image, you can bring up the Text Wrap dialog by selecting it from the Window menu (or hitting Command-Alt-W). The default setting is for no wrapping, as indicated by the row of icons along the top of the palette. The second icon wraps text around the bounding box of the placed image – in other words, wrapping around a rectangular shape that holds the image, even if the image is a cutout.

Once any form of wrapping is active, the panel beneath the icons comes into play. Here, you can specify the distance to which text is offset on all four sides of the bounding box. Even when placing a squared-up image within a single column of type, it's worth paying attention to the top and bottom wrapping offset figures here: if type is too close to the bottom of the image, the result will be ungainly and awkward. Beneath the offset pane is a pop-up menu specifying further wrap options, which we'll discuss presently.

Every image requires a caption. The most common way to create this is as a separate text block, to the same width as the picture, placed directly beneath it. We can use the Text Wrap dialog to apply to this block of text as well, forcing the body text out of the way to make room for it. However, it can be fiddly to make the caption and the picture exactly the same width, especially if the pair are placed between two columns rather than in a single column line.

One solution is to increase the Bottom Offset on the image wrap, so it extends below the caption and pushes the body text out of the way to make room for it. Now, however,

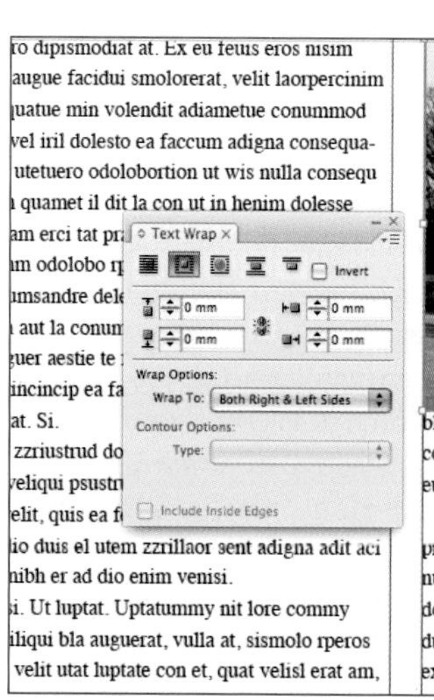

▲ It's important to check the offset beneath a placed image: it's easy for the text to butt right up against the picture.

▲ By increasing the offset, we force the text to the next baseline grid step (if these have been used) for a more appealing result.

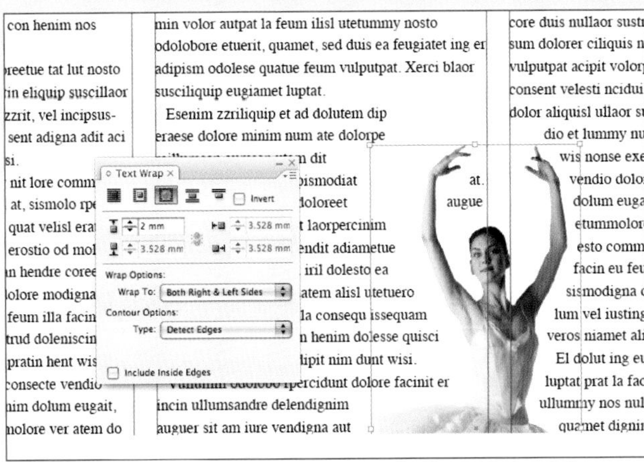

▲ Wrapped text can sometimes inadvertently wrap inside an object, as is the case with the words inside the ballerina's arms.

▲ By changing the Wrap Options to Largest Area, you can prevent this sort of error – the stray words have gone from between the arms.

you'll find that the image wrap pushes the caption itself out of the way. To fix this, select the block of caption text and bring up the Text Frame Options dialog box (Object menu, or use the Command-B shortcut). At the bottom-left of this dialog box is a checkbox marked Ignore Text Wrap: check this to allow this block of text to override the wrapping set by the object above it.

If you're placing a cutout object on the page, you select the third icon for the wrapping method: wrap around object shape. At this point, however, the options get a little more complicated.

First, you have to decide how the text will wrap around the object, and that depends on the nature of the cutout. If it's an image with an embedded clipping path, you can choose Same as Clipping from the pop-up Contour Options menu. Now, the four numeric fields that specified the top, bottom, left and right offsets will change to a single field: there will be a uniform offset all the way around the cutout. You'll see that this is shown as a faint blue line around the cutout.

It may be that you have an outline path in Photoshop, but it hasn't been specifically defined as a clipping path; or there may be multiple paths in the file. In this case, you can choose the path you want to use from the pop-up list. If the image is a cutout with transparency – that is, a Photoshop, Tiff or PNG file with no background layer – you can specify Alpha Channel in the Contour Options pop-up menu, again setting the offset value we require.

If you're working with a simple cutout on a white background, you can use the Detect Edges method. Here, InDesign will interpret where the edges of the cutout are and will generally make an intelligent guess. However, if your placed image has any white near its edges, it's likely that InDesign will be unable to distinguish between the image and the white background.

You can see any wrapping errors marked by the blue bounding line, which marks the offset. What's useful here is that this bounding line is itself an editable path: you can use the Direct Selection tool (shortcut: press A) to select and move individual anchor points along this path to correct any errors.

The final pop-up menu that you need to look at is Wrap Options. This sets whether the text wraps to both sides of the image or just to one side. If you're placing your cutout between two columns of text, then you'll want the text to wrap on both sides – in other words, both columns will be offset to bend around the image. If you've placed a cutout on the right of a single column of text though,

▲ When set to auto-detect edges, InDesign can easily mistake white within an image for part of the background. It's simple enough to select the wrapping path, shown offset in blue, and adjust the anchor points with the Pen or Direct Selection tools, so that they better fit the true contour.

it will look awkward if one or two words appear to the right of it. Here, you can specify that the text should only wrap on the left of the object.

In the case of the ballerina in our example (above), she's placed between two columns of text, but the nature of the wrapping is such that a couple of stray words appear between her arms. You can't specify only left or right wrapping, since you want both columns to be affected. You could manually edit the wrapping path, but there's a better way: choosing Largest Area from the Wrap Options pop-up will eliminate all such minor inaccuracies.

The two final wrapping icons are Jump object, which wraps only above and below the image – useful if you want to place a narrow object in a column of text without the text wrapping around its sides – and Jump to the next column, which forces a column break above the object.

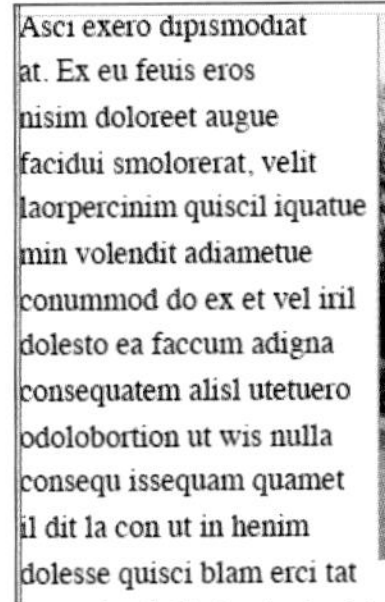

▲ Always check that there isn't a paragraph break too close to a wrapped image. This will make the page look ungainly, as if the image is unbalancing the text.

X: X and Y axes

You'll remember these from school, but in the world of design they've broken out of spreadsheets and graphs, and are now key to accurate positioning.

X and Y can stand for unknown quantities in mathematics or the chromosome difference between men and women. But it's also a way of describing an item's location in two-dimensional space in Cartesian geometry – a coordinate system devised by the French philosopher René Descartes.

Moving a layer or selection around in Photoshop, Illustrator or any layout program involves changing the X and Y coordinates of the object's location. Generally, we're unaware of the mathematics, as we are with most of the complex algorithms that underlie graphics applications' effects. But coordinates are an invaluable aid for moving items by a precise amount; rather than dragging an object we can enter numerical values for every move.

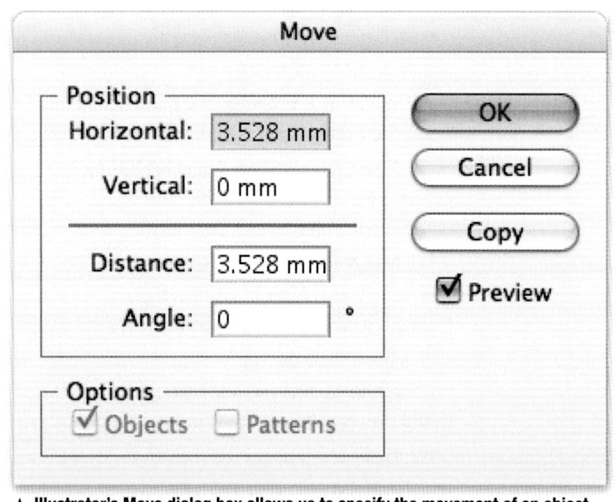

▲ Illustrator's Move dialog box allows us to specify the movement of an object precisely in the units of our choice.

▲ The Free Transform command in Photoshop enables us to specify the movement of a layer or selection in any unit. Clicking on the triangle icon sets values relative to the object rather than to the canvas.

In Illustrator, pressing the Return or Enter key when any item is selected (and the Move tool is active) will open the Move dialog box. The distance required is typed in here, and pressing Enter again (or pressing the OK button) will move the item a corresponding distance. The units used are defined in the Preferences dialog box but we don't need to stick to them. Even though a dialog box may specify millimetres as the measurement unit, we can change it on the fly simply by typing the appropriate abbreviation – 20 px to move 20 pixels, with 'pt' for point, 'in' for inches and so on.

After typing the value in Illustrator, it will be converted into the default measurement units.

We can use the cursor keys to nudge an object one pixel at a time in either the X or Y axis in Photoshop, and one unit of a predetermined value in Illustrator – the precise value is set in the Preferences dialog box. With both programs, holding Shift while pressing the cursor key will move the object 10 times the standard distance. And by using the cursor keys within the Move dialog it will be nudged up and down by one unit at a time. Also by holding Shift as we press the cursor keys, the value will change by 10 times the standard amount.

In Illustrator though, as values are automatically translated into the default units, typing '1in' to move an object by one inch will turn into 25.4mm; the cursor keys will change this by 1mm at a time rather than in fractions of an inch.

There's no direct equivalent of the Move dialog in Photoshop but we can produce a similar movement using Free Transform. When we press Command-T to enter Free Transform mode, the Options bar displays X and Y coordinates of the current layer's top left corner (as well as its starting size of 100%, and rotation and skew angles of 0%). We can type the distance we want to move a layer in the X and Y fields here.

In Photoshop, however, when we type different measurement units in these fields, they're remembered – not just for the current Free Transform session but also in every Photoshop document until we quit the program. Even better, we can set different units for the X and Y axes. This means that if we're working on an image to fit a magazine layout, for example, we can set the horizontal units to millimetres and the vertical units to point measurements, and these settings will be remembered. Using the cursor keys to increase or decrease values

▲ To create a grid or array, duplicate the layer or selection – then use Free Transform to copy it to the new location.

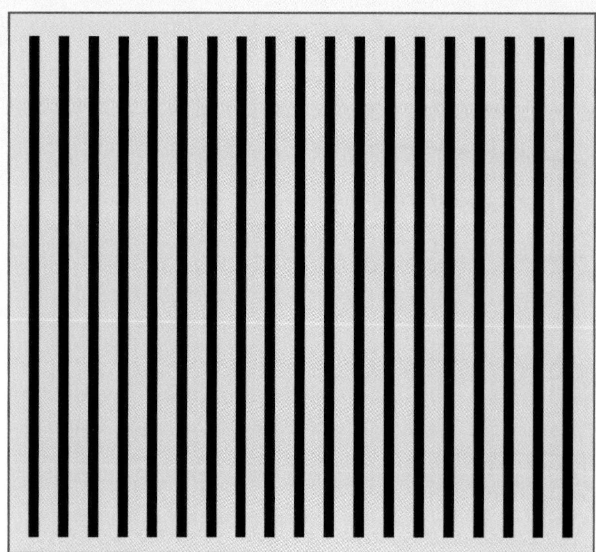

▲ After the grid or array has been copied across, pressing Command-Shift-Alt-T will duplicate it as many times as you wish.

will of course nudge them with the current units rather than the default settings.

While typing in the numerical values in Photoshop the layer or selection will move immediately. Once the desired values have been entered we need to press Return or Enter twice – once to exit the Options bar dialog box and the second time to commit the Free Transform operation. Once a layer has been moved with Free Transform we can repeat the transformation exactly, using Shift-Command-T. What is less well known is that it's possible to duplicate a transformation by pressing Alt-Shift-Command-T. This will move a copy of the layer or selection, leaving the original in place. In turn, this makes it easy to set up grids in Photoshop, with precise spacing between the items.

Each time we press Alt-Shift-Command-T we create a new instance of the item, so we can keep the Alt, Shift and Command keys held down, and then repeatedly press the T key to build an entire array in just a matter of seconds.

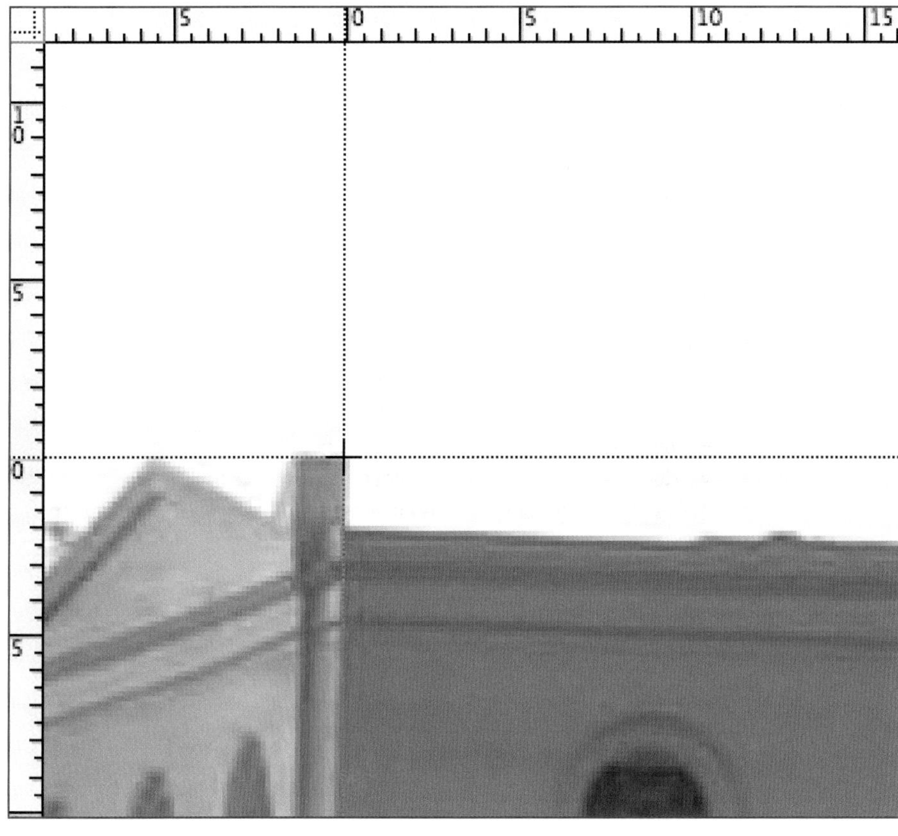

When we first enter Free Transform, the position of the object is shown relative to the zero position of the rulers. By default this will be the top left corner of the document. If we click on the small triangle icon between the X and Y values in the Options bar, we're able to specify the movement relative to the object itself rather than relative to the document. The X and Y values are set to 0, so we can enter the distance we want to move it without having to add a value to the current position.

Although the absolute position is initially set relative to the top-left corner, in reality it's relative to the zero position on the rulers. We can set this zero position anywhere we choose within the document by choosing Show Rulers from the View menu (shortcut Command-R). The rulers will always show the measurement units set in the Preferences. At the top-left corner is a square ruler icon and we can drag this to any position we like within the document: this will now be set as the zero point, and all measurements will be taken as positive and negative X and Y values relative to this position. Double-clicking this ruler icon will reset the rulers to the top left corner again.

The ruler is also used for dragging guides on to the artwork. These are non-printing vertical or horizontal rules that can help to align objects or which can be set up to work in a similar way to a baseline grid in a page layout application. As well as positioning guides by hand, we can use the New Guide option under the View menu to set guides with precise numerical values.

◄ With the Rulers visible, we can drag the cross hairs from the top-left corner to set the zero point at any location within the image.

Z: Z axis

The key to understanding 3D is mastering the mysterious Z axis, which positions your objects in space. Here, we explain how it interacts with X and Y.

In the last section, we looked at X and Y coordinates. Moving objects around in two dimensions is simple since the mouse itself moves on a 2D plane – and if you use a graphics tablet, there's a 1:1 correspondence between stylus movement and cursor position.

When working with 3D modelling applications, the relationship between mouse movements and object position and orientation is far less straightforward. Dragging an object will tend to move it in the Z axis as well as X and Y, which means the simple relationship between mouse and cursor has been broken. When we position two objects relative to each other, they may seem to be perfectly aligned in one view. But when seen from a different angle we frequently find that one is further into the distance than the other.

Movement in the Z axis is a problem that should have been resolved decades ago. The trouble is that each 3D modelling application has its own approach to dealing with the issue. In the absence of overall conformity we have to learn the technique separately for each program. In some applications, for example, dragging an object will always move it in the X-Y plane, while holding the Z key will move it backwards and forwards.

The problem here is: how do you define that X-Y plane? Is it an absolute relative to the geometry of the scene, or a plane that's always precisely facing the user, whatever angle he or she happens to be viewing the scene from? It's further complicated by the fact that we want to both move an object around in 3D space and to move our camera position independently of the objects within the scene.

Ironically it tends to be the cheaper, lower-end modelling applications that offer a more intuitive solution. This is probably because while users of Maya, FormZ and Cinema4D have shelled out a lot of cash and can therefore be expected to take the time to research the methods and learn the required techniques, those who pick up Bryce or Poser on an impulse want more immediate access to the toolset.

Users of the free Google Sketchup want to get modelling in minutes, so it's in these consumer applications that we tend to see the biggest interface enhancements. Professional users on the other hand are content to continue using the perhaps outdated methods they've rigorously learned.

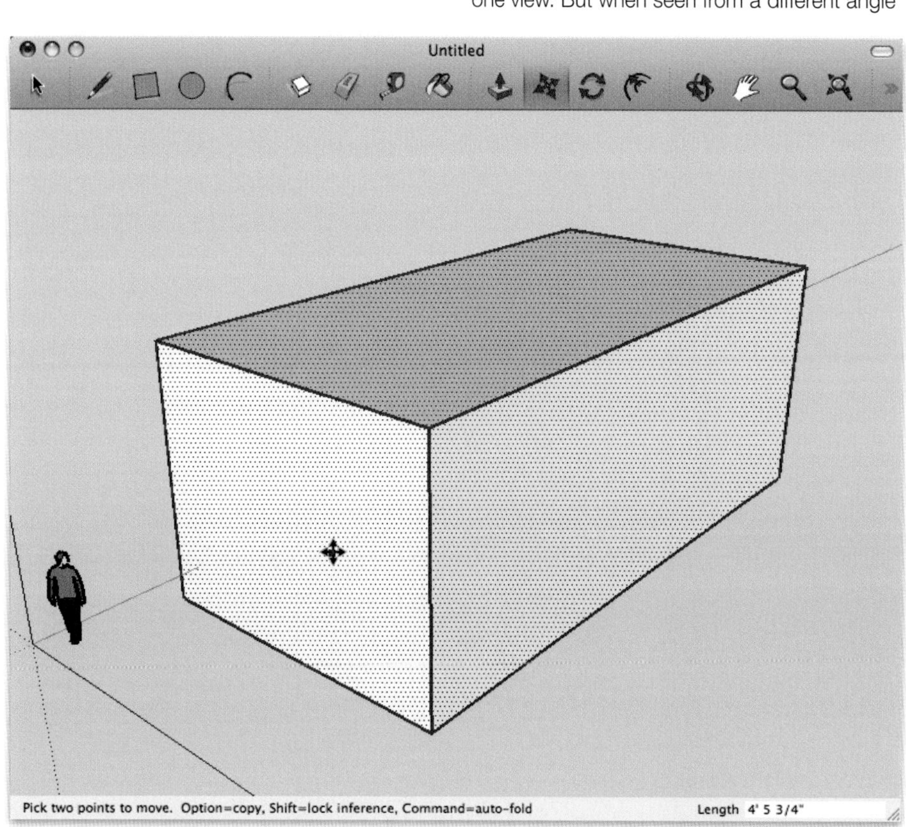

◄ **Moving objects in Google Sketchup involves first selecting the direction with the cursor keys, then holding the Shift key to constrain motion in that direction. Clumsy – but practical when you get the hang of it.**

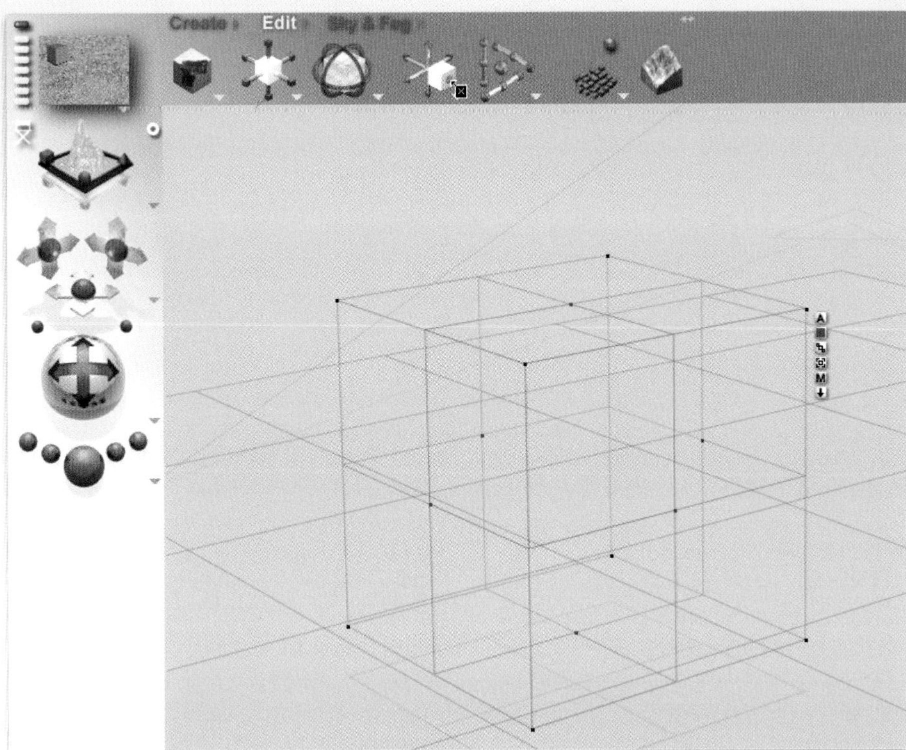

▲ **Toolbar icons in Bryce allow us to move, scale and rotate objects in each direction by dragging on the corresponding handle. It's all too easy for an object to zoom off the screen and disappear though.**

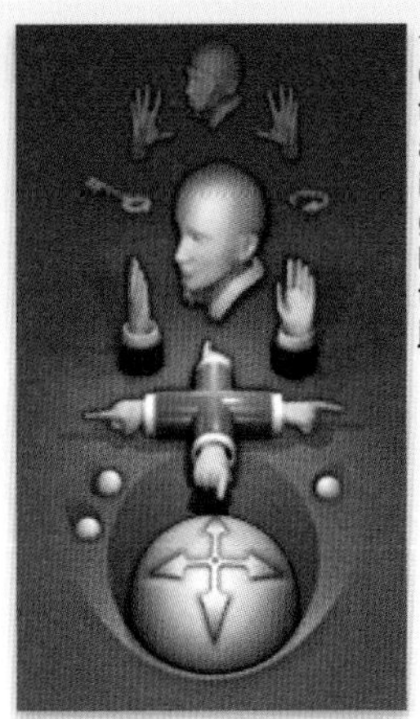

◄ **Characteristically quirky, the Poser icons for moving in the X, Y and Z planes are intuitive and easy to grasp. The icons may be too kitsch for some tastes but they do their job effectively.**

Sketchup uses a straightforward approach to 3D movement: we press the up, down, left and right cursor keys to set the direction of movement, then hold the Shift key while dragging with the Move tool to constrain movement of objects to those directions. It's not ideal and is a little clumsy in operation; but for basic modelling it's a competent if somewhat inelegant method of manipulating in 3D space.

In Bryce, arguably the most approachable 3D modeller of all, we can move objects using the Move icon on the toolbar. This displays a cube with arrows coming out of it in the positive and negative X, Y and Z axes – dragging on this icon in any of these directions will correspondingly move the object. A cube surrounded by hoops in each dimension allows us to rotate the object in each direction as well.

Poser, known for its quirky interface, has a equally quirky method for moving objects. A hand with its palm towards us is the tool for moving in the X and Y plane; a hand viewed side-on moves in Y and Z. A four-way arm with pointing fingers moves in the X and Z plane; and a recessed ball is used to rotate in all three dimensions. It sounds clumsy, but it works. Best of all though, Poser offers a split window that can contain multiple views of the scene: typically, you'd want to view front, left (or right) and top, with the fourth pane showing the camera view. This does mean that each working space is only a quarter of the size it could be.

The result is that objects can be manipulated in any one pane while being viewed in all the others simultaneously. Thus we get more control over the object's absolute position and avoid the errors normally associated with aligning objects in three dimensions. This multi-pane view is the system used by high-end 3D modelling applications and is the most satisfactory method for ensuring that what we see from one angle is indeed what we want to achieve.

A 3D controller makes the job easier. Take 3D Connexion's Space Navigator, a controller that fits in the palm of your hand. It moves in three dimensions: not just forward and backward, side to side and twisting left and right, but also up and down. Within a matter of minutes the motion becomes second nature, whether rotating scenes in Sketchup, positioning 3D objects in Photoshop CS3 Extended or flying over a landscape in Google Earth. Better still, it costs just £39.

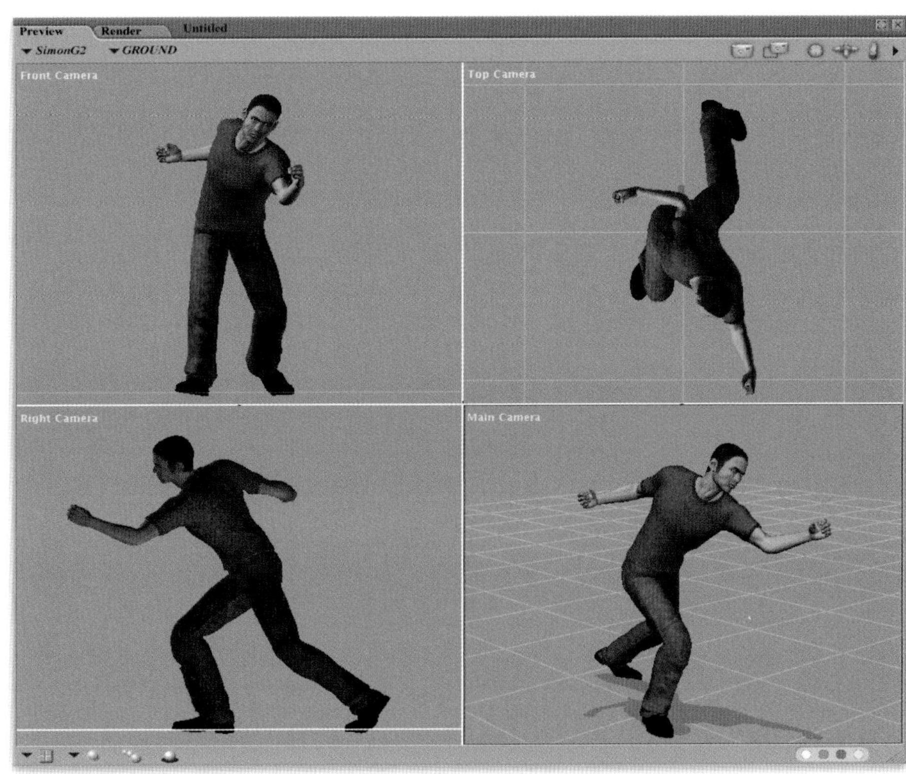

► **The four-up view offered by Poser, used by all high-end modellers, gives us the most control by showing the top, side, front and camera views simultaneously. This makes object modelling and alignment that much more assured.**

Z: Zooming images

There are several ways to enlarge your images on screen so that you can work with greater accuracy. Here are the most common, and most useful.

Zooming in and out of images is a task you have to perform dozens, if not hundreds, of times a day. You need to zoom right in to check the detail in a Photoshop file, or to select anchor points in Illustrator, or to align elements in InDesign; but you then have to zoom out again to see the entire image or layout. The Adobe applications offer a range of tools and keystrokes for managing the zoom level of your files, and you can save a lot of time by using the right ones.

All graphics and design applications include a Zoom tool, shaped like a magnifying glass. You can use this on your image to zoom in by a standard amount: normally, each time you click, you'll zoom from 100% to 200%, then 300%, 400% and so on. If you hold down the Alt key, you'll zoom out, and once you get below 100%, you'll zoom to 67%, then 50%, then 33%, and so on. You can also drag with the Zoom tool to magnify an area of the image. As you drag, you'll trace a rectangular marquee-like shape; when you release the mouse button, this area is enlarged to fit the size of your monitor.

If you have a mouse with a scroll wheel, you can use this to zoom in and out of the image – this feature can be enabled or disabled in the General section of the Preferences dialog box.

More useful, though, is the existence of keyboard shortcuts that mean you don't have to change the tool that you're in. Holding down Command-Spacebar gives you temporary access to the Zoom tool and enables you to zoom in on an image, centred around the point you click. Holding down Alt-Spacebar will zoom out. You may find the default settings of either Exposé or Spotlight in Mac OS X interfere with these shortcuts. If so, you should use System Preferences to change the Exposé and Spotlight settings.

You can also hold down the Command key and press the plus and minus keys to zoom in and out of the image one step at a time, without having to click on the image or change tool.

In Photoshop, when you zoom out so far that the image appears smaller than your monitor, one of two things can happen. Either the image window will shrink to fit the image, or it will remain the same size and the image will be surrounded by a grey background. Both of these methods have their pros and cons: if you're performing transformations, for instance, the grey background can make it easier for you to drag transformation handles outside the image area. You can set the behaviour in the Preferences dialog.

In Photoshop CS4, zooming into an image at magnifications of higher than 500% will show a fine line around each pixel, dividing them into a visible grid. That's because at this magnification, it's expected that you'll be working on individual pixels – perhaps drawing a bitmap image. In this case, the ability to see the grid is a real bonus. This feature can be turned off in the Preferences dialog box.

To zoom to specific magnifications, you can make use of a range of keyboard shortcuts. In Adobe applications, pressing Command-0 (that's zero, rather than the letter O) will display

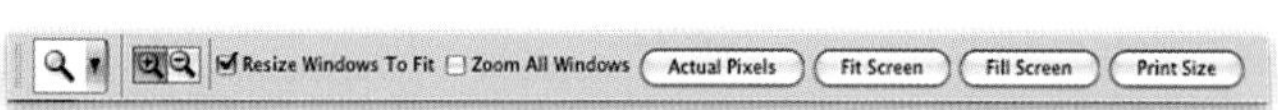

▲ **When you choose the Zoom tool in Photoshop, the Options Bar presents you with a range of choices for how you want to view your image.**

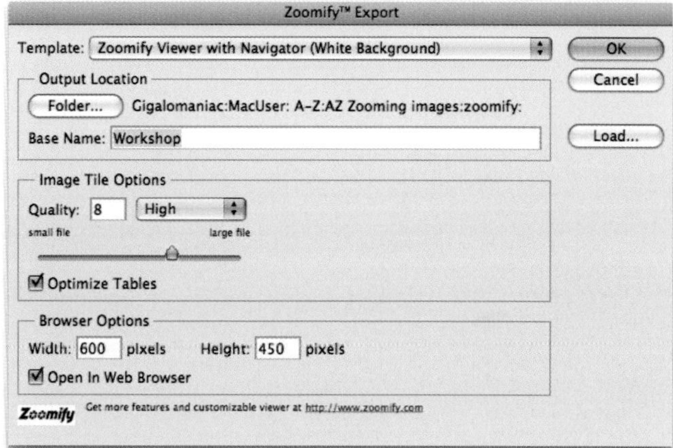

▲ **The excellent Zoomify export feature, found in Photoshop CS3 and later versions, lets you build zoomable web images in an instant.**

▲ When the end user zooms or pans a zoomed image in the Zoomify viewer, it's initially shown as a low-resolution preview…

▲ …which is then brought into crisp focus as the tile loads. Note the inset view of the whole image, and the blue rectangle showing the zoomed area.

the image as large as it will go within the window, and pressing Command-1 will generally zoom the image to 100%. By 100%, we mean that each pixel in the image is the size of a single pixel on the monitor: this isn't the same as print size (see below).

You should be aware that in earlier versions of Photoshop, viewing an image at other than halves or doubles of full size – that is, at sizes other than 25%, 50%, 100%, 200% and so on – would produce somewhat ragged results, as pixel values are estimated for intermediate zoom levels. This has been fixed with the new rendering engine in CS4, and images now look smooth at any magnification. If you have an earlier version of Photoshop, you'll need to choose the reduction closest to your monitor size for a decent view of the image.

Photoshop also has a setting called Print size, which attempts to display the image at the size it will appear on the printed page, bearing in mind the resolution at which the image is created. The trouble is, this is rarely anything like the size at which the image will be printed, and we need to compensate for it. If we're working on an image at 300dpi, for example, Photoshop will show a 'print size' view of 24%. In fact, this is way off the mark: the true print size is shown with the image at 38.4% magnification. The exact size will vary, depending on the size and resolution of your monitor, but it's easy to calibrate by creating a new image of, say, 20cm wide, and then adjusting the view size until the image on the screen measures exactly 20cm.

The current magnification is shown at the bottom left of each window; you can click there and type any value you want. Once you know the right setting for our combination of monitor and image resolution, you can simply type this in each time to see your image truly at the size it will be printed.

To enable web users to zoom into your images, Photoshop CS3 and above includes an export feature called Export to Zoomify. This produces a small thumbnail of your image, together with up to a hundred or so tiles showing the image at larger magnifications, all bound together with an html page. When the end user views the image, it appears as fast as any low-resolution Jpeg, but controls allow it to be zoomed and panned, each new tile appearing at full resolution as it's called up by the software. Zoomify uses a Flash plug-in to render the images, and should work with any modern browser, such as Firefox, Safari and Internet Explorer.

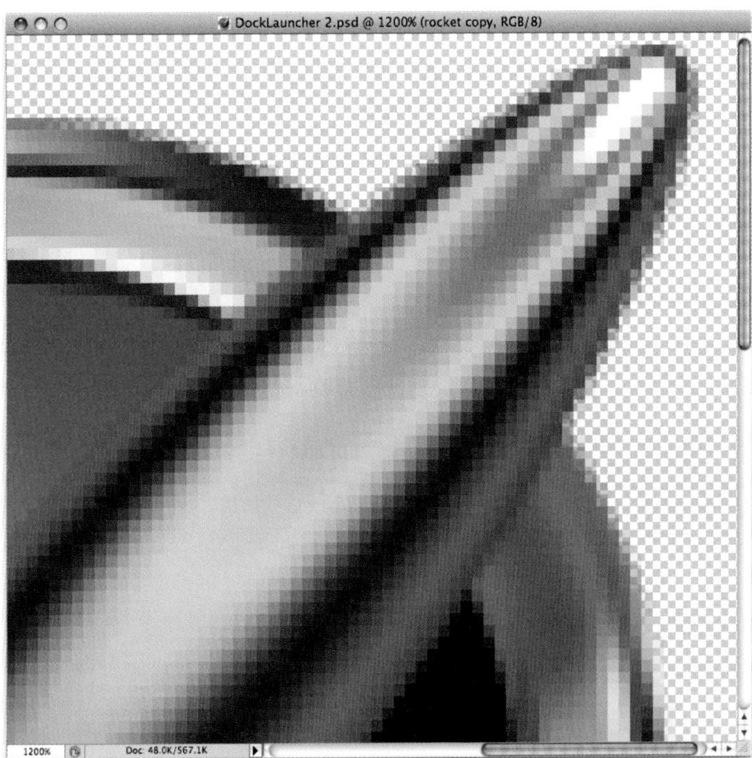

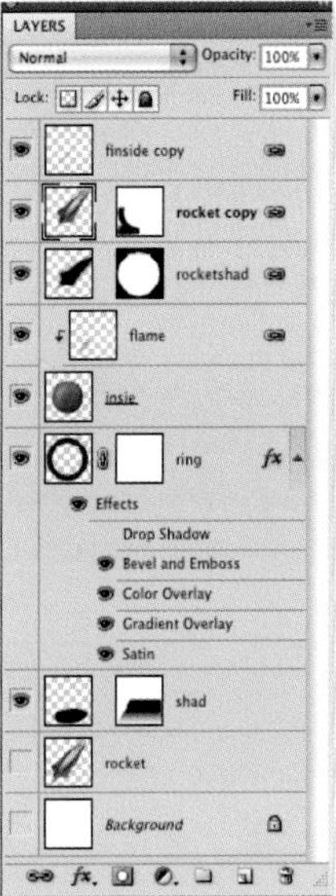

▲ When working on very small images such as logos, it can help to have two views open. Zoom right in to pixel level on one, but keep the other at 100% so you get an overview of the full image at all times.

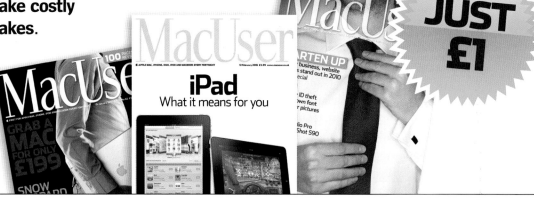